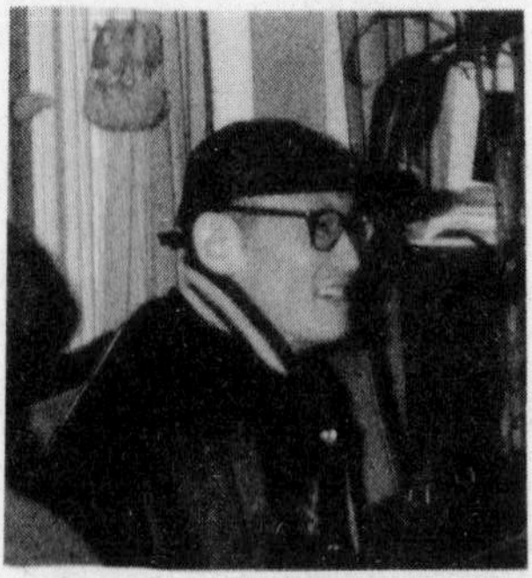

桂 正和

Masakazu Katsura

I'm sure you've already noticed, but this comic is told from one character's point of view. Revealing only the main character's (Ichitaka's) feelings is the foundation. Even though *Video Girl* was a love story too, unlike this comic, every character's feelings were shown. Doing this from only one character's perspective isn't easy because every incident has to somehow involve Ichitaka. I'm having a really hard time with it. I broke the rule a bit in this volume.

When Masakazu Katsura was a high school student, he entered a story he had drawn into a manga contest in hopes of winning money to buy a stereo. He won the contest and was soon published in the immensely popular weekly manga anthology magazine *WEEKLY SHONEN JUMP*. Katsura was quickly propelled into manga-artist stardom, and his subsequent comic series, *WINGMAN*, *VIDEO GIRL AI*, *DNA²*, and *SHADOW LADY* are perennial fan favorites. *I"S*, which began publication in 1997, also inspired an original video series. Katsura lives in Tokyo and possesses an extensive collection of Batman memorabilia.

I"s
VOL. 6: BYE BYE
The SHONEN JUMP ADVANCED Manga Edition

STORY AND ART BY
MASAKAZU KATSURA

English Adaptation/Lance Caselman
Translation/Joe Yamazaki
Touch-up Art & Lettering/Freeman Wong
Design/Hidemi Sahara
Editor/Nancy Thistlethwaite

Managing Editor/Elizabeth Kawasaki
Director of Production/Noboru Watanabe
Vice President of Publishing/Alvin Lu
Vice President & Editor in Chief/Yumi Hoashi
Sr. Director of Acquisitions/Rika Inouye
Vice President of Sales & Marketing/Liza Coppola
Publisher/Hyoe Narita

Printed in the U.S.A.

Published by VIZ Media, LLC
P.O. Box 77010
San Francisco, CA 94107

SHONEN JUMP ADVANCED Manga Edition
10 9 8 7 6 5 4 3 2 1
First printing, March 2006

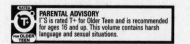

PARENTAL ADVISORY
I"S is rated T+ for Older Teen and is recommended
for ages 16 and up. This volume contains harsh
language and sexual situations.

THE WORLD'S MOST
CUTTING-EDGE MANGA

www.viz.com
www.shonenjump.com

SHONEN JUMP ADVANCED MANGA

I"s™
アイズ

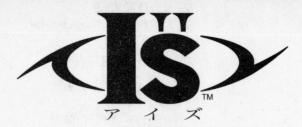

Vol. 6
BYE BYE

STORY & ART BY
MASAKAZU KATSURA

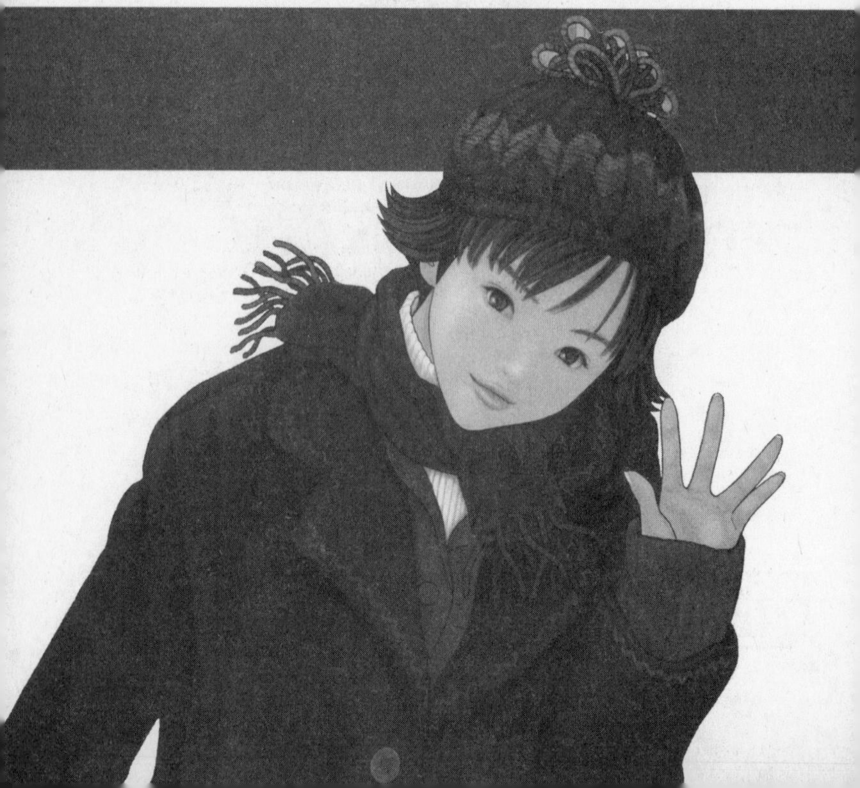

I"s

アイズ

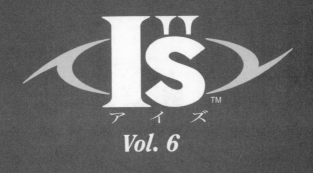

Vol. 6

CONTENTS

I"s

アイズ

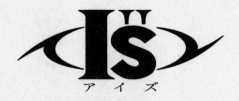

Chapter 46: In Your Own Way

IS

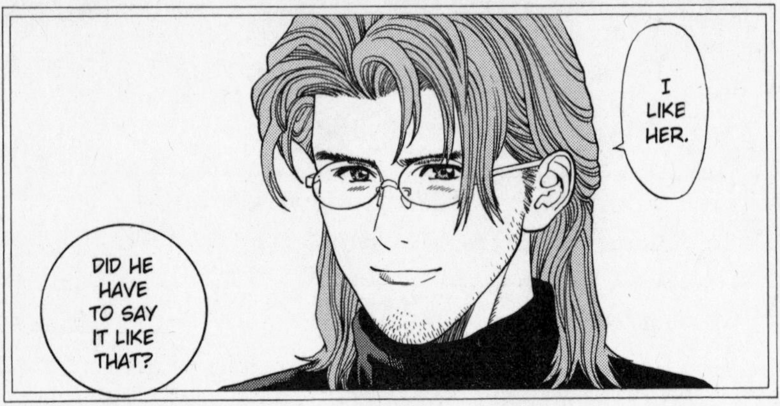
I LIKE HER.
DID HE HAVE TO SAY IT LIKE THAT?

THAT HIT ME HARD.

I FEEL SO DEPRESSED NOW.

I JUST WANT TO BE ALONE.

BUT TERATANI ALWAYS SHOWS UP...

...WHETHER HE'S WANTED OR NOT...

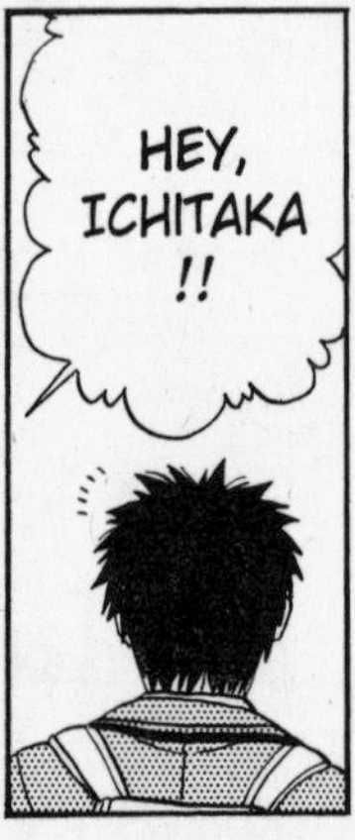
HEY, ICHITAKA!!

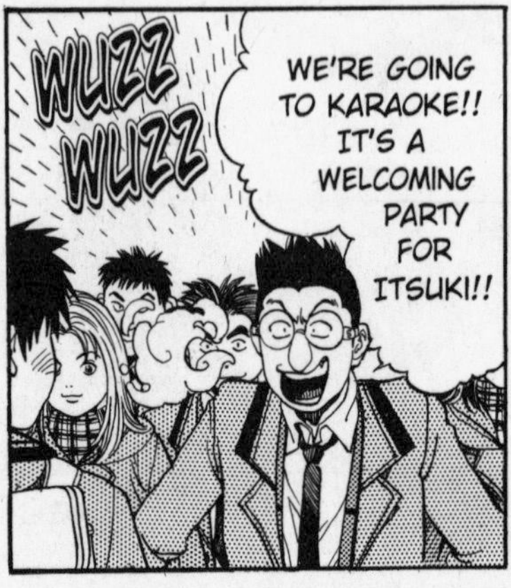
WUZZ WUZZ
WE'RE GOING TO KARAOKE!! IT'S A WELCOMING PARTY FOR ITSUKI!!

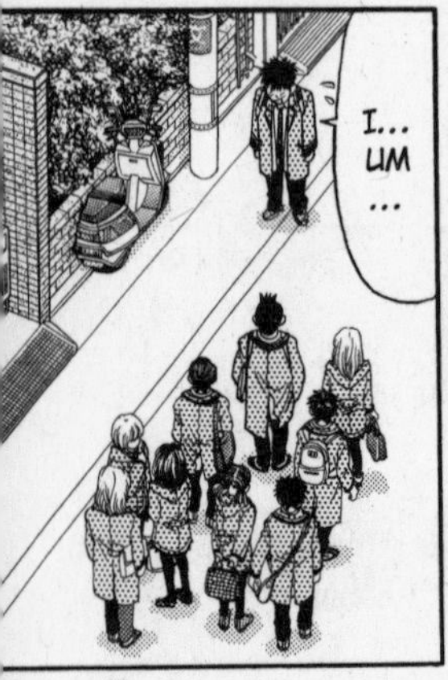
I... UM ...

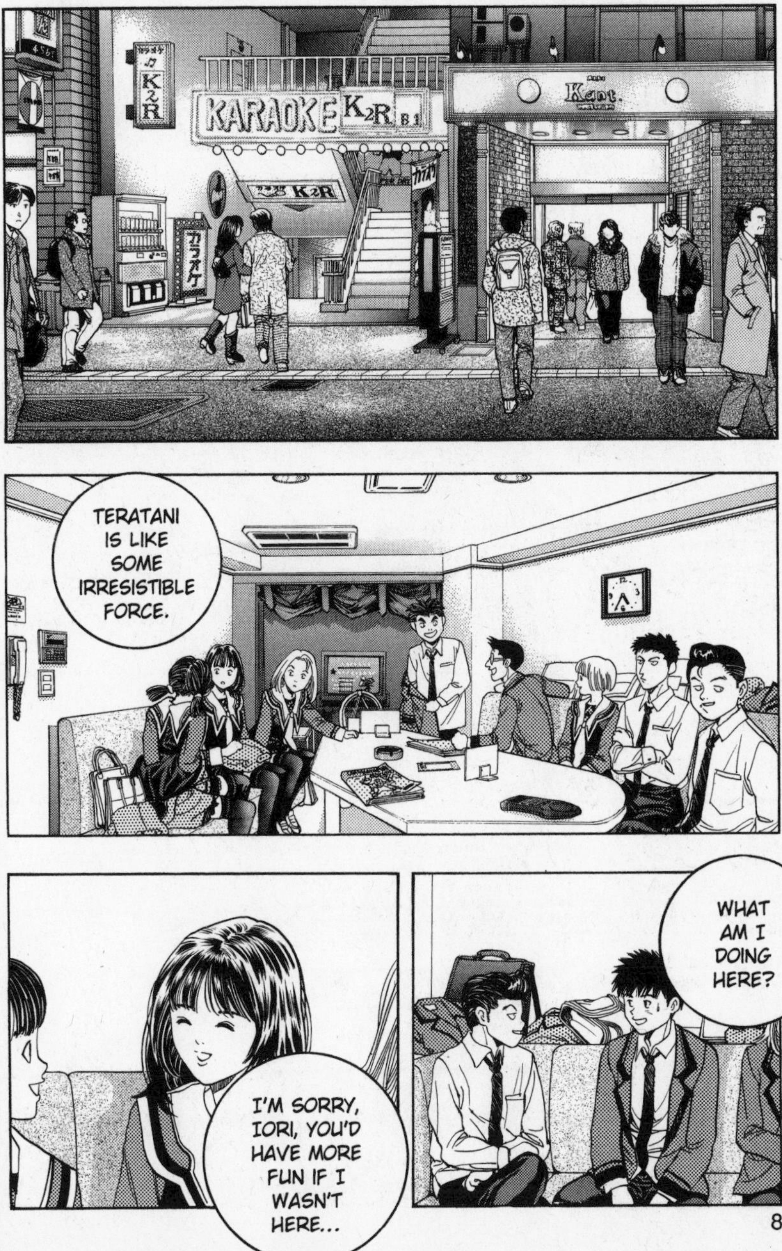
KARAOKE K2R B1
K2R
Kent
TERATANI IS LIKE SOME IRRESISTIBLE FORCE.
WHAT AM I DOING HERE?
I'M SORRY, IORI, YOU'D HAVE MORE FUN IF I WASN'T HERE...

READ THIS WAY

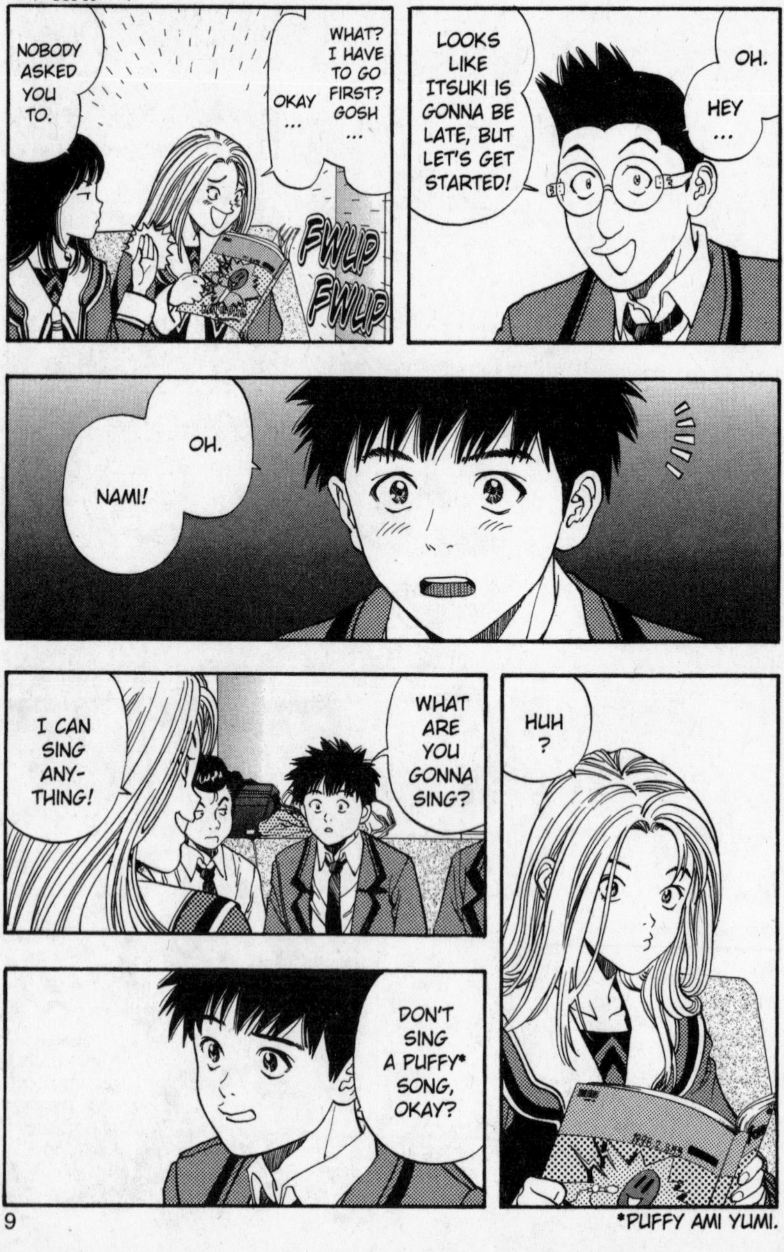
OH.
HEY ...
LOOKS LIKE ITSUKI IS GONNA BE LATE, BUT LET'S GET STARTED!
WHAT? I HAVE TO GO FIRST? GOSH ...
OKAY ...
FWLP FWLP
NOBODY ASKED YOU TO.
OH.
NAMI!
HUH?
WHAT ARE YOU GONNA SING?
I CAN SING ANYTHING!
DON'T SING A PUFFY* SONG, OKAY?

*PUFFY AMI YUMI.

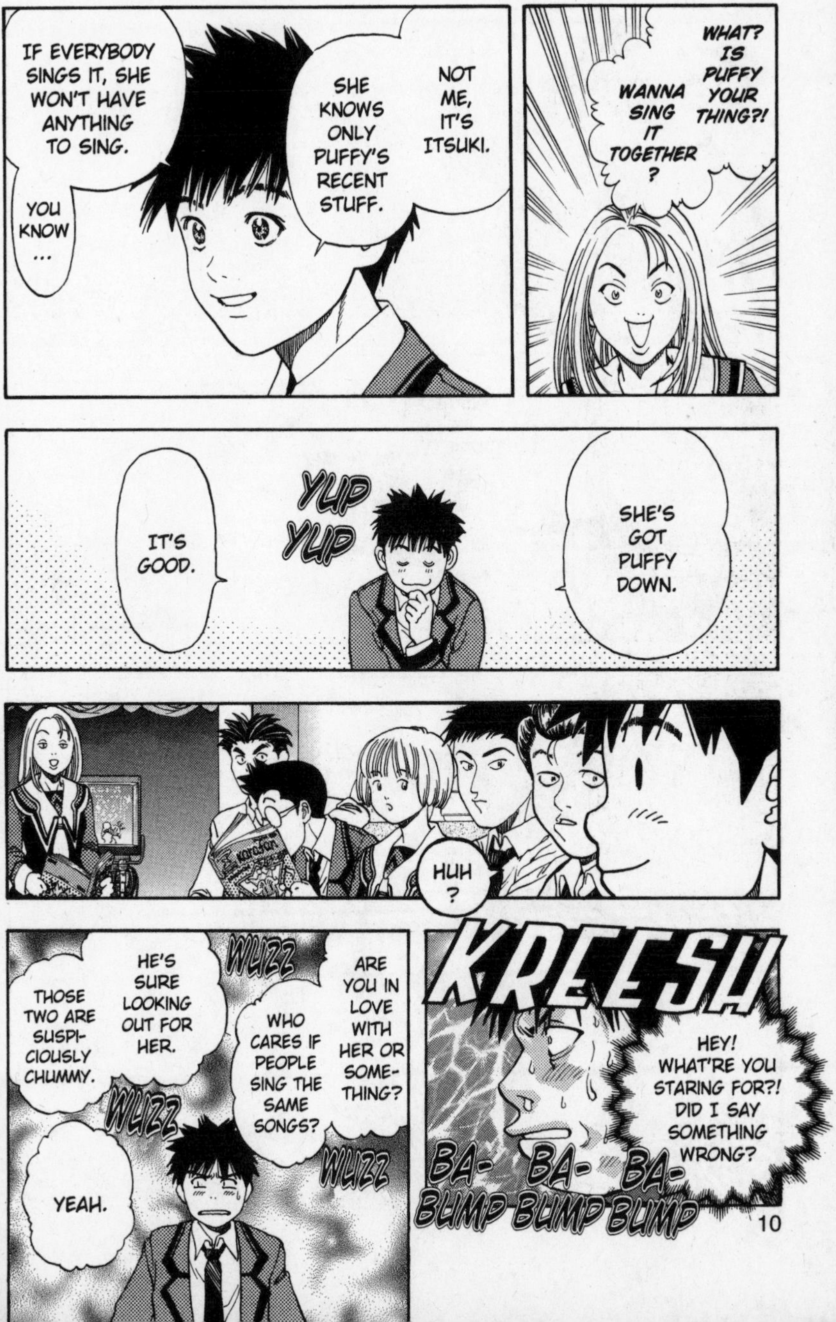
WHAT? IS PUFFY YOUR THING?!
WANNA SING IT TOGETHER?
NOT ME, IT'S ITSUKI.
SHE KNOWS ONLY PUFFY'S RECENT STUFF.
IF EVERYBODY SINGS IT, SHE WON'T HAVE ANYTHING TO SING.
YOU KNOW...
SHE'S GOT PUFFY DOWN.
YUP YUP
IT'S GOOD.
HUH?
KREESH
HEY! WHAT'RE YOU STARING FOR?! DID I SAY SOMETHING WRONG?
BA-BUMP BA-BUMP BA-BUMP
ARE YOU IN LOVE WITH HER OR SOMETHING?
WUZZ
HE'S SURE LOOKING OUT FOR HER.
WHO CARES IF PEOPLE SING THE SAME SONGS?
THOSE TWO ARE SUSPICIOUSLY CHUMMY.
WUZZ
WUZZ
YEAH.

READ THIS WAY

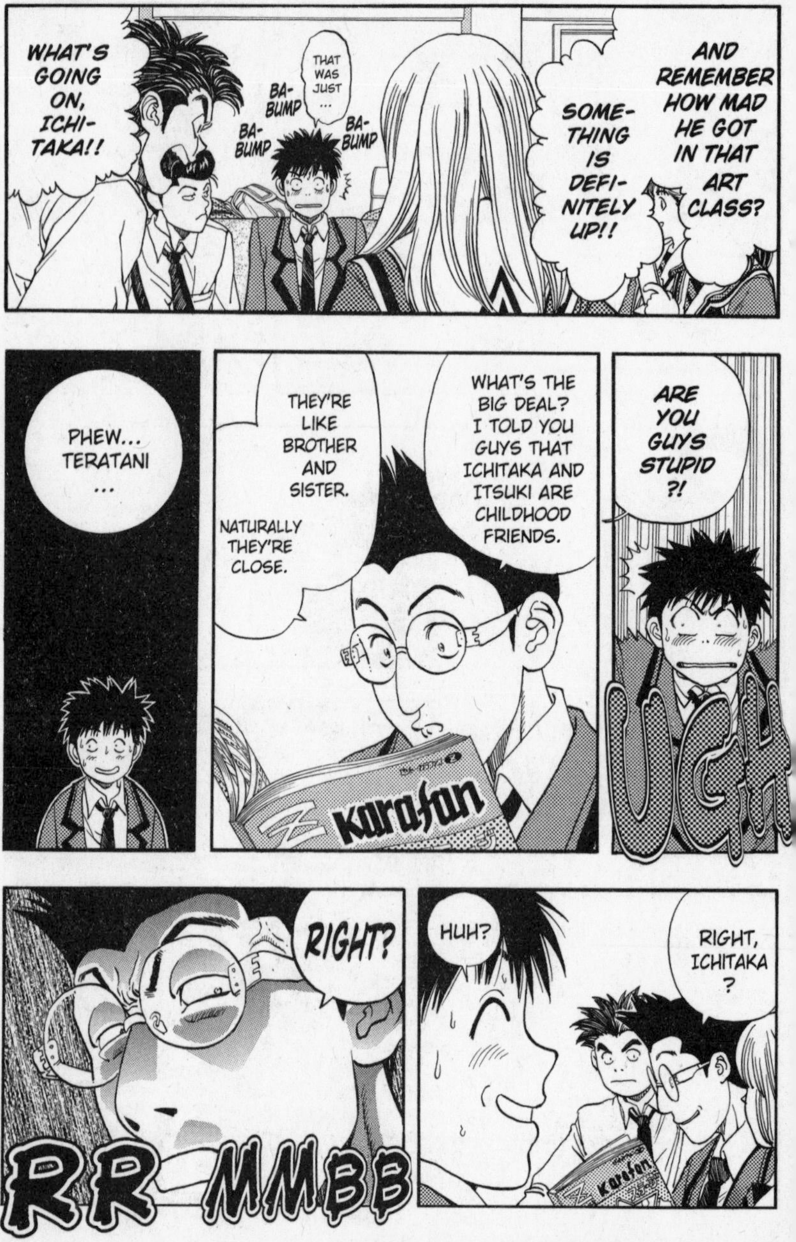
AND REMEMBER HOW MAD HE GOT IN THAT ART CLASS?
SOMETHING IS DEFINITELY UP!!
BA-BUMP
THAT WAS JUST ...
BA-BUMP
BA-BUMP
WHAT'S GOING ON, ICHITAKA!!
ARE YOU GUYS STUPID?!
UGH
WHAT'S THE BIG DEAL? I TOLD YOU GUYS THAT ICHITAKA AND ITSUKI ARE CHILDHOOD FRIENDS.
THEY'RE LIKE BROTHER AND SISTER.
NATURALLY THEY'RE CLOSE.
Karafan
PHEW... TERATANI ...
RIGHT, ICHITAKA?
HUH?
Karafan
RIGHT?
RR MMBB

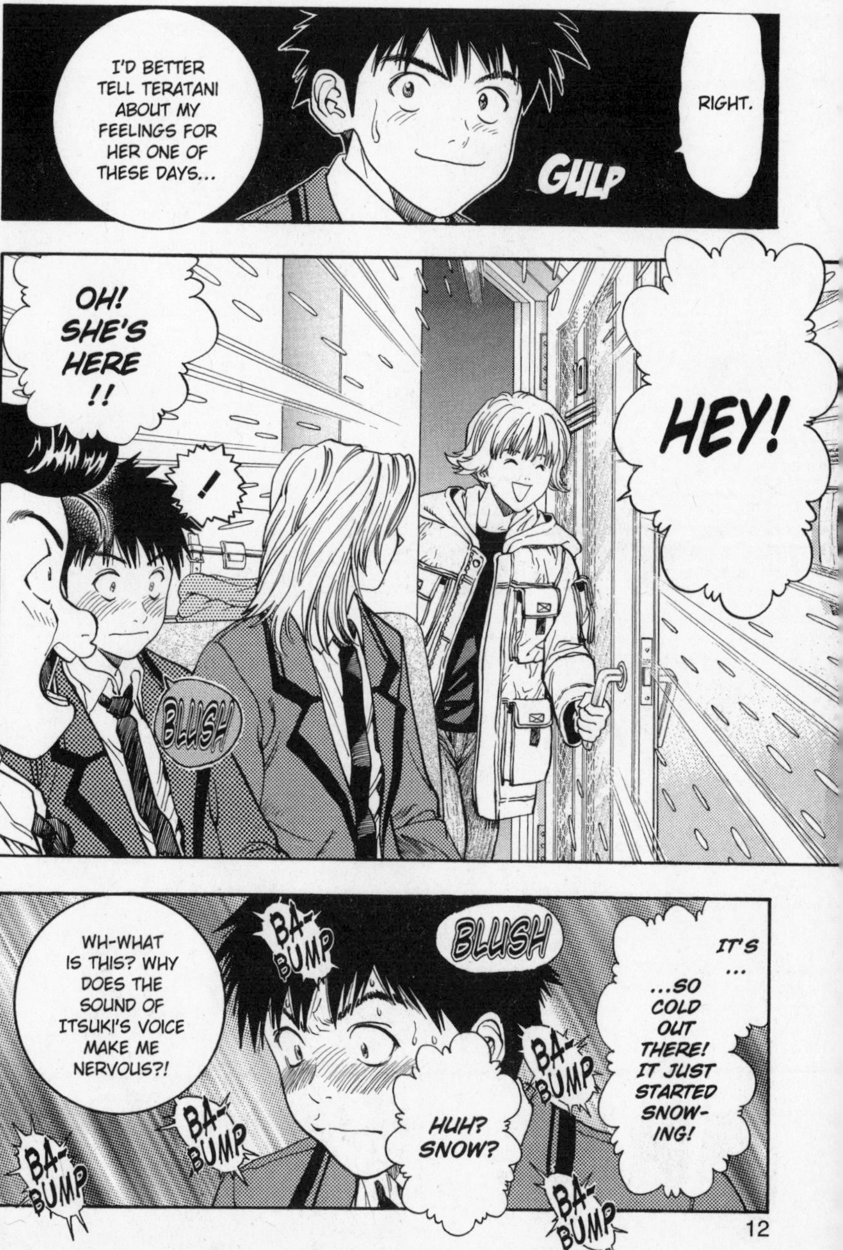
RIGHT.
GULP
I'D BETTER TELL TERATANI ABOUT MY FEELINGS FOR HER ONE OF THESE DAYS...
HEY!
OH! SHE'S HERE !!
!
BLUSH
IT'S ...
...SO COLD OUT THERE! IT JUST STARTED SNOW-ING!
BLUSH
BA-BUMP
WH-WHAT IS THIS? WHY DOES THE SOUND OF ITSUKI'S VOICE MAKE ME NERVOUS?!
BA-BUMP
HUH? SNOW?
BA-BUMP
BA-BUMP
BA-BUMP

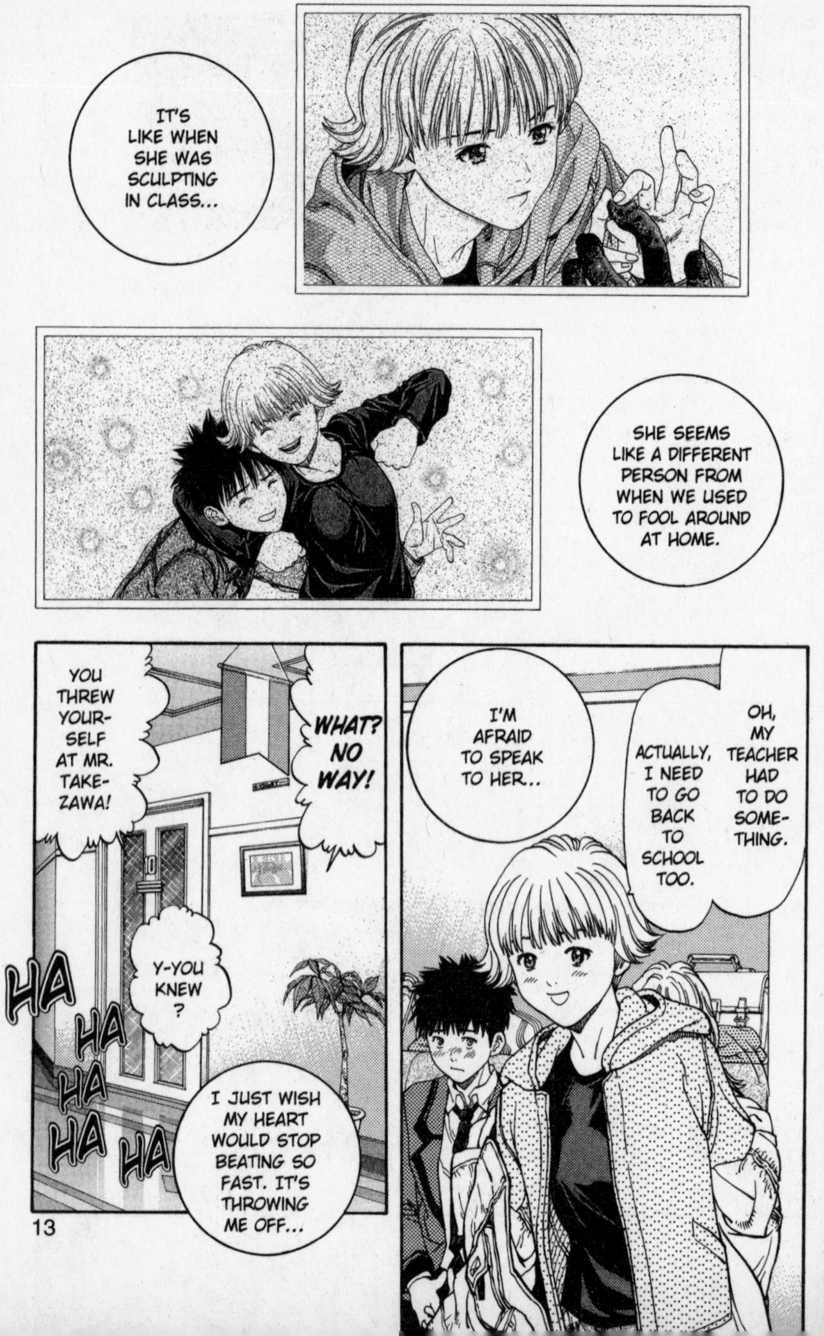
IT'S LIKE WHEN SHE WAS SCULPTING IN CLASS...
SHE SEEMS LIKE A DIFFERENT PERSON FROM WHEN WE USED TO FOOL AROUND AT HOME.
OH, MY TEACHER HAD TO DO SOMETHING.
ACTUALLY, I NEED TO GO BACK TO SCHOOL TOO.
I'M AFRAID TO SPEAK TO HER...
WHAT? NO WAY!
YOU THREW YOURSELF AT MR. TAKEZAWA!
Y-YOU KNEW?
HA HA HA HA HA
I JUST WISH MY HEART WOULD STOP BEATING SO FAST. IT'S THROWING ME OFF...

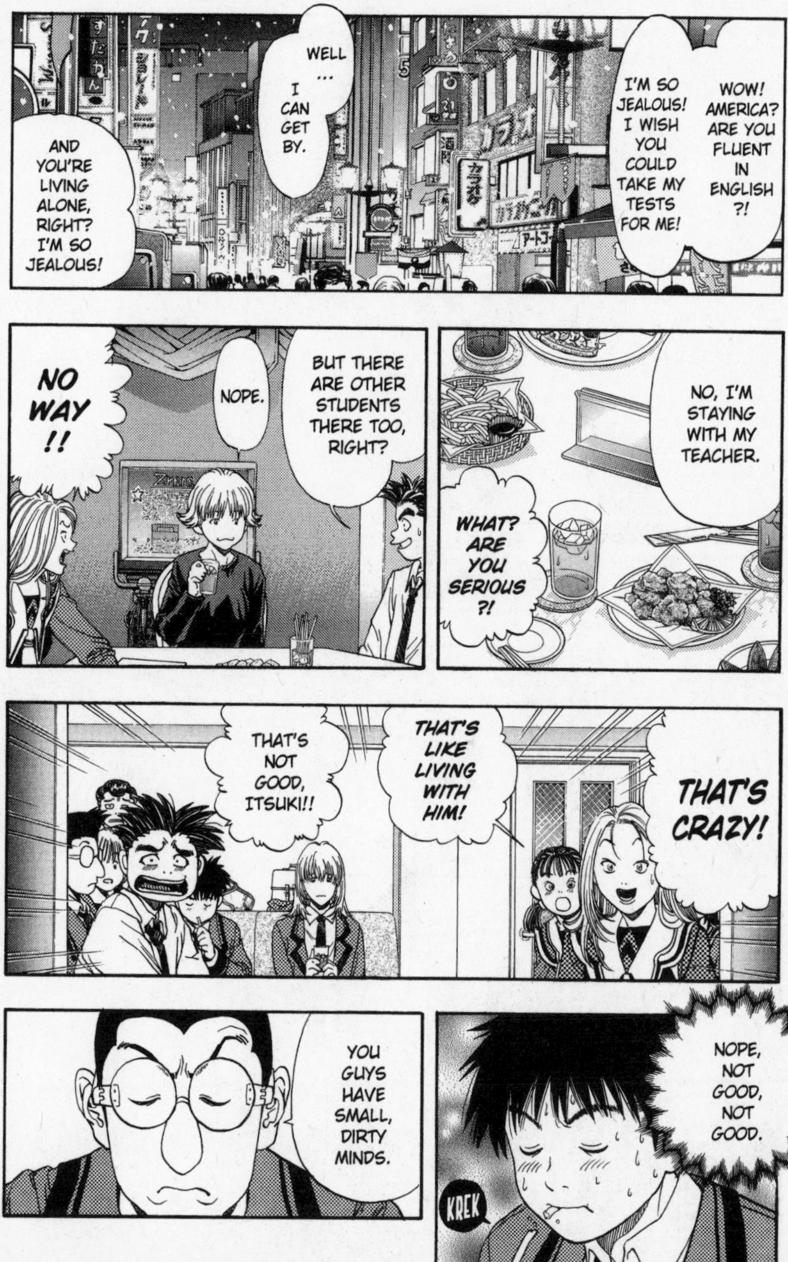
WOW! AMERICA? ARE YOU FLUENT IN ENGLISH?!
I'M SO JEALOUS! I WISH YOU COULD TAKE MY TESTS FOR ME!
WELL... I CAN GET BY.
AND YOU'RE LIVING ALONE, RIGHT? I'M SO JEALOUS!
NO, I'M STAYING WITH MY TEACHER.
WHAT? ARE YOU SERIOUS?!
BUT THERE ARE OTHER STUDENTS THERE TOO, RIGHT?
NOPE.
NO WAY!!
THAT'S CRAZY!
THAT'S LIKE LIVING WITH HIM!
THAT'S NOT GOOD, ITSUKI!!
NOPE, NOT GOOD, NOT GOOD.
KREK
YOU GUYS HAVE SMALL, DIRTY MINDS.

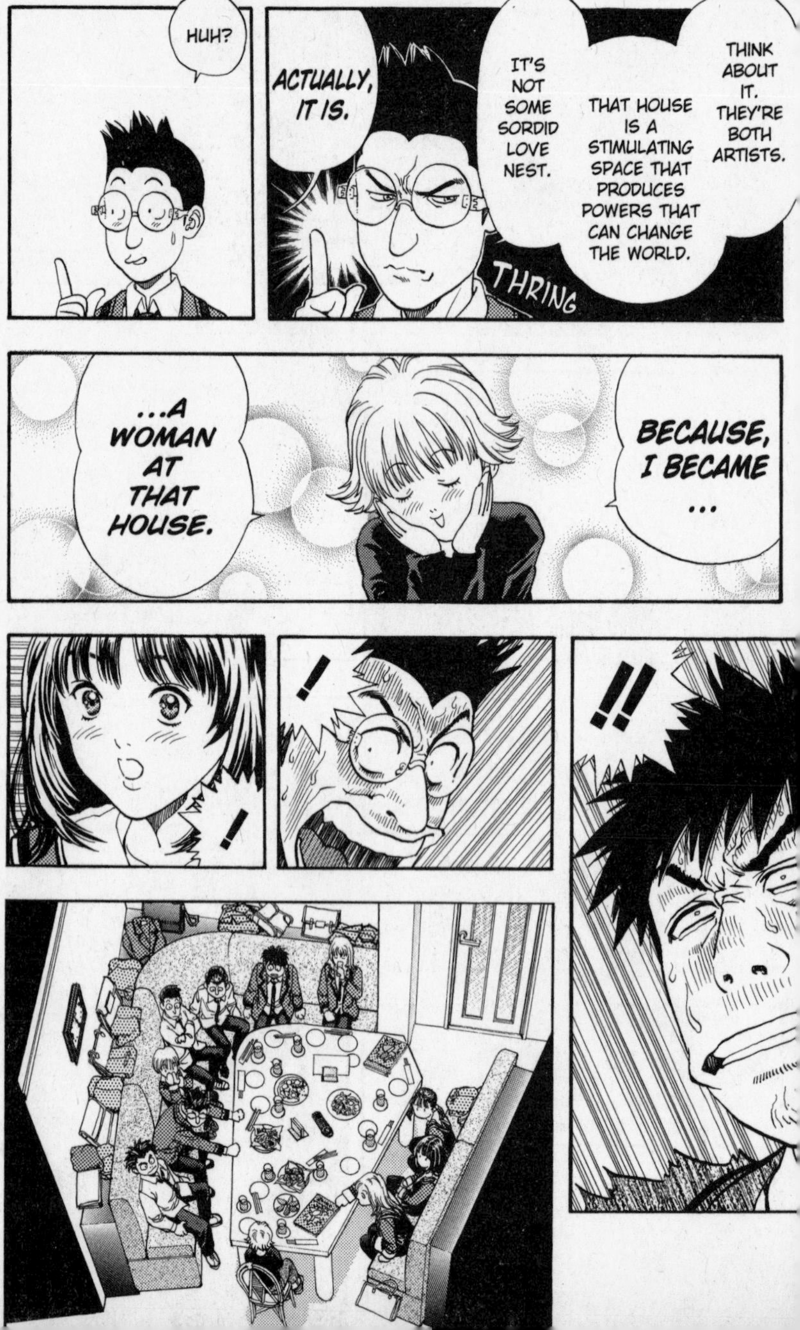
THINK ABOUT IT. THEY'RE BOTH ARTISTS.
THAT HOUSE IS A STIMULATING SPACE THAT PRODUCES POWERS THAT CAN CHANGE THE WORLD.
IT'S NOT SOME SORDID LOVE NEST.
ACTUALLY, IT IS.
THRING
HUH?
BECAUSE, I BECAME ...
...A WOMAN AT THAT HOUSE.
!!
!
!

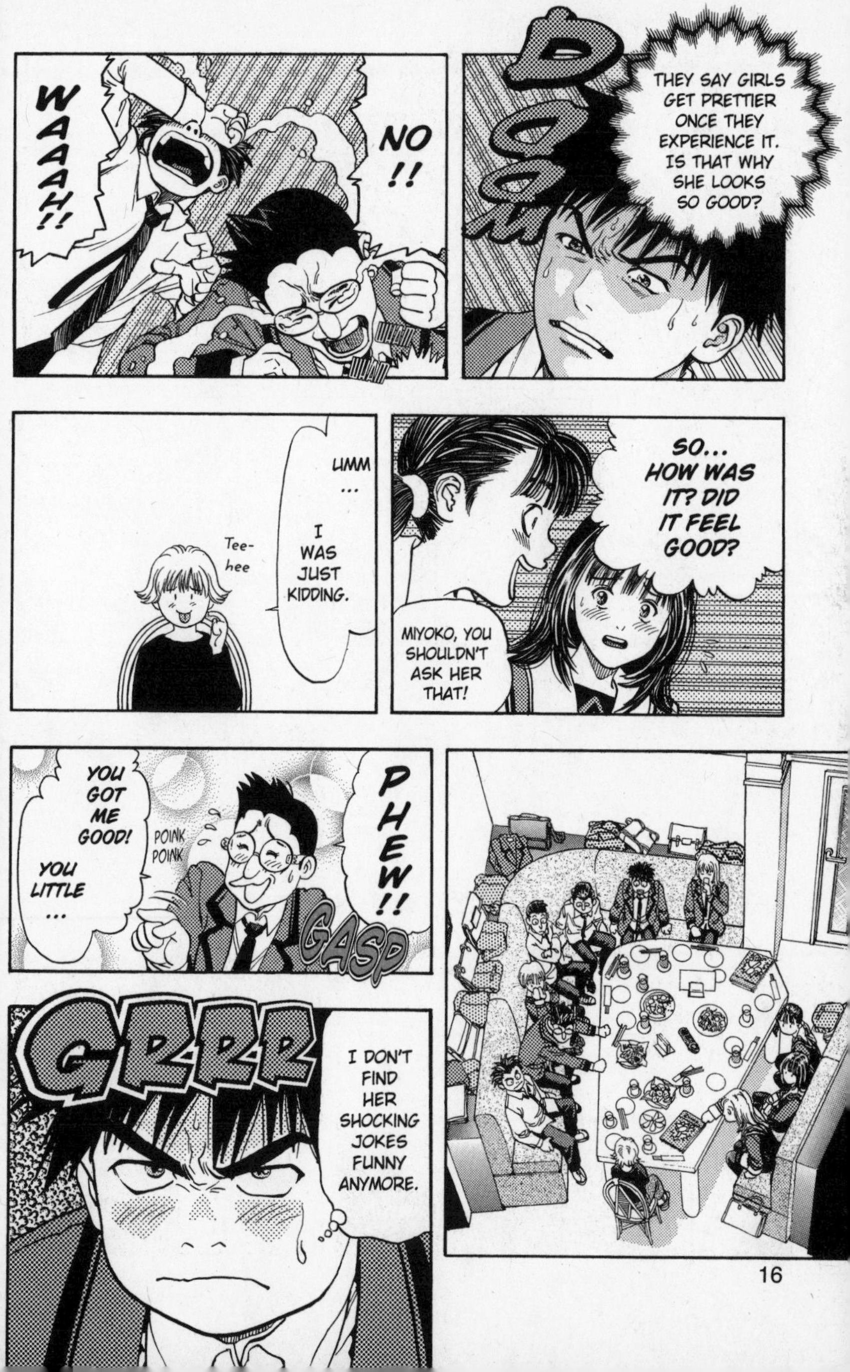
THEY SAY GIRLS GET PRETTIER ONCE THEY EXPERIENCE IT. IS THAT WHY SHE LOOKS SO GOOD?
NO !!
WAAAH!!
SO... HOW WAS IT? DID IT FEEL GOOD?
MIYOKO, YOU SHOULDN'T ASK HER THAT!
UMM ... I WAS JUST KIDDING.
Tee-hee
PHEW!!
GASP
YOU GOT ME GOOD!
POINK POINK
YOU LITTLE ...
GRRR
I DON'T FIND HER SHOCKING JOKES FUNNY ANYMORE.

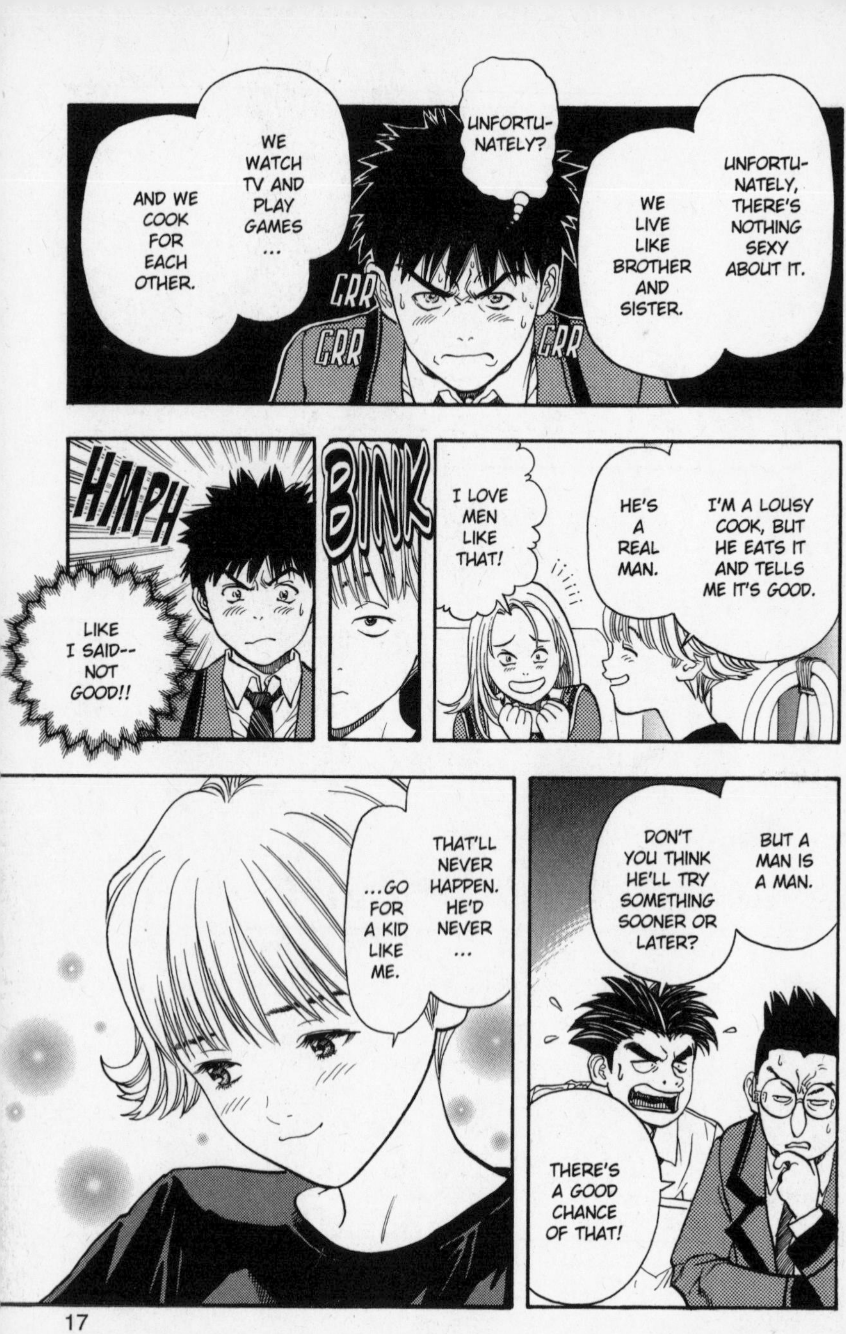
UNFORTUNATELY, THERE'S NOTHING SEXY ABOUT IT.
WE LIVE LIKE BROTHER AND SISTER.
WE WATCH TV AND PLAY GAMES ...
AND WE COOK FOR EACH OTHER.
UNFORTUNATELY?
GRR
GRR
GRR
I'M A LOUSY COOK, BUT HE EATS IT AND TELLS ME IT'S GOOD.
HE'S A REAL MAN.
I LOVE MEN LIKE THAT!
BINK
HMPH
LIKE I SAID-- NOT GOOD!!
BUT A MAN IS A MAN.
DON'T YOU THINK HE'LL TRY SOMETHING SOONER OR LATER?
THERE'S A GOOD CHANCE OF THAT!
THAT'LL NEVER HAPPEN. HE'D NEVER ...
...GO FOR A KID LIKE ME.

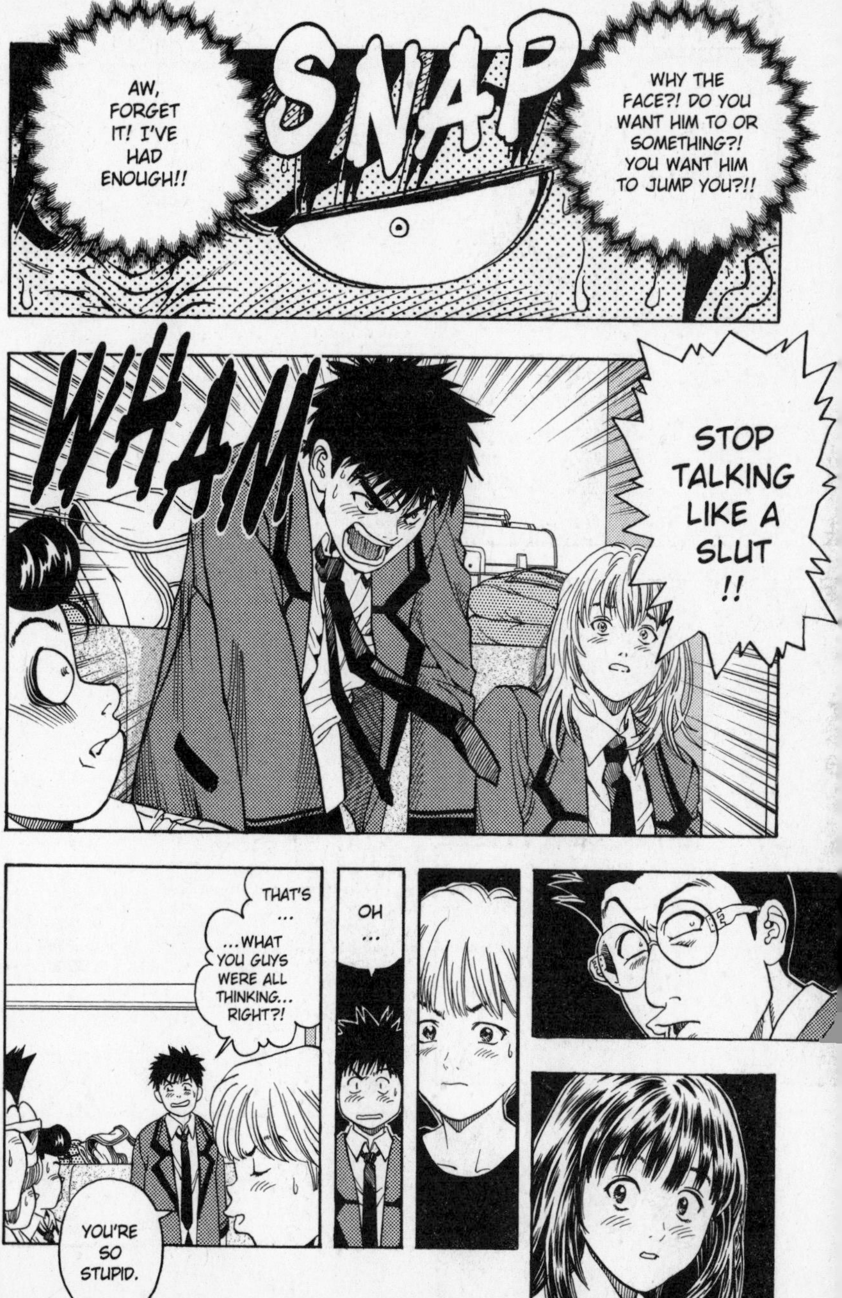
WHY THE FACE?! DO YOU WANT HIM TO OR SOMETHING?! YOU WANT HIM TO JUMP YOU?!!
SNAP
AW, FORGET IT! I'VE HAD ENOUGH!!
STOP TALKING LIKE A SLUT !!
WHAM
OH ...
THAT'S ... ...WHAT YOU GUYS WERE ALL THINKING... RIGHT?!
YOU'RE SO STUPID.

READ THIS WAY

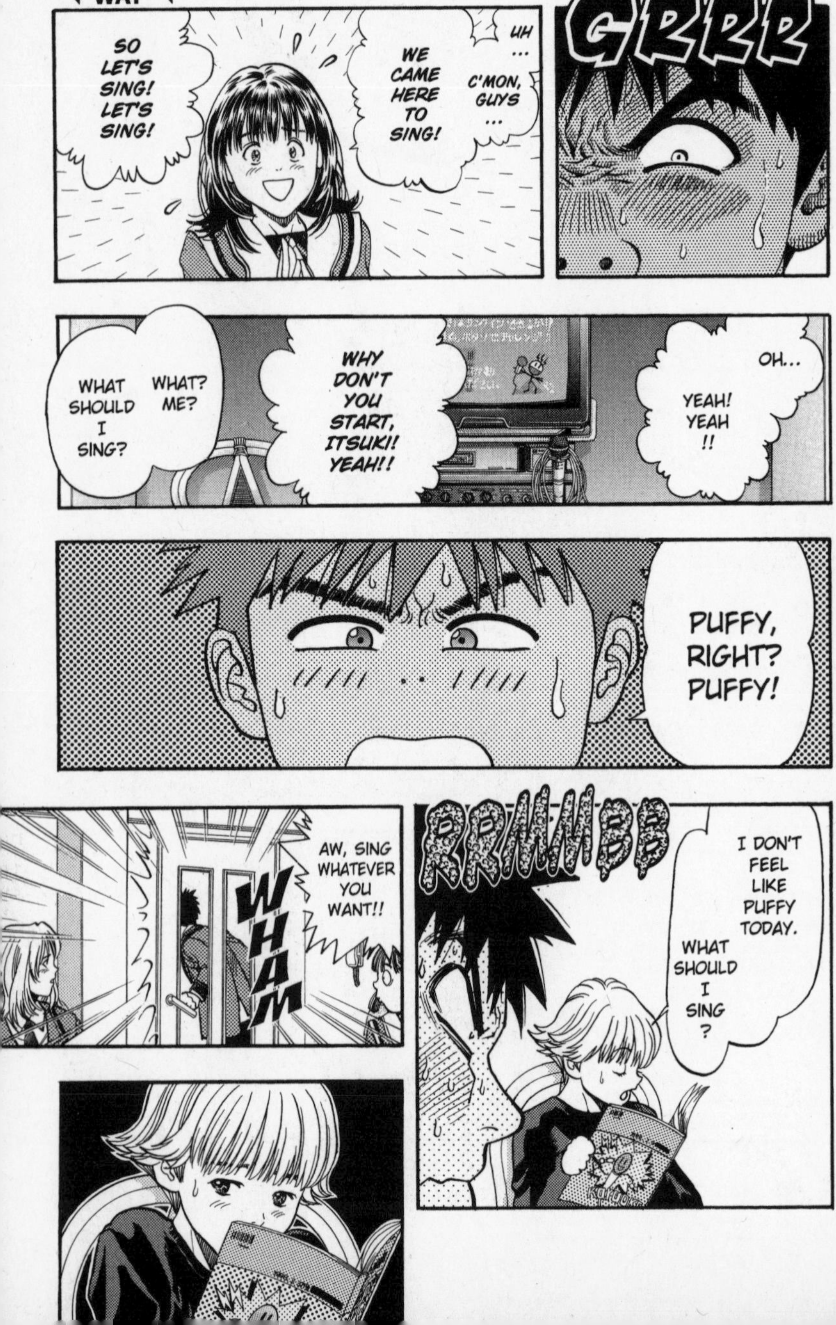
GRRR
UH ... C'MON, GUYS ...
WE CAME HERE TO SING!
SO LET'S SING! LET'S SING!
OH...
YEAH! YEAH !!
WHY DON'T YOU START, ITSUKI! YEAH!!
WHAT? ME?
WHAT SHOULD I SING?
PUFFY, RIGHT? PUFFY!
RRMMBB
I DON'T FEEL LIKE PUFFY TODAY.
WHAT SHOULD I SING ?
AW, SING WHATEVER YOU WANT!!
WHAM

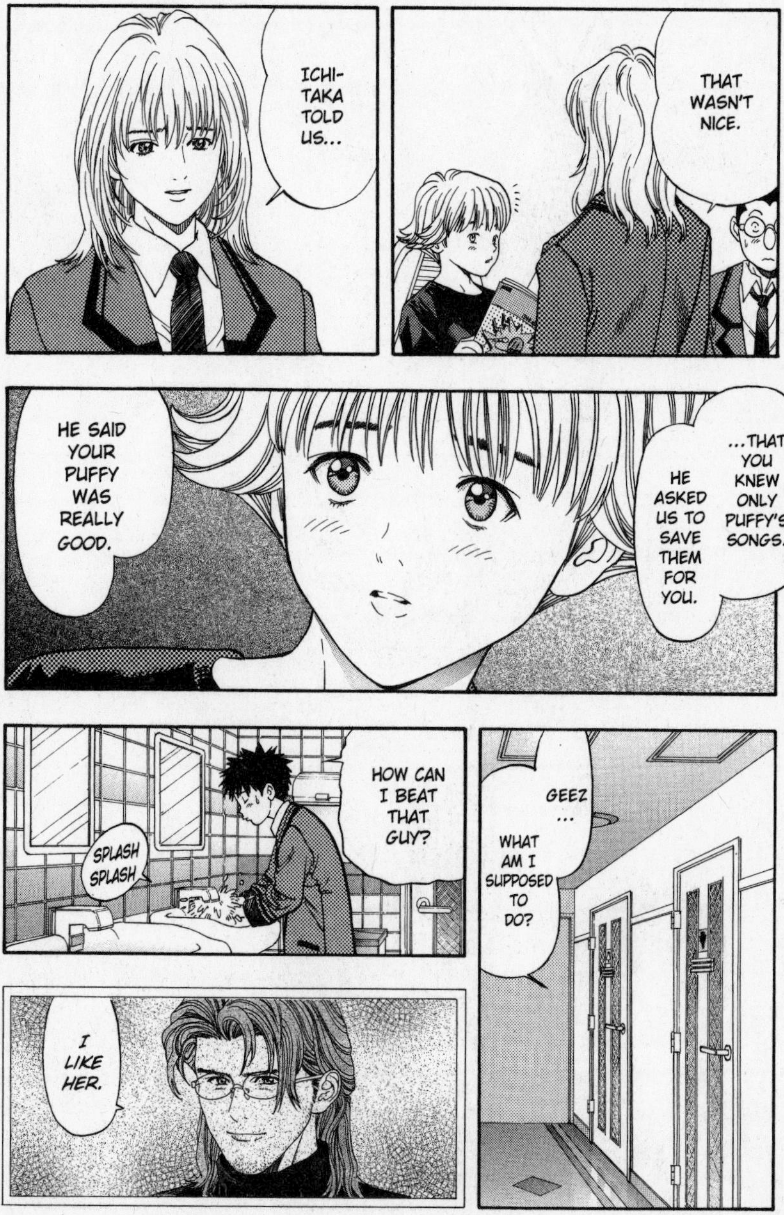
THAT WASN'T NICE.
ICHI-TAKA TOLD US...
...THAT YOU KNEW ONLY PUFFY'S SONGS.
HE ASKED US TO SAVE THEM FOR YOU.
HE SAID YOUR PUFFY WAS REALLY GOOD.
GEEZ...
WHAT AM I SUPPOSED TO DO?
HOW CAN I BEAT THAT GUY?
SPLASH SPLASH
I LIKE HER.

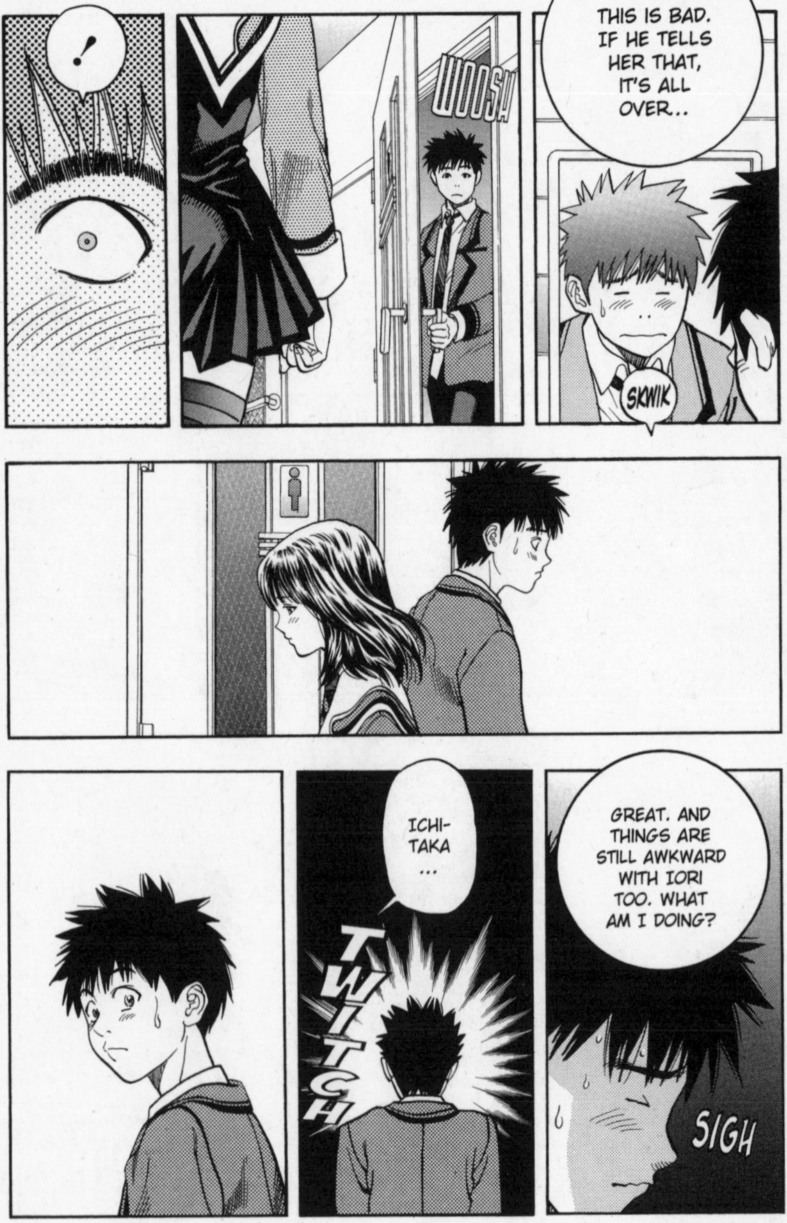
THIS IS BAD. IF HE TELLS HER THAT, IT'S ALL OVER...
SKWIK
WOOSH
!
GREAT. AND THINGS ARE STILL AWKWARD WITH IORI TOO. WHAT AM I DOING?
SIGH
ICHI-TAKA ...
TWITCH

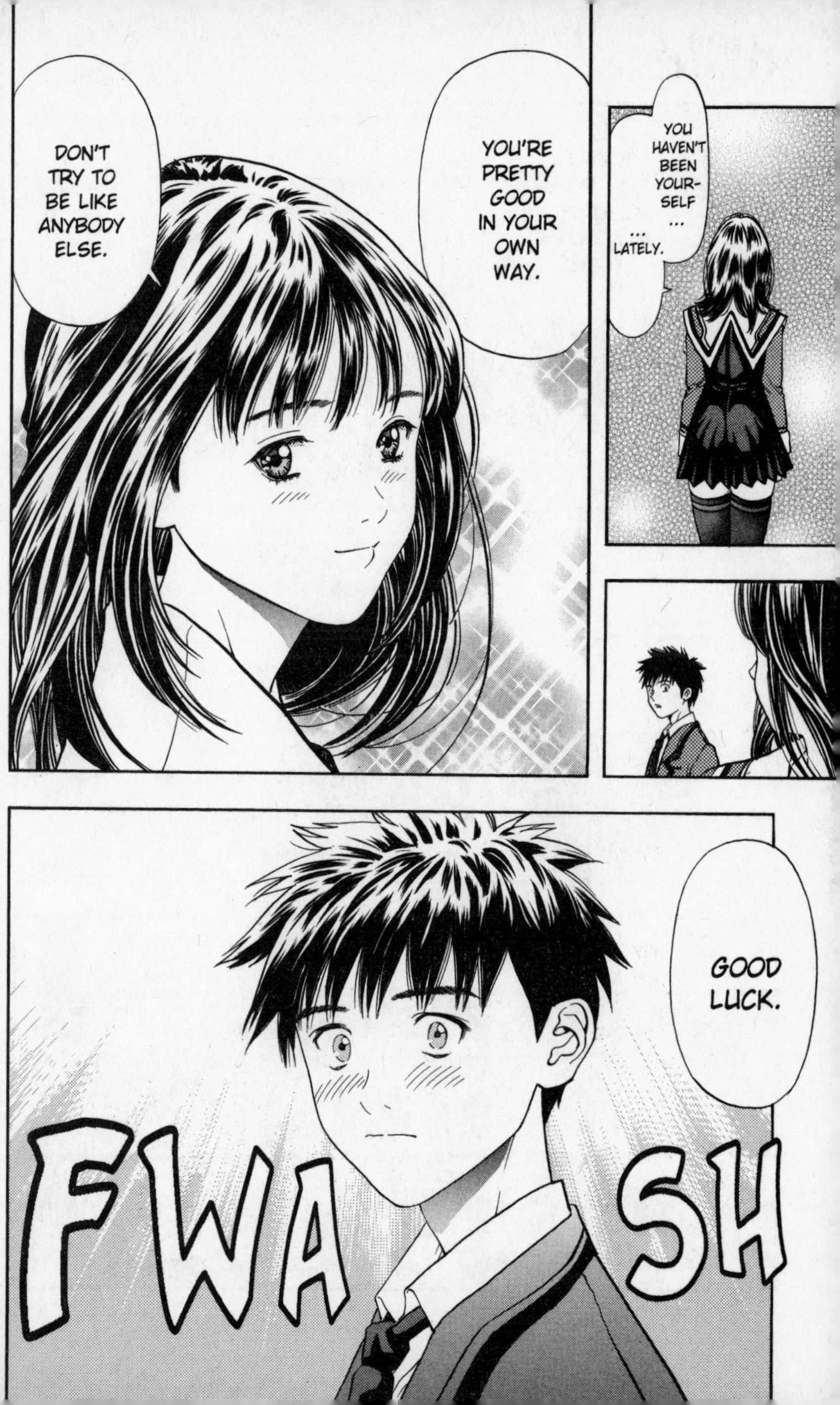
YOU HAVEN'T BEEN YOURSELF ... ...LATELY.
YOU'RE PRETTY GOOD IN YOUR OWN WAY.
DON'T TRY TO BE LIKE ANYBODY ELSE.
GOOD LUCK.
FWASH

READ THIS WAY

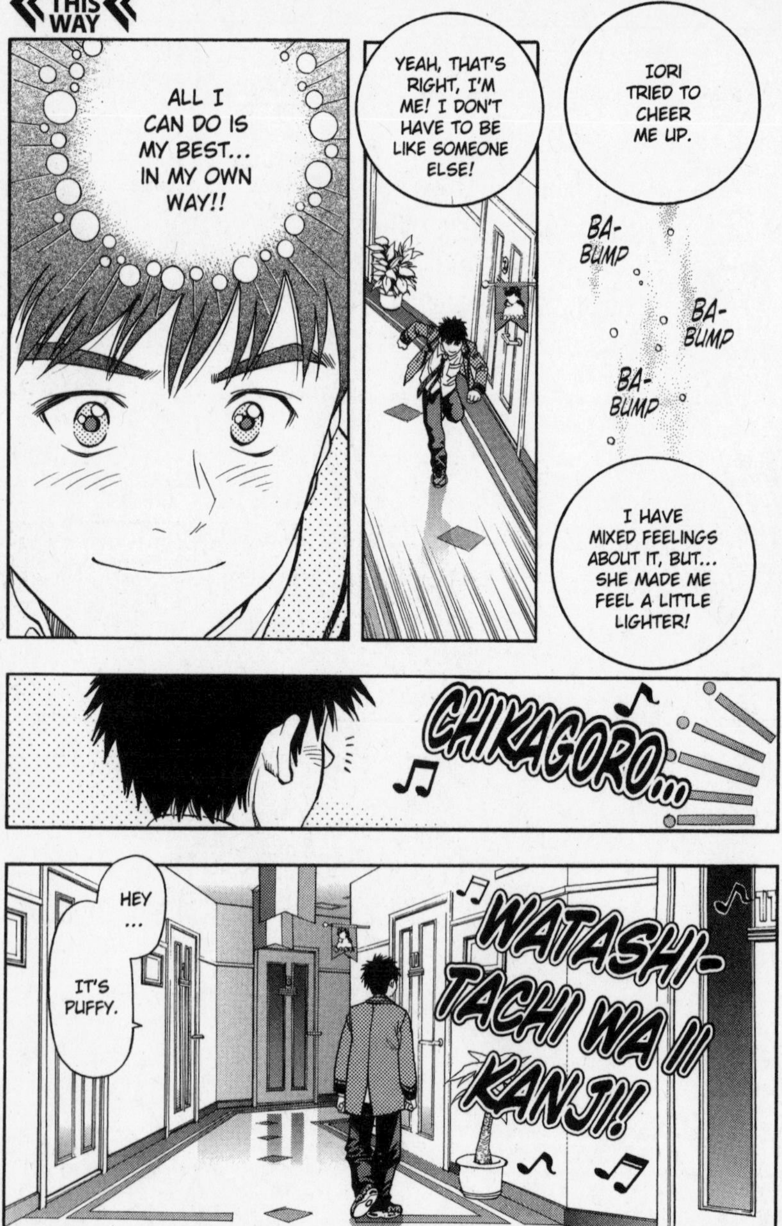
IORI TRIED TO CHEER ME UP.
BA-BUMP
BA-BUMP
BA-BUMP
I HAVE MIXED FEELINGS ABOUT IT, BUT... SHE MADE ME FEEL A LITTLE LIGHTER!
YEAH, THAT'S RIGHT, I'M ME! I DON'T HAVE TO BE LIKE SOMEONE ELSE!
ALL I CAN DO IS MY BEST... IN MY OWN WAY!!
CHIKAGORO...
WATASHI-TACHI WA II KANJI!
HEY...
IT'S PUFFY.

I"s

アイズ

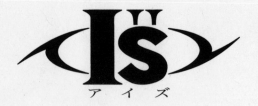

Chapter 47:
A New Attitude

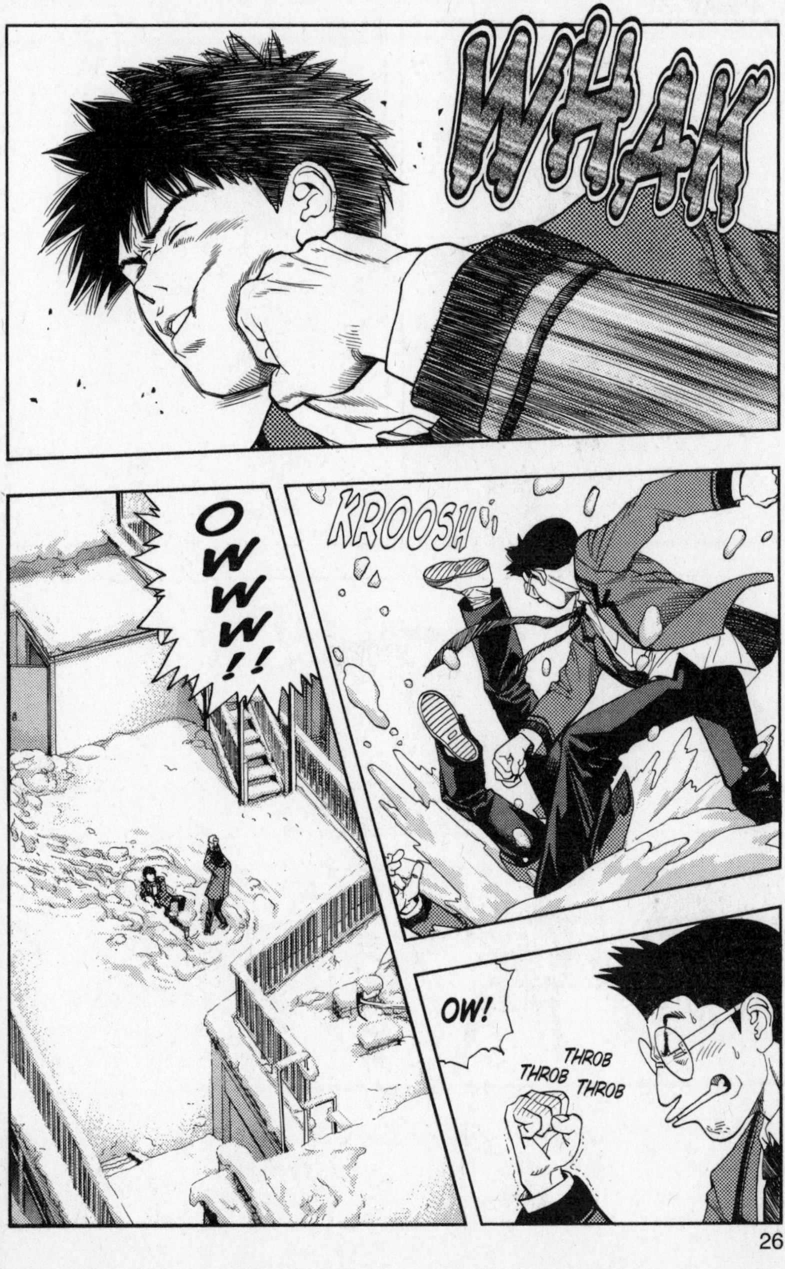
WHAK
KROOSH
OW!
THROB
THROB THROB
OWWW!!

READ THIS WAY

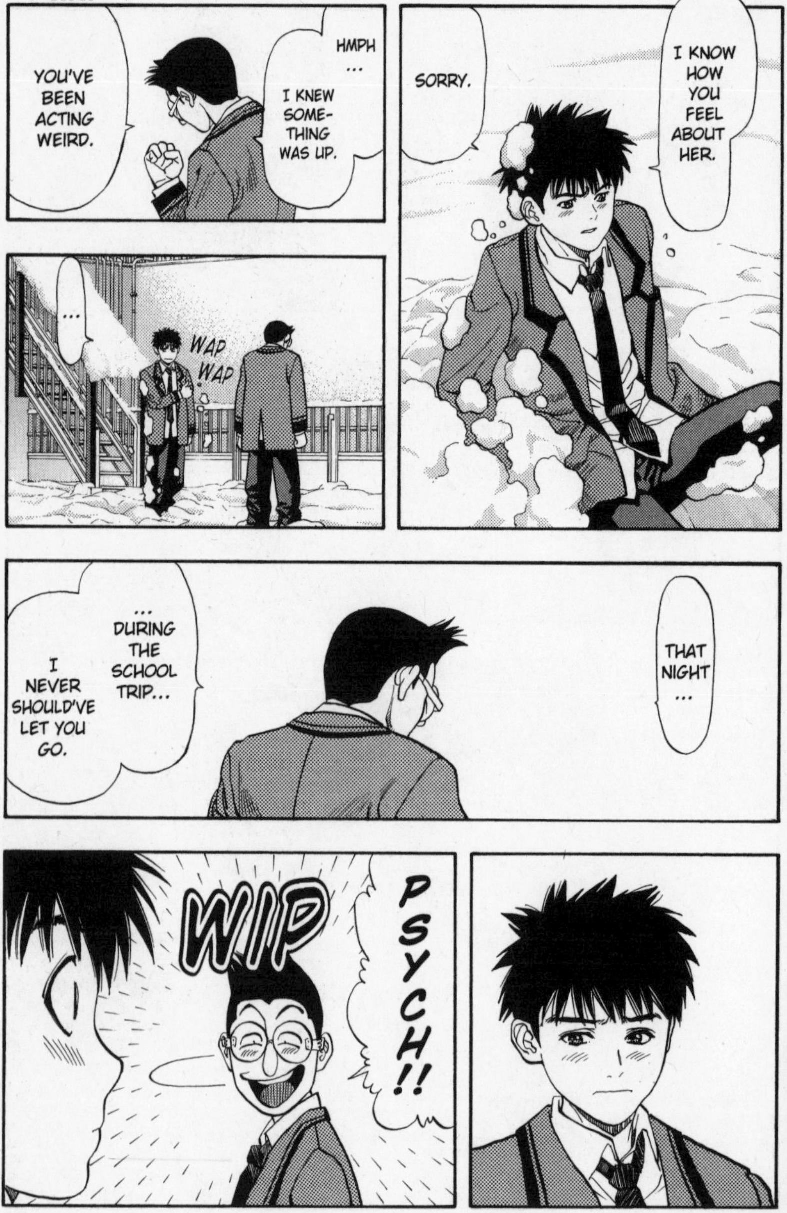

I KNOW HOW YOU FEEL ABOUT HER.
SORRY.
HMPH ... I KNEW SOME-THING WAS UP.
YOU'VE BEEN ACTING WEIRD.
...
WAP WAP
THAT NIGHT ...
... DURING THE SCHOOL TRIP...
I NEVER SHOULD'VE LET YOU GO.
PSYCH!!
WIP

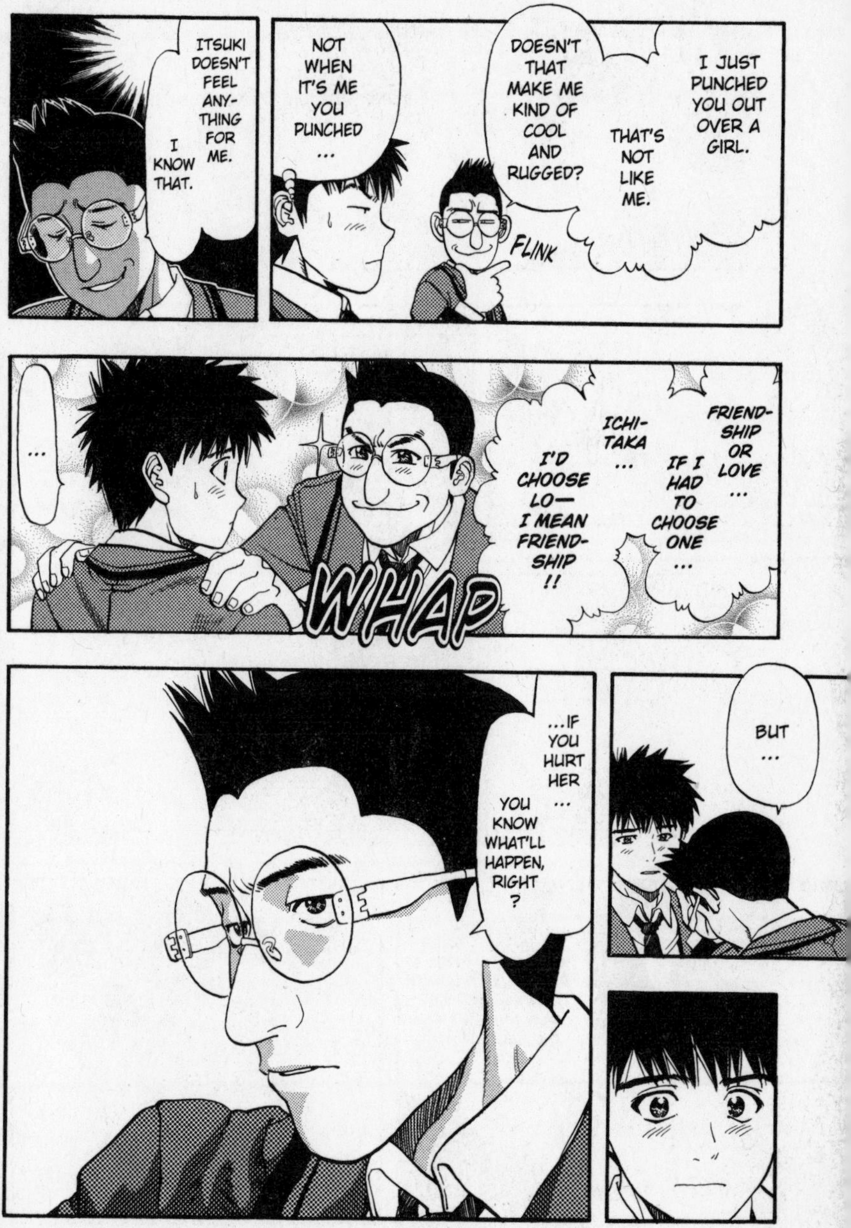
I JUST PUNCHED YOU OUT OVER A GIRL.
THAT'S NOT LIKE ME.
DOESN'T THAT MAKE ME KIND OF COOL AND RUGGED?
FLINK
NOT WHEN IT'S ME YOU PUNCHED ...
ITSUKI DOESN'T FEEL ANY-THING FOR ME.
I KNOW THAT.
FRIEND-SHIP OR LOVE ...
IF I HAD TO CHOOSE ONE ...
ICHI-TAKA ...
I'D CHOOSE LO— I MEAN FRIEND-SHIP !!
WHAP
...
BUT ...
...IF YOU HURT HER ...
YOU KNOW WHAT'LL HAPPEN, RIGHT ?

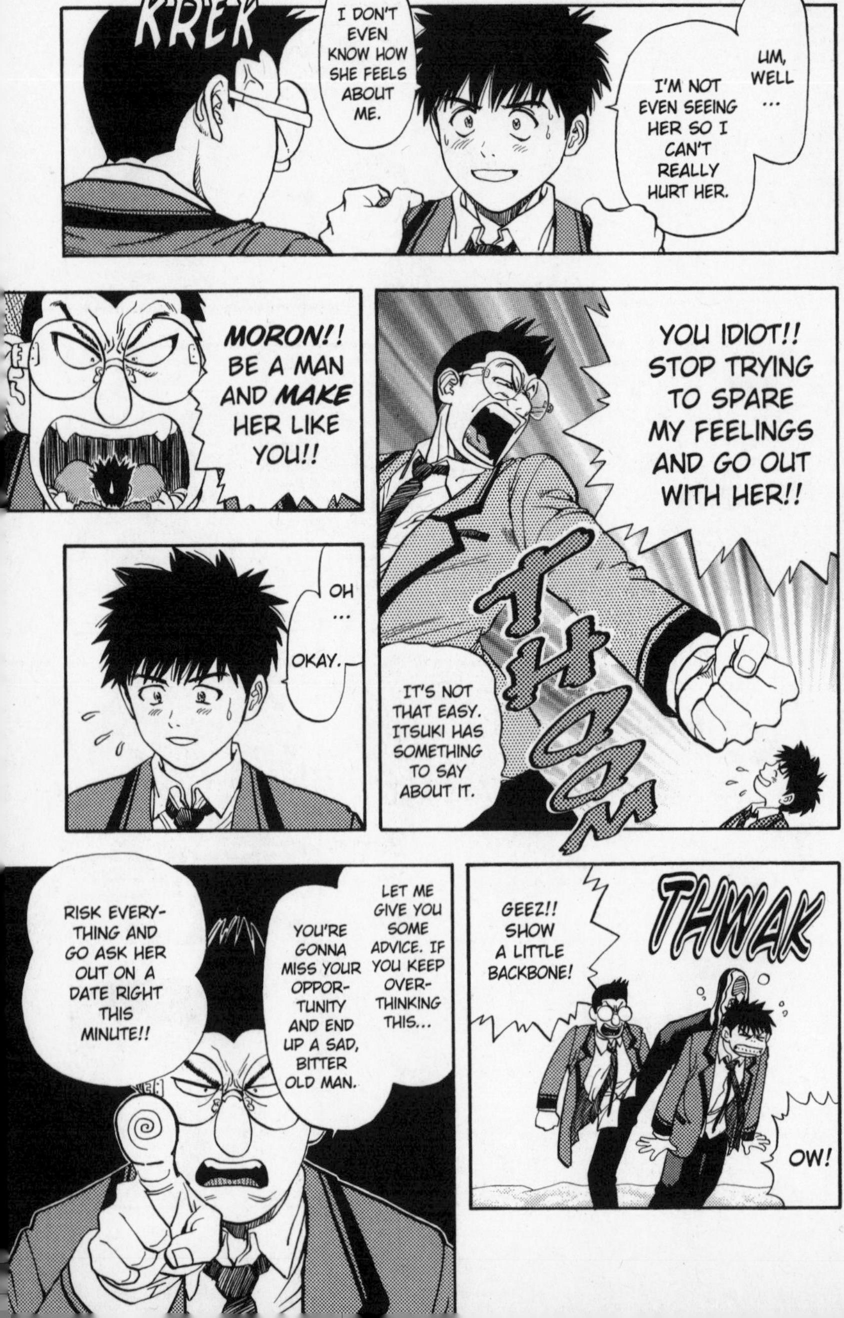
UM, WELL ...
I'M NOT EVEN SEEING HER SO I CAN'T REALLY HURT HER.
I DON'T EVEN KNOW HOW SHE FEELS ABOUT ME.
KREK
YOU IDIOT!! STOP TRYING TO SPARE MY FEELINGS AND GO OUT WITH HER!!
THOOM
IT'S NOT THAT EASY. ITSUKI HAS SOMETHING TO SAY ABOUT IT.
MORON!! BE A MAN AND MAKE HER LIKE YOU!!
OH ... OKAY.
THWAK
GEEZ!! SHOW A LITTLE BACKBONE!
OW!
LET ME GIVE YOU SOME ADVICE. IF YOU KEEP OVER-THINKING THIS...
YOU'RE GONNA MISS YOUR OPPOR-TUNITY AND END UP A SAD, BITTER OLD MAN.
RISK EVERY-THING AND GO ASK HER OUT ON A DATE RIGHT THIS MINUTE!!

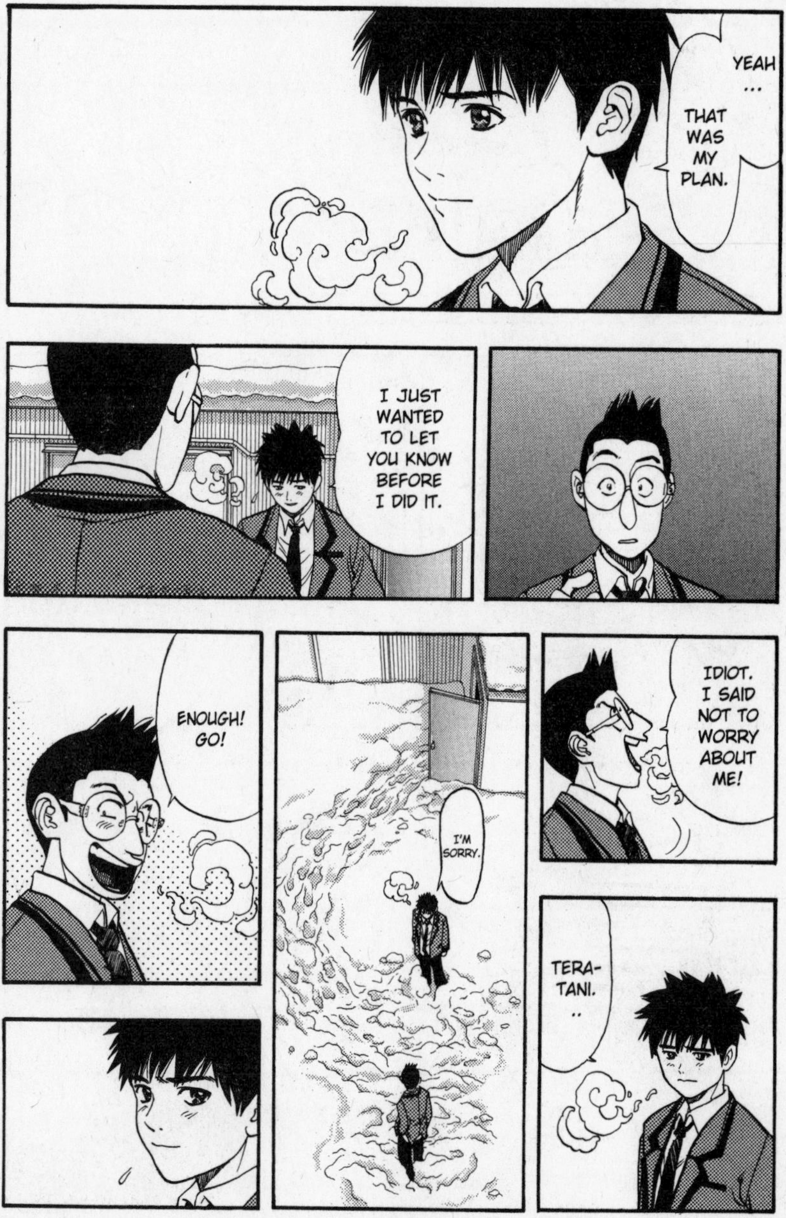
YEAH ...
THAT WAS MY PLAN.
I JUST WANTED TO LET YOU KNOW BEFORE I DID IT.
IDIOT. I SAID NOT TO WORRY ABOUT ME!
TERA-TANI...
I'M SORRY.
ENOUGH! GO!

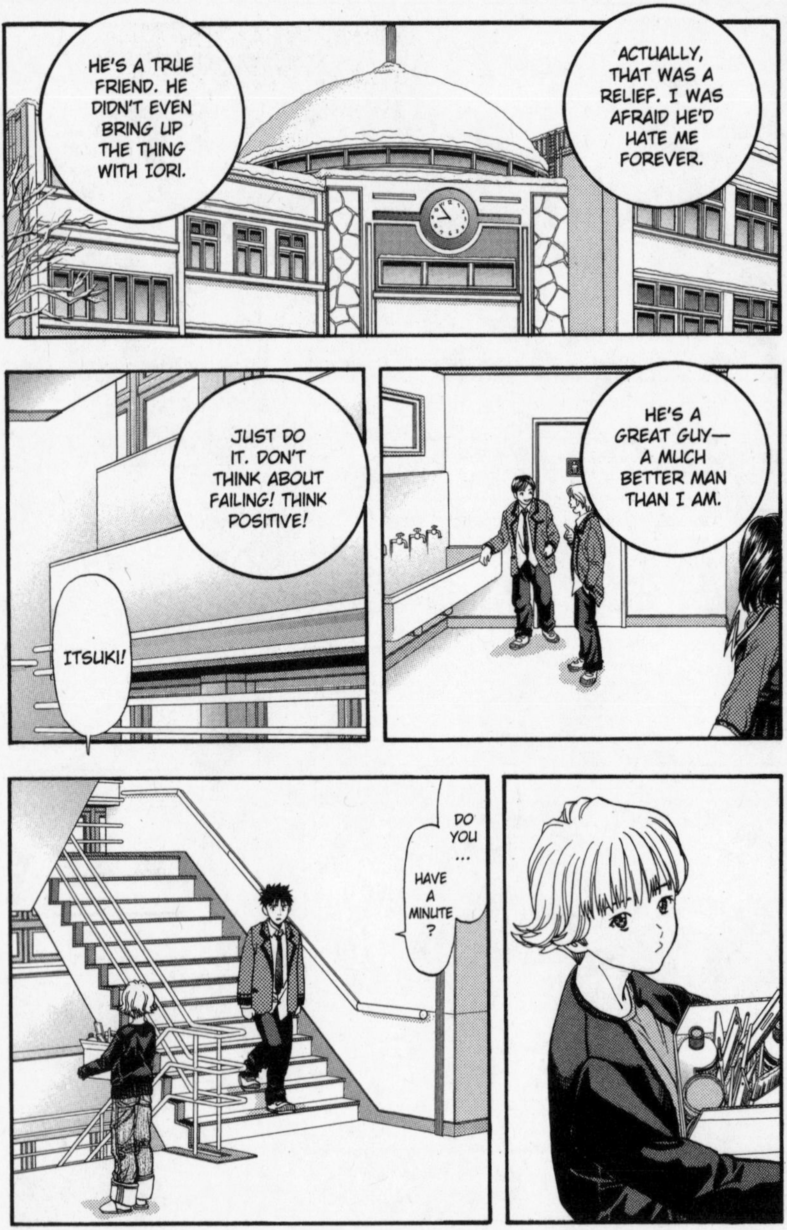
ACTUALLY, THAT WAS A RELIEF. I WAS AFRAID HE'D HATE ME FOREVER.
HE'S A TRUE FRIEND. HE DIDN'T EVEN BRING UP THE THING WITH IORI.
HE'S A GREAT GUY— A MUCH BETTER MAN THAN I AM.
JUST DO IT. DON'T THINK ABOUT FAILING! THINK POSITIVE!
ITSUKI!
DO YOU... HAVE A MINUTE?

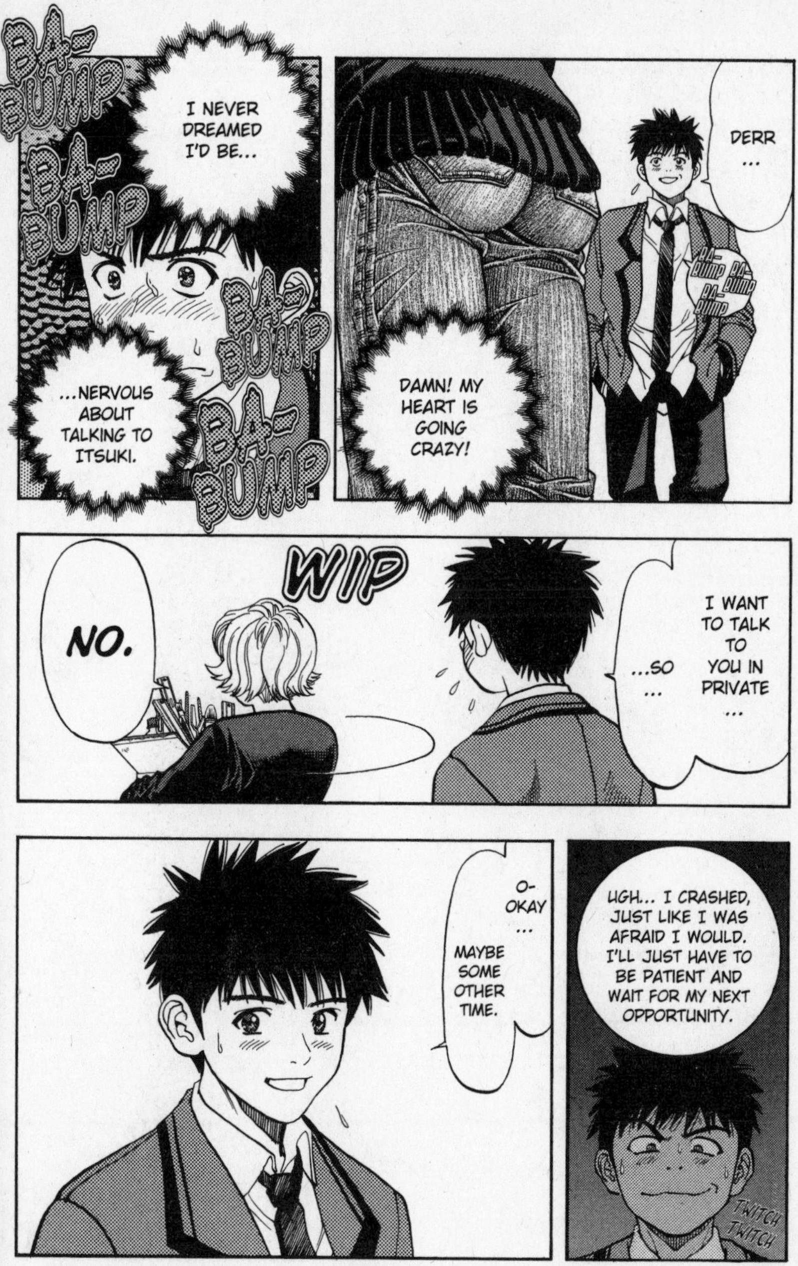
DERR ...
BA-BUMP BA-BUMP BA-BUMP
DAMN! MY HEART IS GOING CRAZY!
BA-BUMP
BA-BUMP
I NEVER DREAMED I'D BE...
BA-BUMP
BA-BUMP
...NERVOUS ABOUT TALKING TO ITSUKI.
I WANT TO TALK TO YOU IN PRIVATE ...
...SO ...
WIP
NO.
UGH... I CRASHED, JUST LIKE I WAS AFRAID I WOULD. I'LL JUST HAVE TO BE PATIENT AND WAIT FOR MY NEXT OPPORTUNITY.
TWITCH TWITCH
O-OKAY ...
MAYBE SOME OTHER TIME.

READ THIS WAY

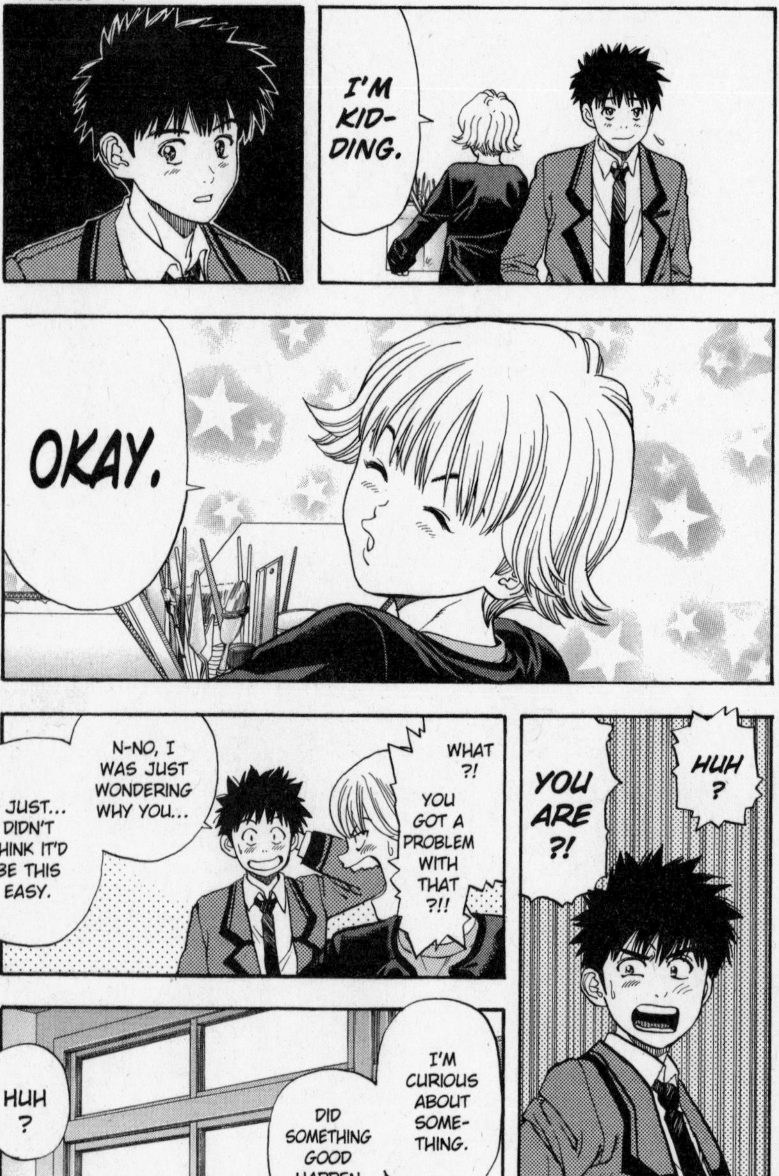
I'M KIDDING.
OKAY.
HUH ?
YOU ARE ?!
WHAT ?! YOU GOT A PROBLEM WITH THAT ?!!
N-NO, I WAS JUST WONDERING WHY YOU...
I JUST... DIDN'T THINK IT'D BE THIS EASY.
I'M CURIOUS ABOUT SOME-THING.
DID SOMETHING GOOD HAPPEN TO YOU?
HUH ?

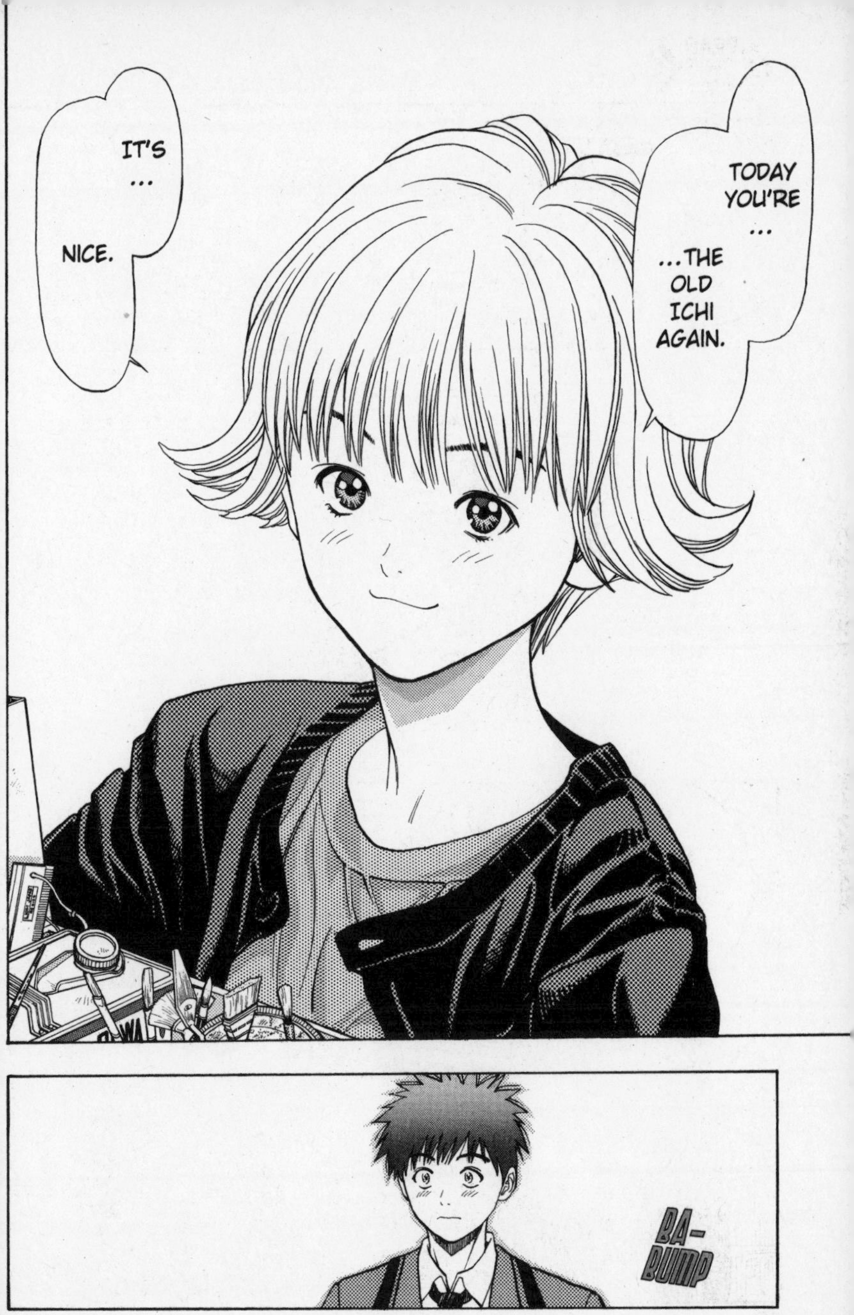
TODAY YOU'RE ... ...THE OLD ICHI AGAIN.
IT'S ... NICE.
BA-BUMP

READ THIS WAY

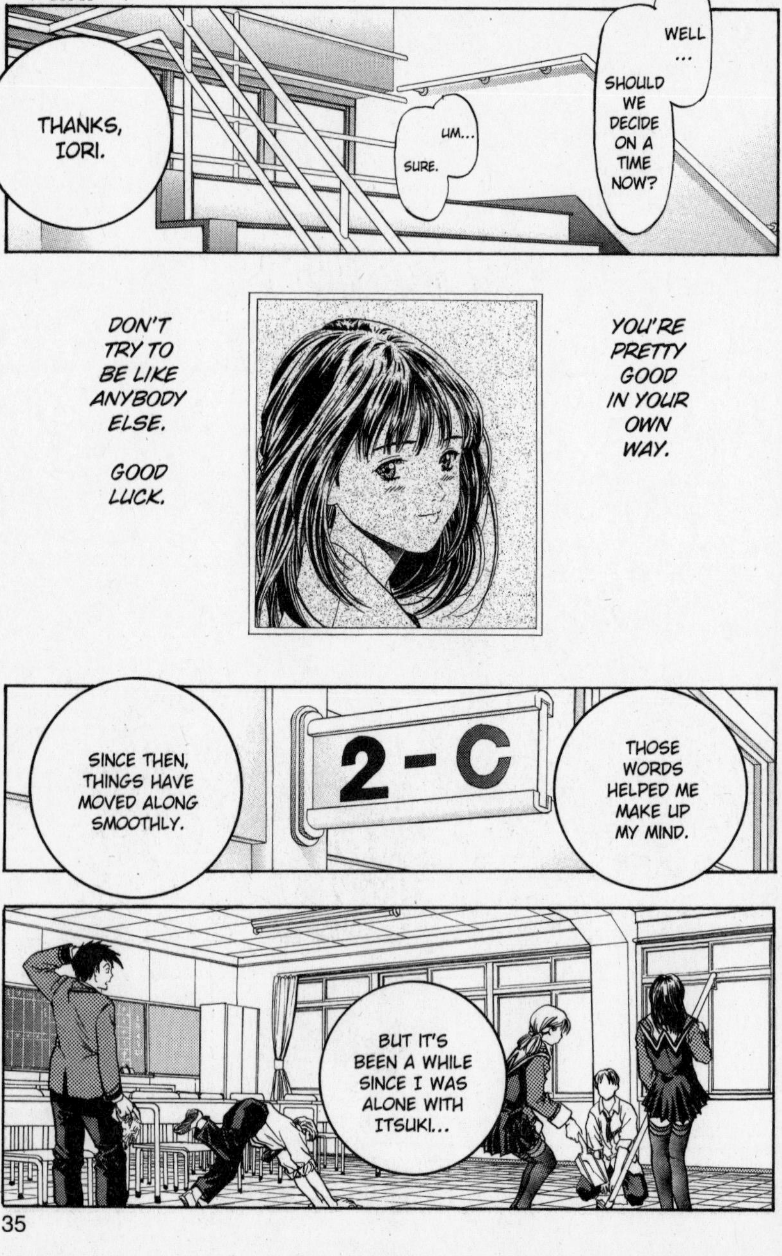
WELL... SHOULD WE DECIDE ON A TIME NOW?
UM... SURE.
THANKS, IORI.
YOU'RE PRETTY GOOD IN YOUR OWN WAY.
DON'T TRY TO BE LIKE ANYBODY ELSE.
GOOD LUCK.
THOSE WORDS HELPED ME MAKE UP MY MIND.
2-C
SINCE THEN, THINGS HAVE MOVED ALONG SMOOTHLY.
BUT IT'S BEEN A WHILE SINCE I WAS ALONE WITH ITSUKI...

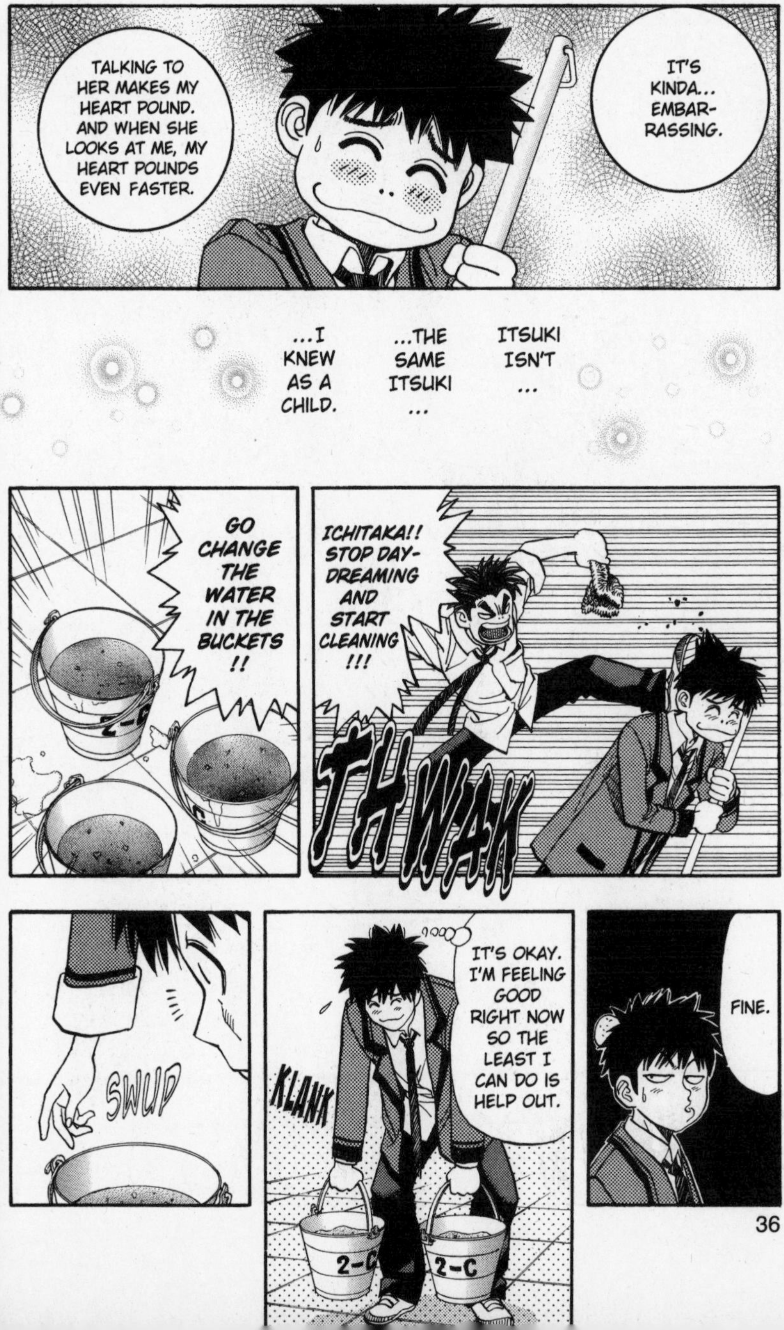

IT'S KINDA... EMBARRASSING.
TALKING TO HER MAKES MY HEART POUND. AND WHEN SHE LOOKS AT ME, MY HEART POUNDS EVEN FASTER.
ITSUKI ISN'T ...
...THE SAME ITSUKI ...
...I KNEW AS A CHILD.
ICHITAKA!! STOP DAY-DREAMING AND START CLEANING!!!
THWAK
GO CHANGE THE WATER IN THE BUCKETS!!
FINE.
IT'S OKAY. I'M FEELING GOOD RIGHT NOW SO THE LEAST I CAN DO IS HELP OUT.
KLANK
SWUP

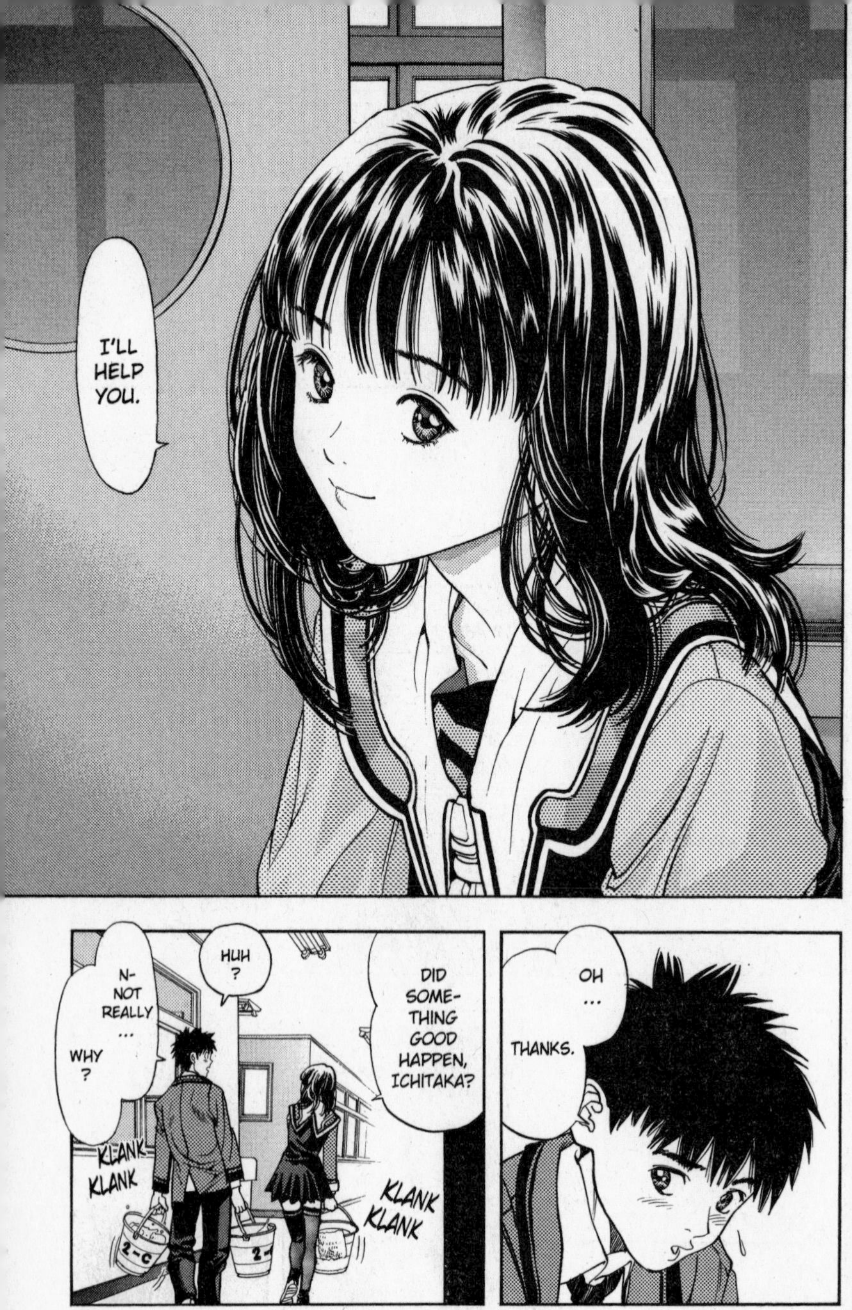
I'LL HELP YOU.
OH ...
THANKS.
DID SOME-THING GOOD HAPPEN, ICHITAKA?
HUH ?
N-NOT REALLY ...
WHY ?
KLANK KLANK
KLANK KLANK

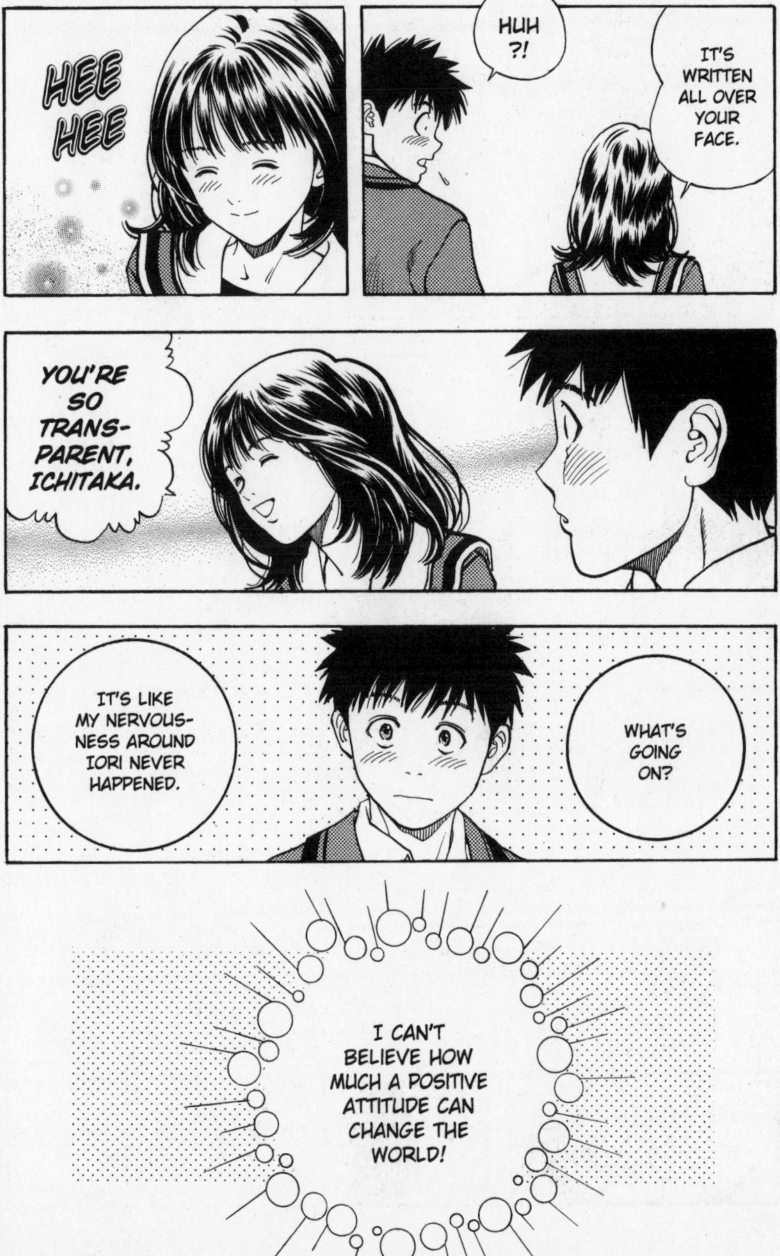
IT'S WRITTEN ALL OVER YOUR FACE.
HUH ?!
HEE HEE
YOU'RE SO TRANS-PARENT, ICHITAKA.
WHAT'S GOING ON?
IT'S LIKE MY NERVOUS-NESS AROUND IORI NEVER HAPPENED.
I CAN'T BELIEVE HOW MUCH A POSITIVE ATTITUDE CAN CHANGE THE WORLD!

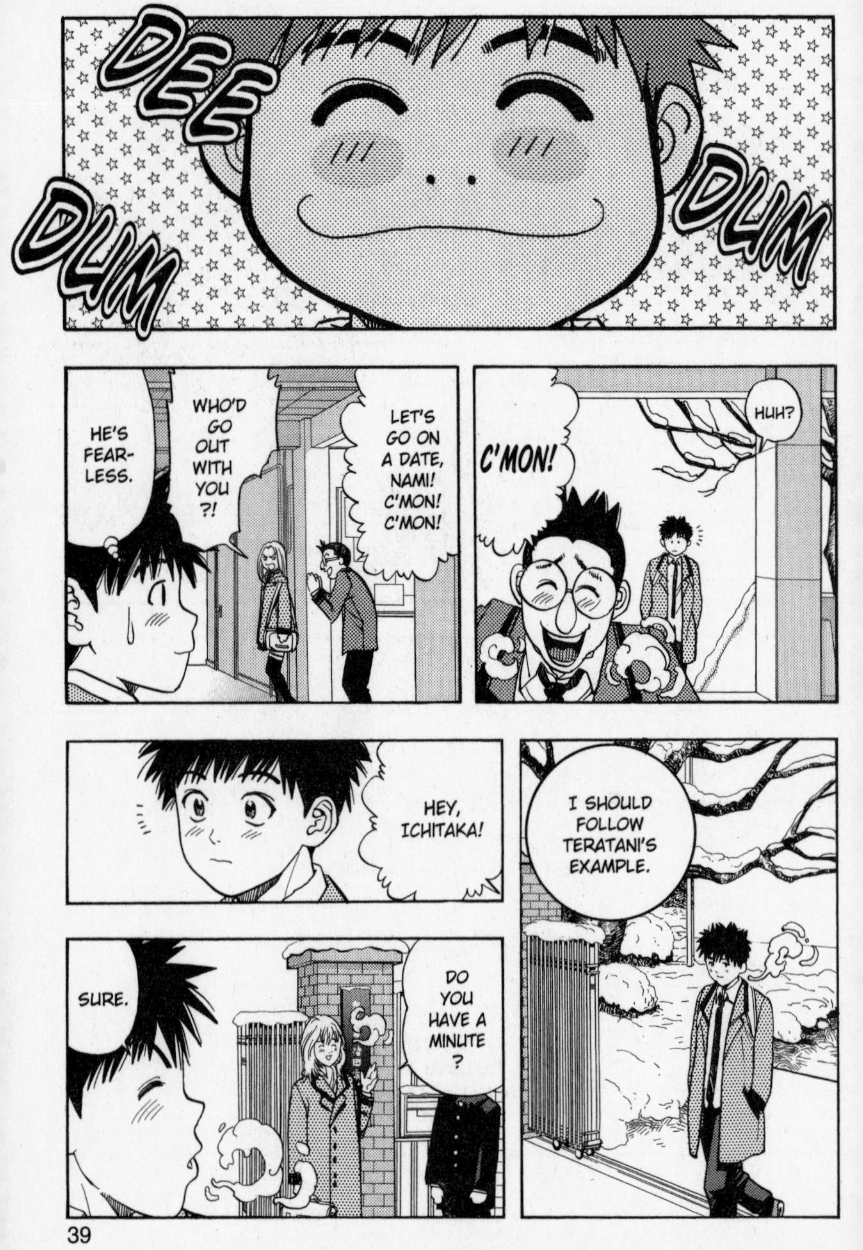
DEE
DUM
DUM
HUH?
C'MON!
LET'S GO ON A DATE, NAMI! C'MON! C'MON!
WHO'D GO OUT WITH YOU?!
HE'S FEARLESS.
I SHOULD FOLLOW TERATANI'S EXAMPLE.
HEY, ICHITAKA!
DO YOU HAVE A MINUTE?
SURE.

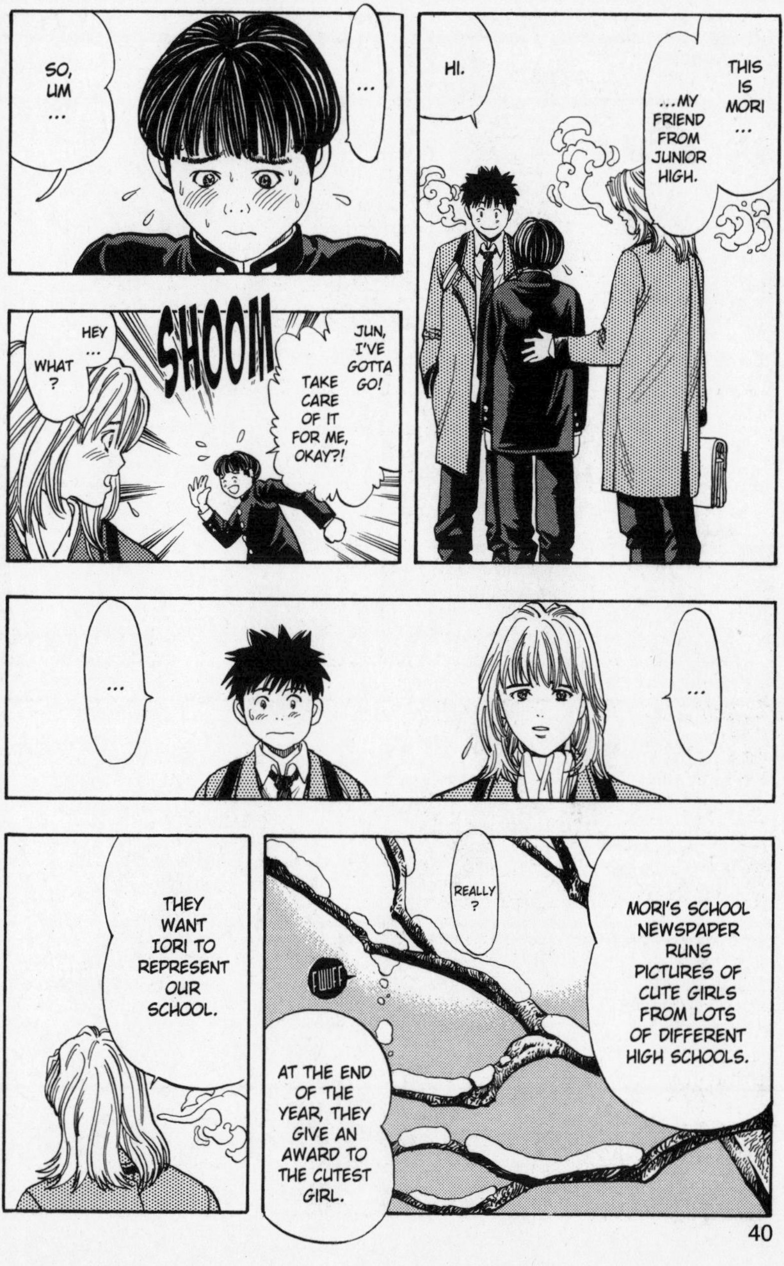
THIS IS MORI ...
...MY FRIEND FROM JUNIOR HIGH.
HI.
...
SO, UM ...
JUN, I'VE GOTTA GO!
TAKE CARE OF IT FOR ME, OKAY?!
SHOOM
HEY ...
WHAT ?
...
...
MORI'S SCHOOL NEWSPAPER RUNS PICTURES OF CUTE GIRLS FROM LOTS OF DIFFERENT HIGH SCHOOLS.
REALLY ?
FWUFF
AT THE END OF THE YEAR, THEY GIVE AN AWARD TO THE CUTEST GIRL.
THEY WANT IORI TO REPRESENT OUR SCHOOL.

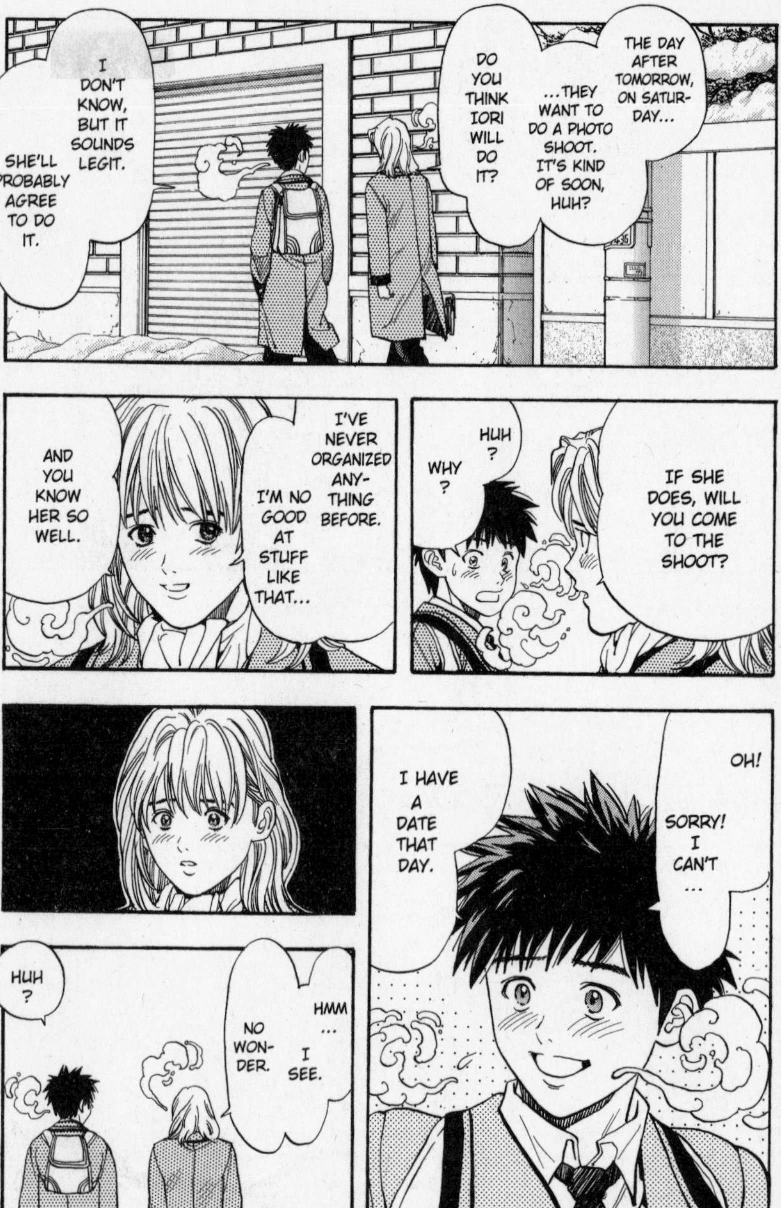
THE DAY AFTER TOMORROW, ON SATURDAY...
...THEY WANT TO DO A PHOTO SHOOT. IT'S KIND OF SOON, HUH?
DO YOU THINK IORI WILL DO IT?
I DON'T KNOW, BUT IT SOUNDS LEGIT.
SHE'LL PROBABLY AGREE TO DO IT.
IF SHE DOES, WILL YOU COME TO THE SHOOT?
HUH?
WHY?
I'VE NEVER ORGANIZED ANYTHING BEFORE.
I'M NO GOOD AT STUFF LIKE THAT...
AND YOU KNOW HER SO WELL.
OH!
SORRY! I CAN'T ...
I HAVE A DATE THAT DAY.
HMM... I SEE.
NO WONDER.
HUH?

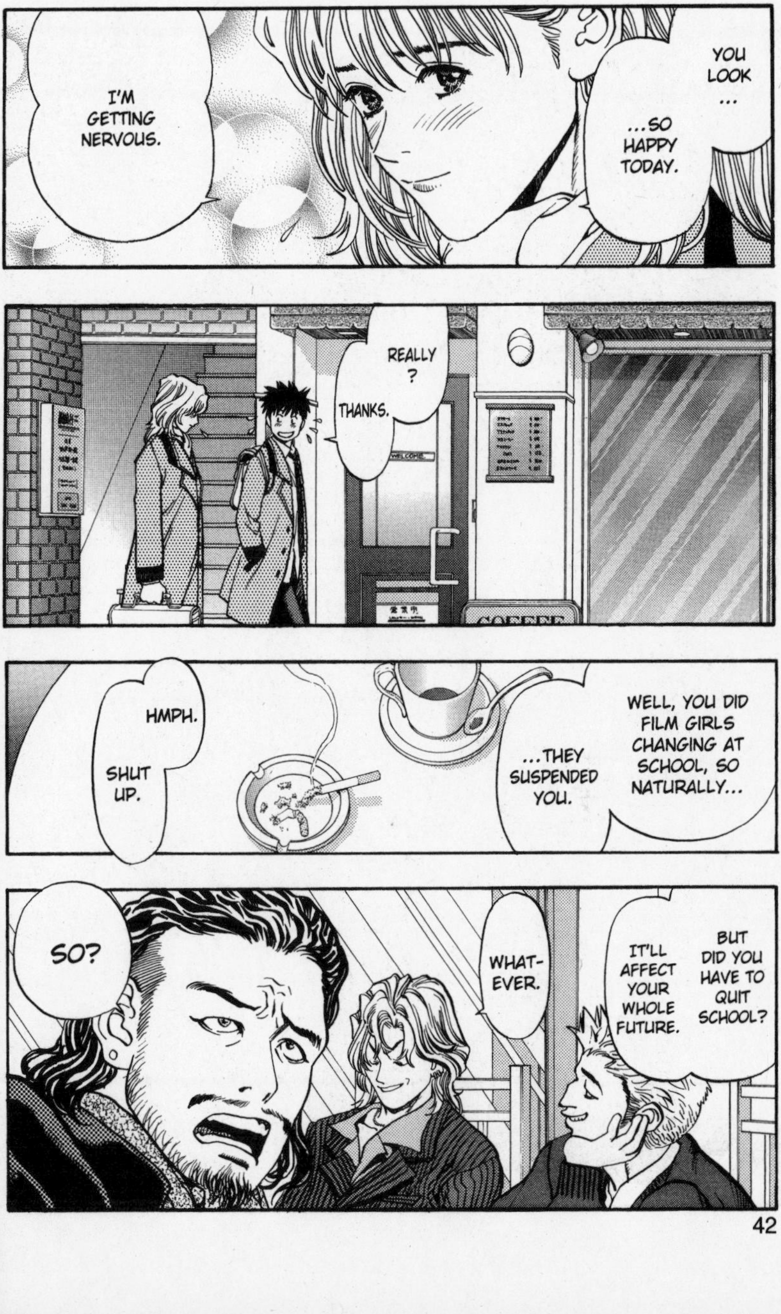
YOU LOOK... ...SO HAPPY TODAY.
I'M GETTING NERVOUS.
REALLY? THANKS.
WELL, YOU DID FILM GIRLS CHANGING AT SCHOOL, SO NATURALLY... ...THEY SUSPENDED YOU.
HMPH. SHUT UP.
BUT DID YOU HAVE TO QUIT SCHOOL? IT'LL AFFECT YOUR WHOLE FUTURE.
WHAT-EVER.
SO?

READ THIS WAY

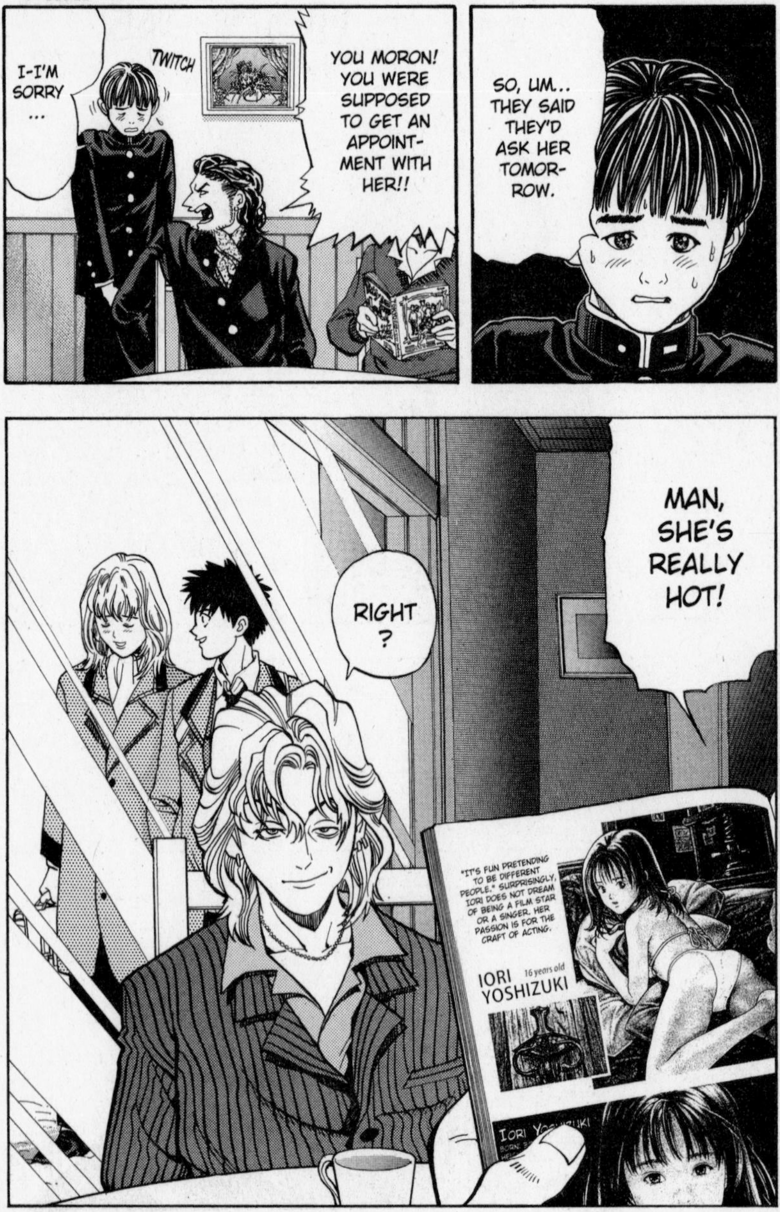

SO, UM... THEY SAID THEY'D ASK HER TOMORROW.
YOU MORON! YOU WERE SUPPOSED TO GET AN APPOINTMENT WITH HER!!
TWITCH
I-I'M SORRY ...
MAN, SHE'S REALLY HOT!
RIGHT ?
"IT'S FUN PRETENDING TO BE DIFFERENT PEOPLE." SURPRISINGLY, IORI DOES NOT DREAM OF BEING A FILM STAR OR A SINGER. HER PASSION IS FOR THE CRAFT OF ACTING.
IORI YOSHIZUKI
16 years old

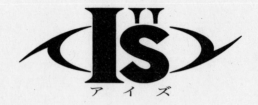

アイズ

Chapter 48:
A Strange Phone Call

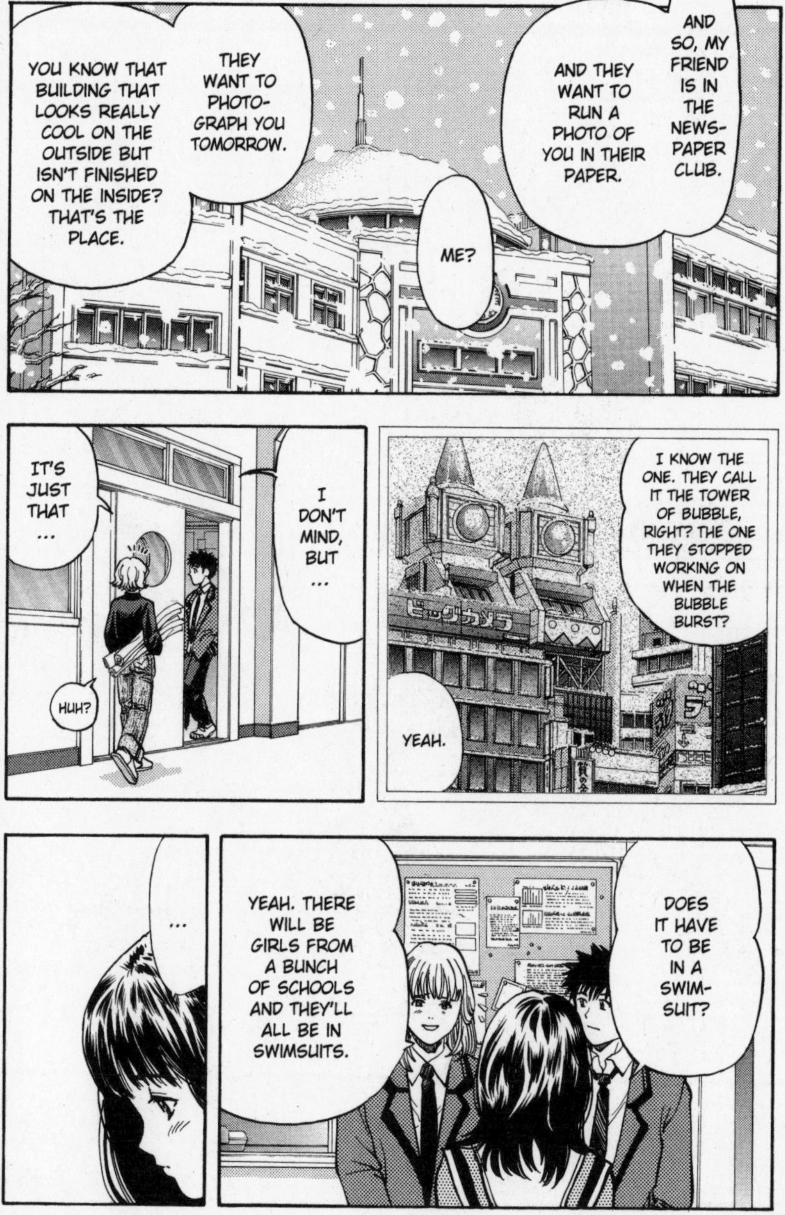
AND SO, MY FRIEND IS IN THE NEWS-PAPER CLUB.
AND THEY WANT TO RUN A PHOTO OF YOU IN THEIR PAPER.
ME?
THEY WANT TO PHOTO-GRAPH YOU TOMORROW.
YOU KNOW THAT BUILDING THAT LOOKS REALLY COOL ON THE OUTSIDE BUT ISN'T FINISHED ON THE INSIDE? THAT'S THE PLACE.
I KNOW THE ONE. THEY CALL IT THE TOWER OF BUBBLE, RIGHT? THE ONE THEY STOPPED WORKING ON WHEN THE BUBBLE BURST?
YEAH.
I DON'T MIND, BUT ...
IT'S JUST THAT ...
HUH?
DOES IT HAVE TO BE IN A SWIM-SUIT?
YEAH. THERE WILL BE GIRLS FROM A BUNCH OF SCHOOLS AND THEY'LL ALL BE IN SWIMSUITS.
...

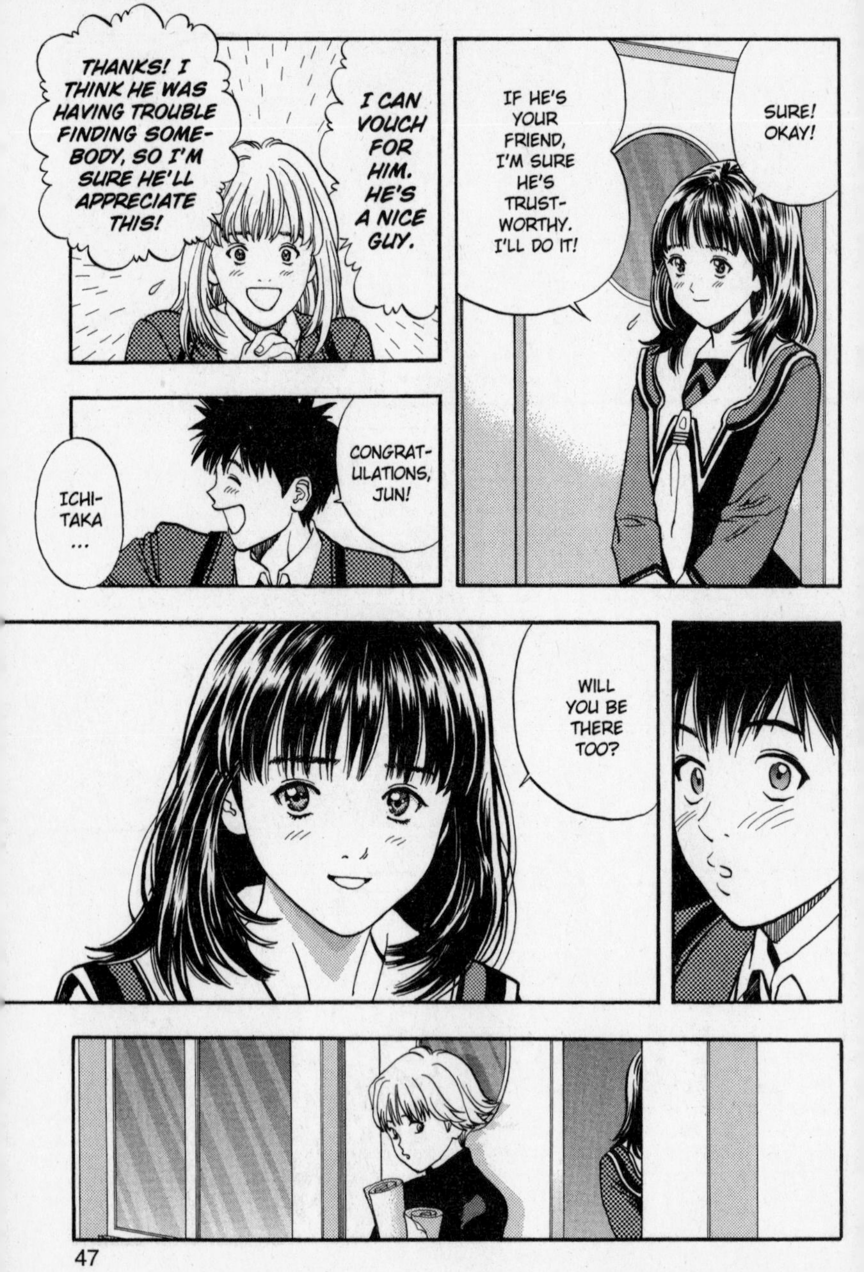
SURE! OKAY!
IF HE'S YOUR FRIEND, I'M SURE HE'S TRUST-WORTHY. I'LL DO IT!
I CAN VOUCH FOR HIM. HE'S A NICE GUY.
THANKS! I THINK HE WAS HAVING TROUBLE FINDING SOME-BODY, SO I'M SURE HE'LL APPRECIATE THIS!
CONGRAT-ULATIONS, JUN!
ICHI-TAKA ...
WILL YOU BE THERE TOO?

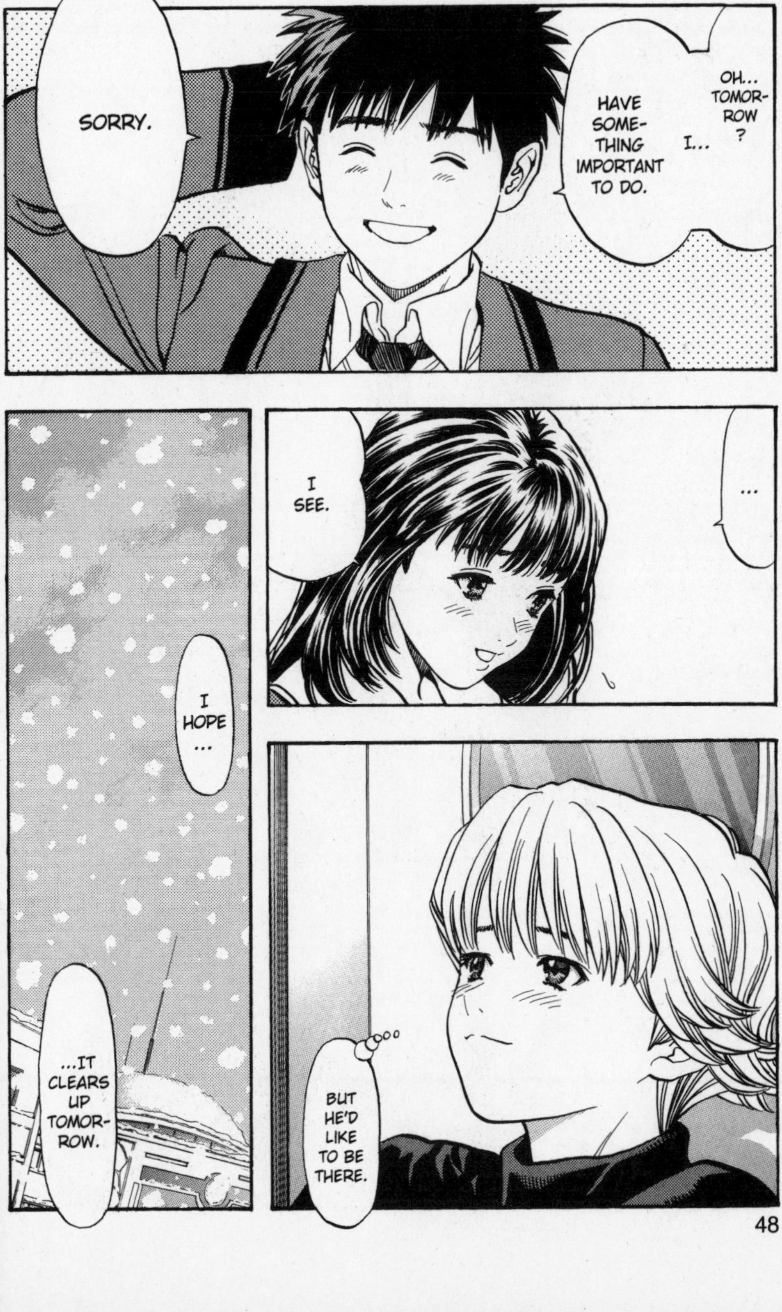
OH... TOMORROW?
I... HAVE SOMETHING IMPORTANT TO DO.
SORRY.
...
I SEE.
BUT HE'D LIKE TO BE THERE.
I HOPE...
...IT CLEARS UP TOMORROW.

READ THIS WAY

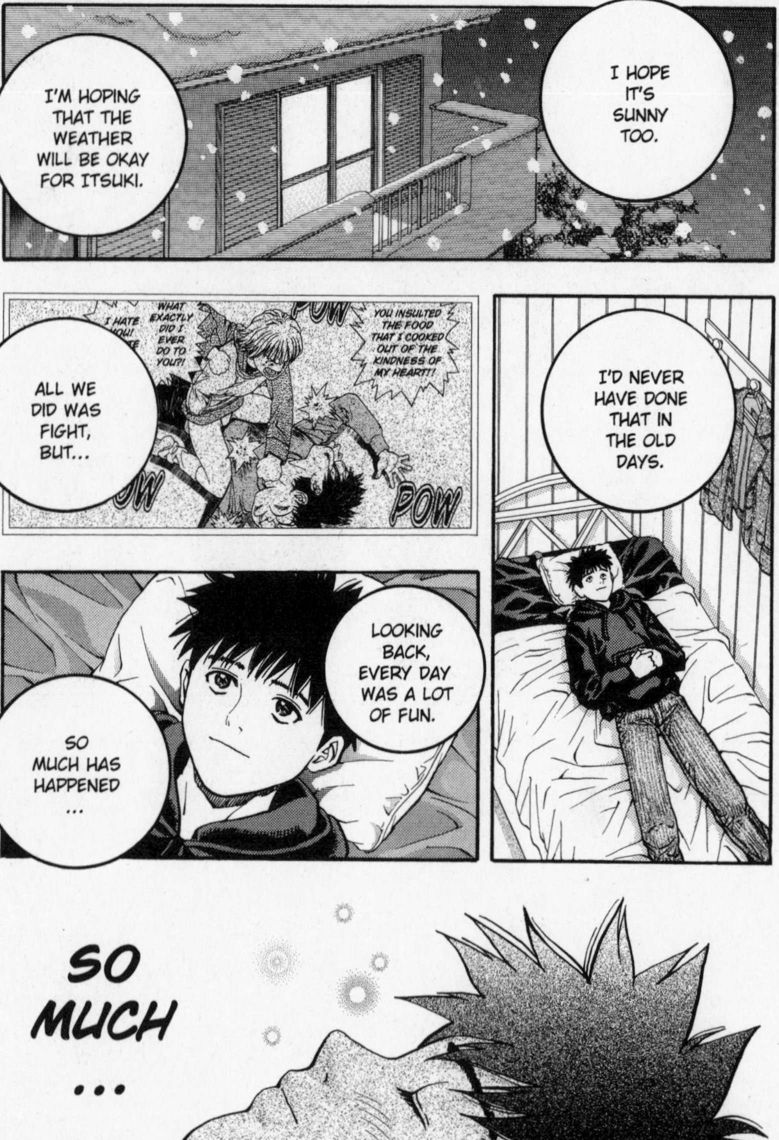

I HOPE IT'S SUNNY TOO.
I'M HOPING THAT THE WEATHER WILL BE OKAY FOR ITSUKI.
I'D NEVER HAVE DONE THAT IN THE OLD DAYS.
YOU INSULTED THE FOOD THAT I COOKED OUT OF THE KINDNESS OF MY HEART!!
POW
WHAT EXACTLY DID I EVER DO TO YOU?!
I HATE
ALL WE DID WAS FIGHT, BUT...
POW
LOOKING BACK, EVERY DAY WAS A LOT OF FUN.
SO MUCH HAS HAPPENED ...
SO MUCH ...

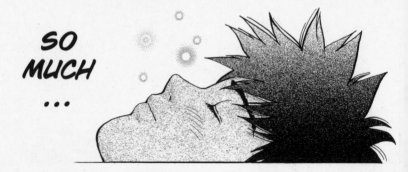

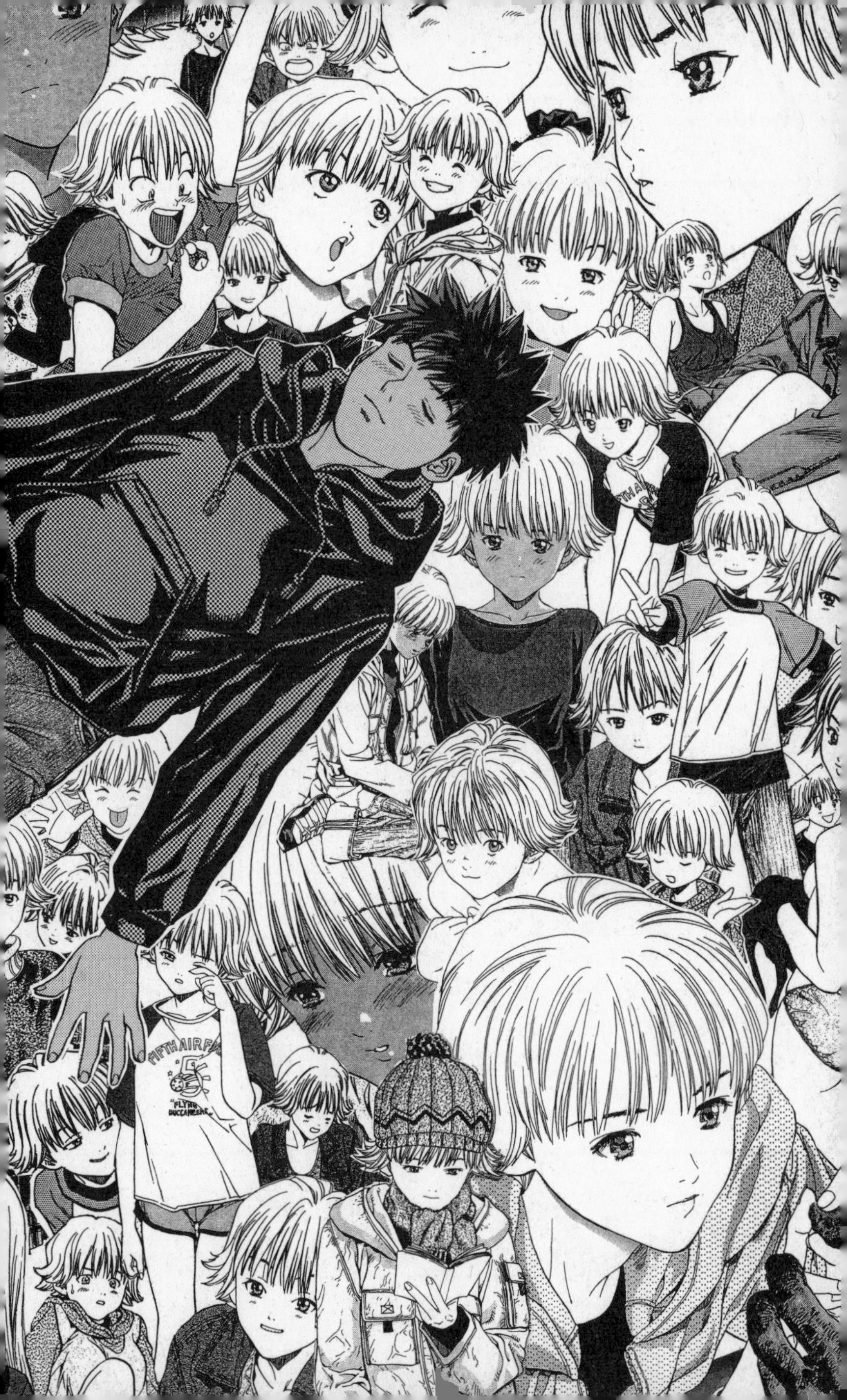

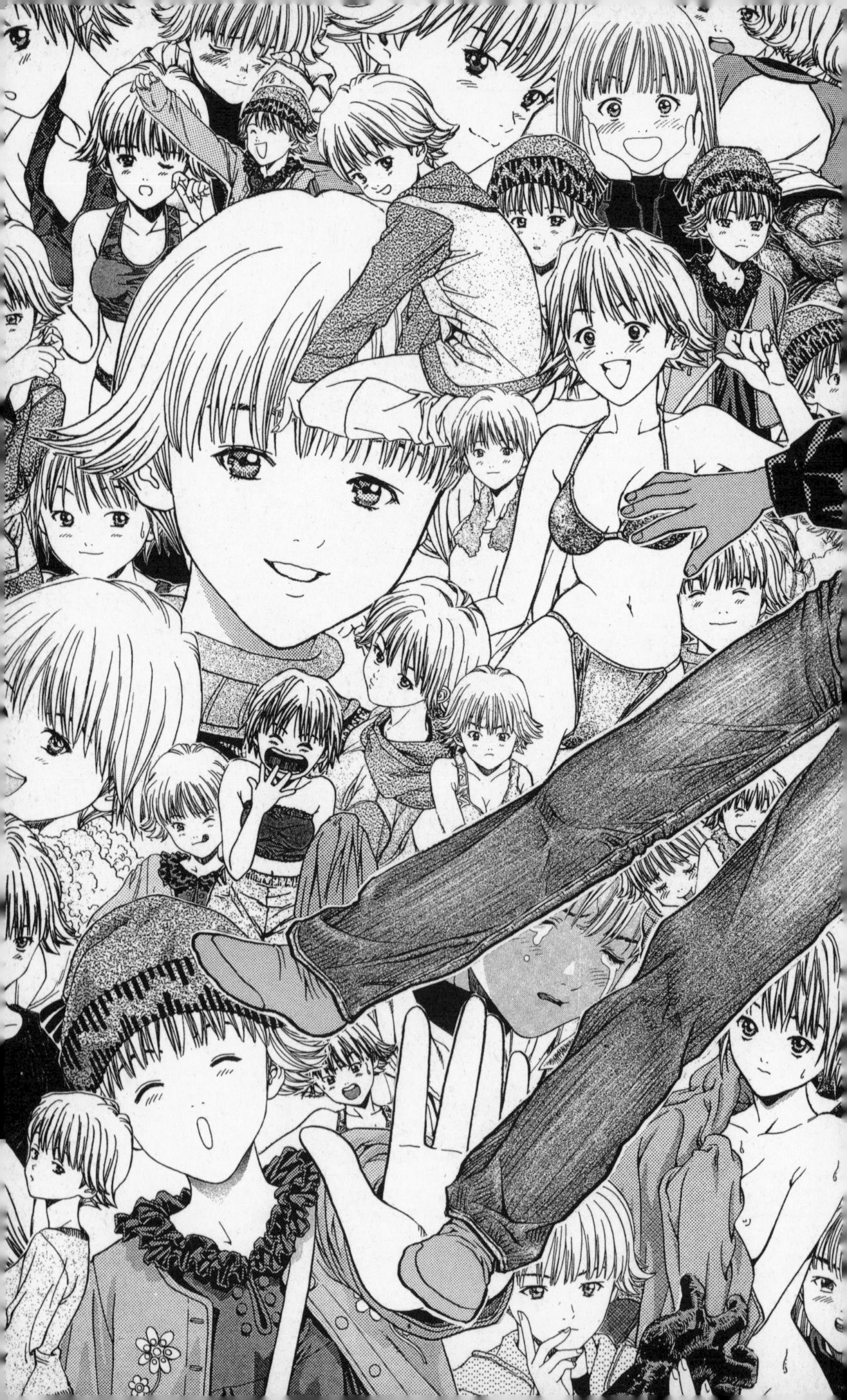

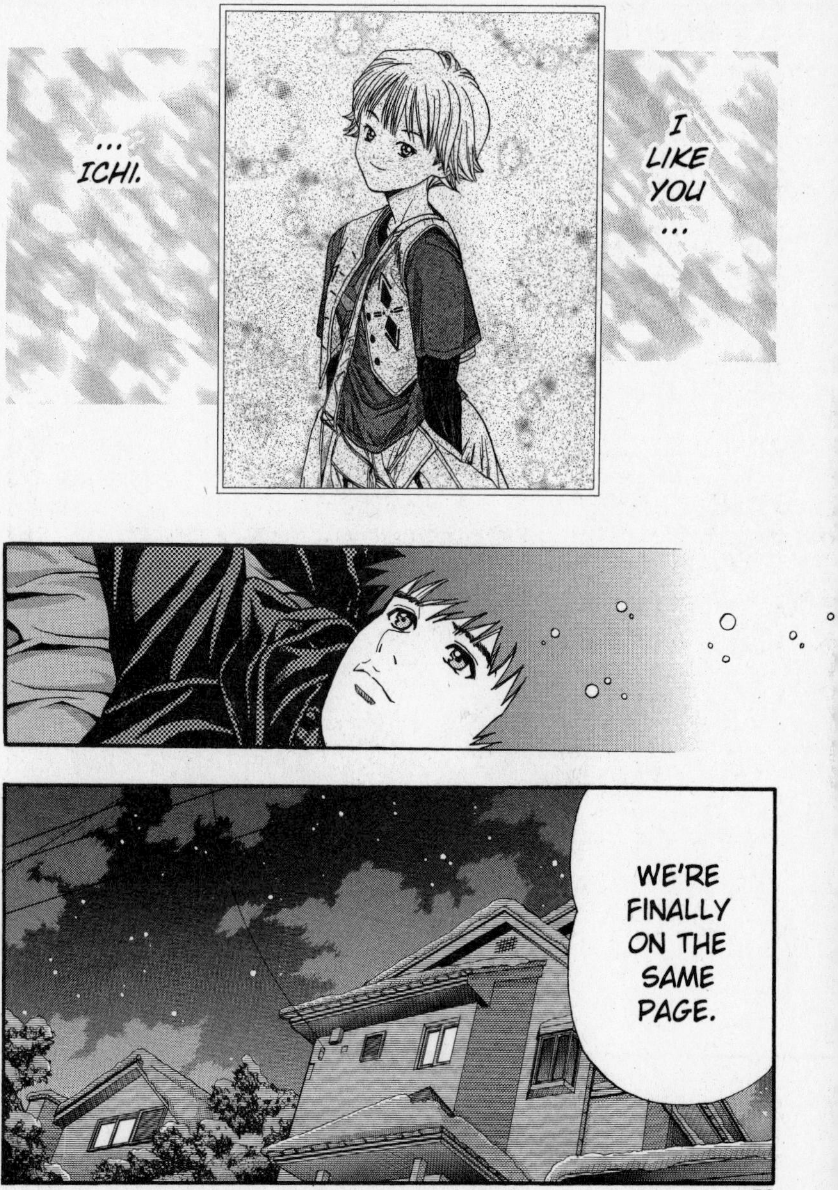
I LIKE YOU ...
... ICHI.
WE'RE FINALLY ON THE SAME PAGE.

READ THIS WAY

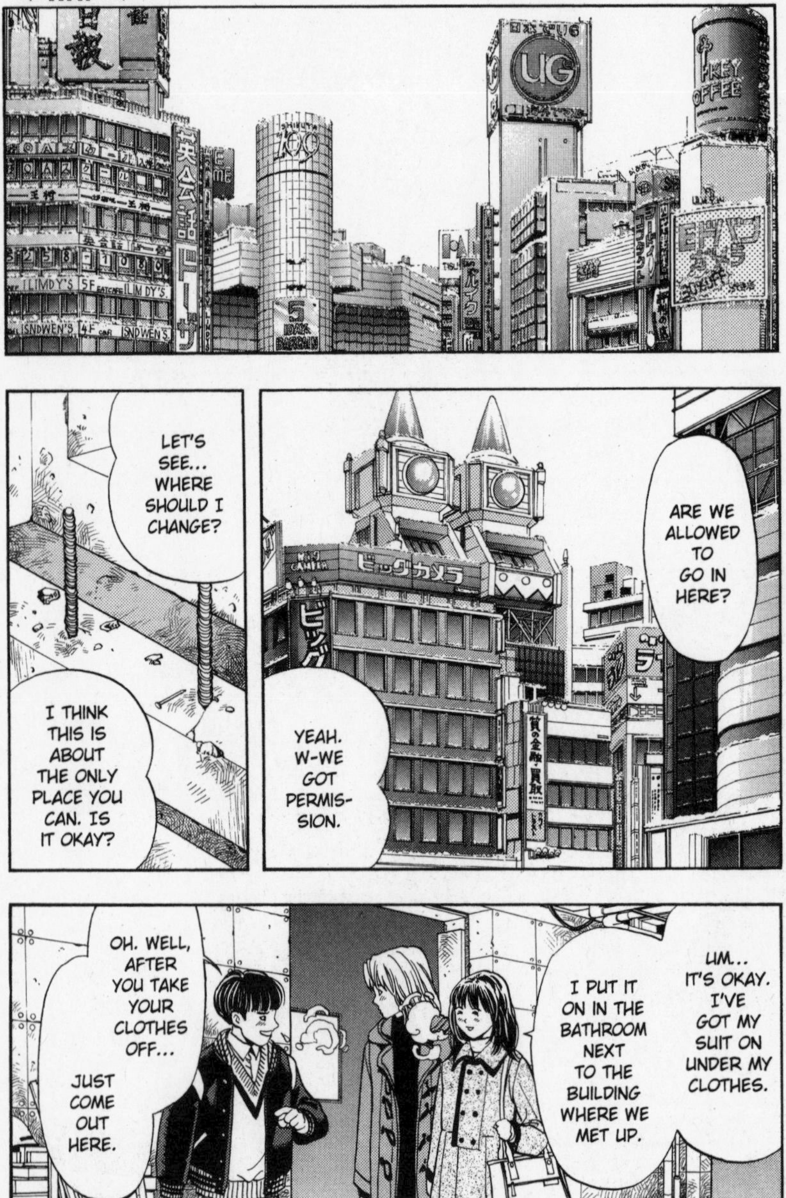
ARE WE ALLOWED TO GO IN HERE?
YEAH. W-WE GOT PERMIS-SION.
LET'S SEE... WHERE SHOULD I CHANGE?
I THINK THIS IS ABOUT THE ONLY PLACE YOU CAN. IS IT OKAY?
UM... IT'S OKAY. I'VE GOT MY SUIT ON UNDER MY CLOTHES.
I PUT IT ON IN THE BATHROOM NEXT TO THE BUILDING WHERE WE MET UP.
OH. WELL, AFTER YOU TAKE YOUR CLOTHES OFF...
JUST COME OUT HERE.

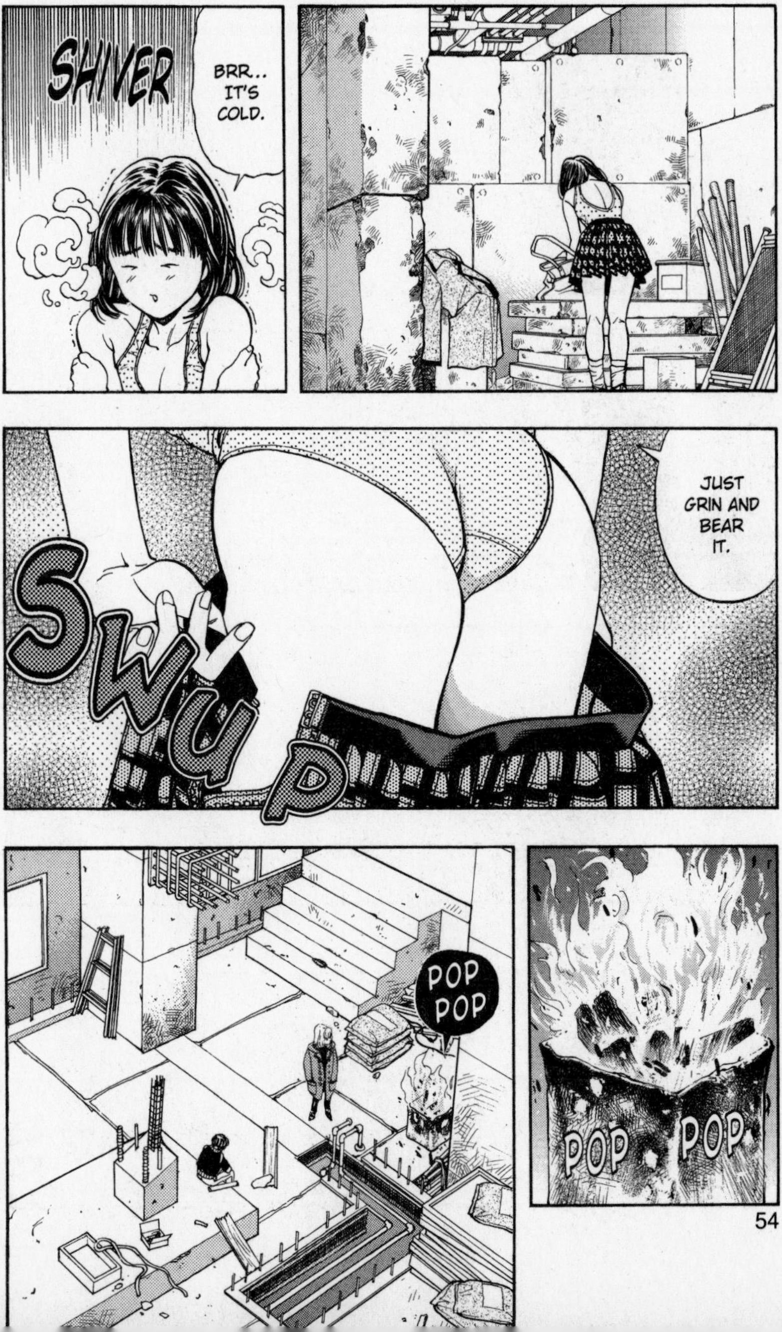
SHIVER
BRR... IT'S COLD.
JUST GRIN AND BEAR IT.
SWUP
POP POP
POP POP

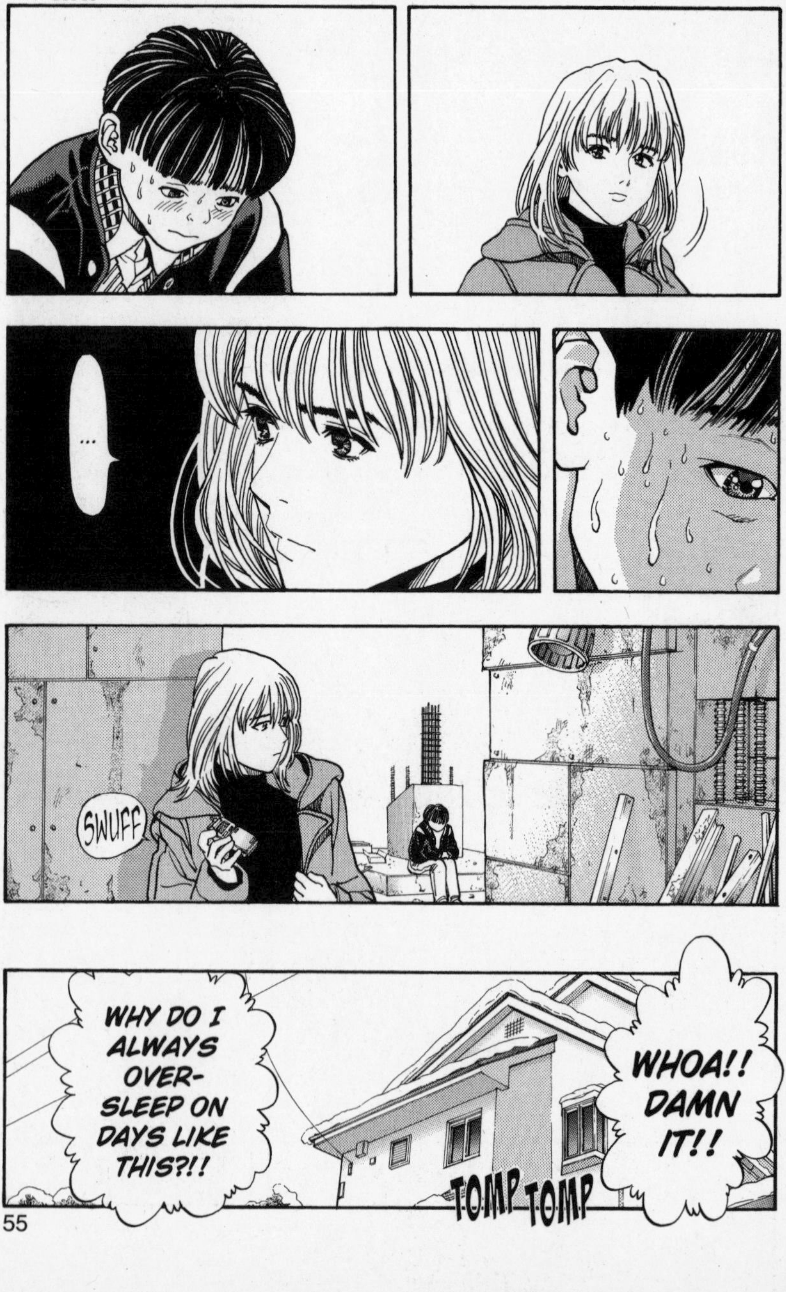
...
SWUFF
WHOA!! DAMN IT!!
WHY DO I ALWAYS OVER-SLEEP ON DAYS LIKE THIS?!!
TOMP TOMP

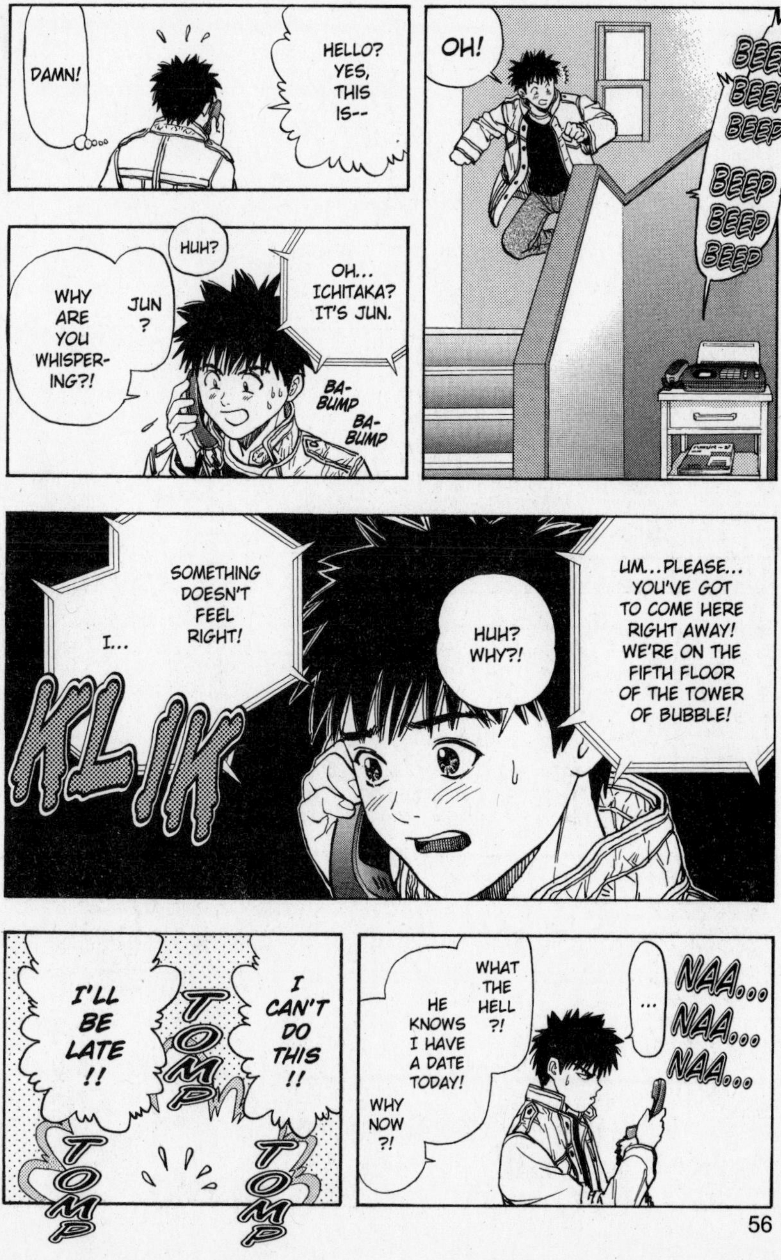
BEEP BEEP BEEP
BEEP BEEP BEEP
OH!
HELLO? YES, THIS IS--
DAMN!
OH... ICHITAKA? IT'S JUN.
HUH?
JUN?
WHY ARE YOU WHISPER-ING?!
BA-BUMP BA-BUMP
UM...PLEASE... YOU'VE GOT TO COME HERE RIGHT AWAY! WE'RE ON THE FIFTH FLOOR OF THE TOWER OF BUBBLE!
HUH? WHY?!
SOMETHING DOESN'T FEEL RIGHT!
I...
KLIK
NAA... NAA... NAA...
...
WHAT THE HELL?!
HE KNOWS I HAVE A DATE TODAY!
WHY NOW?!
I CAN'T DO THIS!!
TOMP
I'LL BE LATE!!
TOMP
TOMP

READ THIS WAY

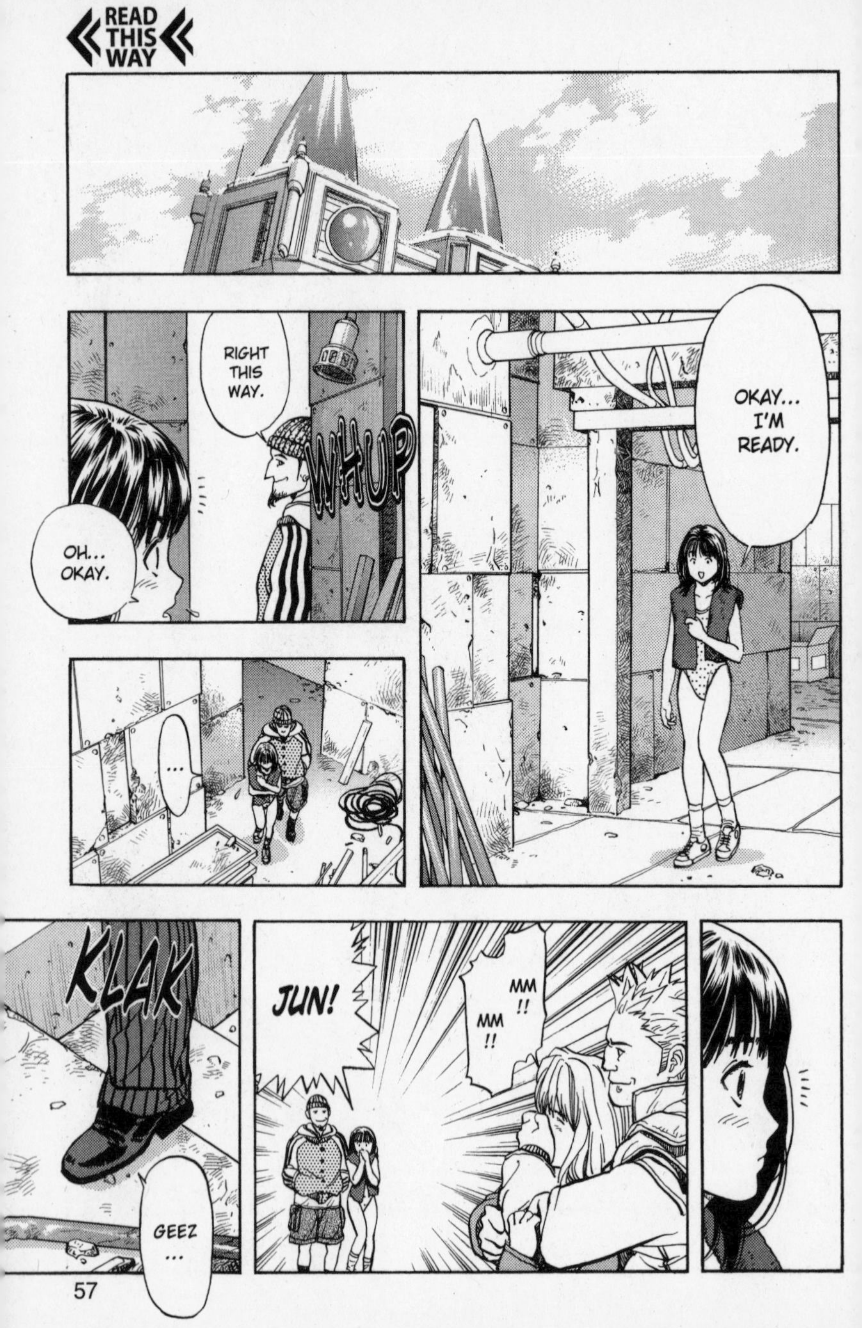
OKAY... I'M READY.
RIGHT THIS WAY.
WHUP
OH... OKAY.
...
MM!!
MM!!
JUN!
KLAK
GEEZ...

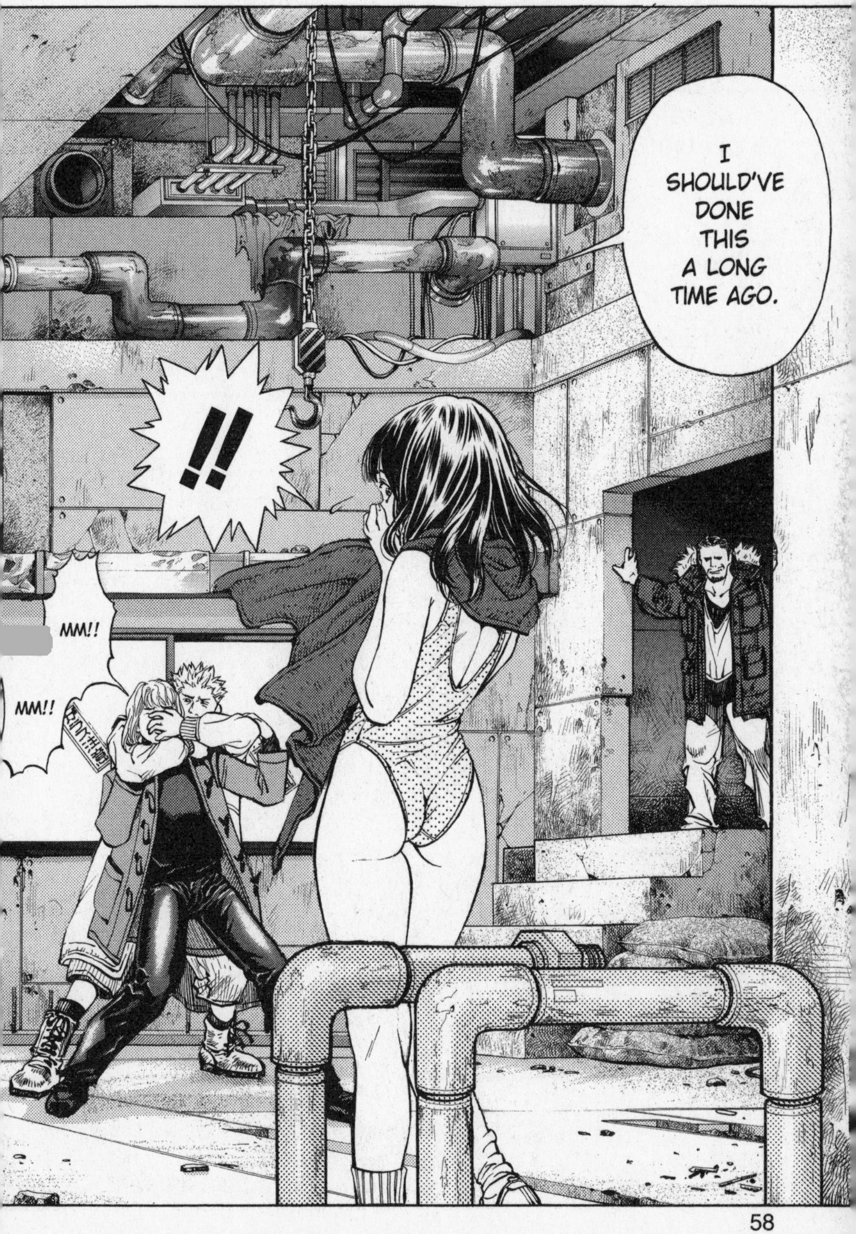
I SHOULD'VE DONE THIS A LONG TIME AGO.
!!
MM!!
MM!!

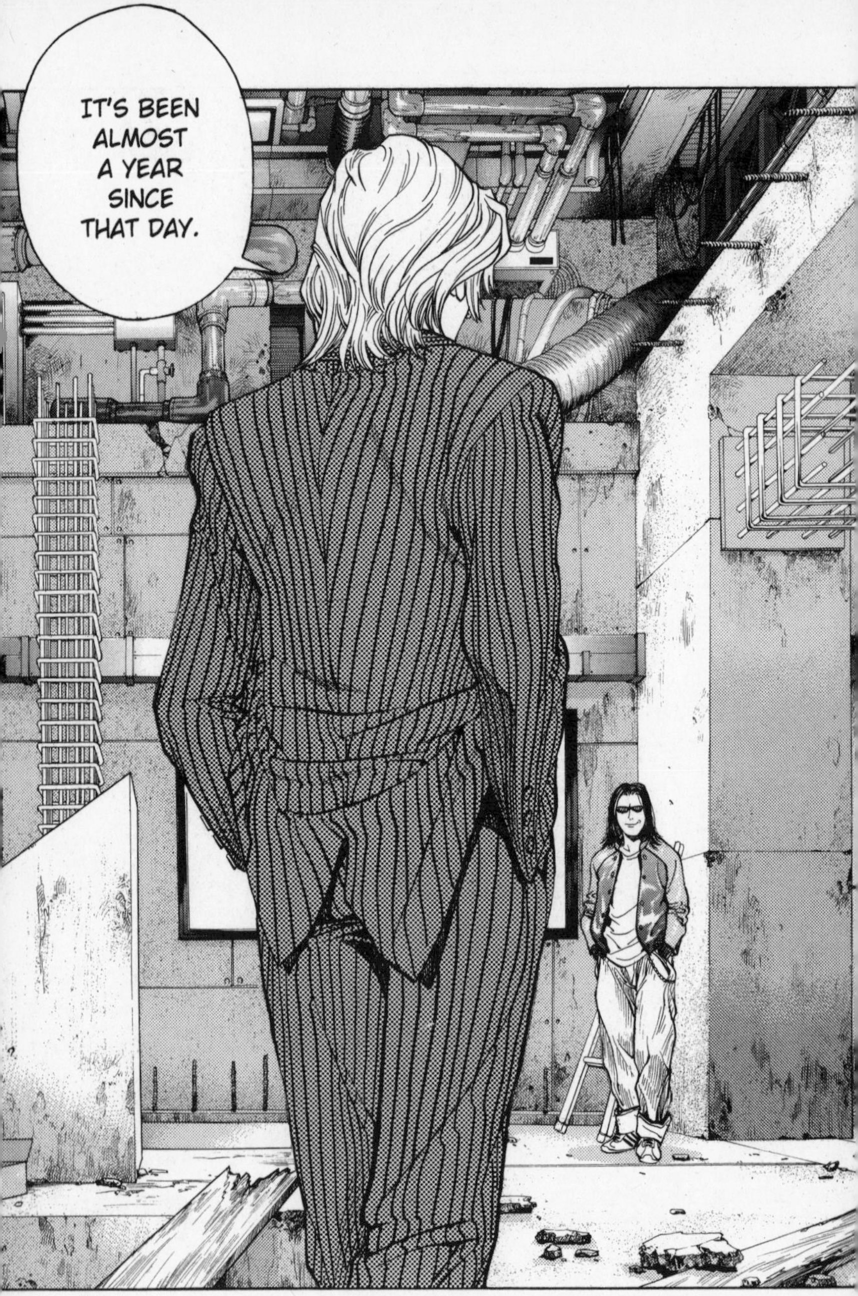
IT'S BEEN ALMOST A YEAR SINCE THAT DAY.

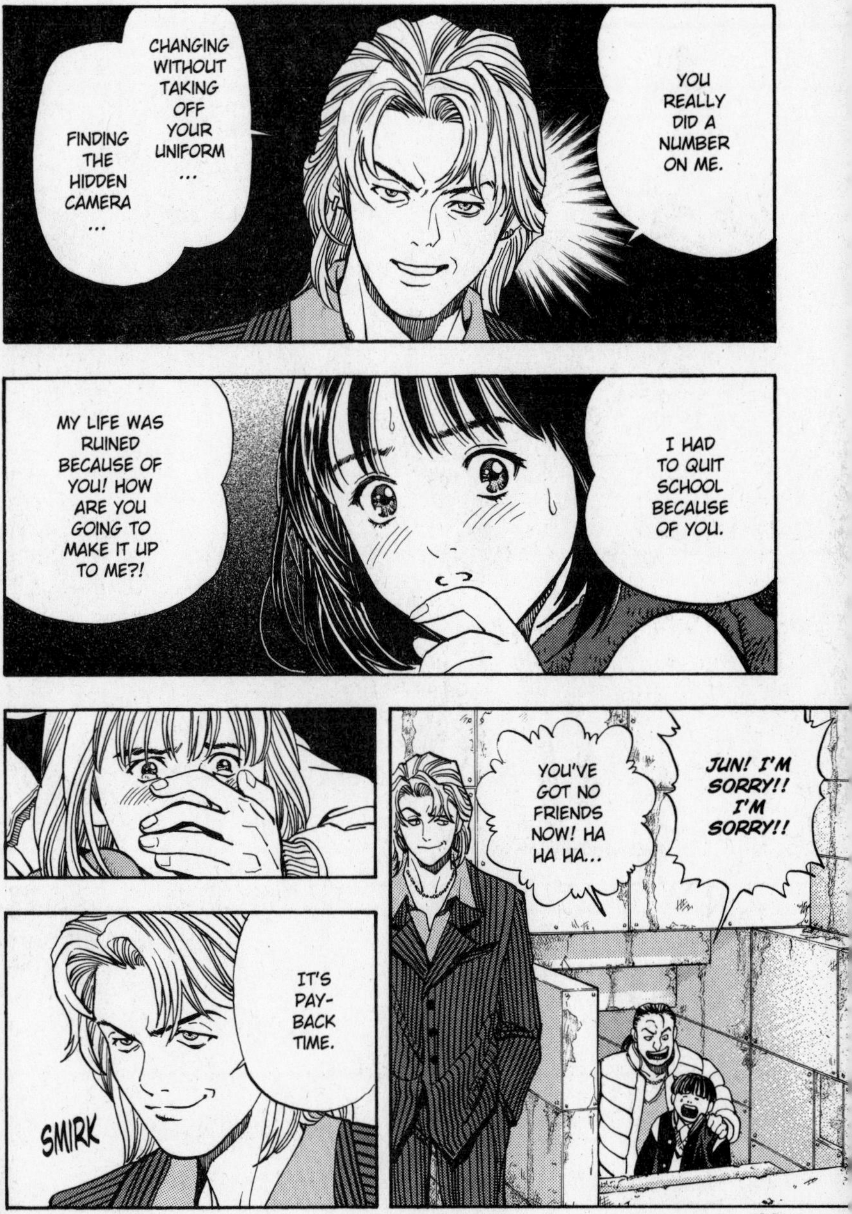
YOU REALLY DID A NUMBER ON ME.
CHANGING WITHOUT TAKING OFF YOUR UNIFORM ...
FINDING THE HIDDEN CAMERA ...
I HAD TO QUIT SCHOOL BECAUSE OF YOU.
MY LIFE WAS RUINED BECAUSE OF YOU! HOW ARE YOU GOING TO MAKE IT UP TO ME?!
JUN! I'M SORRY!! I'M SORRY!!
YOU'VE GOT NO FRIENDS NOW! HA HA HA...
IT'S PAY-BACK TIME.
SMIRK

READ THIS WAY

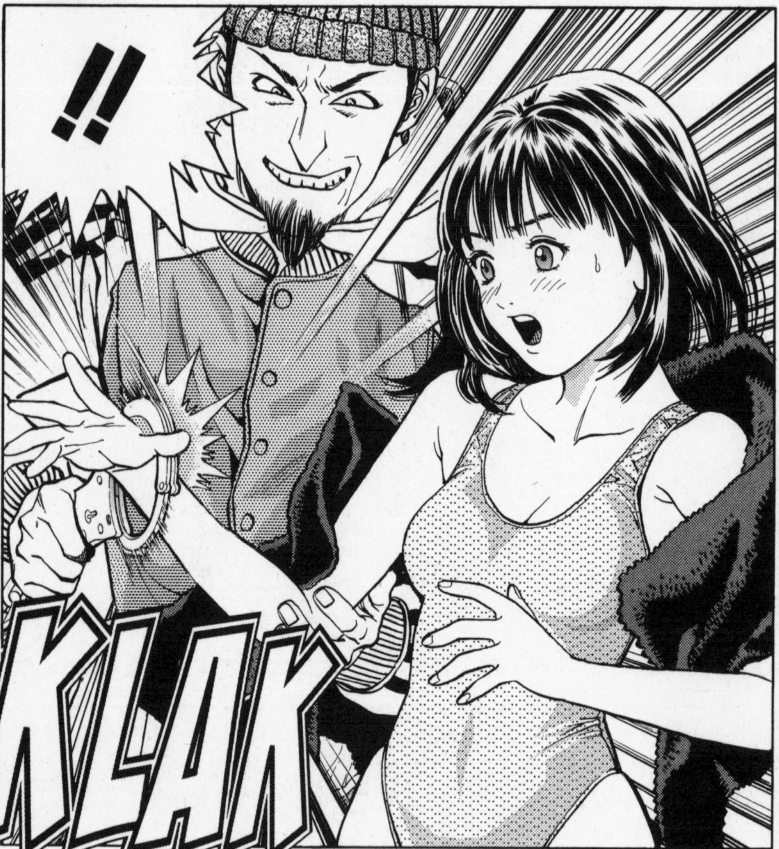
!!
KLAK

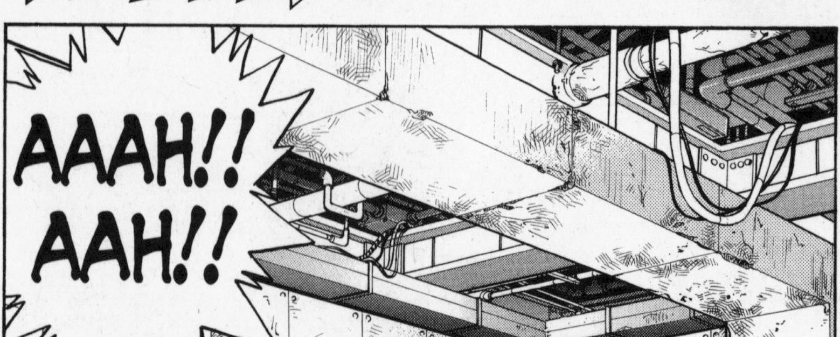
AAAH!! AAH!!

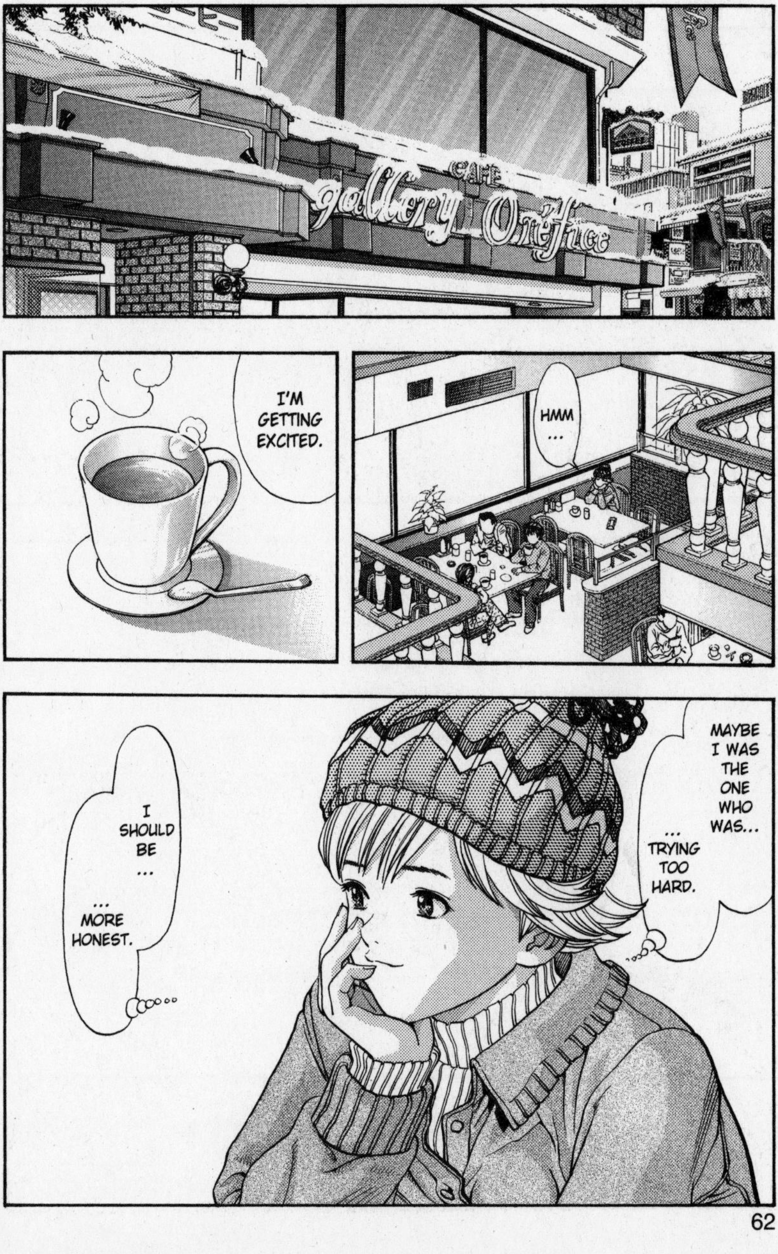
CAFE
gallery Oréfice
HMM ...
I'M GETTING EXCITED.
MAYBE I WAS THE ONE WHO WAS...
... TRYING TOO HARD.
I SHOULD BE ...
... MORE HONEST.

READ THIS WAY

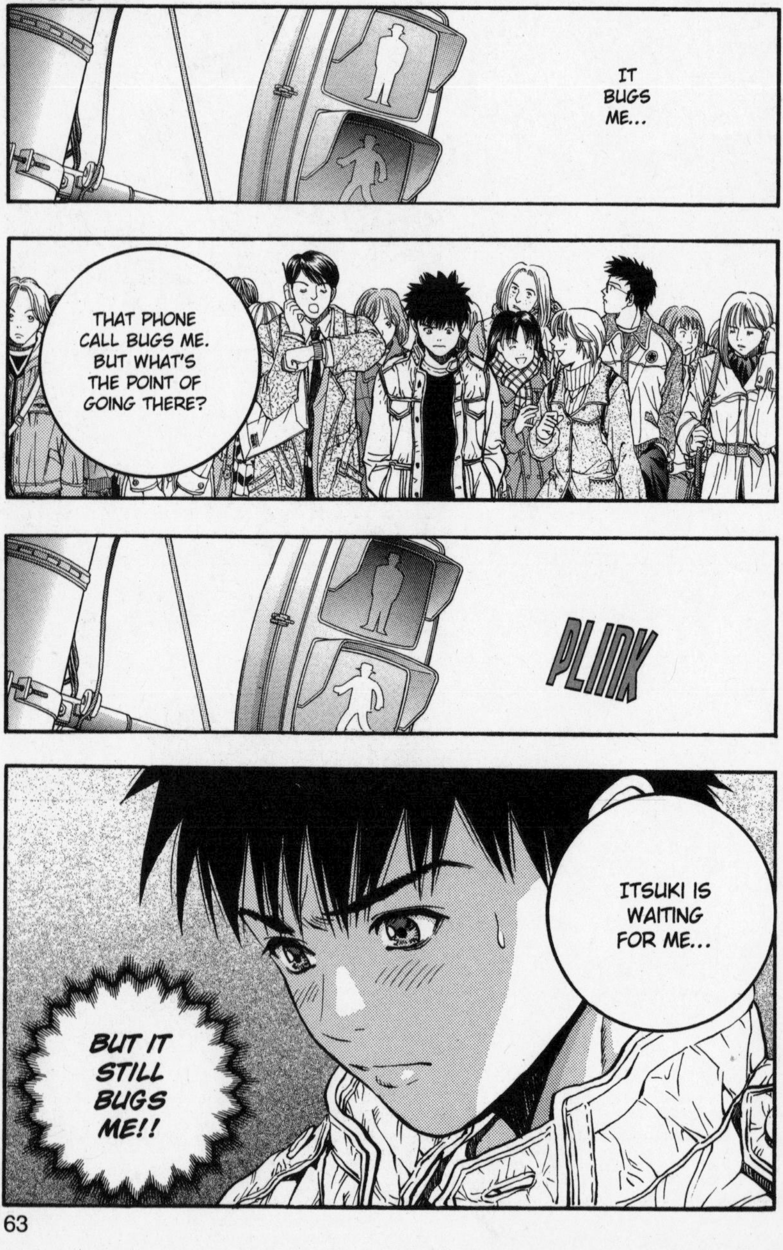
IT BUGS ME...
THAT PHONE CALL BUGS ME. BUT WHAT'S THE POINT OF GOING THERE?
PLINK
ITSUKI IS WAITING FOR ME...
BUT IT STILL BUGS ME!!

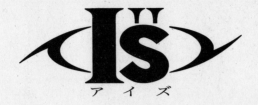

アイズ

Chapter 49:
Begins Right Now

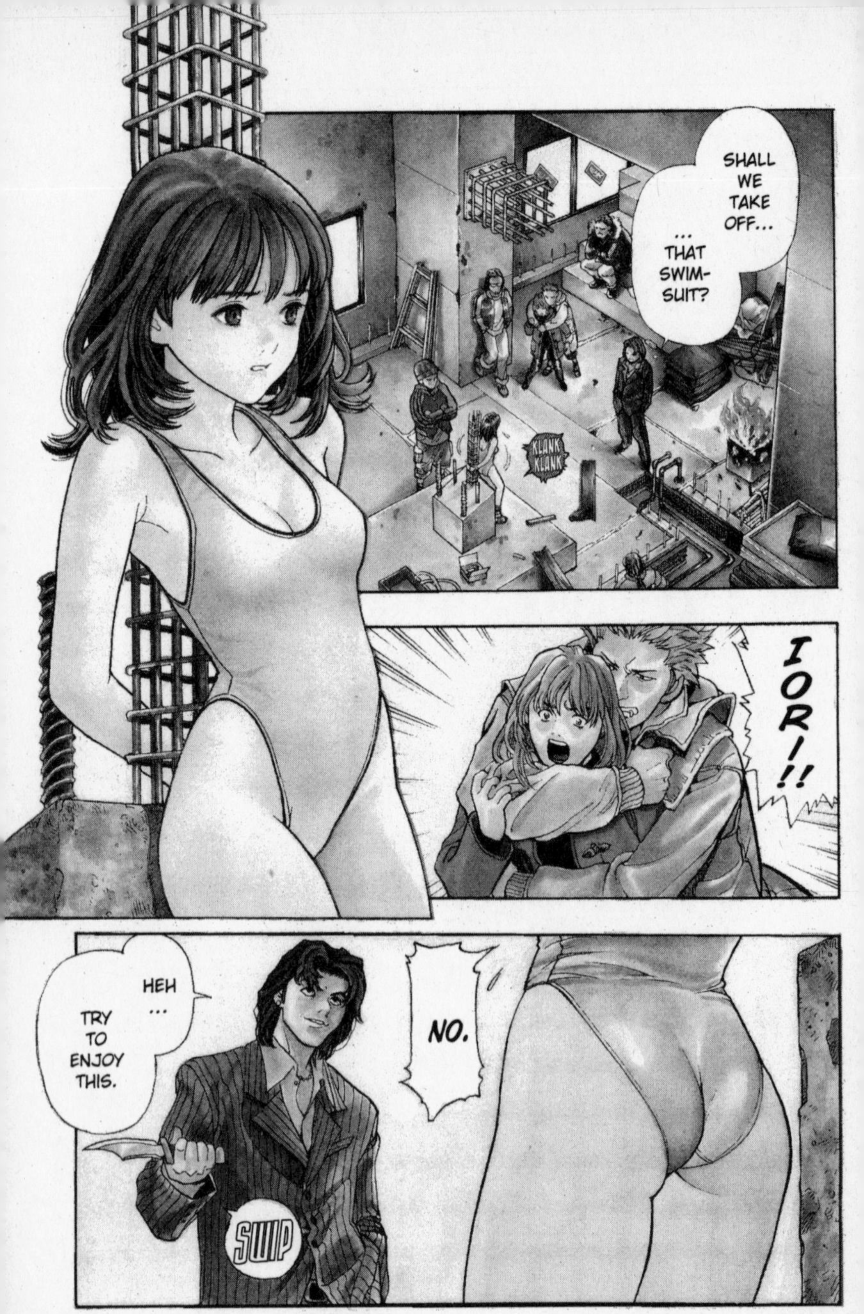
SHALL WE TAKE OFF...
...THAT SWIM-SUIT?
KLANK KLANK
IORI!!
NO.
HEH...
TRY TO ENJOY THIS.
SWIP

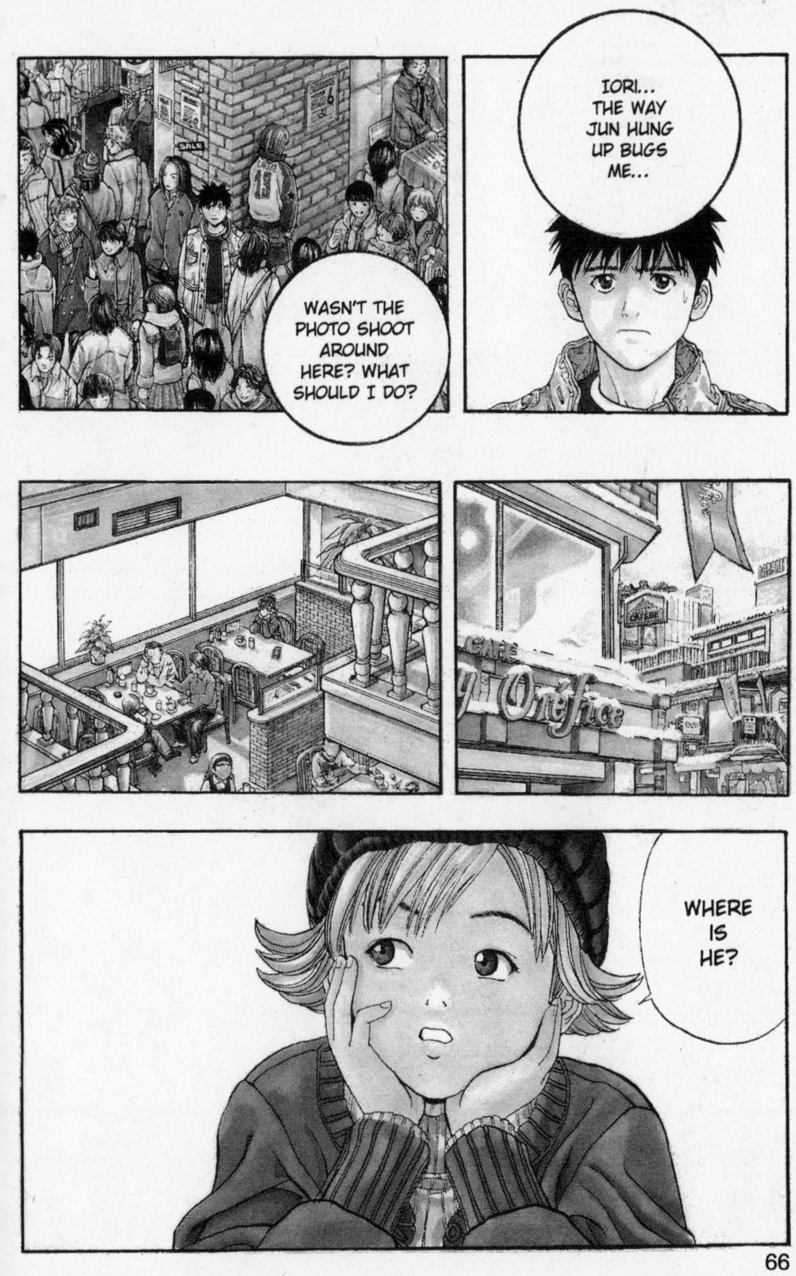
IORI... THE WAY JUN HUNG UP BUGS ME...
WASN'T THE PHOTO SHOOT AROUND HERE? WHAT SHOULD I DO?
WHERE IS HE?

READ THIS WAY

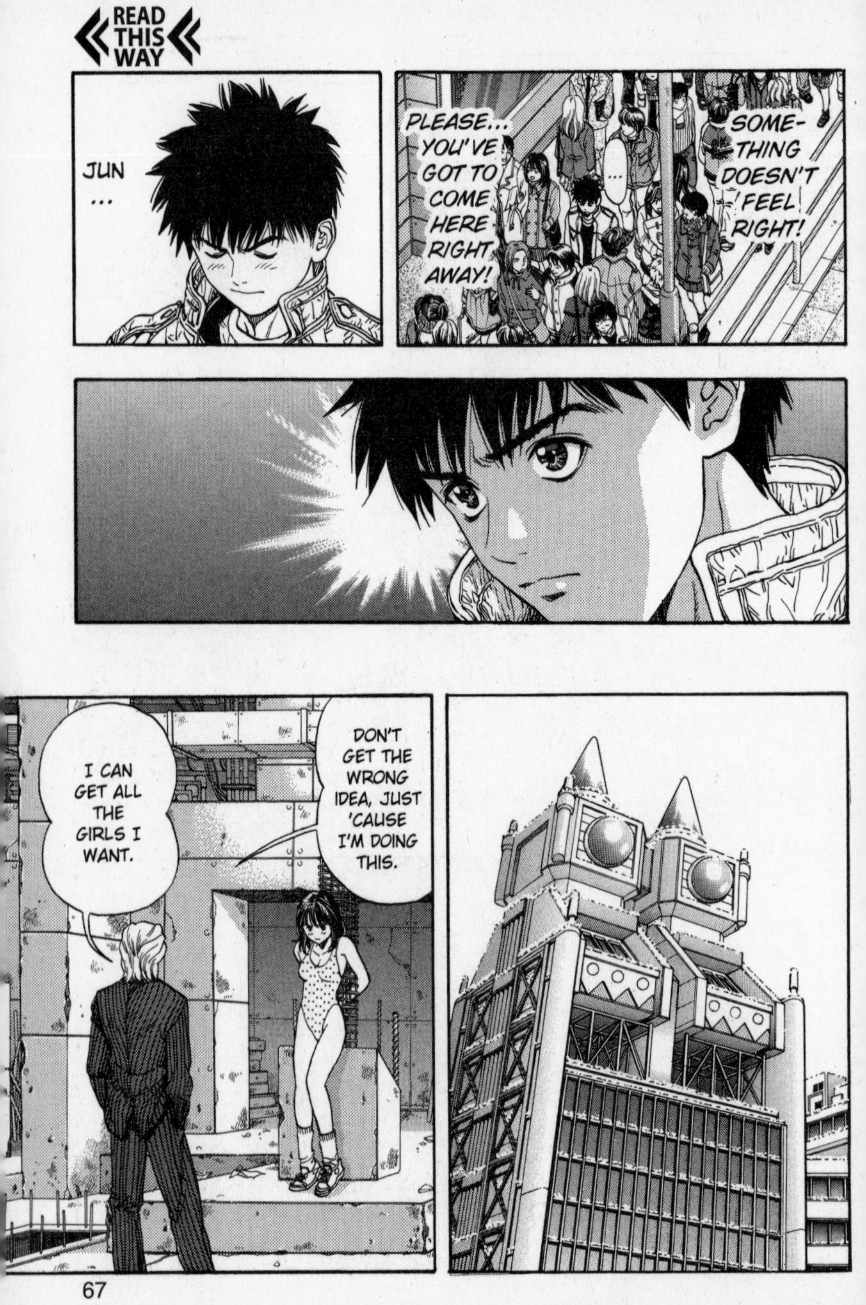
SOME-THING DOESN'T FEEL RIGHT!
...
PLEASE... YOU'VE GOT TO COME HERE RIGHT AWAY!
JUN ...
DON'T GET THE WRONG IDEA, JUST 'CAUSE I'M DOING THIS.
I CAN GET ALL THE GIRLS I WANT.

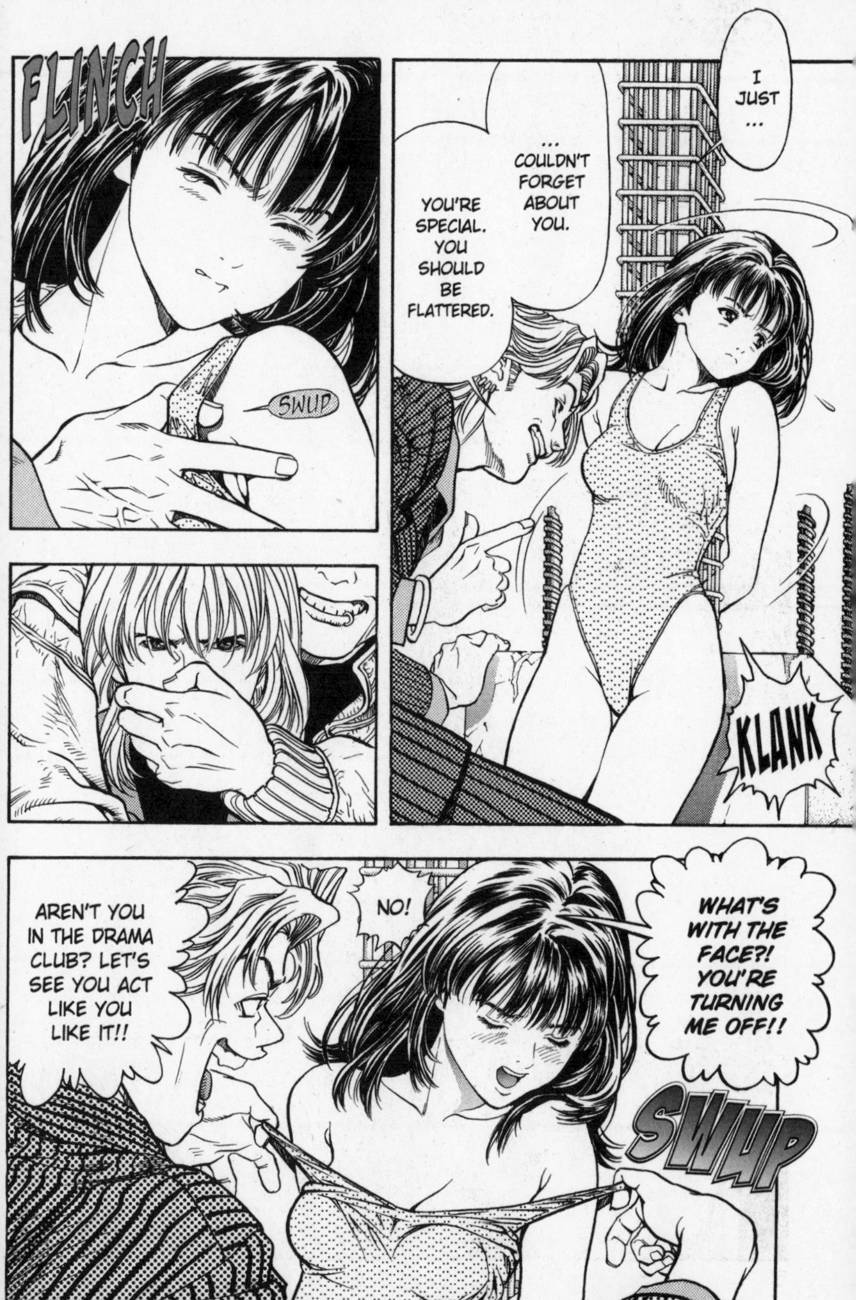
I JUST ...
... COULDN'T FORGET ABOUT YOU.
YOU'RE SPECIAL. YOU SHOULD BE FLATTERED.
KLANK
FLINCH
SWUP
WHAT'S WITH THE FACE?! YOU'RE TURNING ME OFF!!
SWUP
NO!
AREN'T YOU IN THE DRAMA CLUB? LET'S SEE YOU ACT LIKE YOU LIKE IT!!

READ THIS WAY

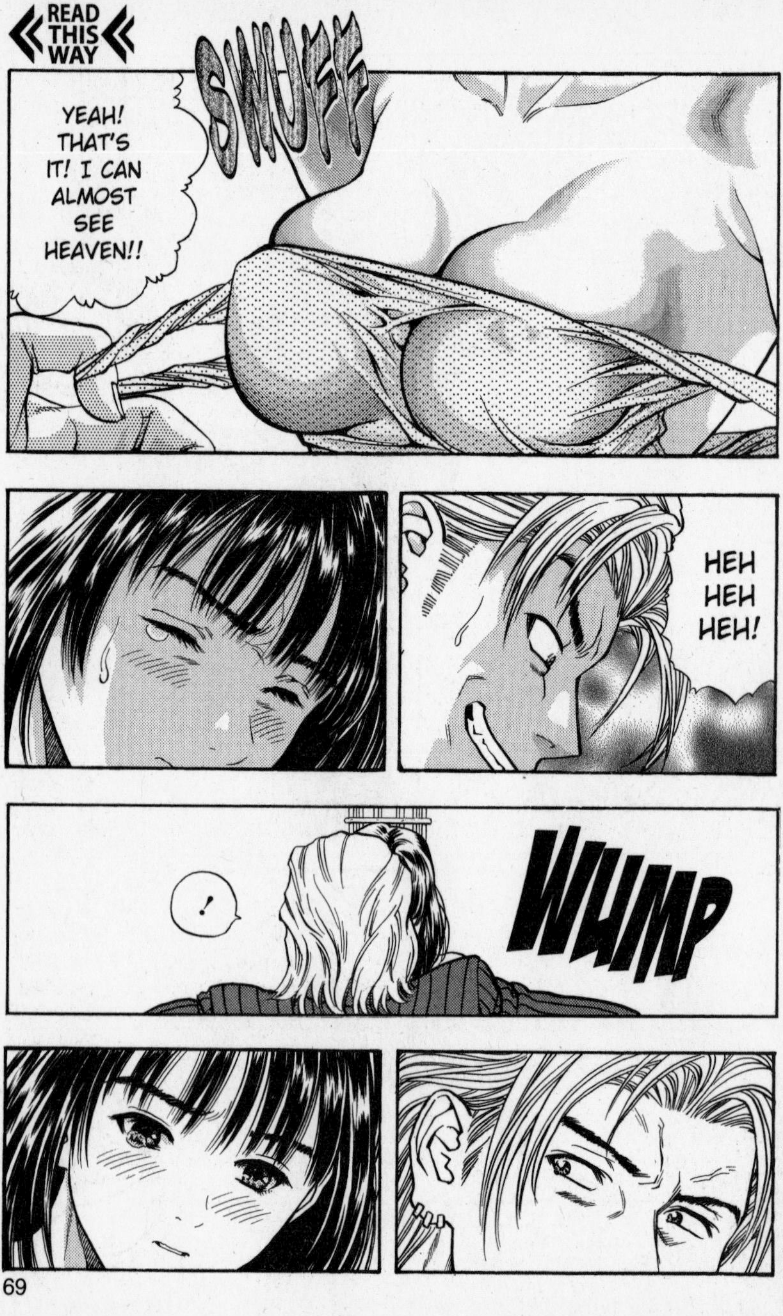
SNIFF
YEAH! THAT'S IT! I CAN ALMOST SEE HEAVEN!!
HEH HEH HEH!
WUMP
!

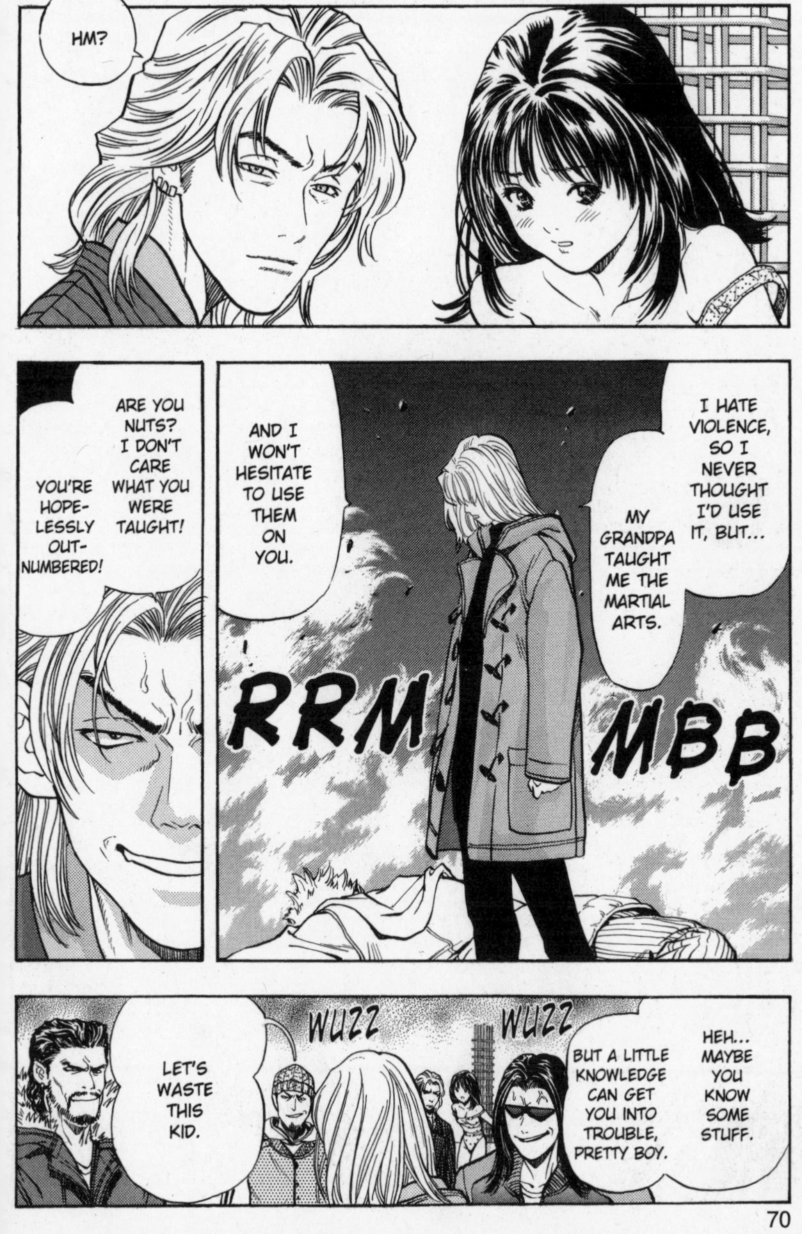
HM?
I HATE VIOLENCE, SO I NEVER THOUGHT I'D USE IT, BUT...
MY GRANDPA TAUGHT ME THE MARTIAL ARTS.
AND I WON'T HESITATE TO USE THEM ON YOU.
RRM MBB
ARE YOU NUTS? I DON'T CARE WHAT YOU WERE TAUGHT!
YOU'RE HOPE-LESSLY OUT-NUMBERED!
HEH... MAYBE YOU KNOW SOME STUFF.
BUT A LITTLE KNOWLEDGE CAN GET YOU INTO TROUBLE, PRETTY BOY.
WUZZ
WUZZ
LET'S WASTE THIS KID.

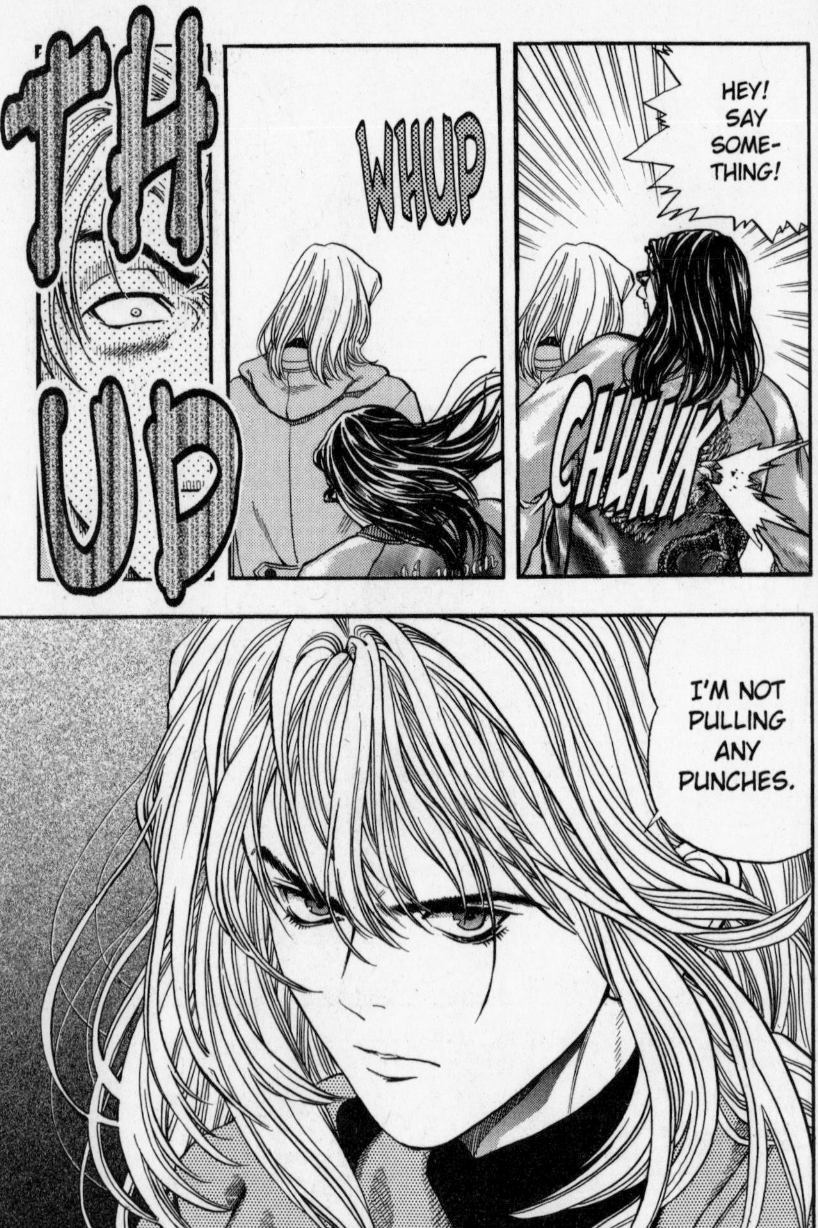
HEY! SAY SOME-THING!
CHUNK
WHUP
THUD
I'M NOT PULLING ANY PUNCHES.

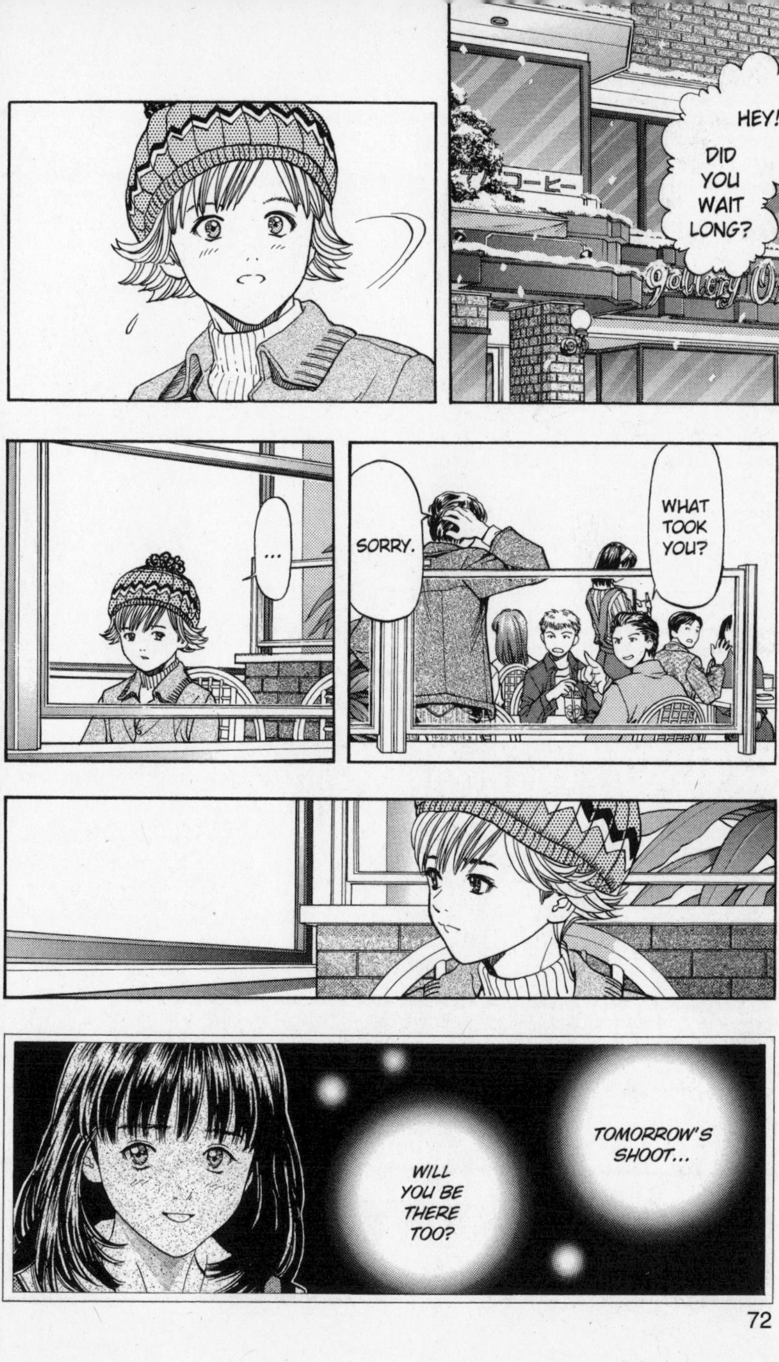
HEY! DID YOU WAIT LONG?
WHAT TOOK YOU?
SORRY.
...
TOMORROW'S SHOOT...
WILL YOU BE THERE TOO?

READ THIS WAY

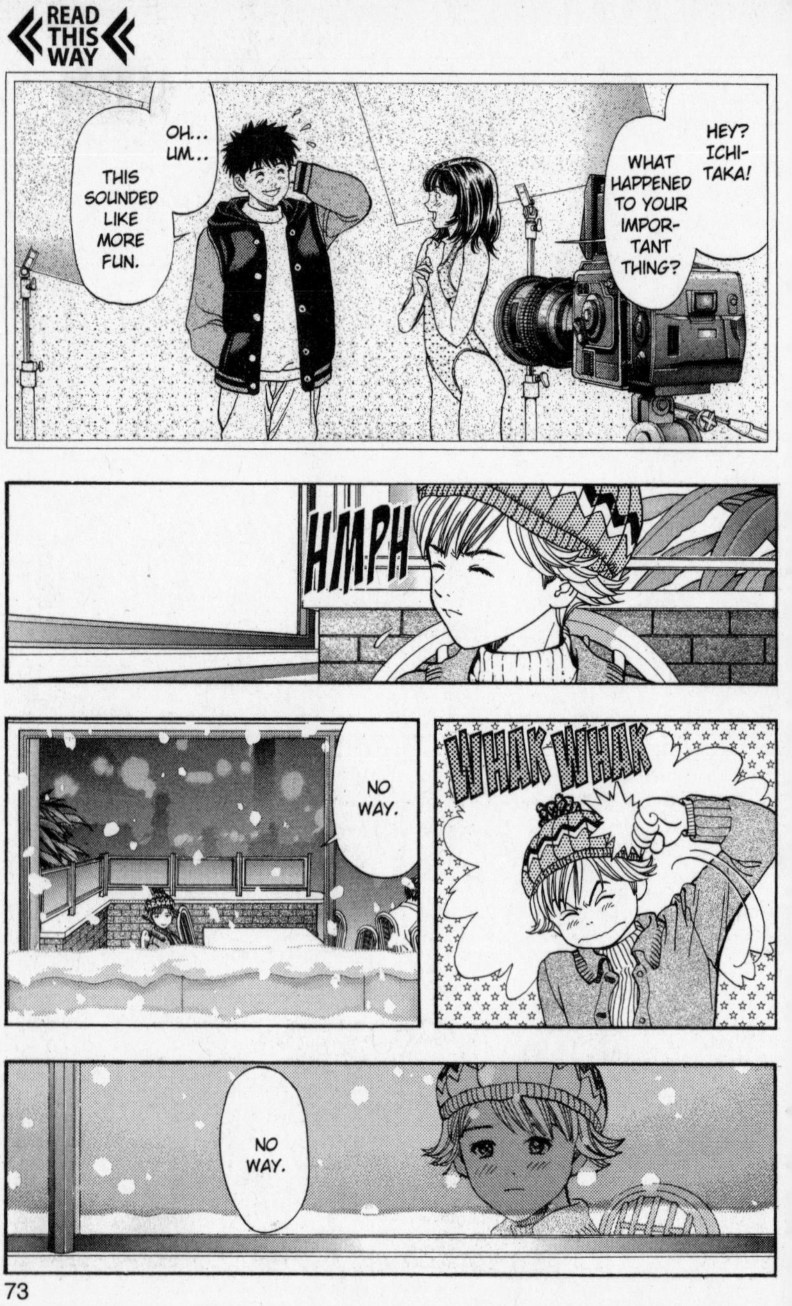
HEY? ICHI-TAKA!
WHAT HAPPENED TO YOUR IMPOR-TANT THING?
OH... UM...
THIS SOUNDED LIKE MORE FUN.
HMPH
WHAK WHAK
NO WAY.
NO WAY.

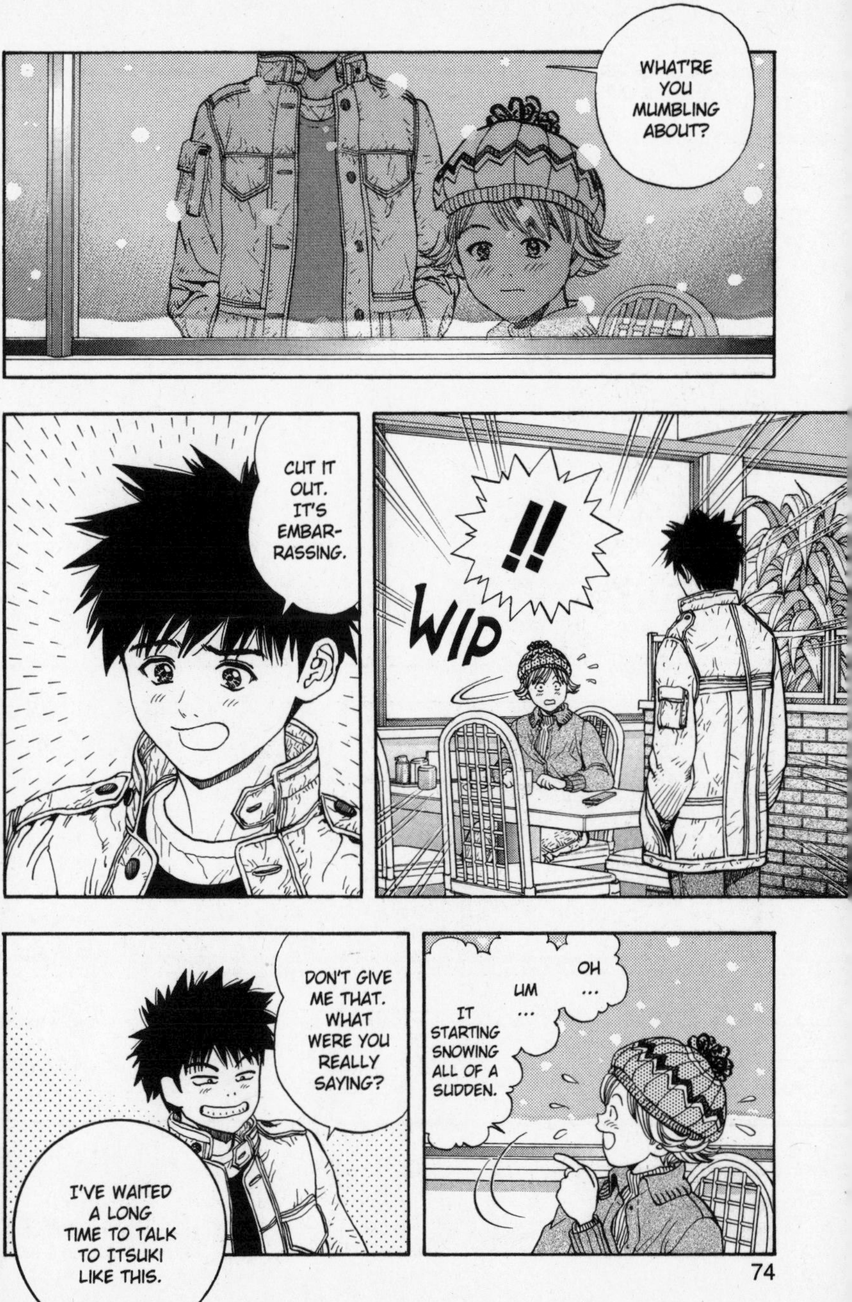
WHAT'RE YOU MUMBLING ABOUT?
!!
WIP
CUT IT OUT. IT'S EMBAR-RASSING.
OH ...
UM ...
IT STARTING SNOWING ALL OF A SUDDEN.
DON'T GIVE ME THAT. WHAT WERE YOU REALLY SAYING?
I'VE WAITED A LONG TIME TO TALK TO ITSUKI LIKE THIS.

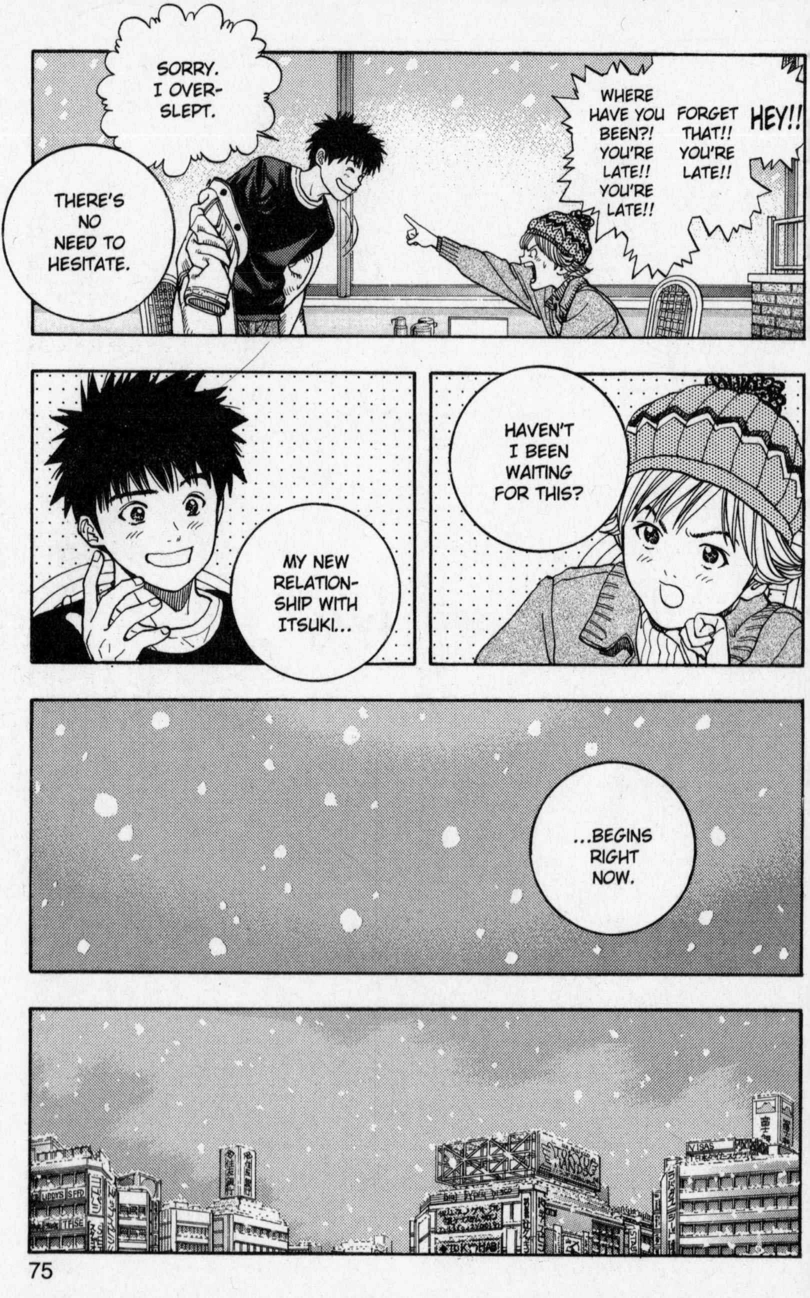
HEY!!
FORGET THAT!! YOU'RE LATE!!
WHERE HAVE YOU BEEN?! YOU'RE LATE!! YOU'RE LATE!!
SORRY. I OVER-SLEPT.
THERE'S NO NEED TO HESITATE.
HAVEN'T I BEEN WAITING FOR THIS?
MY NEW RELATION-SHIP WITH ITSUKI...
...BEGINS RIGHT NOW.

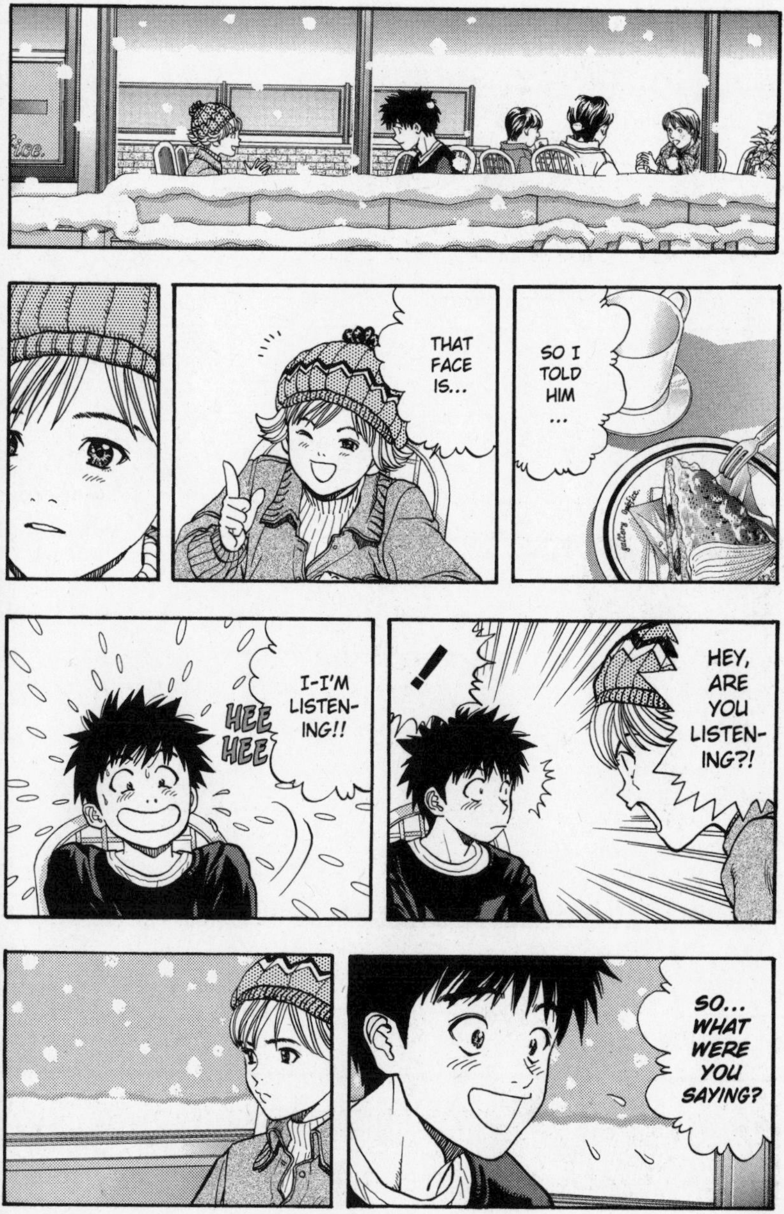
SO I TOLD HIM ...
THAT FACE IS...
HEY, ARE YOU LISTEN-ING?!
!
I-I'M LISTEN-ING!!
HEE HEE
SO... WHAT WERE YOU SAYING?

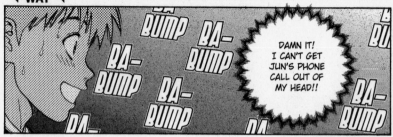

DAMN IT!
I CAN'T GET
JUN'S PHONE
CALL OUT OF
MY HEAD!!

BA-
BUMP

BA-
BUMP

BA-
BUMP

BA-
BUMP

BA-
BUMP

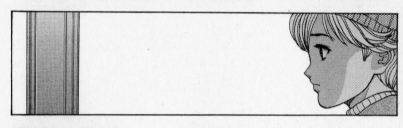

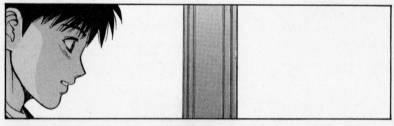

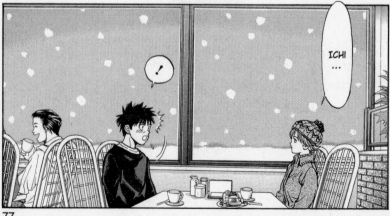

!

ICHI
...

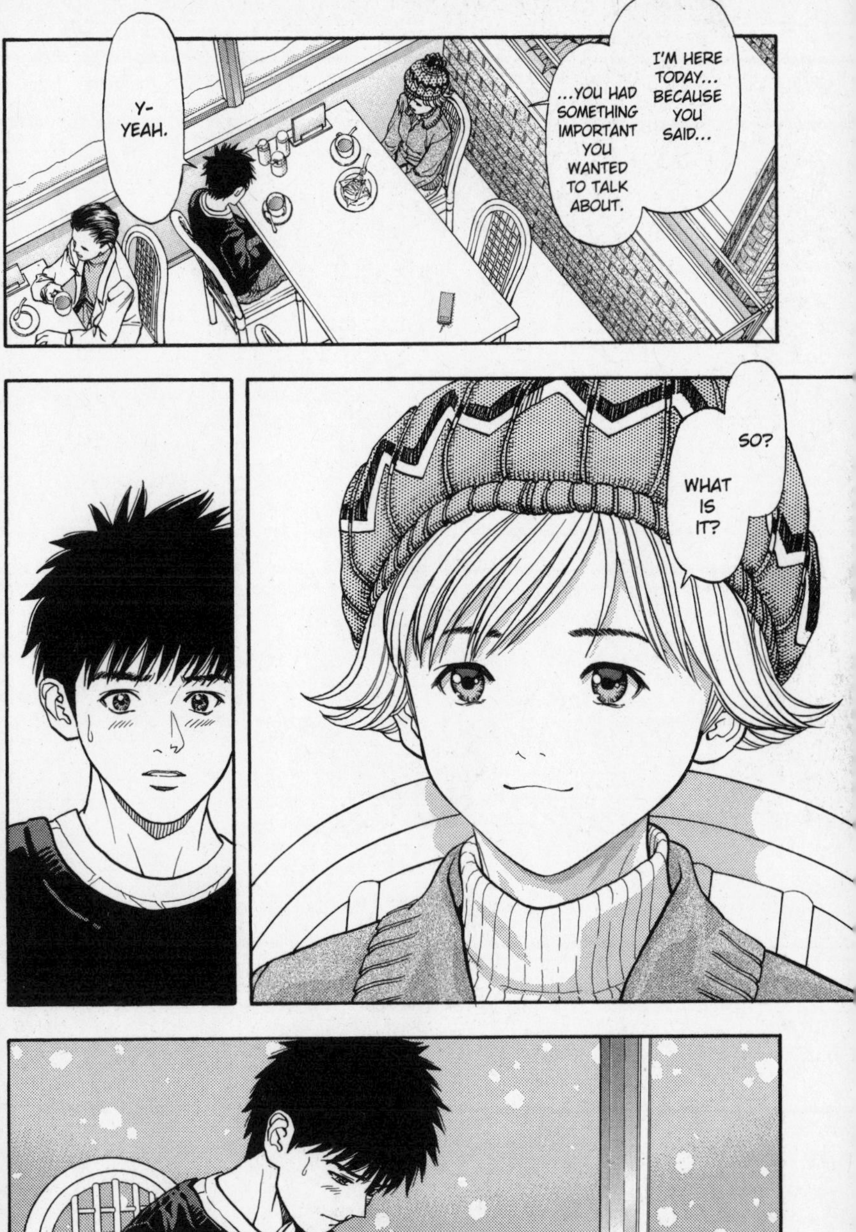
I'M HERE TODAY... BECAUSE YOU SAID...
...YOU HAD SOMETHING IMPORTANT YOU WANTED TO TALK ABOUT.
Y-YEAH.
SO?
WHAT IS IT?

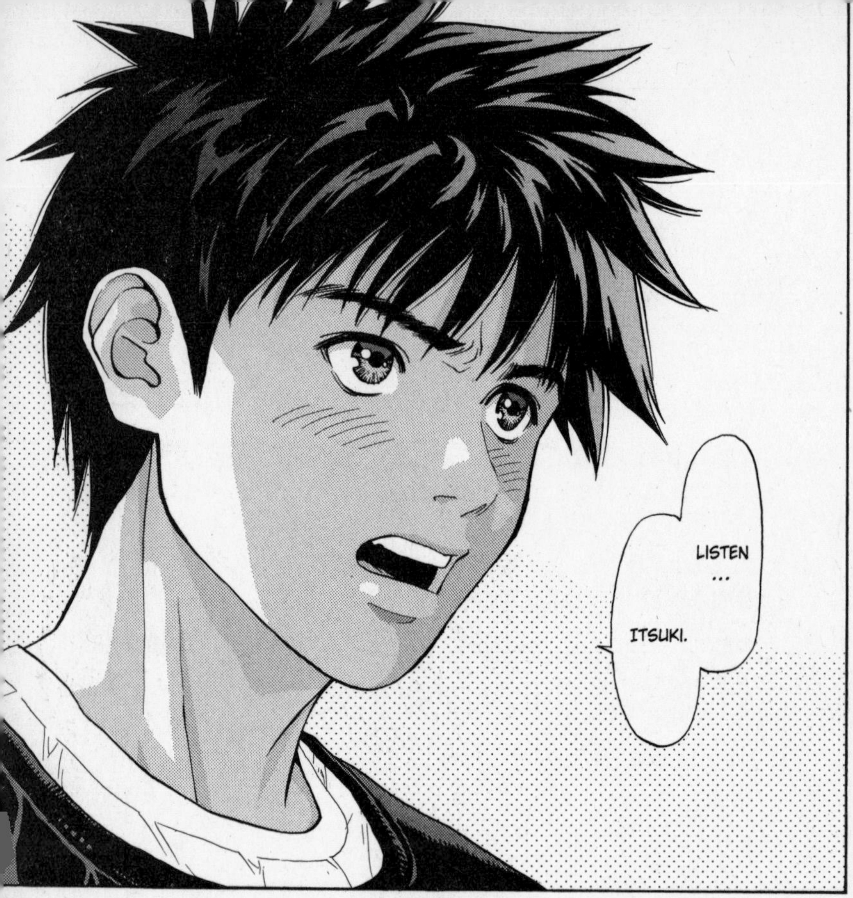
LISTEN ... ITSUKI.

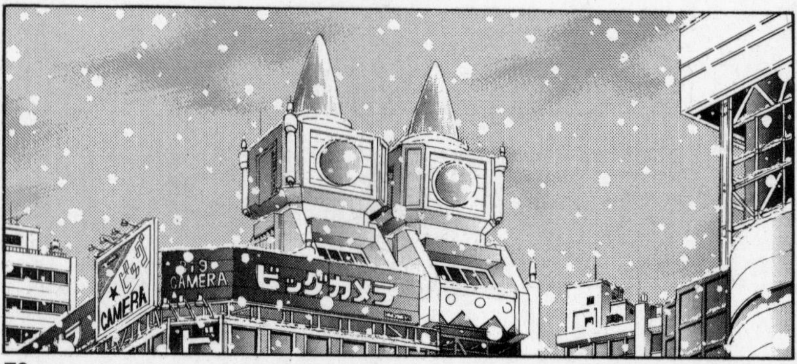
CAMERA
CAMERA

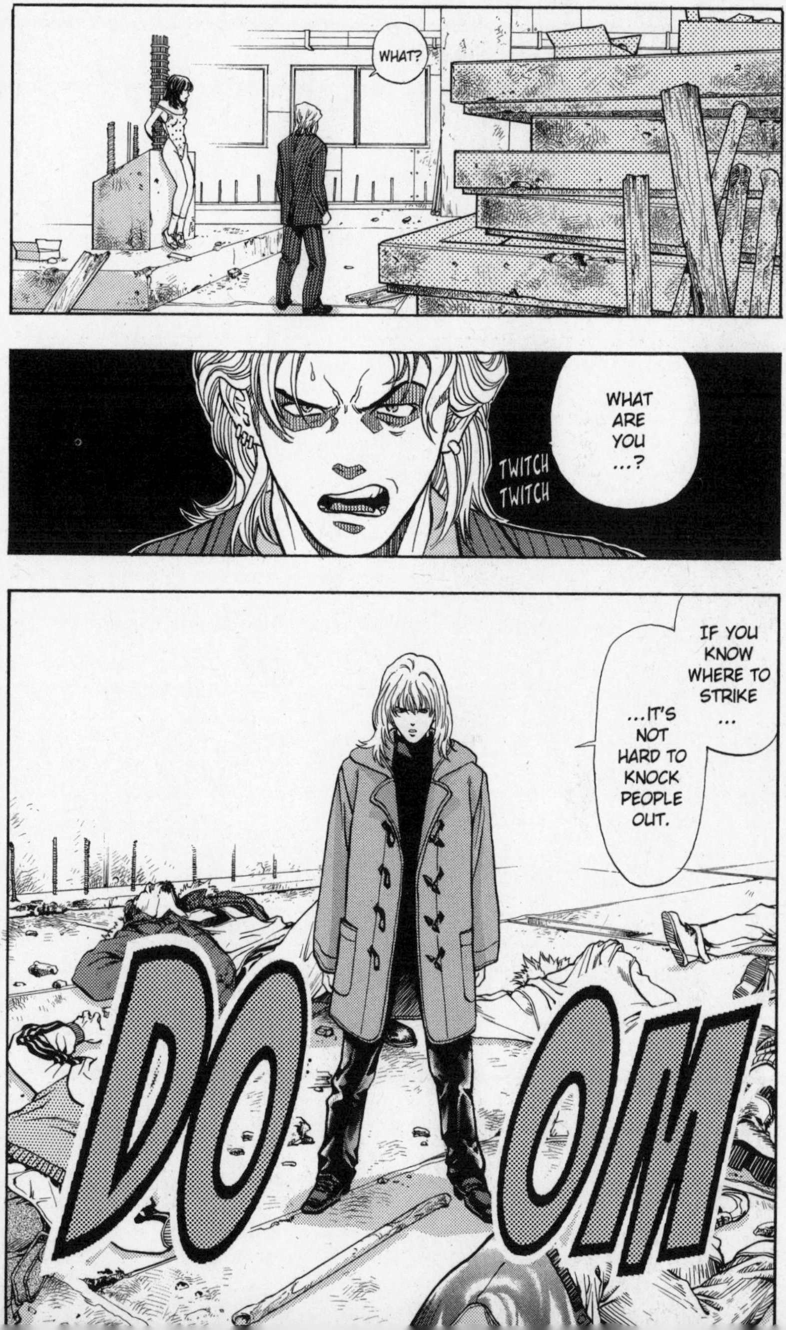
WHAT?
WHAT ARE YOU ...?
TWITCH TWITCH
IF YOU KNOW WHERE TO STRIKE ...
...IT'S NOT HARD TO KNOCK PEOPLE OUT.
DOOM

READ THIS WAY

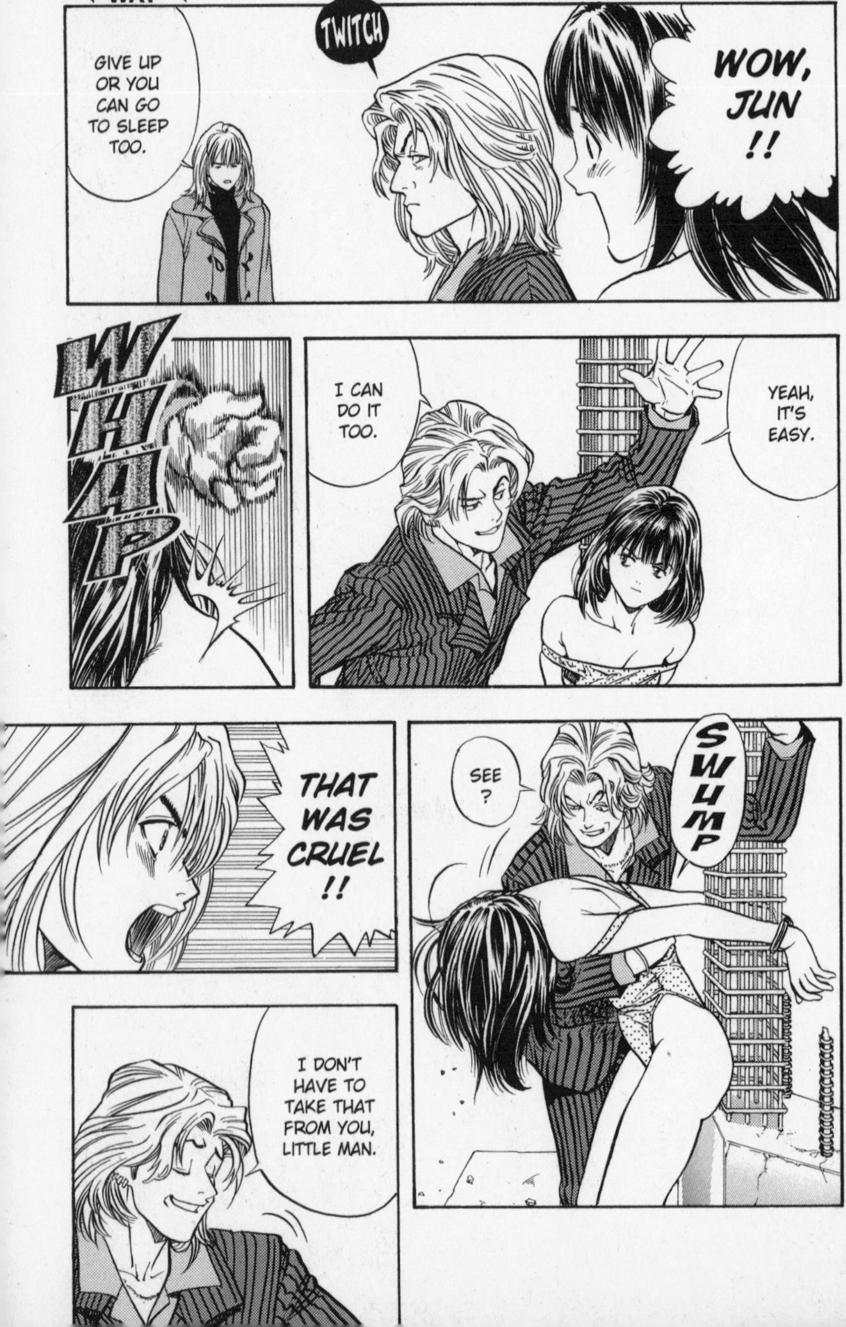
WOW, JUN !!
TWITCH
GIVE UP OR YOU CAN GO TO SLEEP TOO.
YEAH, IT'S EASY.
I CAN DO IT TOO.
WHAP
SWUMP
SEE ?
THAT WAS CRUEL !!
I DON'T HAVE TO TAKE THAT FROM YOU, LITTLE MAN.

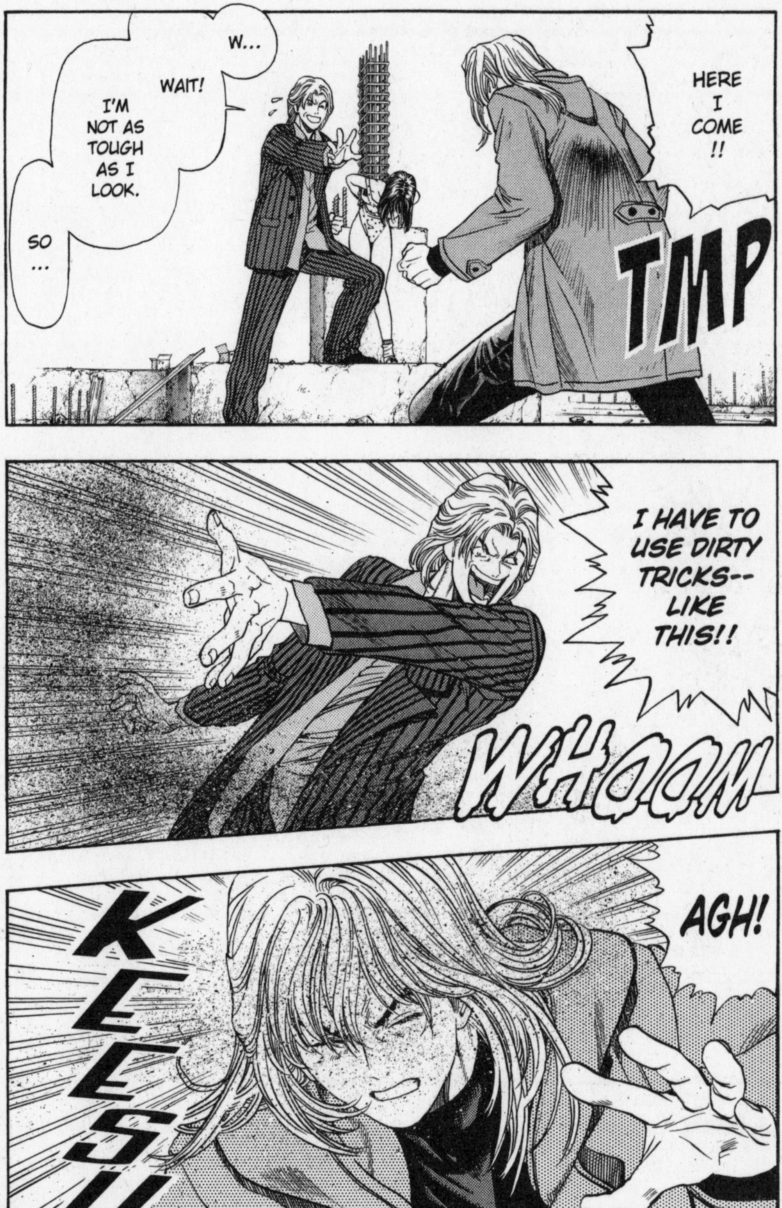
HERE I COME !!
TMP
W...
WAIT!
I'M NOT AS TOUGH AS I LOOK.
SO ...
I HAVE TO USE DIRTY TRICKS-- LIKE THIS!!
WHOOM
AGH!
KEESH

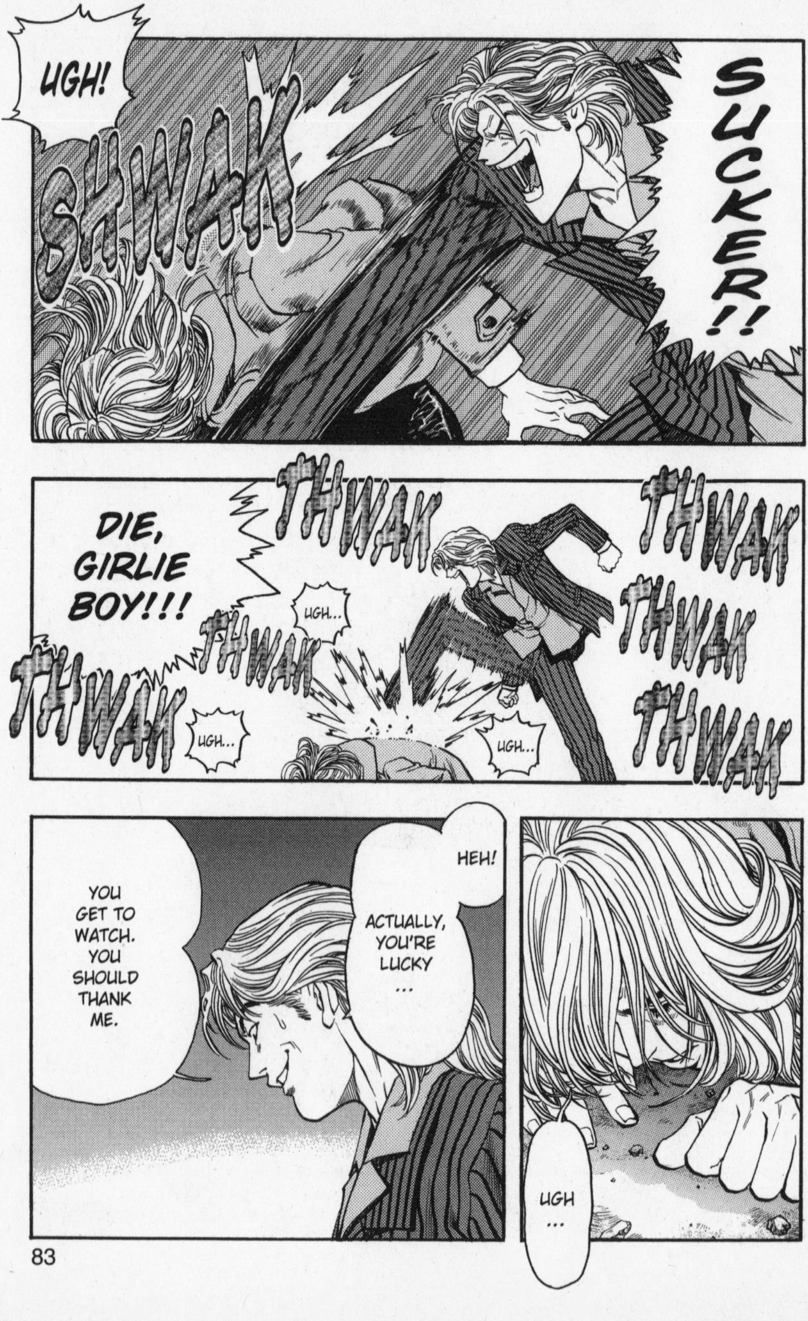
SUCKER!!
UGH!
SHWAK
THWAK
THWAK
THWAK
THWAK
DIE, GIRLIE BOY!!!
UGH...
THWAK
THWAK
UGH...
UGH...
UGH ...
HEH!
ACTUALLY, YOU'RE LUCKY ...
YOU GET TO WATCH. YOU SHOULD THANK ME.

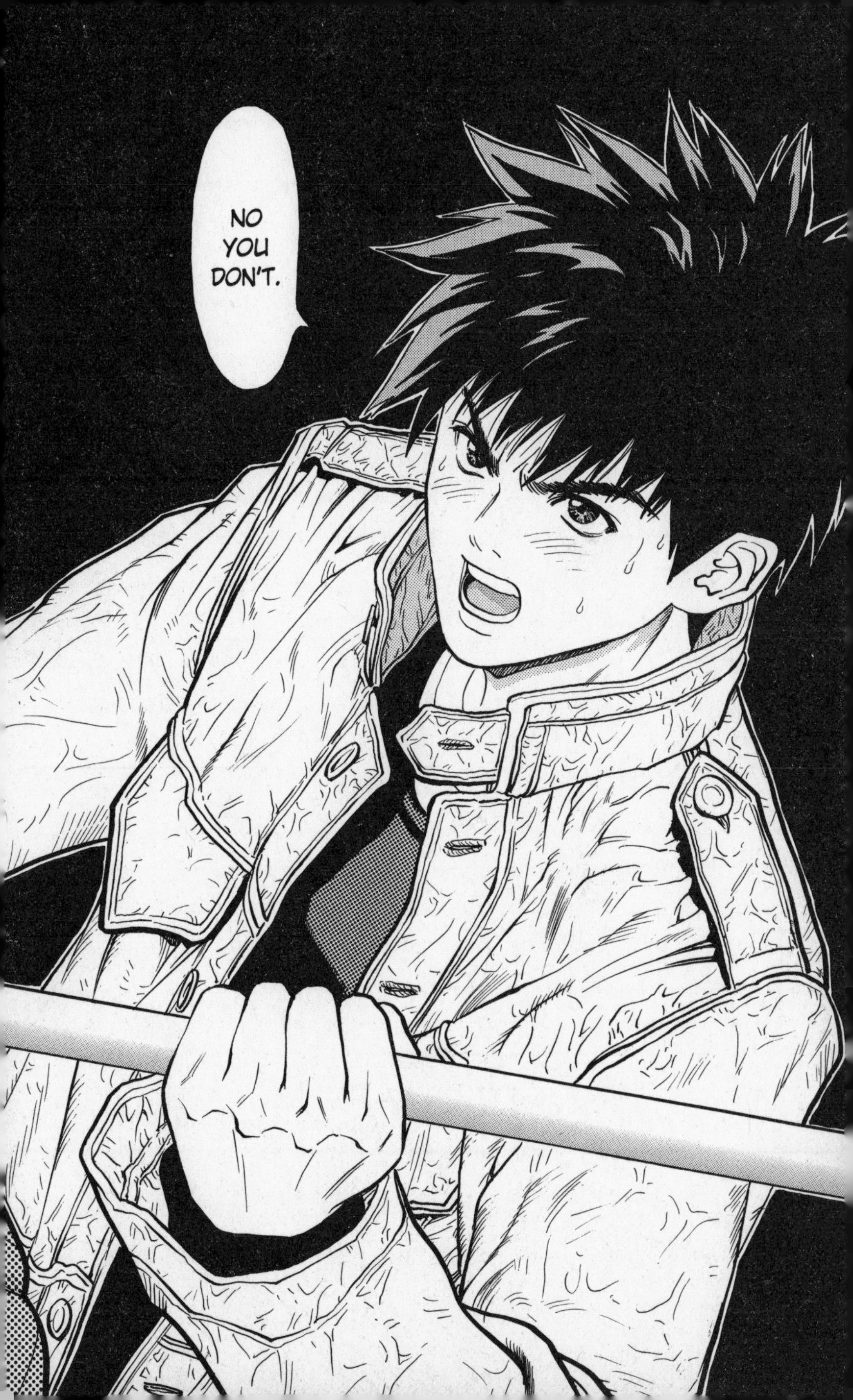
NO YOU DON'T.

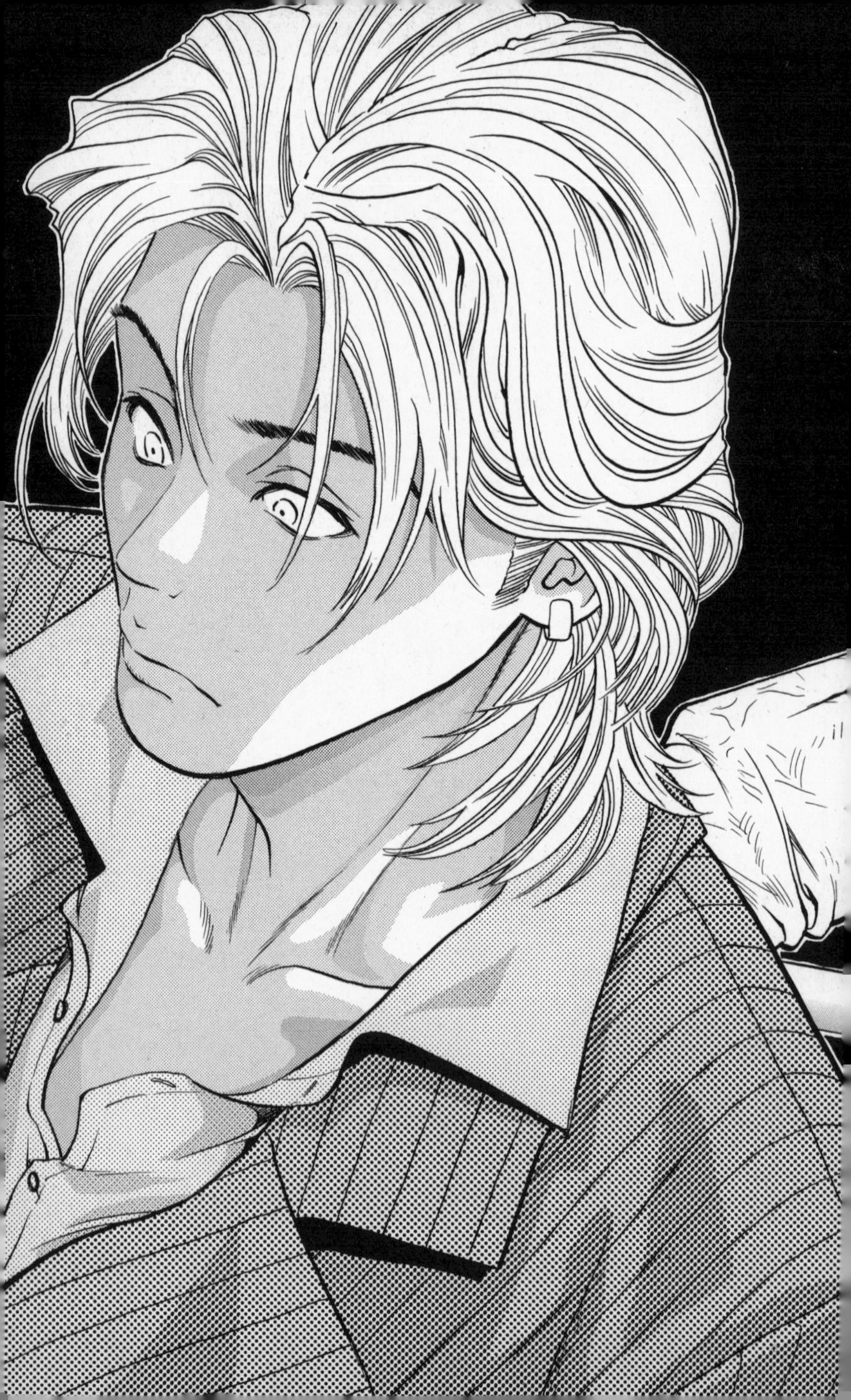

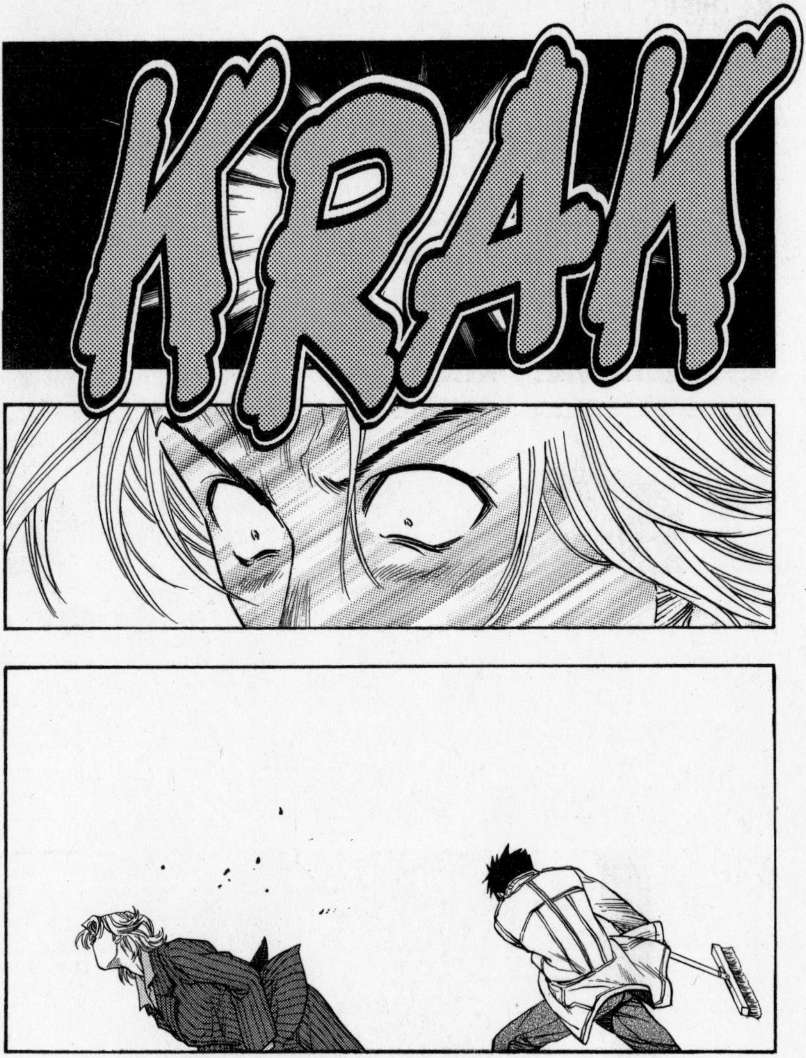
KRAK
WHUMP

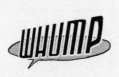

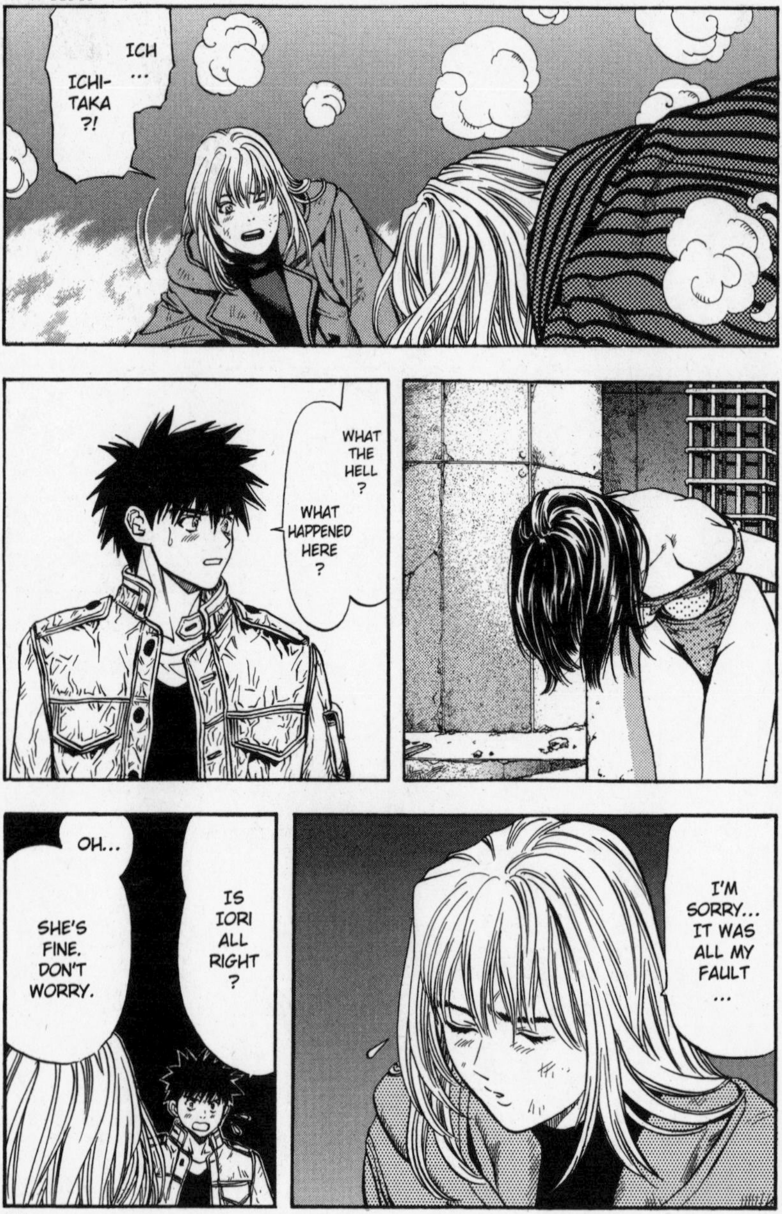
ICH ...
ICHI-TAKA ?!
WHAT THE HELL ?
WHAT HAPPENED HERE ?
I'M SORRY... IT WAS ALL MY FAULT ...
OH...
IS IORI ALL RIGHT ?
SHE'S FINE. DON'T WORRY.

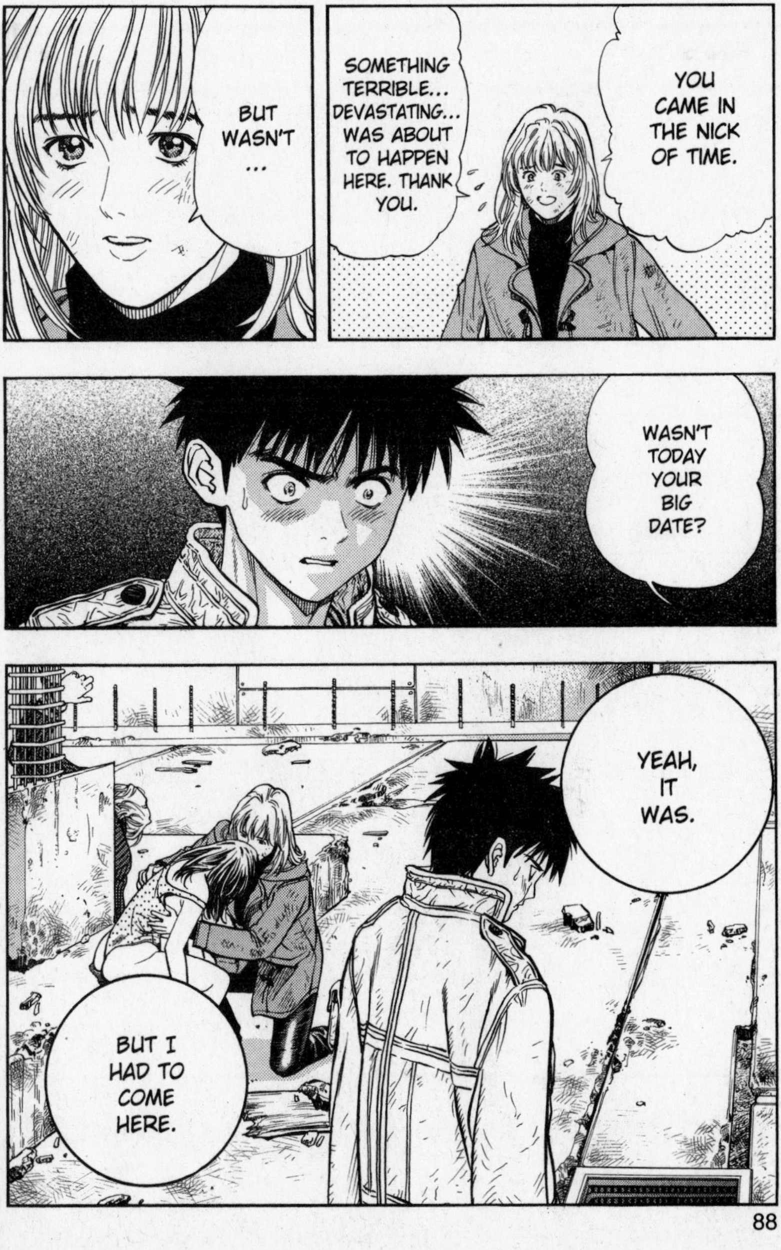
YOU CAME IN THE NICK OF TIME.
SOMETHING TERRIBLE... DEVASTATING... WAS ABOUT TO HAPPEN HERE. THANK YOU.
BUT WASN'T ...
WASN'T TODAY YOUR BIG DATE?
YEAH, IT WAS.
BUT I HAD TO COME HERE.

READ THIS WAY

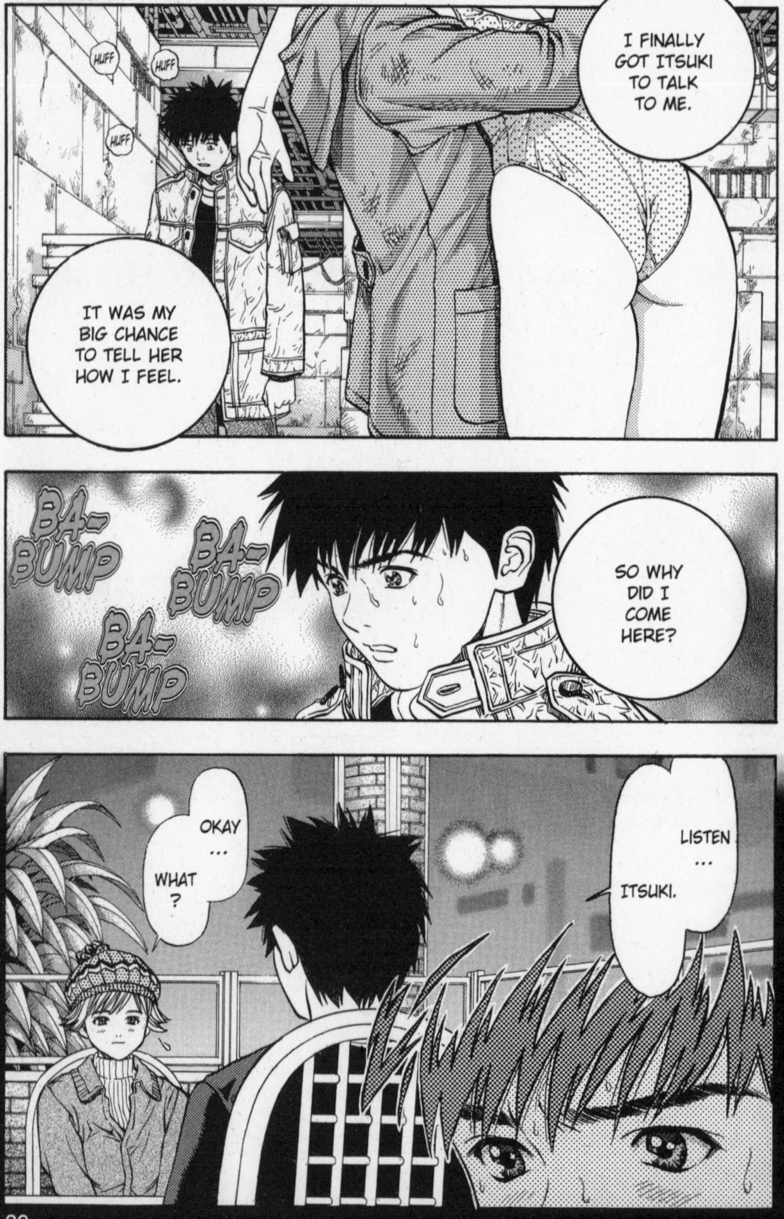
I FINALLY GOT ITSUKI TO TALK TO ME.
HUFF
HUFF
HUFF
IT WAS MY BIG CHANCE TO TELL HER HOW I FEEL.
SO WHY DID I COME HERE?
BA-BUMP
BA-BUMP
BA-BUMP
LISTEN ... ITSUKI.
OKAY ... WHAT?

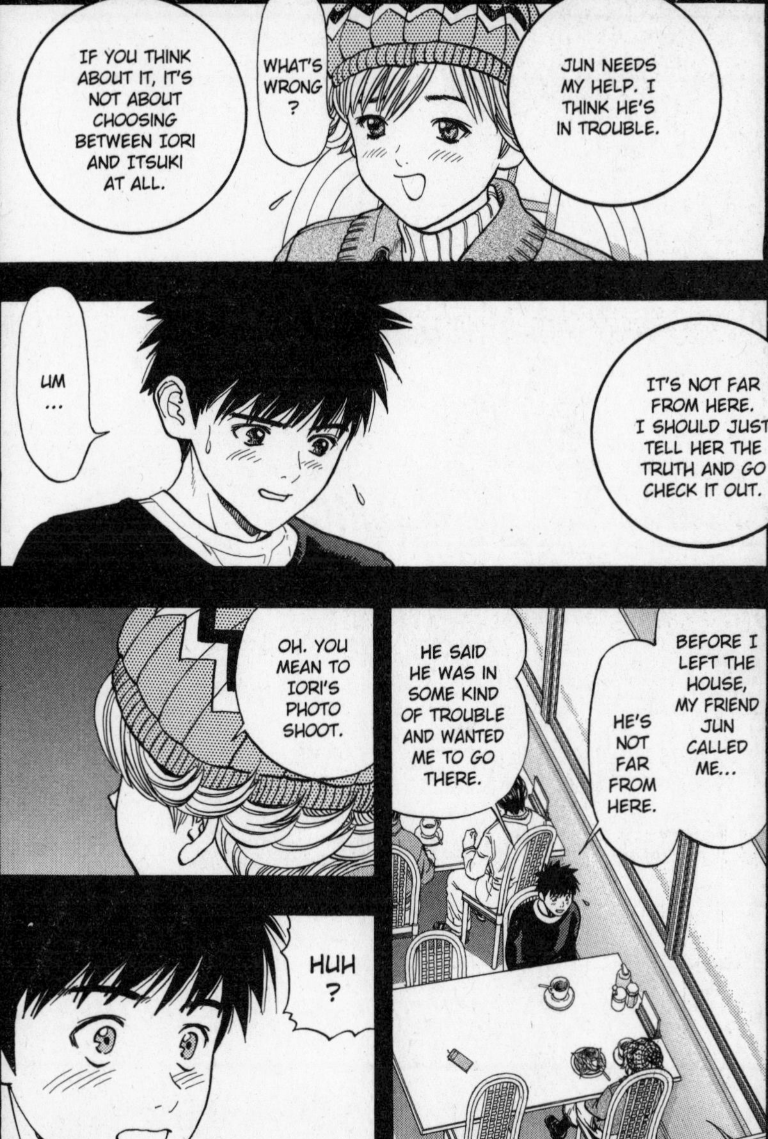
JUN NEEDS MY HELP. I THINK HE'S IN TROUBLE.
WHAT'S WRONG?
IF YOU THINK ABOUT IT, IT'S NOT ABOUT CHOOSING BETWEEN IORI AND ITSUKI AT ALL.
IT'S NOT FAR FROM HERE. I SHOULD JUST TELL HER THE TRUTH AND GO CHECK IT OUT.
UM ...
BEFORE I LEFT THE HOUSE, MY FRIEND JUN CALLED ME...
HE SAID HE WAS IN SOME KIND OF TROUBLE AND WANTED ME TO GO THERE.
HE'S NOT FAR FROM HERE.
OH. YOU MEAN TO IORI'S PHOTO SHOOT.
HUH?

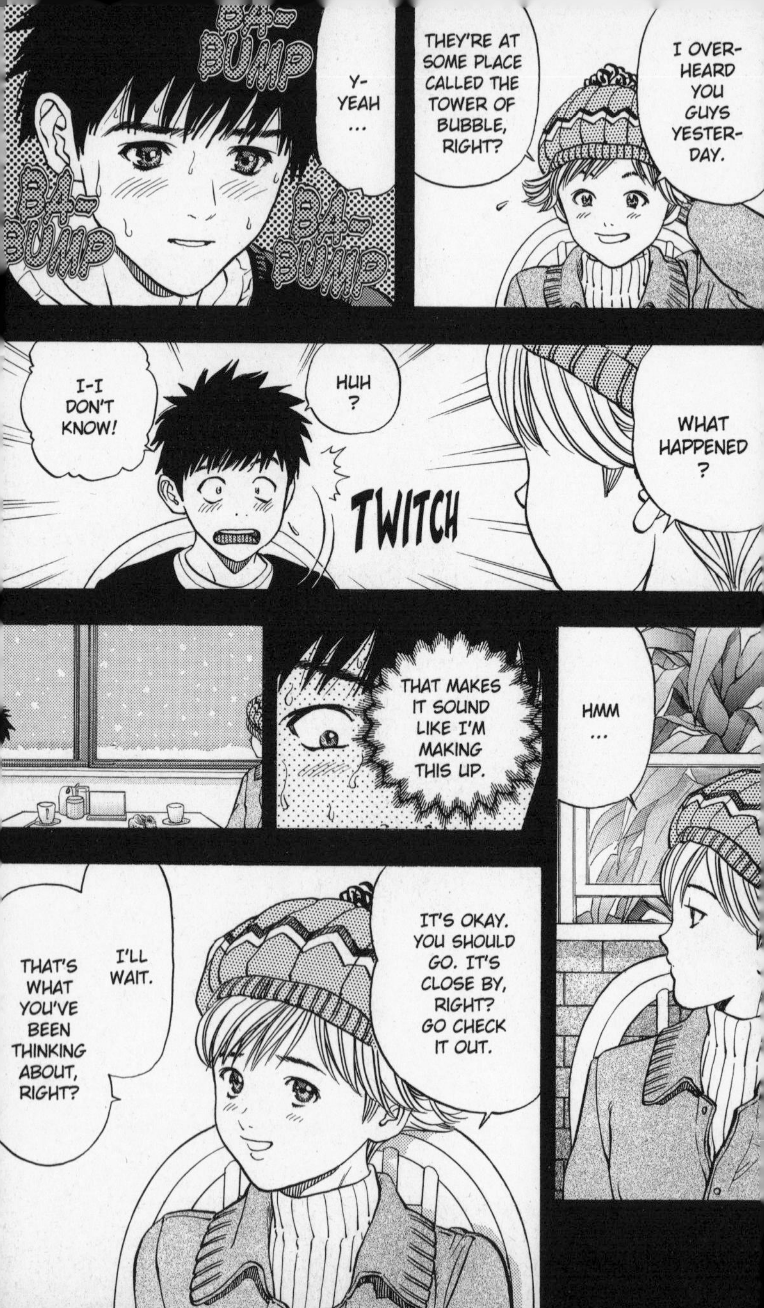
I OVER-HEARD YOU GUYS YESTER-DAY.
THEY'RE AT SOME PLACE CALLED THE TOWER OF BUBBLE, RIGHT?
BA-BUMP
Y-YEAH ...
BA-BUMP
BA-BUMP
WHAT HAPPENED?
HUH?
I-I DON'T KNOW!
TWITCH
HMM ...
THAT MAKES IT SOUND LIKE I'M MAKING THIS UP.
IT'S OKAY. YOU SHOULD GO. IT'S CLOSE BY, RIGHT? GO CHECK IT OUT.
I'LL WAIT.
THAT'S WHAT YOU'VE BEEN THINKING ABOUT, RIGHT?

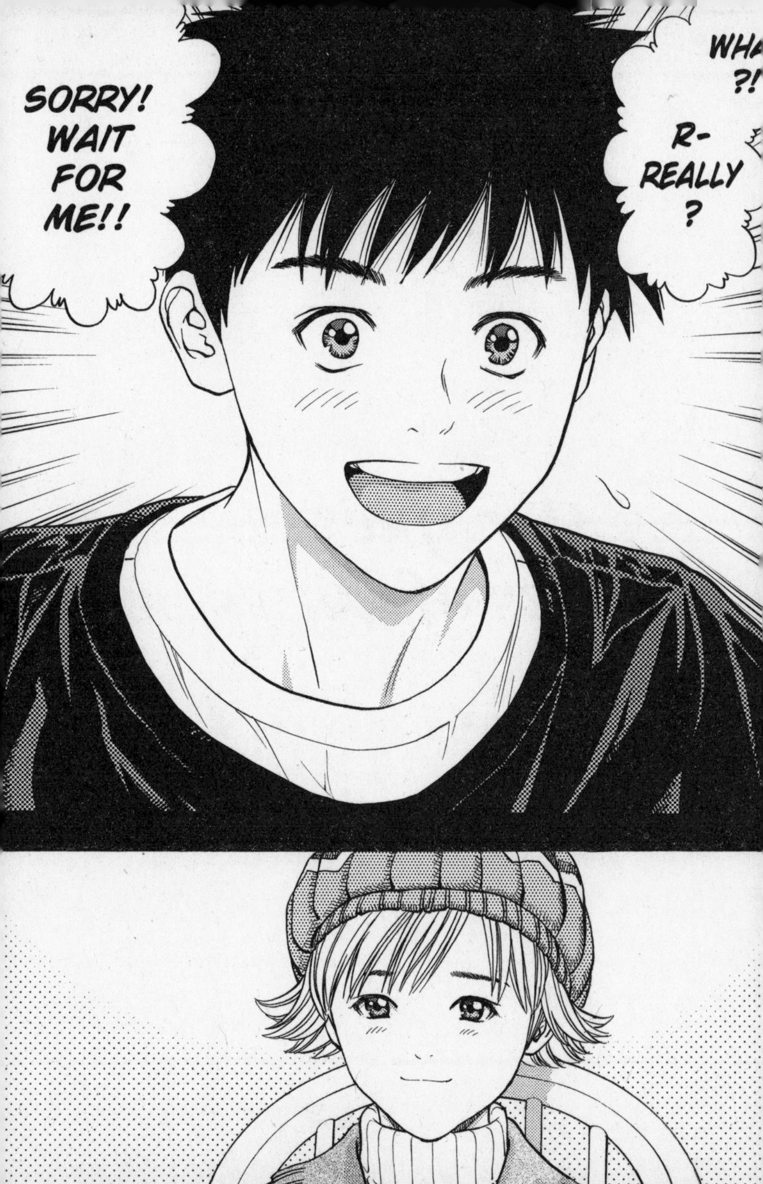
WHA ?! R- REALLY ?
SORRY! WAIT FOR ME!!

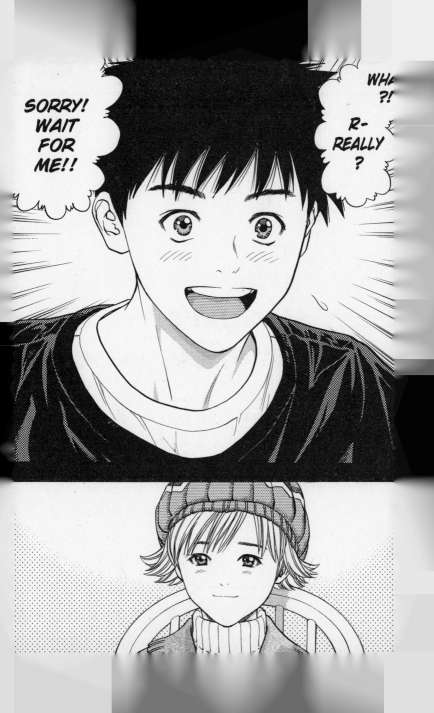

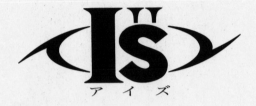

Chapter 50:
Smiles of Difference

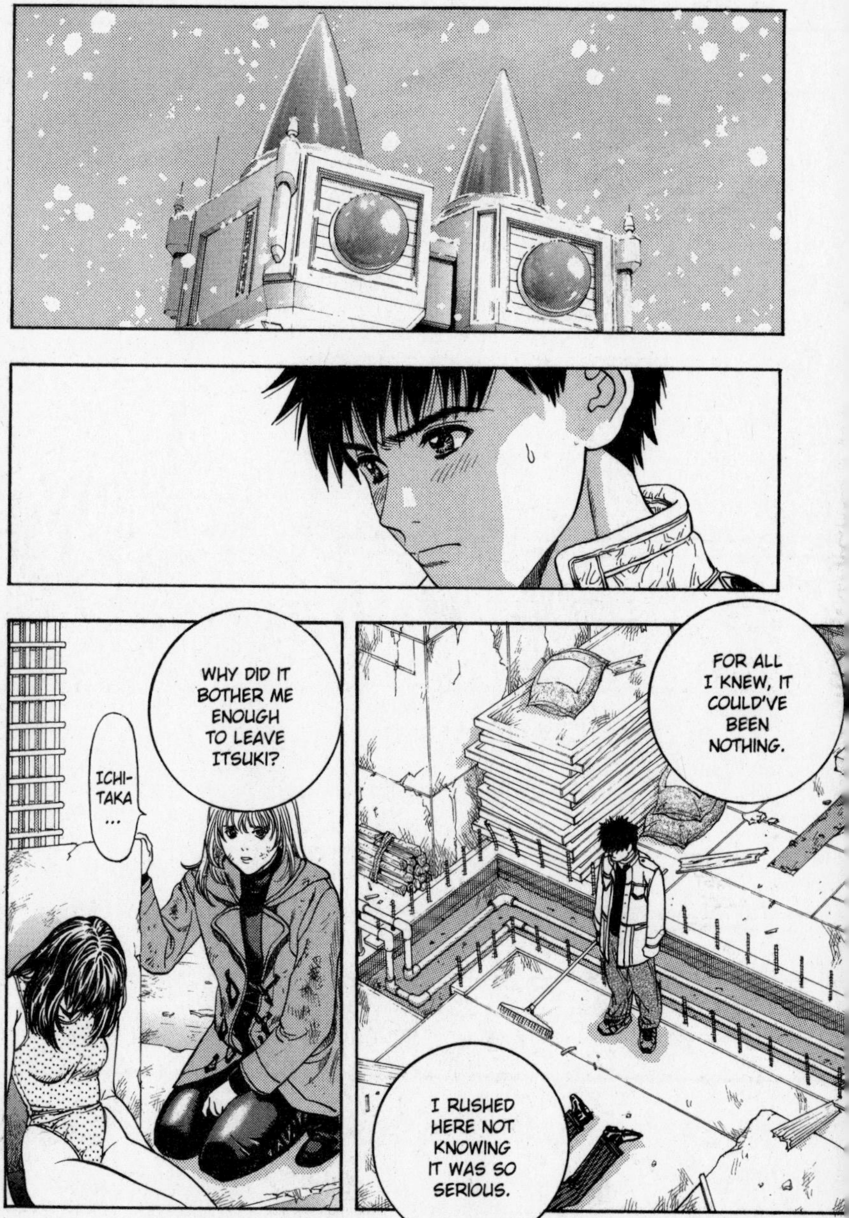
FOR ALL I KNEW, IT COULD'VE BEEN NOTHING.
I RUSHED HERE NOT KNOWING IT WAS SO SERIOUS.
WHY DID IT BOTHER ME ENOUGH TO LEAVE ITSUKI?
ICHI-TAKA...

READ THIS WAY

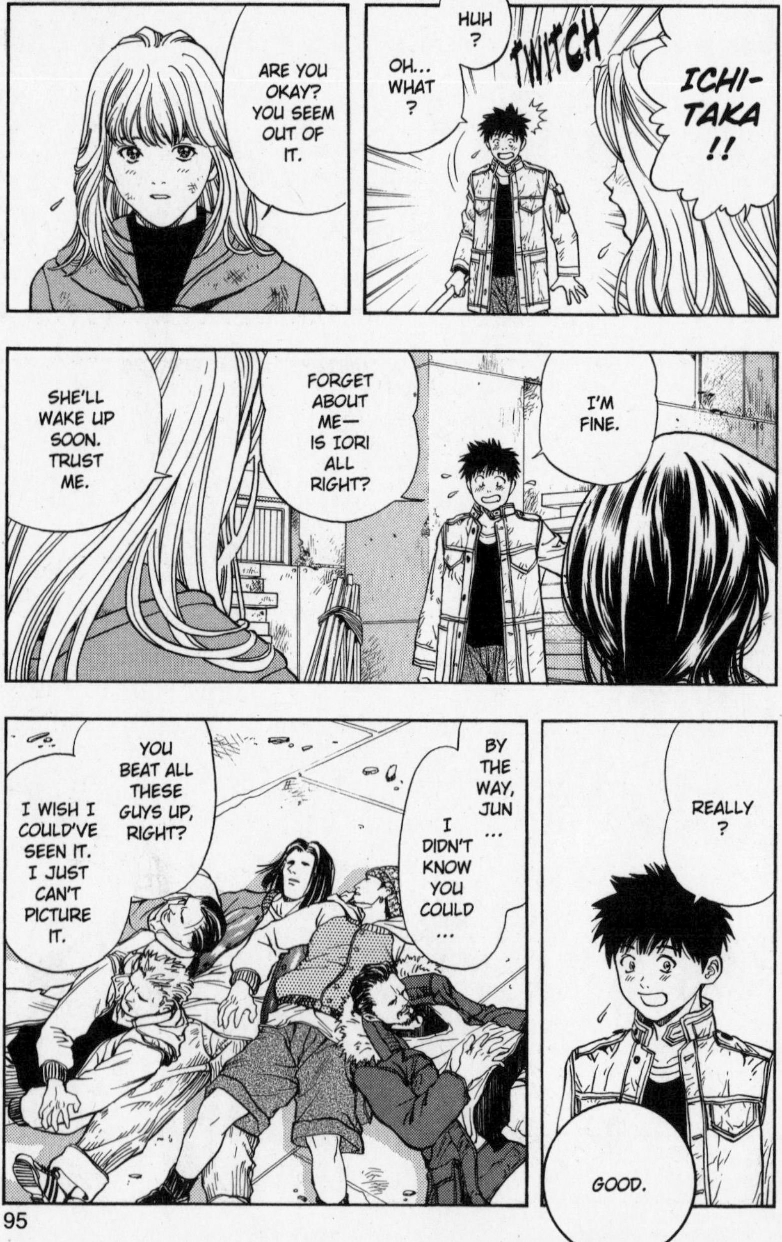

ICHI-TAKA!!
TWITCH
HUH?
OH... WHAT?
ARE YOU OKAY? YOU SEEM OUT OF IT.
I'M FINE.
FORGET ABOUT ME— IS IORI ALL RIGHT?
SHE'LL WAKE UP SOON. TRUST ME.
REALLY?
GOOD.
BY THE WAY, JUN...
I DIDN'T KNOW YOU COULD...
YOU BEAT ALL THESE GUYS UP, RIGHT?
I WISH I COULD'VE SEEN IT. I JUST CAN'T PICTURE IT.

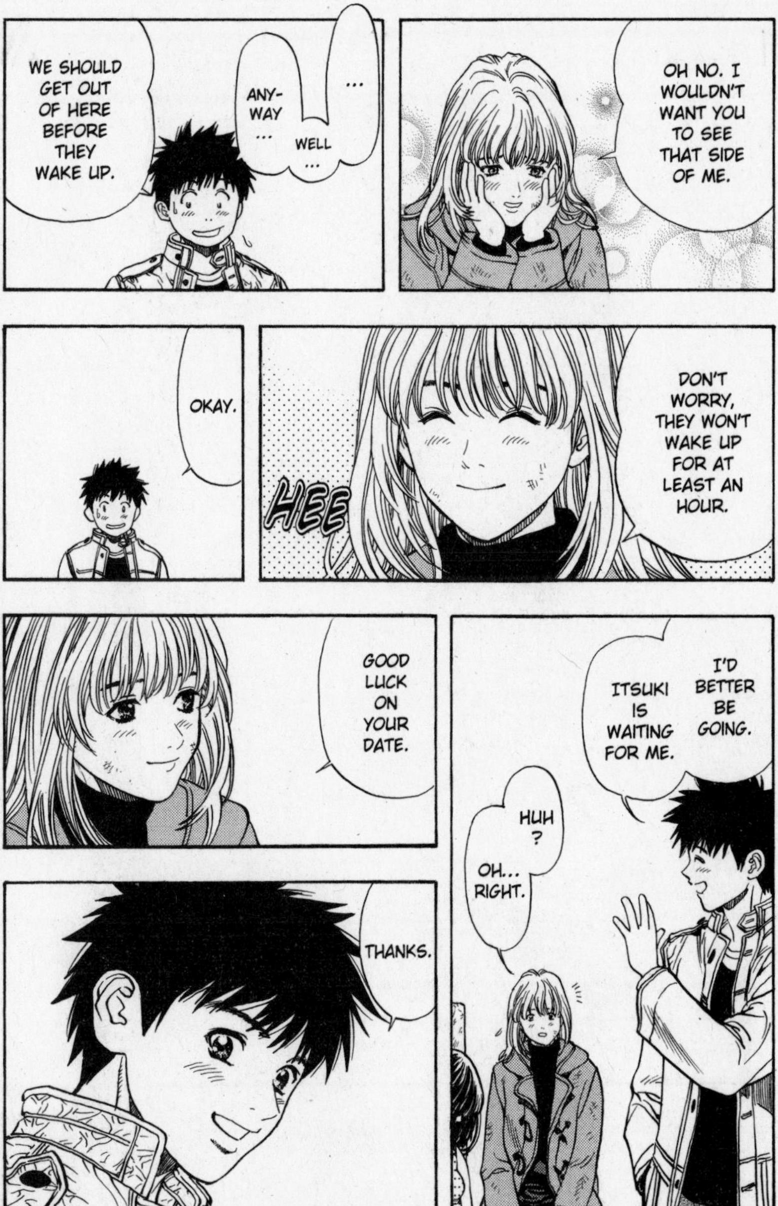
OH NO. I WOULDN'T WANT YOU TO SEE THAT SIDE OF ME.
...
ANY-WAY ... WELL ...
WE SHOULD GET OUT OF HERE BEFORE THEY WAKE UP.
DON'T WORRY, THEY WON'T WAKE UP FOR AT LEAST AN HOUR.
HEE
OKAY.
I'D BETTER BE GOING.
ITSUKI IS WAITING FOR ME.
HUH?
OH... RIGHT.
GOOD LUCK ON YOUR DATE.
THANKS.

READ THIS WAY

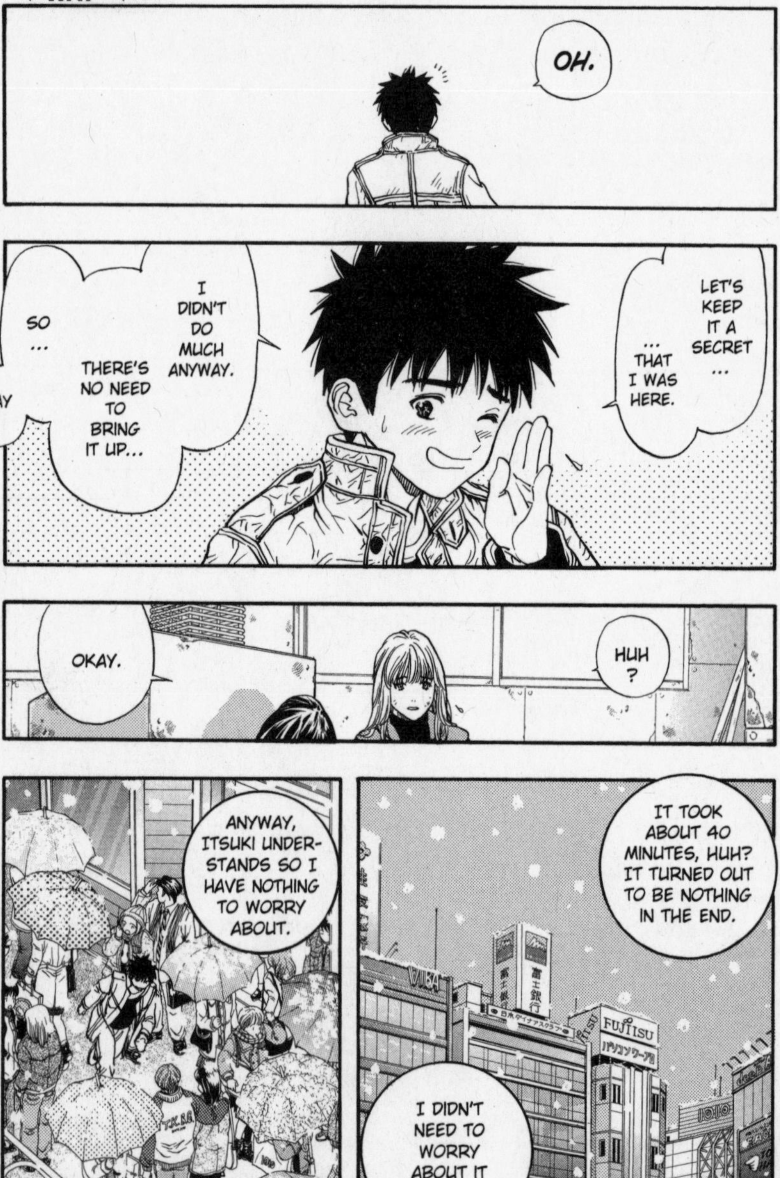
OH.
LET'S KEEP IT A SECRET ...
... THAT I WAS HERE.
I DIDN'T DO MUCH ANYWAY.
SO ... THERE'S NO NEED TO BRING IT UP...
OKAY ?
HUH ?
OKAY.
IT TOOK ABOUT 40 MINUTES, HUH? IT TURNED OUT TO BE NOTHING IN THE END.
I DIDN'T NEED TO WORRY ABOUT IT SO MUCH.
ANYWAY, ITSUKI UNDER-STANDS SO I HAVE NOTHING TO WORRY ABOUT.
FUJITSU

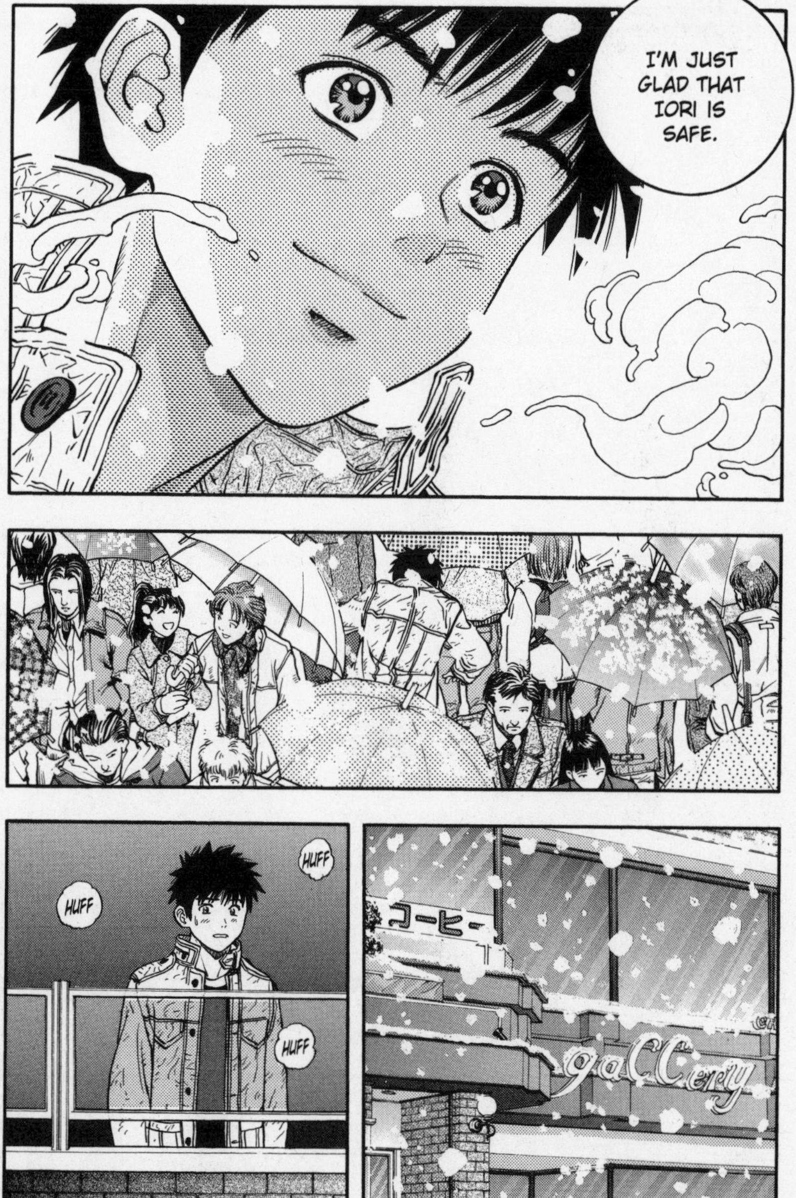
I'M JUST GLAD THAT IORI IS SAFE.
コーヒー
HUFF
HUFF
HUFF

READ THIS WAY

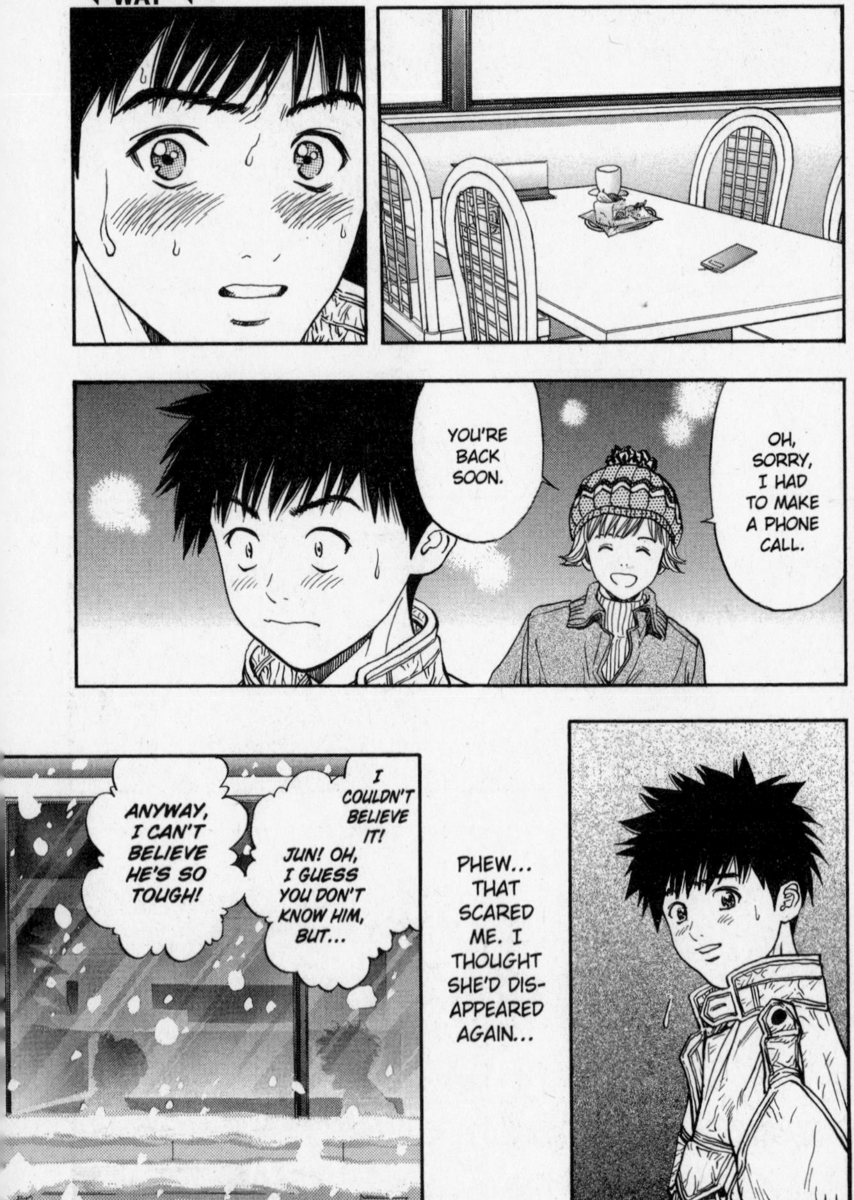
OH, SORRY, I HAD TO MAKE A PHONE CALL.
YOU'RE BACK SOON.
PHEW... THAT SCARED ME. I THOUGHT SHE'D DIS-APPEARED AGAIN...
I COULDN'T BELIEVE IT!
JUN! OH, I GUESS YOU DON'T KNOW HIM, BUT...
ANYWAY, I CAN'T BELIEVE HE'S SO TOUGH!

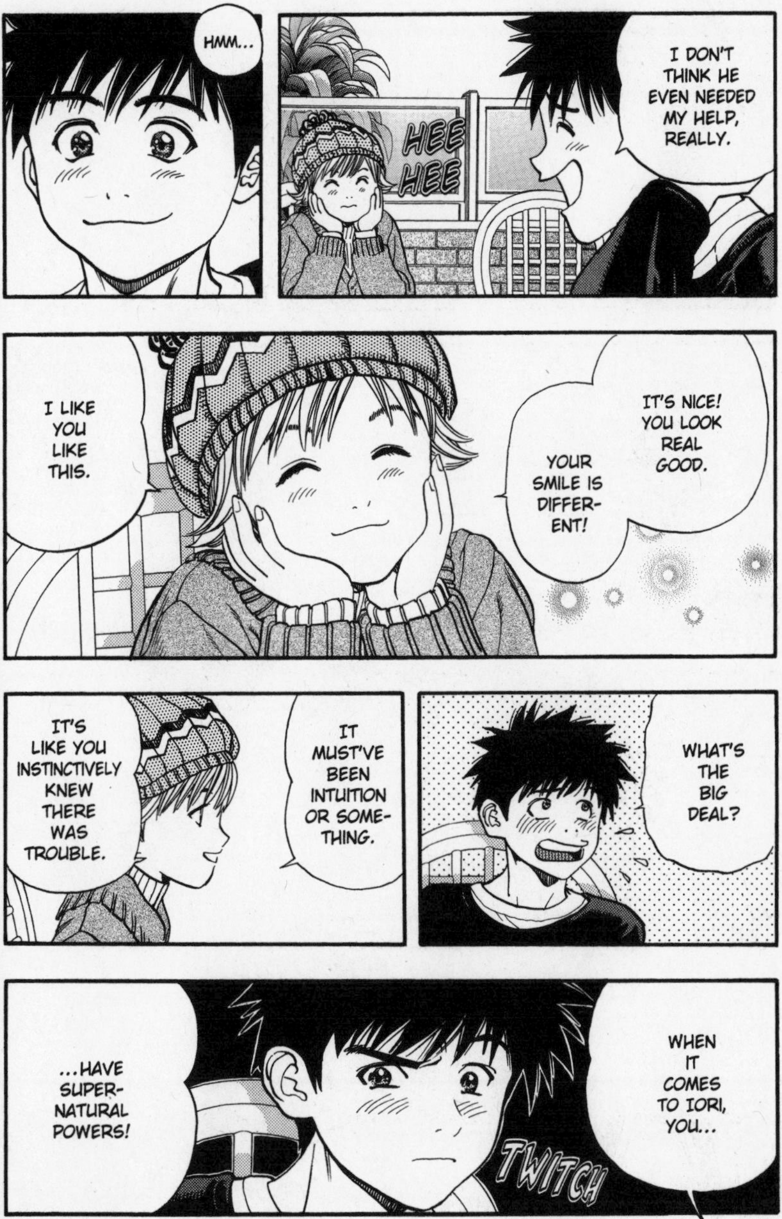
I DON'T THINK HE EVEN NEEDED MY HELP, REALLY.
HEE HEE
HMM...
IT'S NICE! YOU LOOK REAL GOOD.
YOUR SMILE IS DIFFERENT!
I LIKE YOU LIKE THIS.
WHAT'S THE BIG DEAL?
IT MUST'VE BEEN INTUITION OR SOMETHING.
IT'S LIKE YOU INSTINCTIVELY KNEW THERE WAS TROUBLE.
WHEN IT COMES TO IORI, YOU...
TWITCH
...HAVE SUPERNATURAL POWERS!

READ THIS WAY

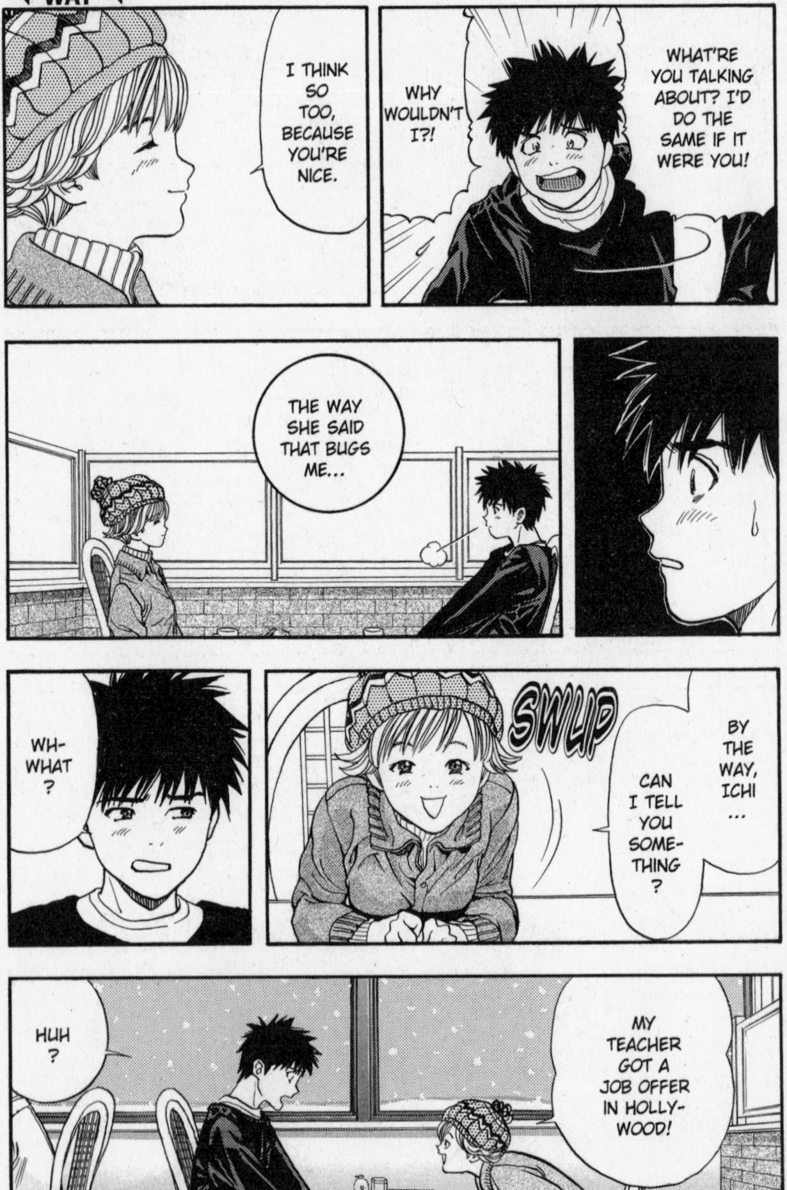
WHAT'RE YOU TALKING ABOUT? I'D DO THE SAME IF IT WERE YOU!
WHY WOULDN'T I?!
I THINK SO TOO, BECAUSE YOU'RE NICE.
THE WAY SHE SAID THAT BUGS ME...
BY THE WAY, ICHI...
CAN I TELL YOU SOMETHING?
SWUP
WH-WHAT?
MY TEACHER GOT A JOB OFFER IN HOLLY-WOOD!
HUH?

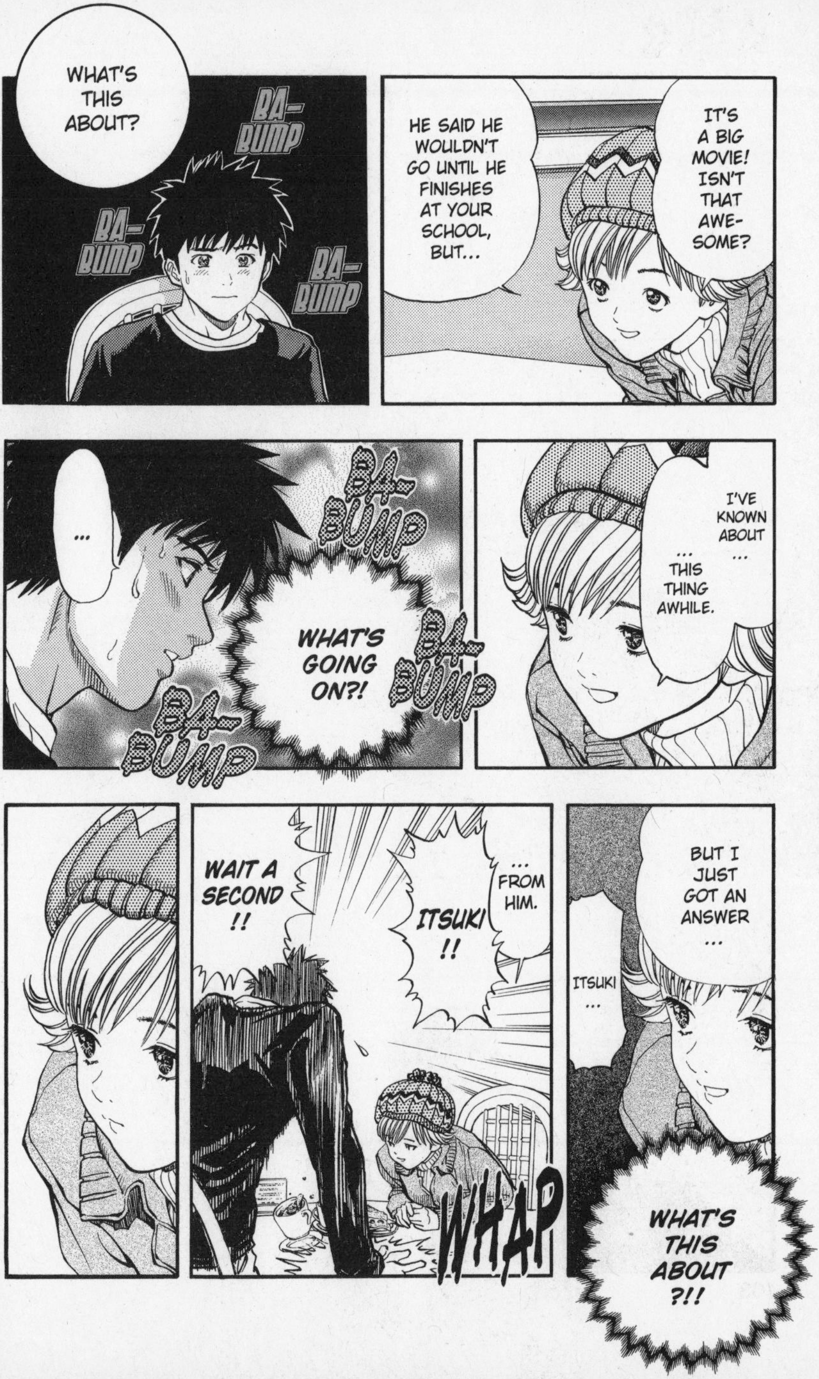
IT'S A BIG MOVIE! ISN'T THAT AWESOME?
HE SAID HE WOULDN'T GO UNTIL HE FINISHES AT YOUR SCHOOL, BUT...
WHAT'S THIS ABOUT?
BA-BUMP
BA-BUMP
BA-BUMP
I'VE KNOWN ABOUT ...
... THIS THING AWHILE.
...
BA-BUMP
WHAT'S GOING ON?!
BA-BUMP
BA-BUMP
BUT I JUST GOT AN ANSWER ...
ITSUKI ...
... FROM HIM.
ITSUKI !!
WAIT A SECOND !!
WHAP
WHAT'S THIS ABOUT ?!!

READ THIS WAY

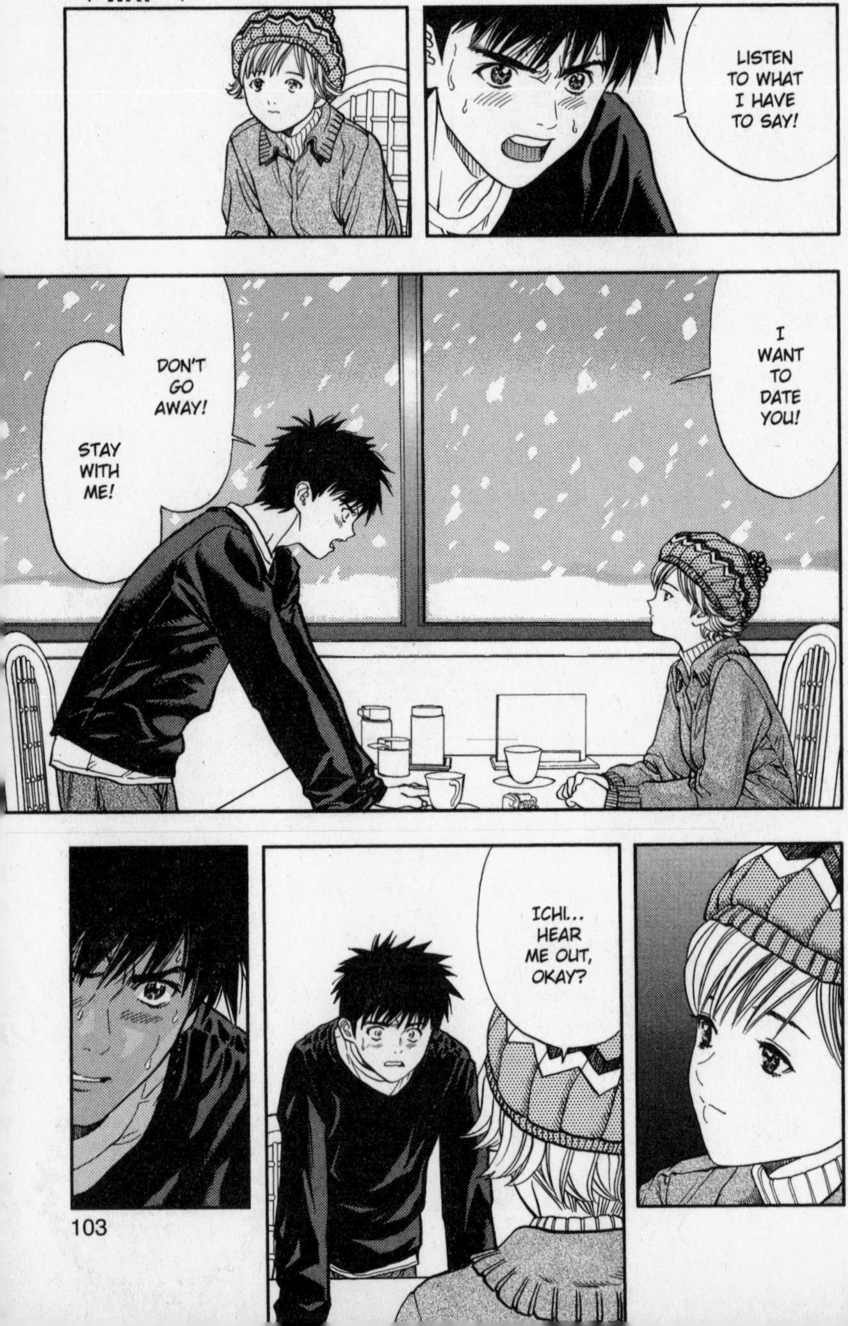
LISTEN TO WHAT I HAVE TO SAY!
I WANT TO DATE YOU!
DON'T GO AWAY!
STAY WITH ME!
ICHI... HEAR ME OUT, OKAY?

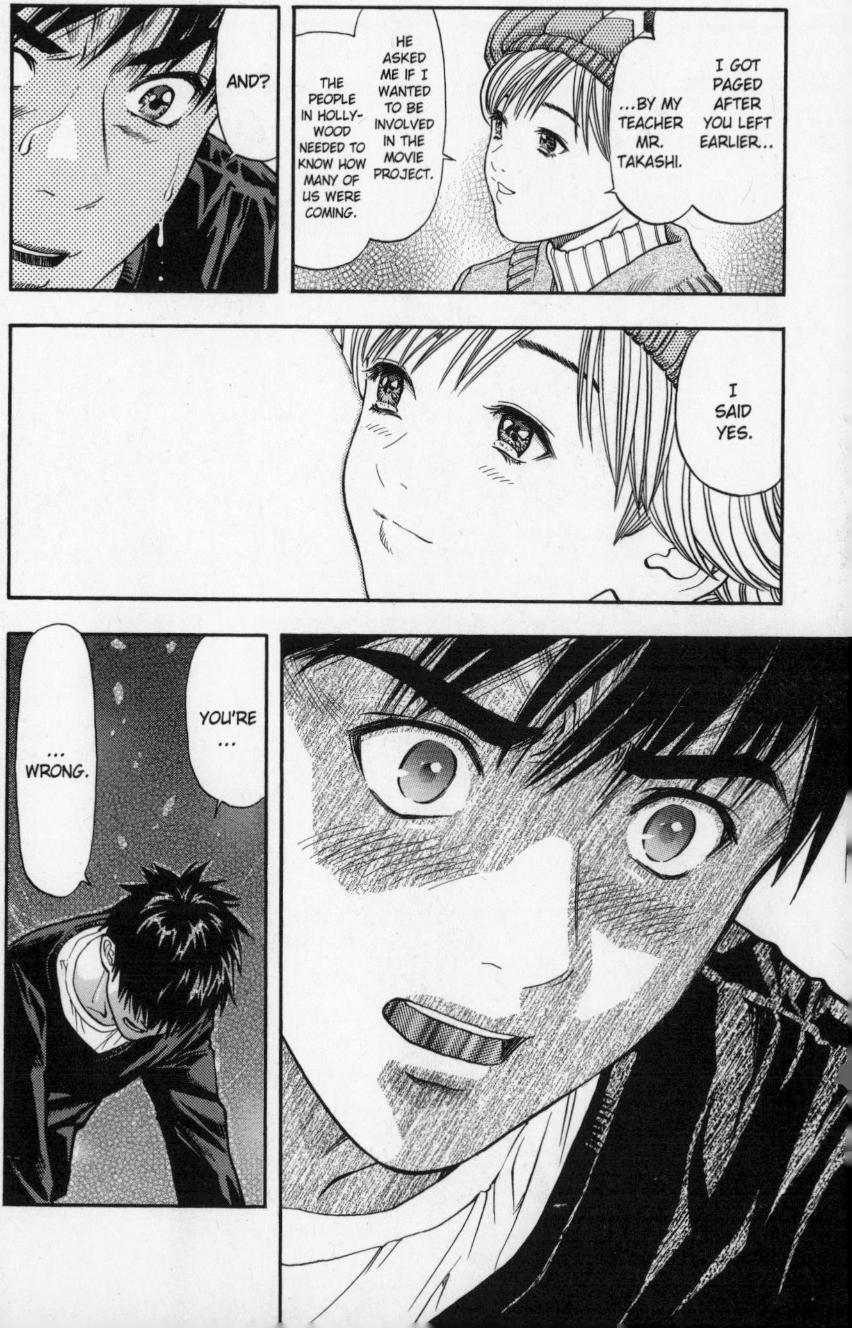
I GOT PAGED AFTER YOU LEFT EARLIER...
...BY MY TEACHER MR. TAKASHI.
HE ASKED ME IF I WANTED TO BE INVOLVED IN THE MOVIE PROJECT.
THE PEOPLE IN HOLLY-WOOD NEEDED TO KNOW HOW MANY OF US WERE COMING.
AND?
I SAID YES.
YOU'RE ...
... WRONG.

READ THIS WAY

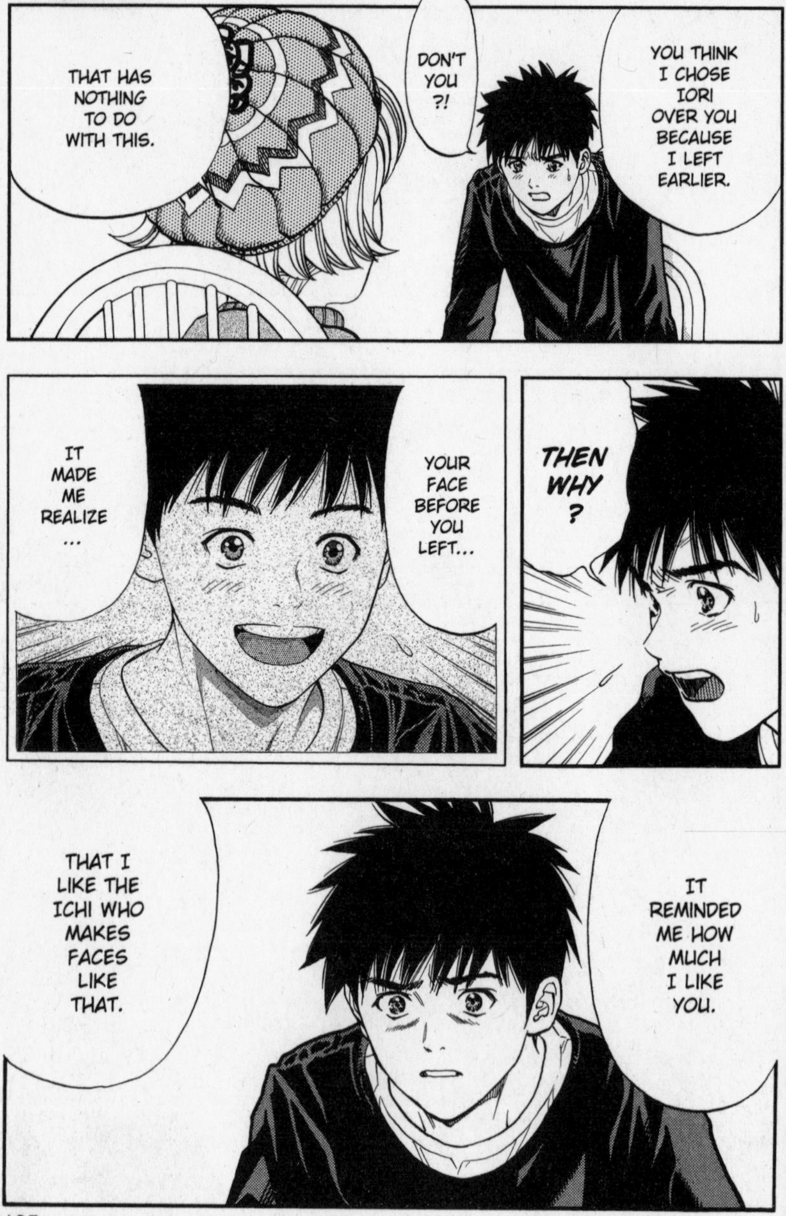
YOU THINK I CHOSE IORI OVER YOU BECAUSE I LEFT EARLIER.
DON'T YOU ?!
THAT HAS NOTHING TO DO WITH THIS.
THEN WHY ?
YOUR FACE BEFORE YOU LEFT...
IT MADE ME REALIZE ...
IT REMINDED ME HOW MUCH I LIKE YOU.
THAT I LIKE THE ICHI WHO MAKES FACES LIKE THAT.

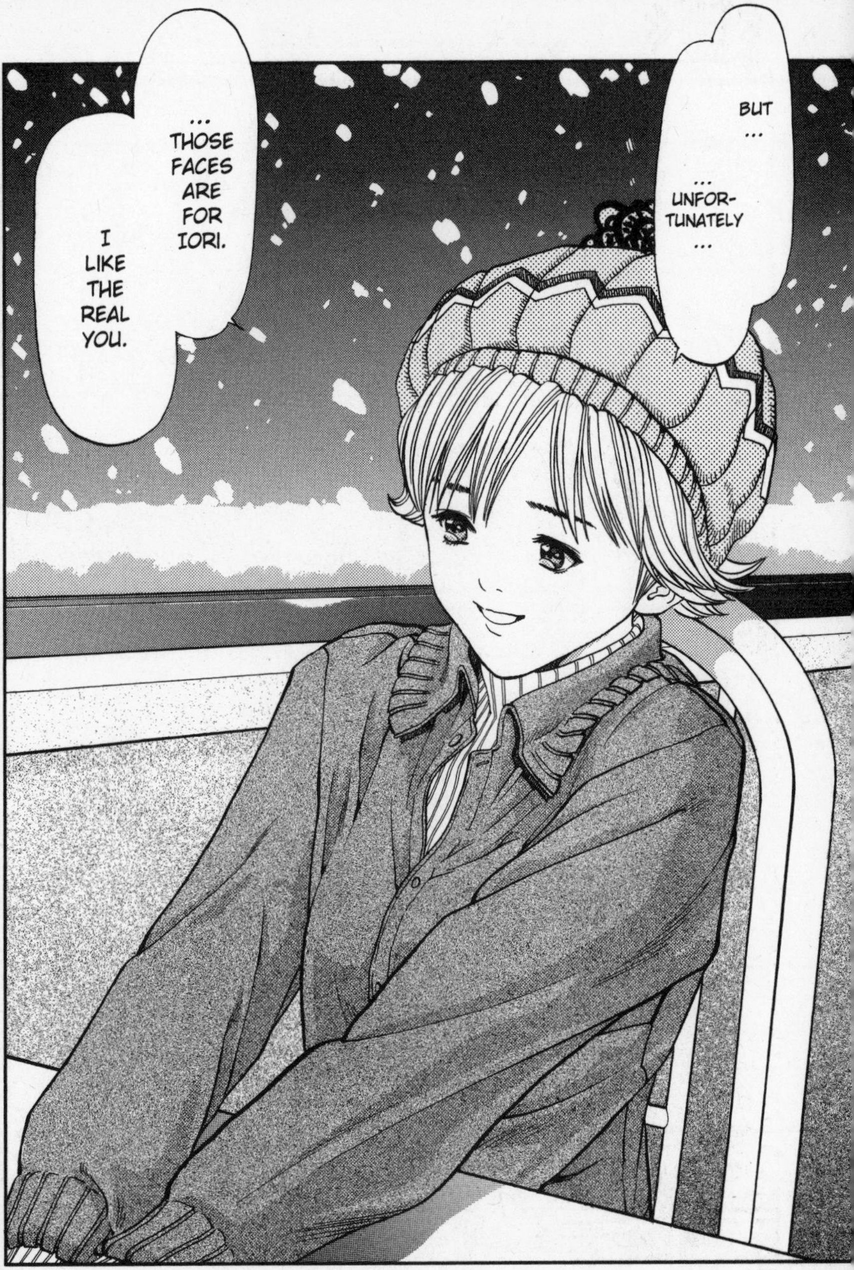
BUT ... ... UNFORTUNATELY ...
... THOSE FACES ARE FOR IORI. I LIKE THE REAL YOU.

READ THIS WAY

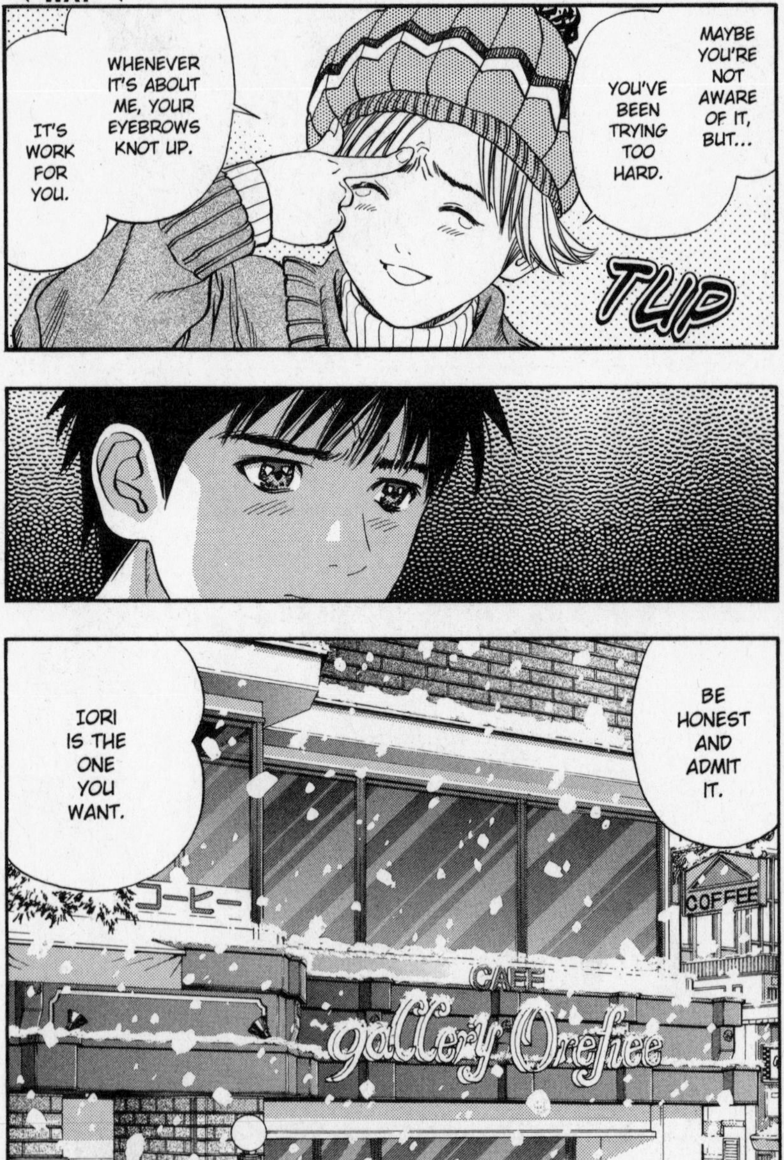
MAYBE YOU'RE NOT AWARE OF IT, BUT...
YOU'VE BEEN TRYING TOO HARD.
WHENEVER IT'S ABOUT ME, YOUR EYEBROWS KNOT UP.
IT'S WORK FOR YOU.
TUP
BE HONEST AND ADMIT IT.
IORI IS THE ONE YOU WANT.
COFFEE
コーヒー
CAFE

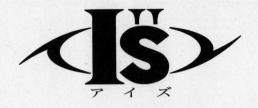

アイズ

Chapter 51: Winter Feelings

ITSUKI WENT BACK TO AMERICA.

THIS IS THE SECOND TIME I'VE HAD TO SAY GOODBYE TO HER.

BUT THIS TIME IT'S DIFFERENT FROM WHEN WE WERE LITTLE KIDS.

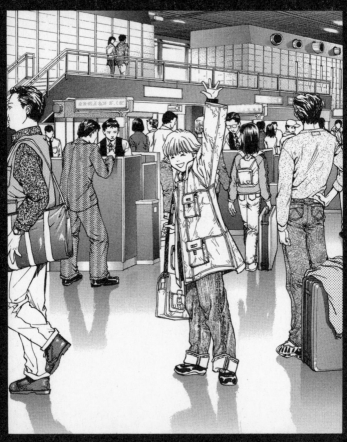

I'M STILL NOT SURE I REALLY UNDER-STAND...

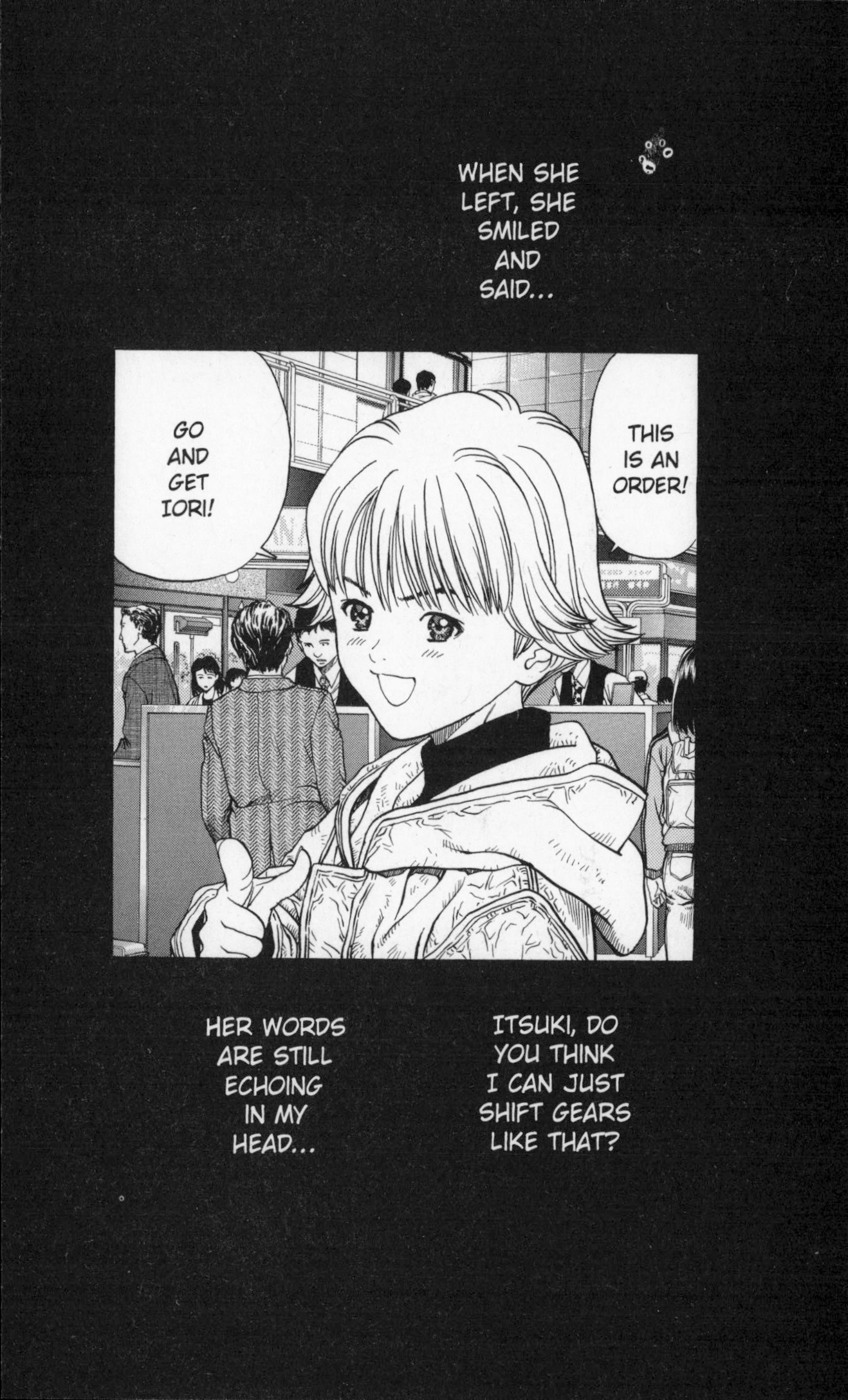
WHEN SHE LEFT, SHE SMILED AND SAID...
THIS IS AN ORDER!
GO AND GET IORI!
ITSUKI, DO YOU THINK I CAN JUST SHIFT GEARS LIKE THAT?
HER WORDS ARE STILL ECHOING IN MY HEAD...

READ THIS WAY

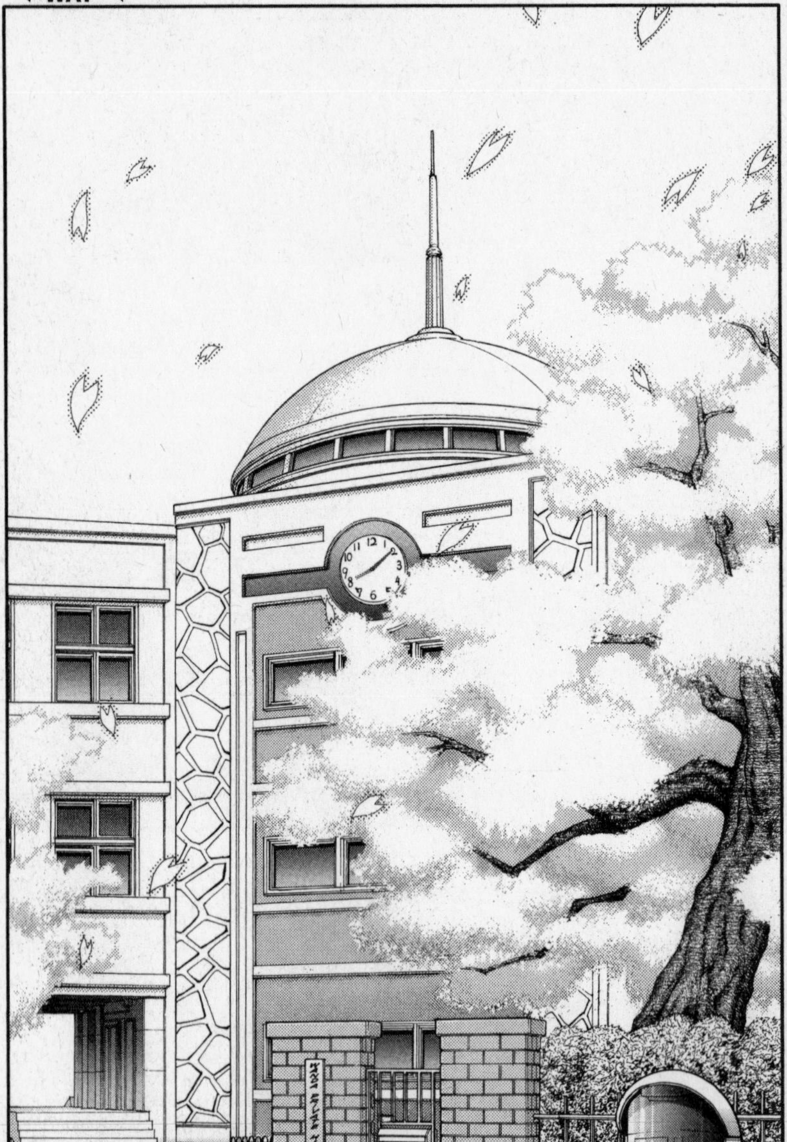

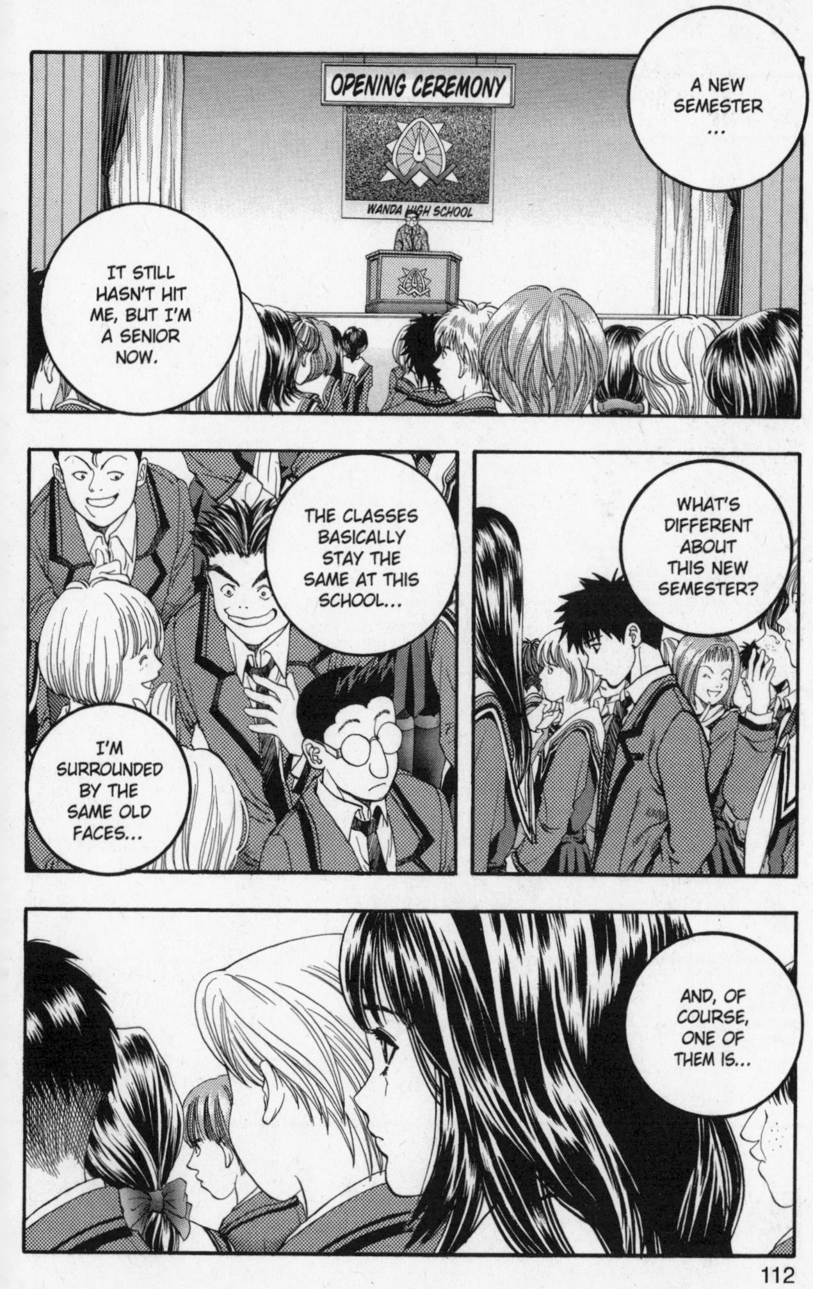
A NEW SEMESTER ...
OPENING CEREMONY
WANDA HIGH SCHOOL
IT STILL HASN'T HIT ME, BUT I'M A SENIOR NOW.
WHAT'S DIFFERENT ABOUT THIS NEW SEMESTER?
THE CLASSES BASICALLY STAY THE SAME AT THIS SCHOOL...
I'M SURROUNDED BY THE SAME OLD FACES...
AND, OF COURSE, ONE OF THEM IS...

READ THIS WAY

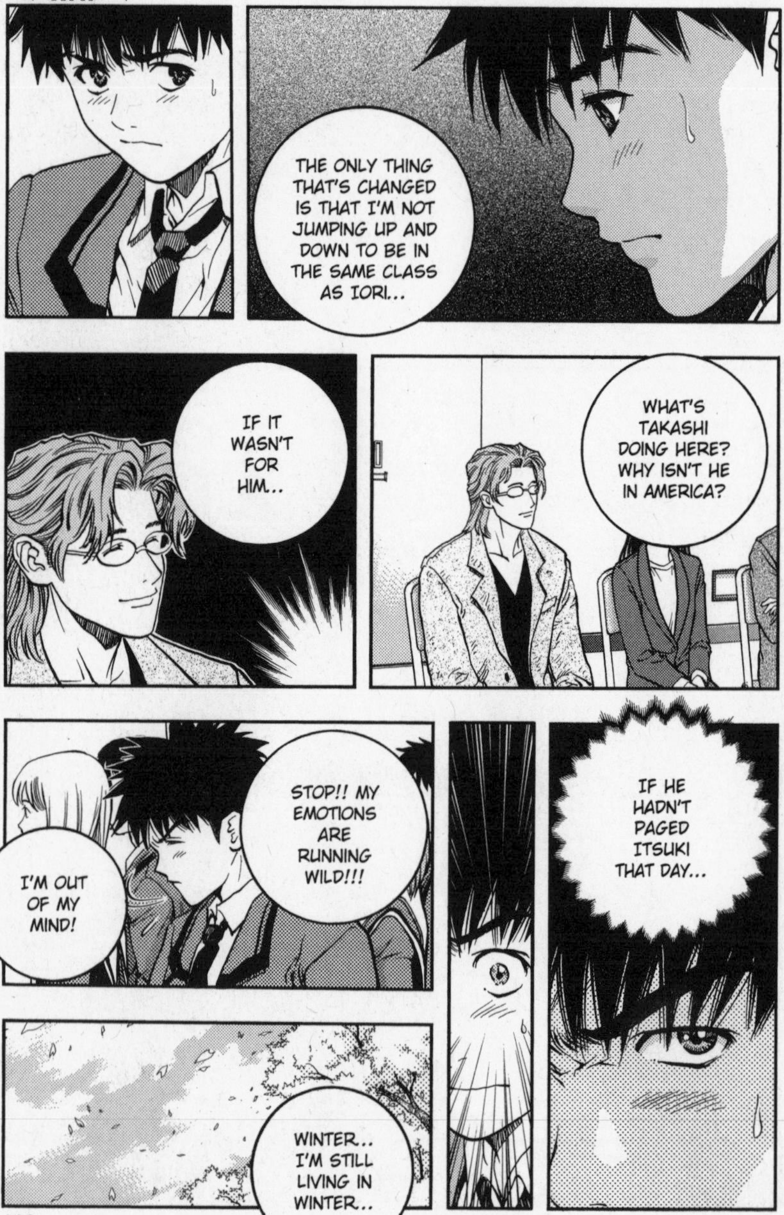
THE ONLY THING THAT'S CHANGED IS THAT I'M NOT JUMPING UP AND DOWN TO BE IN THE SAME CLASS AS IORI...
WHAT'S TAKASHI DOING HERE? WHY ISN'T HE IN AMERICA?
IF IT WASN'T FOR HIM...
IF HE HADN'T PAGED ITSUKI THAT DAY...
STOP!! MY EMOTIONS ARE RUNNING WILD!!!
I'M OUT OF MY MIND!
WINTER... I'M STILL LIVING IN WINTER...

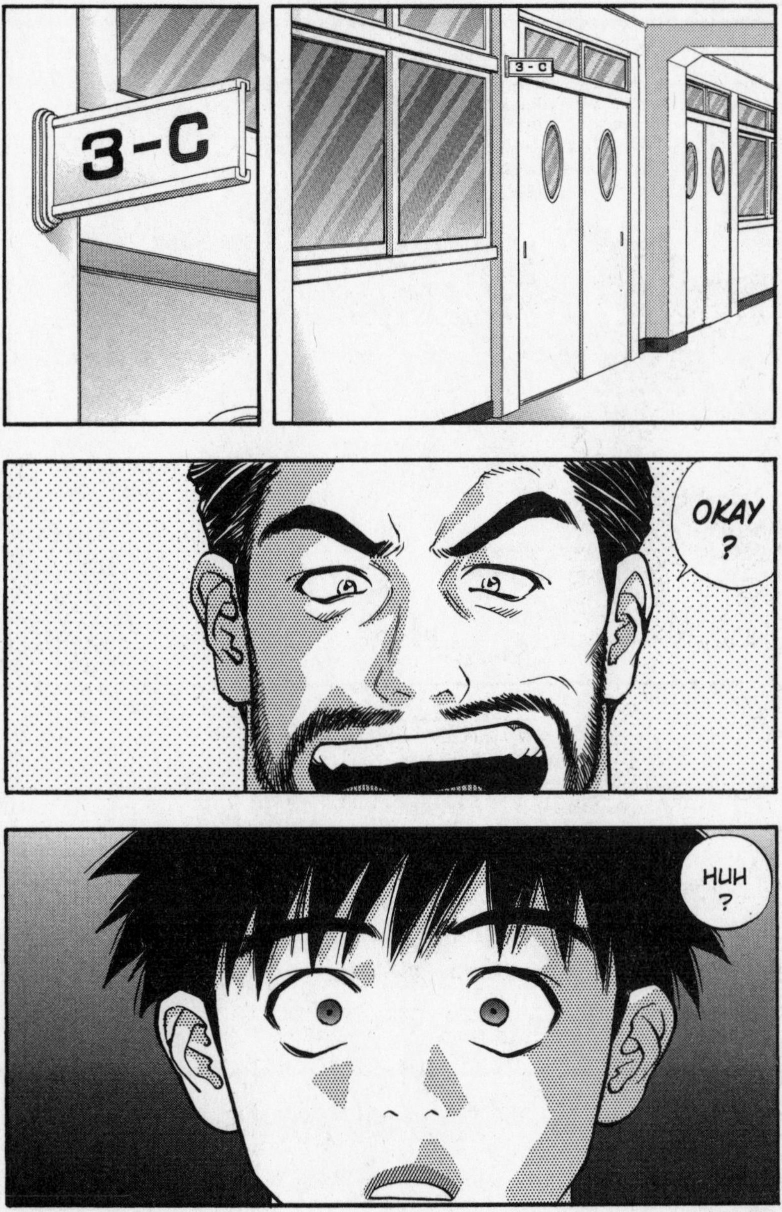
3-C
3-C
OKAY
?
HUH
?

READ THIS WAY

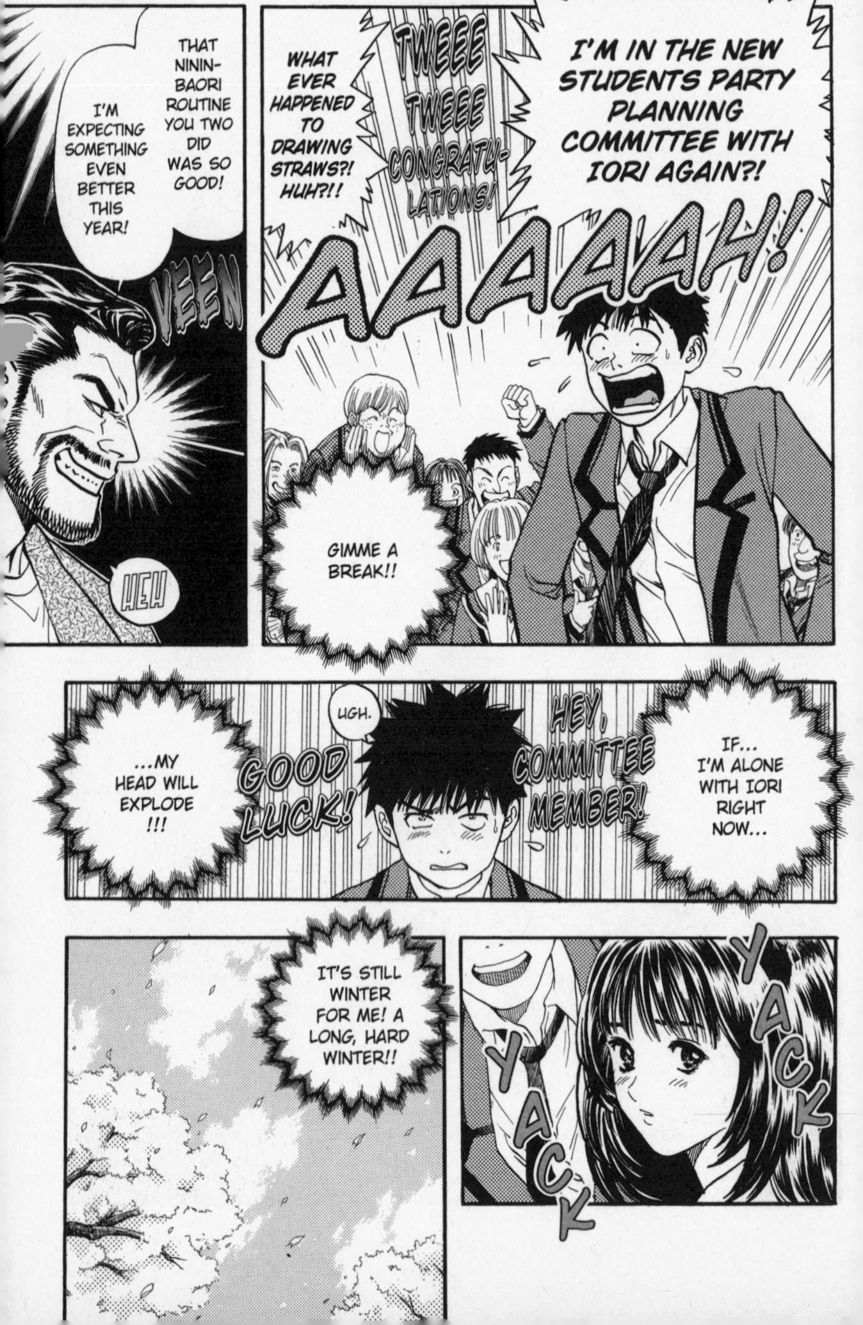
I'M IN THE NEW STUDENTS PARTY PLANNING COMMITTEE WITH IORI AGAIN?!
TWEEE TWEEE CONGRATU-LATIONS!
WHAT EVER HAPPENED TO DRAWING STRAWS?! HUH?!!
AAAAAH!
GIMME A BREAK!!
THAT NININ-BAORI ROUTINE YOU TWO DID WAS SO GOOD!
I'M EXPECTING SOMETHING EVEN BETTER THIS YEAR!
VEEN
HEH
IF... I'M ALONE WITH IORI RIGHT NOW...
HEY, COMMITTEE MEMBER!
UGH.
GOOD LUCK!
...MY HEAD WILL EXPLODE !!!
YACK
YACK
IT'S STILL WINTER FOR ME! A LONG, HARD WINTER!!

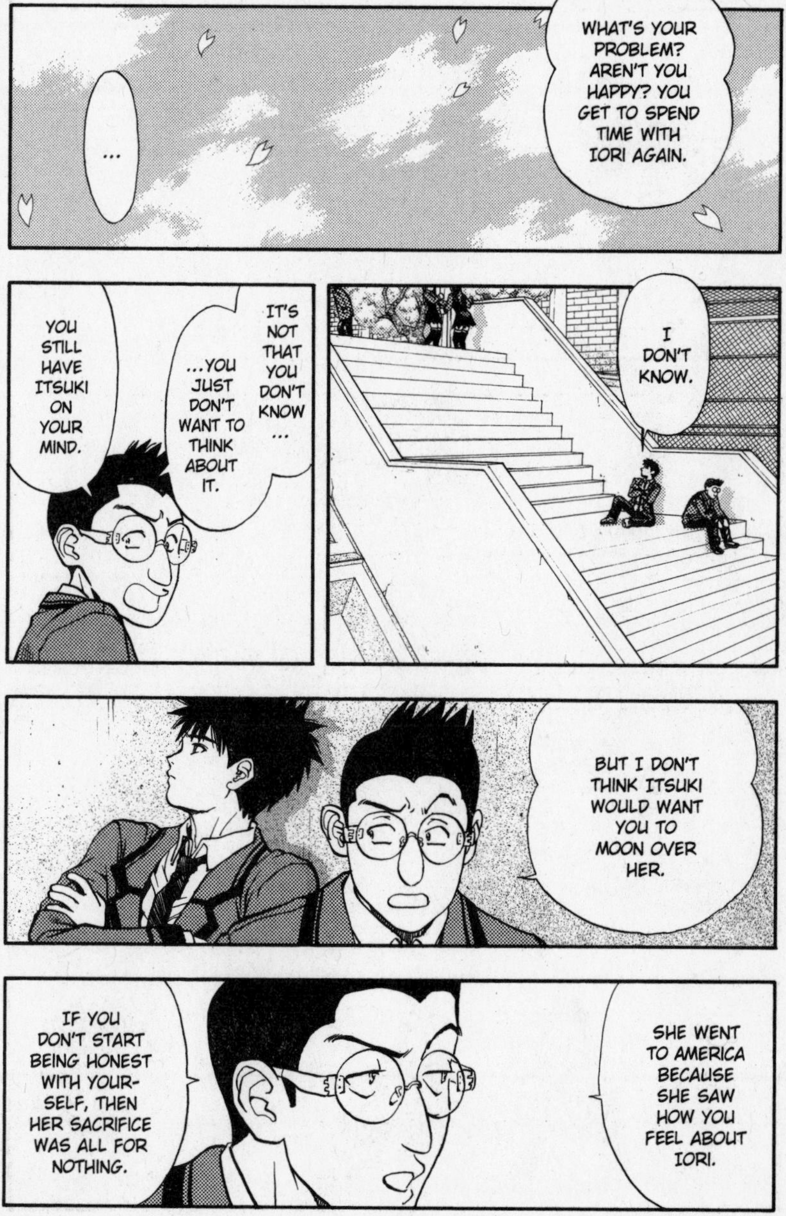
WHAT'S YOUR PROBLEM? AREN'T YOU HAPPY? YOU GET TO SPEND TIME WITH IORI AGAIN.
...
I DON'T KNOW.
IT'S NOT THAT YOU DON'T KNOW...
...YOU JUST DON'T WANT TO THINK ABOUT IT.
YOU STILL HAVE ITSUKI ON YOUR MIND.
BUT I DON'T THINK ITSUKI WOULD WANT YOU TO MOON OVER HER.
SHE WENT TO AMERICA BECAUSE SHE SAW HOW YOU FEEL ABOUT IORI.
IF YOU DON'T START BEING HONEST WITH YOUR-SELF, THEN HER SACRIFICE WAS ALL FOR NOTHING.

READ THIS WAY

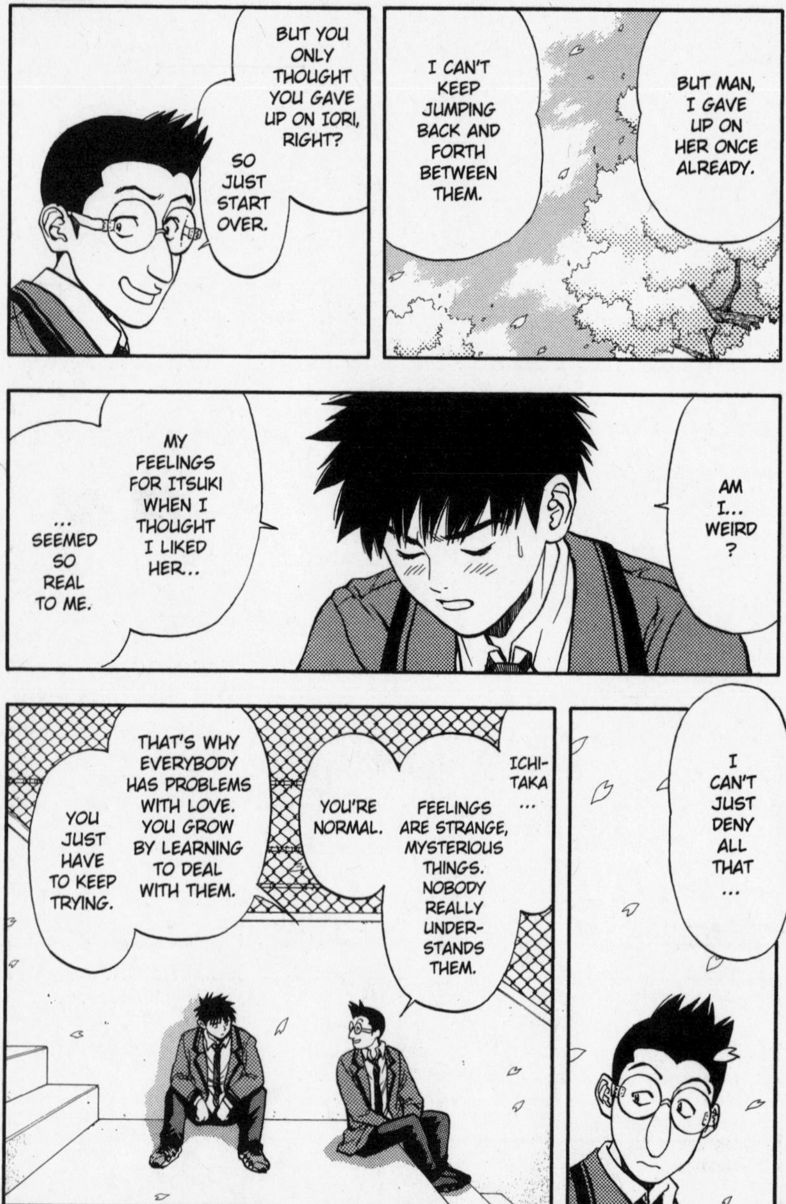
BUT MAN, I GAVE UP ON HER ONCE ALREADY.
I CAN'T KEEP JUMPING BACK AND FORTH BETWEEN THEM.
BUT YOU ONLY THOUGHT YOU GAVE UP ON IORI, RIGHT?
SO JUST START OVER.
AM I... WEIRD?
MY FEELINGS FOR ITSUKI WHEN I THOUGHT I LIKED HER...
...SEEMED SO REAL TO ME.
I CAN'T JUST DENY ALL THAT...
ICHITAKA...
FEELINGS ARE STRANGE, MYSTERIOUS THINGS. NOBODY REALLY UNDERSTANDS THEM.
YOU'RE NORMAL.
THAT'S WHY EVERYBODY HAS PROBLEMS WITH LOVE. YOU GROW BY LEARNING TO DEAL WITH THEM.
YOU JUST HAVE TO KEEP TRYING.

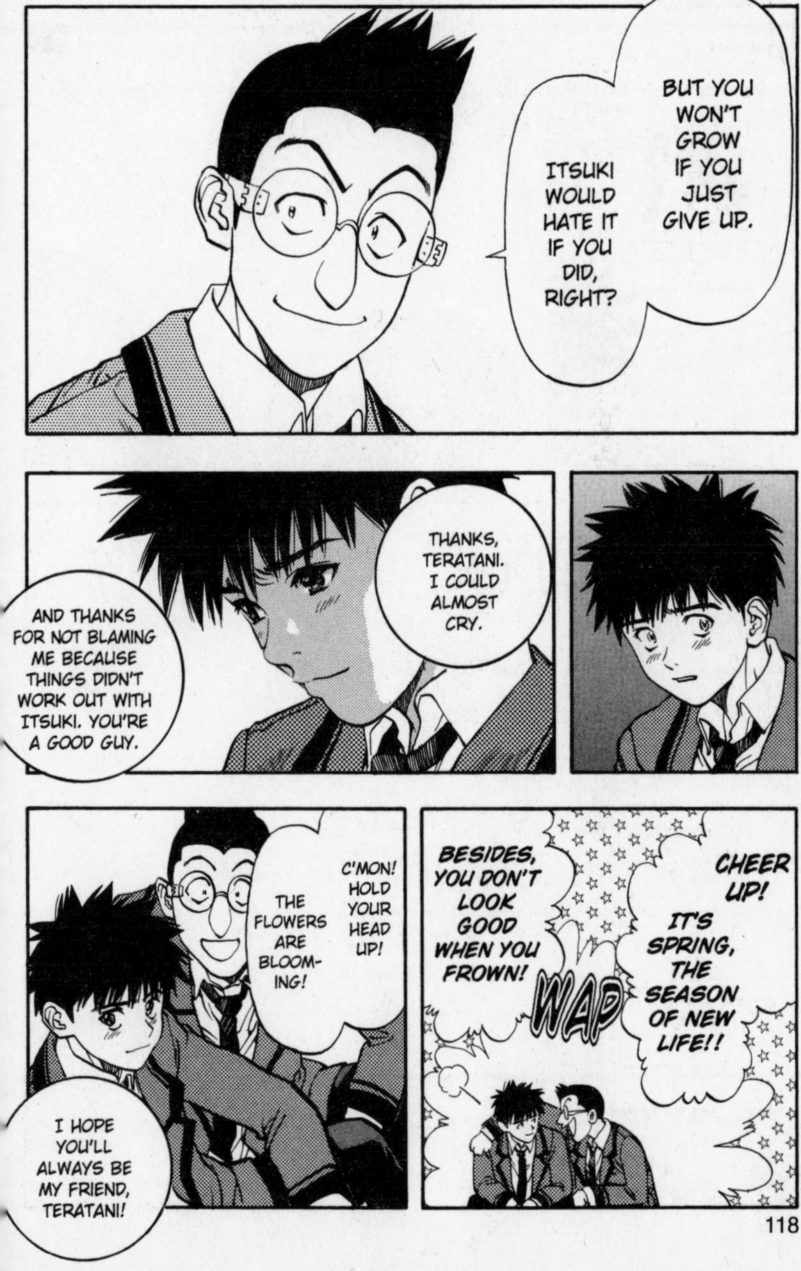

BUT YOU WON'T GROW IF YOU JUST GIVE UP.
ITSUKI WOULD HATE IT IF YOU DID, RIGHT?
THANKS, TERATANI. I COULD ALMOST CRY.
AND THANKS FOR NOT BLAMING ME BECAUSE THINGS DIDN'T WORK OUT WITH ITSUKI. YOU'RE A GOOD GUY.
CHEER UP!
IT'S SPRING, THE SEASON OF NEW LIFE!!
WAP
BESIDES, YOU DON'T LOOK GOOD WHEN YOU FROWN!
C'MON! HOLD YOUR HEAD UP!
THE FLOWERS ARE BLOOM-ING!
I HOPE YOU'LL ALWAYS BE MY FRIEND, TERATANI!

READ THIS WAY

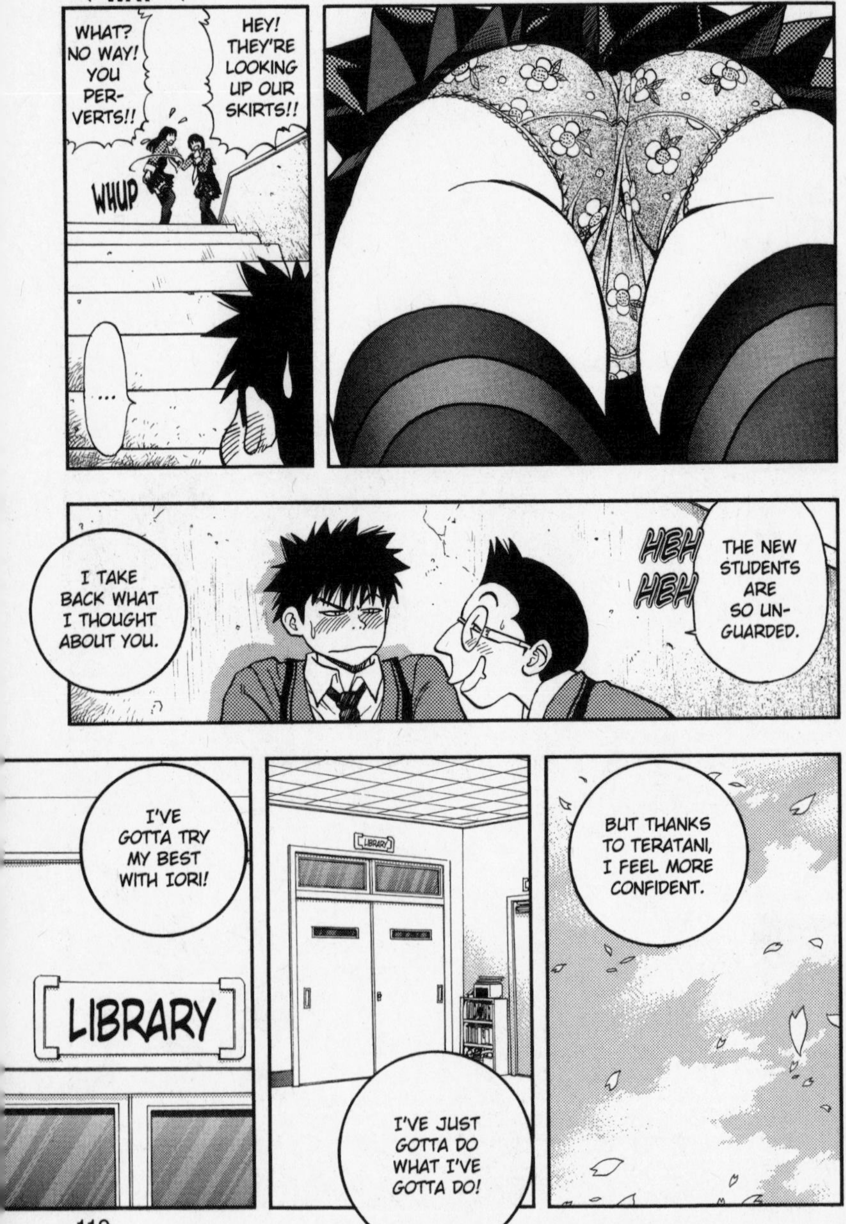

HEY! THEY'RE LOOKING UP OUR SKIRTS!!
WHAT? NO WAY! YOU PER-VERTS!!
WHUP
...
HEH HEH
THE NEW STUDENTS ARE SO UN-GUARDED.
I TAKE BACK WHAT I THOUGHT ABOUT YOU.
BUT THANKS TO TERATANI, I FEEL MORE CONFIDENT.
LIBRARY
I'VE JUST GOTTA DO WHAT I'VE GOTTA DO!
I'VE GOTTA TRY MY BEST WITH IORI!
LIBRARY

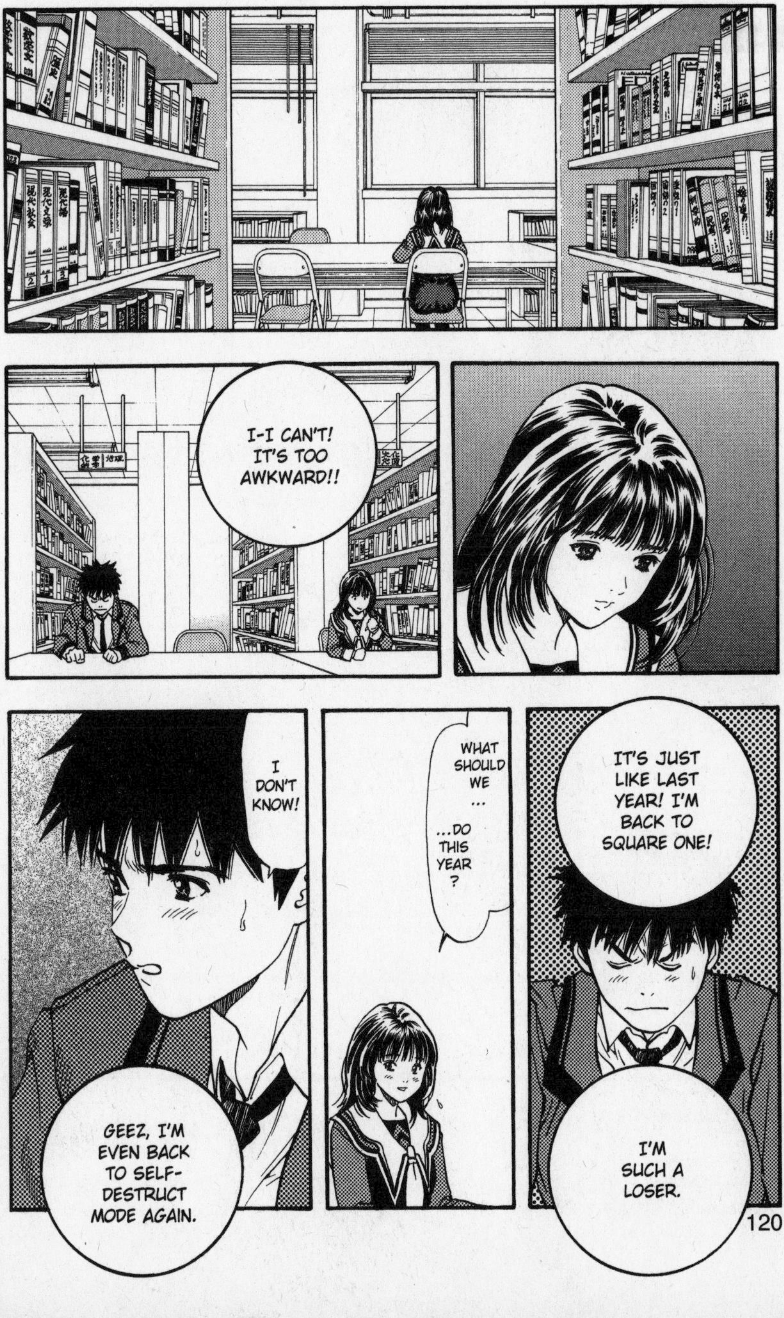
I-I CAN'T! IT'S TOO AWKWARD!!
IT'S JUST LIKE LAST YEAR! I'M BACK TO SQUARE ONE!
I'M SUCH A LOSER.
WHAT SHOULD WE ...
...DO THIS YEAR?
I DON'T KNOW!
GEEZ, I'M EVEN BACK TO SELF-DESTRUCT MODE AGAIN.

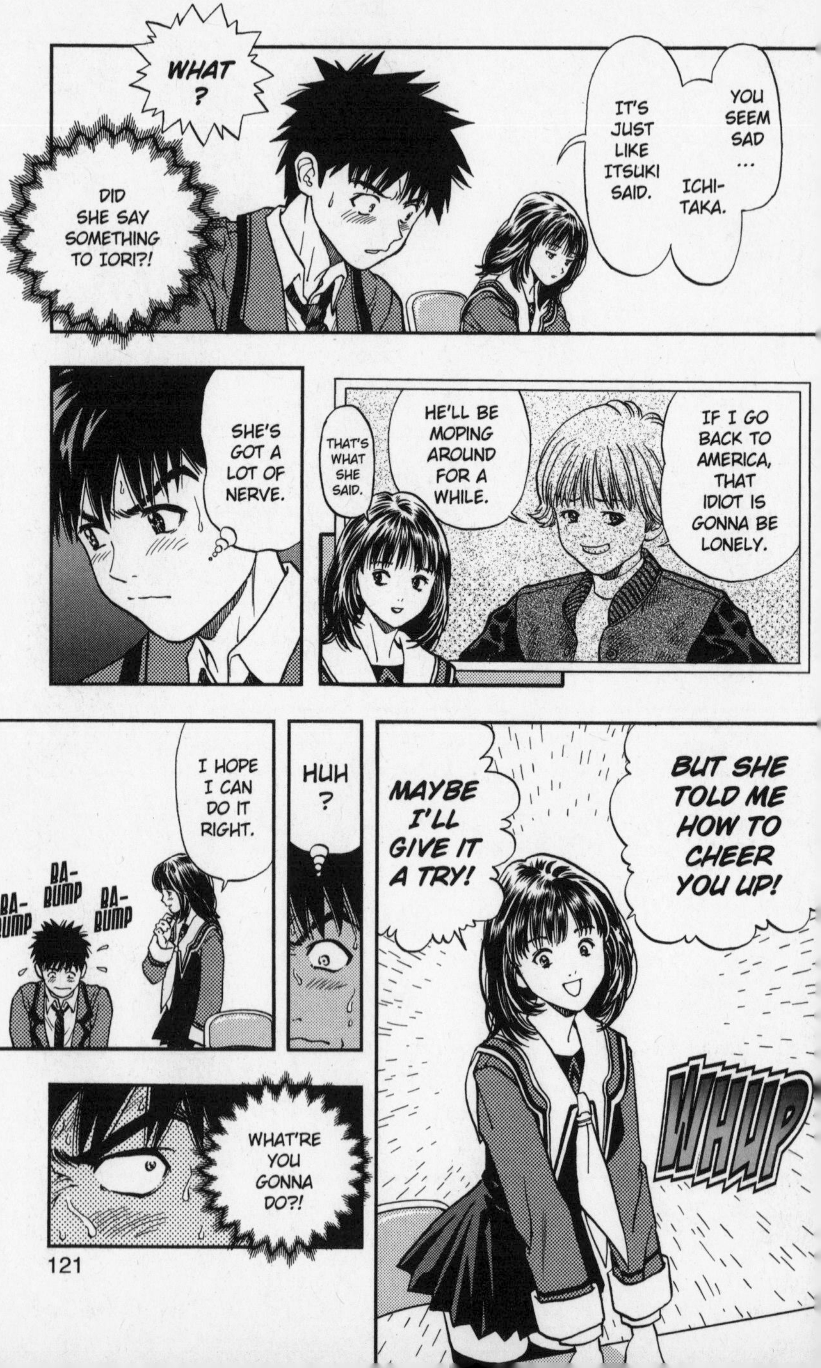
YOU SEEM SAD... ICHI-TAKA.
IT'S JUST LIKE ITSUKI SAID.
WHAT?
DID SHE SAY SOMETHING TO IORI?!
IF I GO BACK TO AMERICA, THAT IDIOT IS GONNA BE LONELY.
HE'LL BE MOPING AROUND FOR A WHILE.
THAT'S WHAT SHE SAID.
SHE'S GOT A LOT OF NERVE.
BUT SHE TOLD ME HOW TO CHEER YOU UP!
MAYBE I'LL GIVE IT A TRY!
WHUP
HUH?
I HOPE I CAN DO IT RIGHT.
BA-BUMP
BA-BUMP
BA-BUMP
WHAT'RE YOU GONNA DO?!

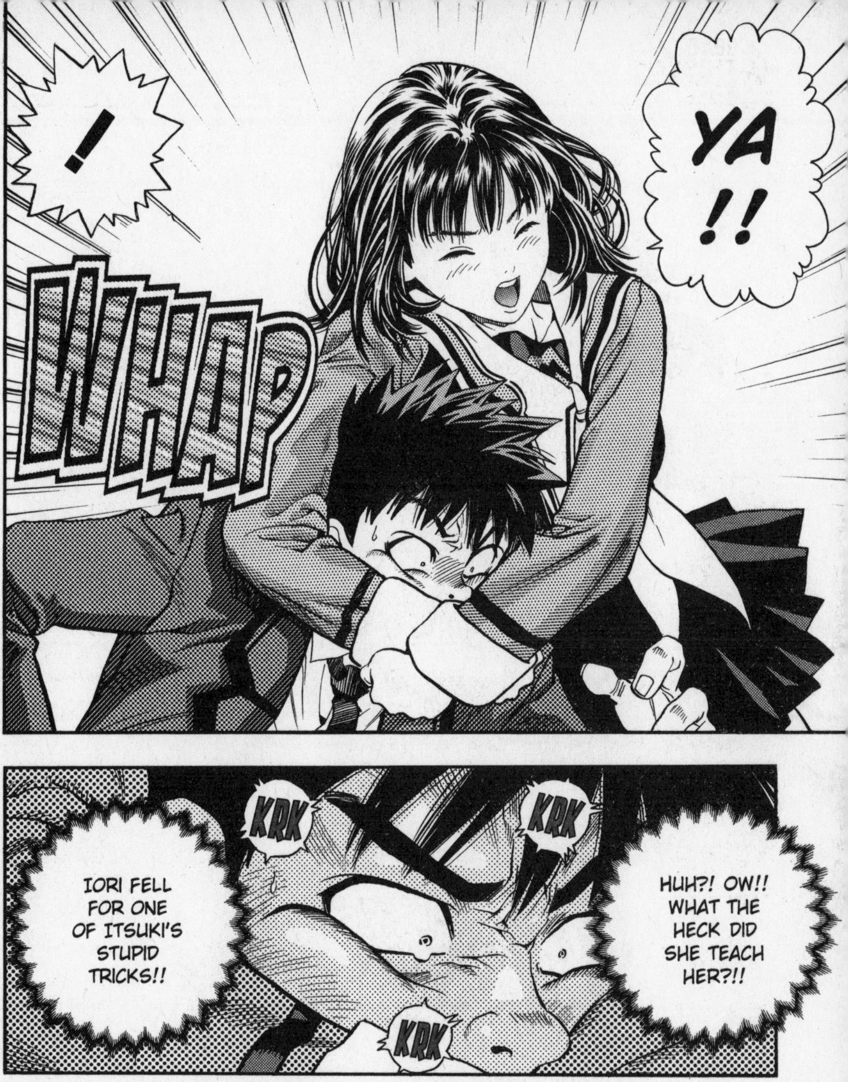
YA!!
!
WHAP
HUH?! OW!! WHAT THE HECK DID SHE TEACH HER?!!
KRK
KRK
IORI FELL FOR ONE OF ITSUKI'S STUPID TRICKS!!
KRK
YA! YA!!
KRK KRK
HEY!
WAIT!
STOP!!

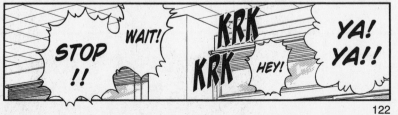

READ THIS WAY

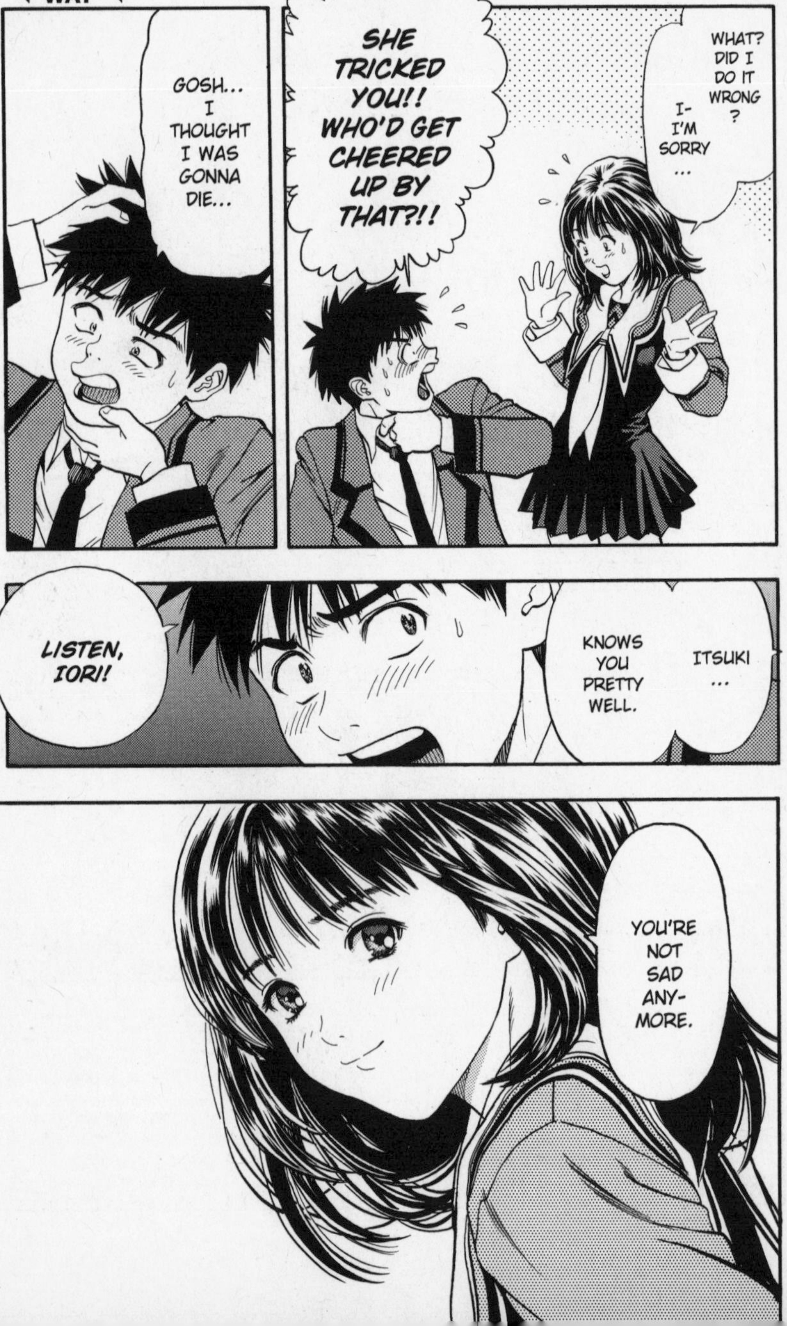
WHAT? DID I DO IT WRONG?
I- I'M SORRY...
SHE TRICKED YOU!! WHO'D GET CHEERED UP BY THAT?!!
GOSH... I THOUGHT I WAS GONNA DIE...
ITSUKI...
KNOWS YOU PRETTY WELL.
LISTEN, IORI!
YOU'RE NOT SAD ANY-MORE.

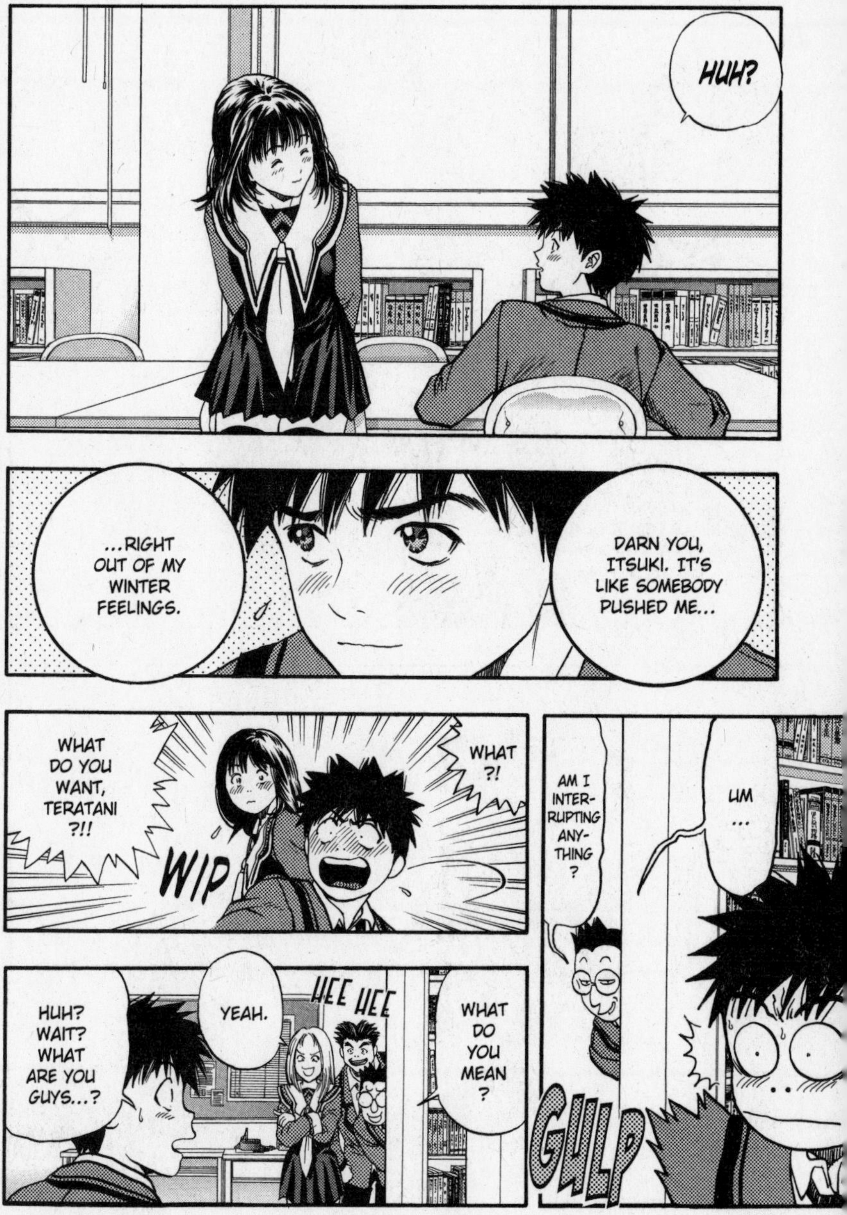
HUH?
DARN YOU, ITSUKI. IT'S LIKE SOMEBODY PUSHED ME...
...RIGHT OUT OF MY WINTER FEELINGS.
UM ...
AM I INTERRUPTING ANYTHING?
GULP
WHAT ?!
WIP
WHAT DO YOU WANT, TERATANI ?!!
WHAT DO YOU MEAN ?
HEE HEE
YEAH.
HUH? WAIT? WHAT ARE YOU GUYS...?

READ THIS WAY

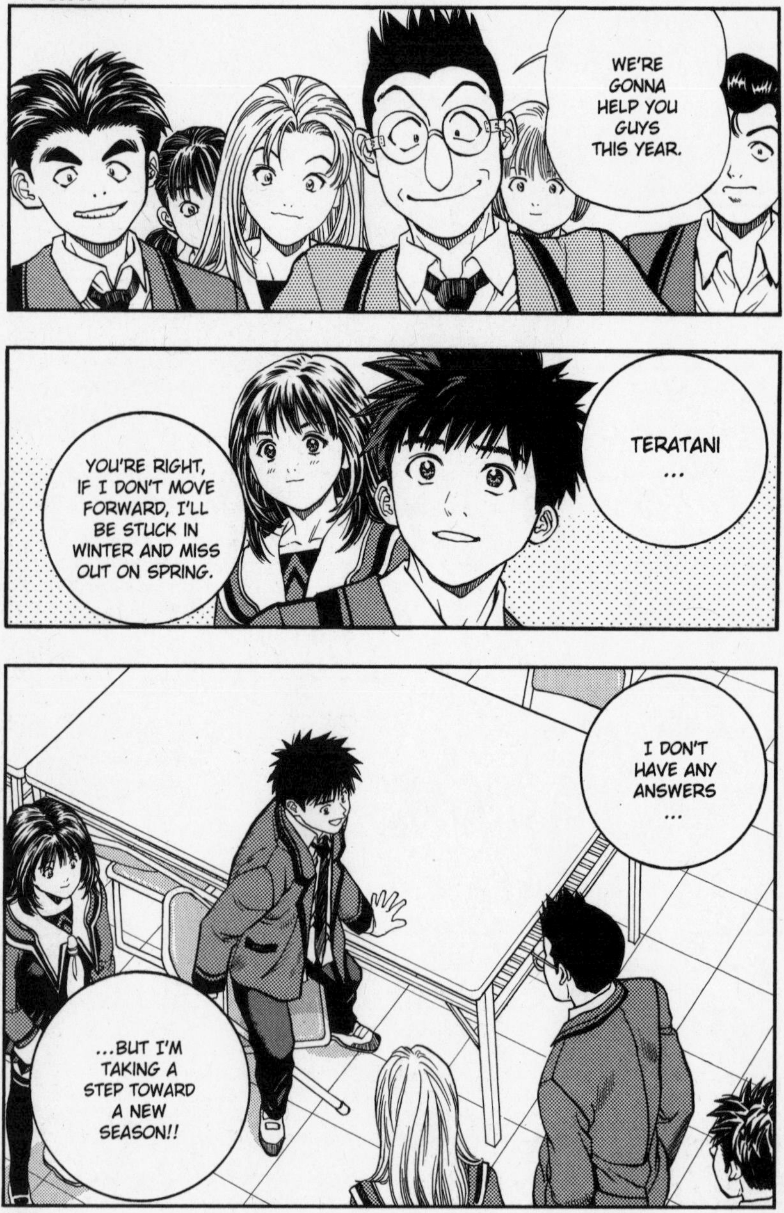
WE'RE GONNA HELP YOU GUYS THIS YEAR.
TERATANI ...
YOU'RE RIGHT, IF I DON'T MOVE FORWARD, I'LL BE STUCK IN WINTER AND MISS OUT ON SPRING.
I DON'T HAVE ANY ANSWERS ...
...BUT I'M TAKING A STEP TOWARD A NEW SEASON!!

I"s

アイズ

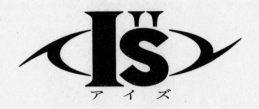

Chapter 52: Can't Hide It

READ THIS WAY

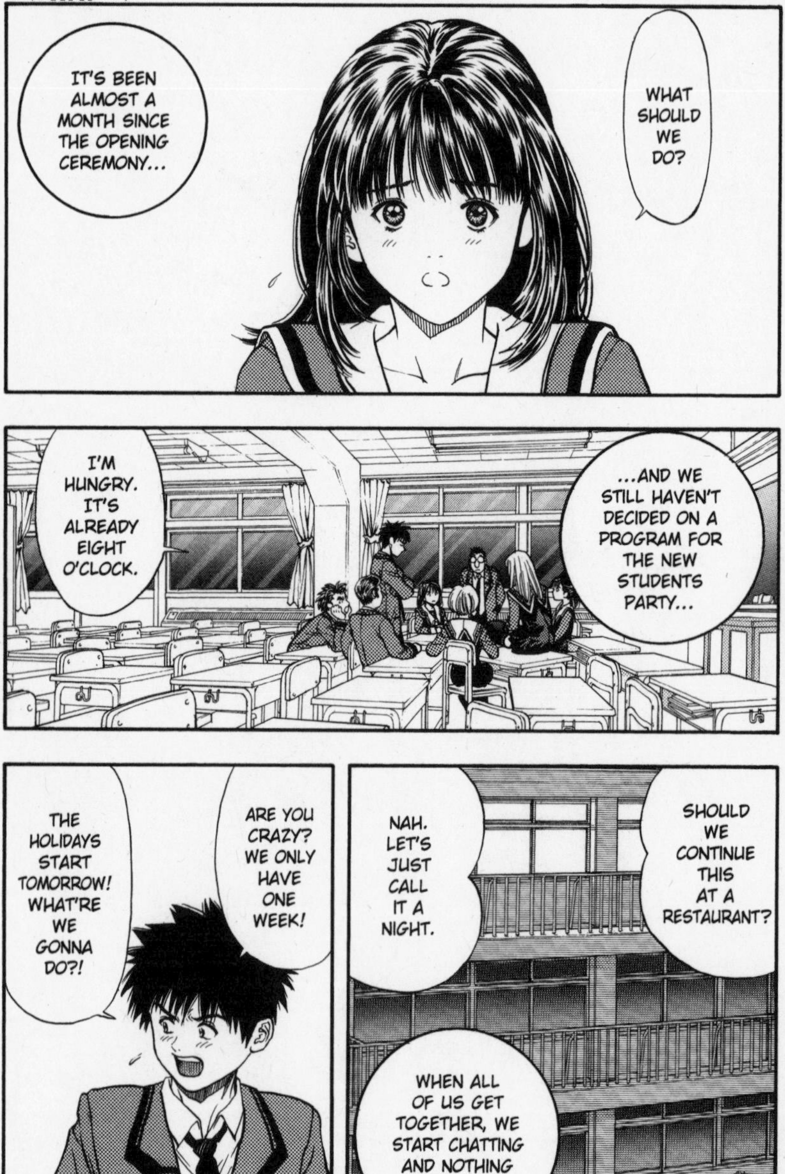
WHAT SHOULD WE DO?
IT'S BEEN ALMOST A MONTH SINCE THE OPENING CEREMONY...
...AND WE STILL HAVEN'T DECIDED ON A PROGRAM FOR THE NEW STUDENTS PARTY...
I'M HUNGRY. IT'S ALREADY EIGHT O'CLOCK.
SHOULD WE CONTINUE THIS AT A RESTAURANT?
NAH. LET'S JUST CALL IT A NIGHT.
WHEN ALL OF US GET TOGETHER, WE START CHATTING AND NOTHING GETS DONE...
ARE YOU CRAZY? WE ONLY HAVE ONE WEEK!
THE HOLIDAYS START TOMORROW! WHAT'RE WE GONNA DO?!

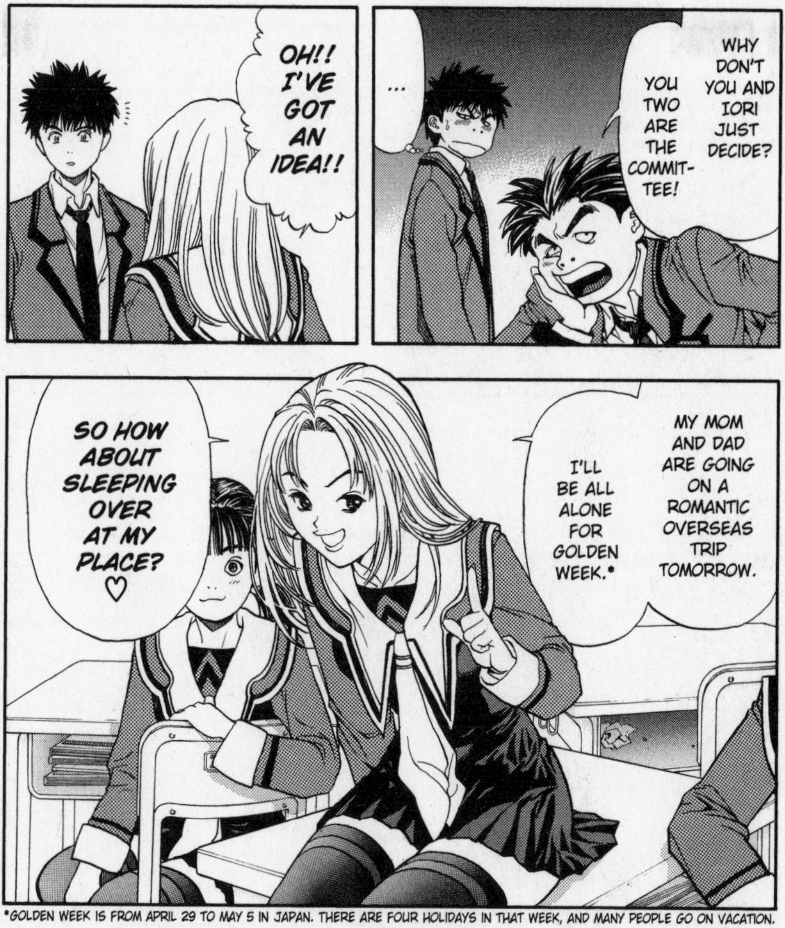
WHY DON'T YOU AND IORI JUST DECIDE?
YOU TWO ARE THE COMMIT-TEE!
...
OH!! I'VE GOT AN IDEA!!
MY MOM AND DAD ARE GOING ON A ROMANTIC OVERSEAS TRIP TOMORROW.
I'LL BE ALL ALONE FOR GOLDEN WEEK.*
SO HOW ABOUT SLEEPING OVER AT MY PLACE? ♡

*GOLDEN WEEK IS FROM APRIL 29 TO MAY 5 IN JAPAN. THERE ARE FOUR HOLIDAYS IN THAT WEEK, AND MANY PEOPLE GO ON VACATION.

AND SO...

READ THIS WAY

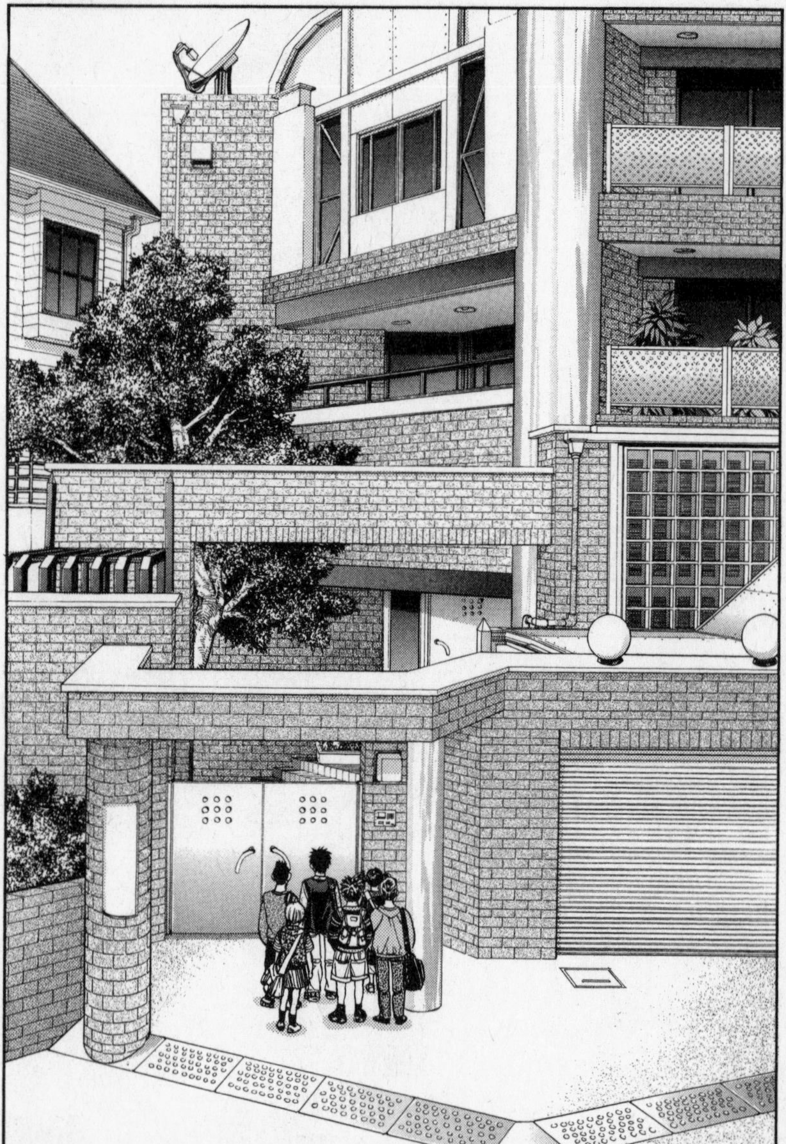

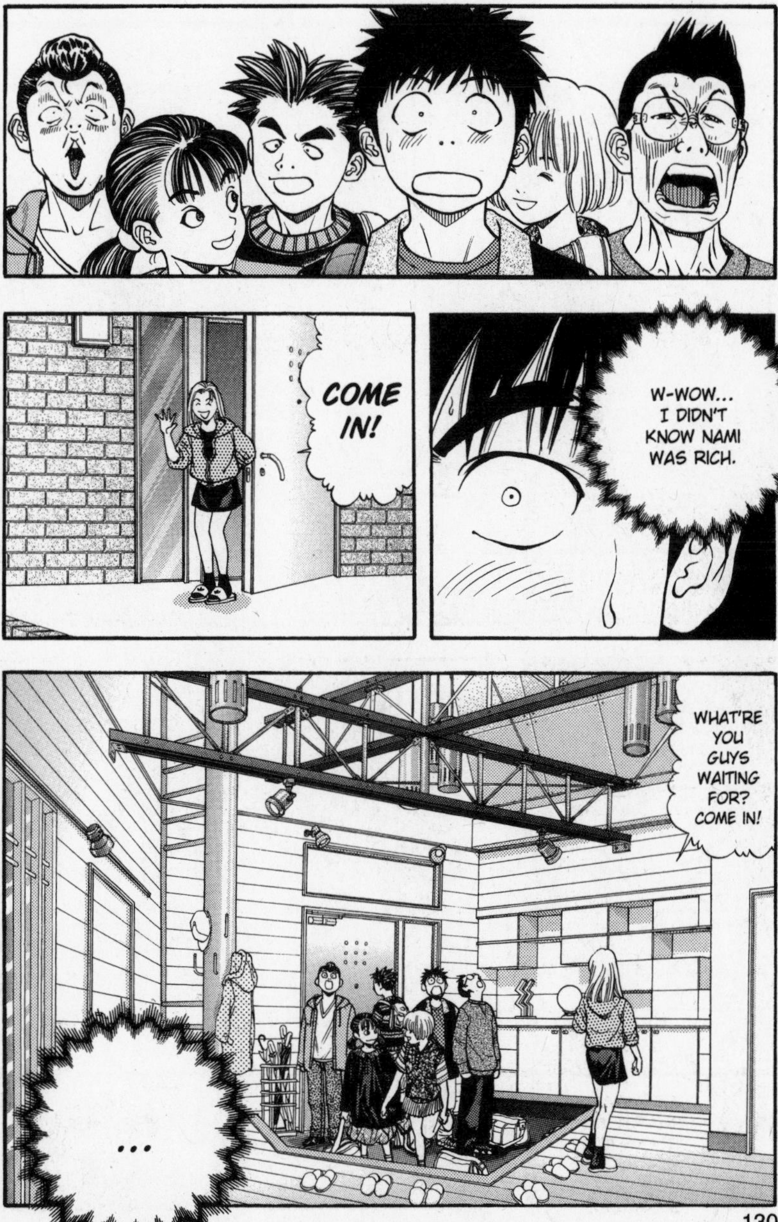
W-WOW... I DIDN'T KNOW NAMI WAS RICH.
COME IN!
WHAT'RE YOU GUYS WAITING FOR? COME IN!
...

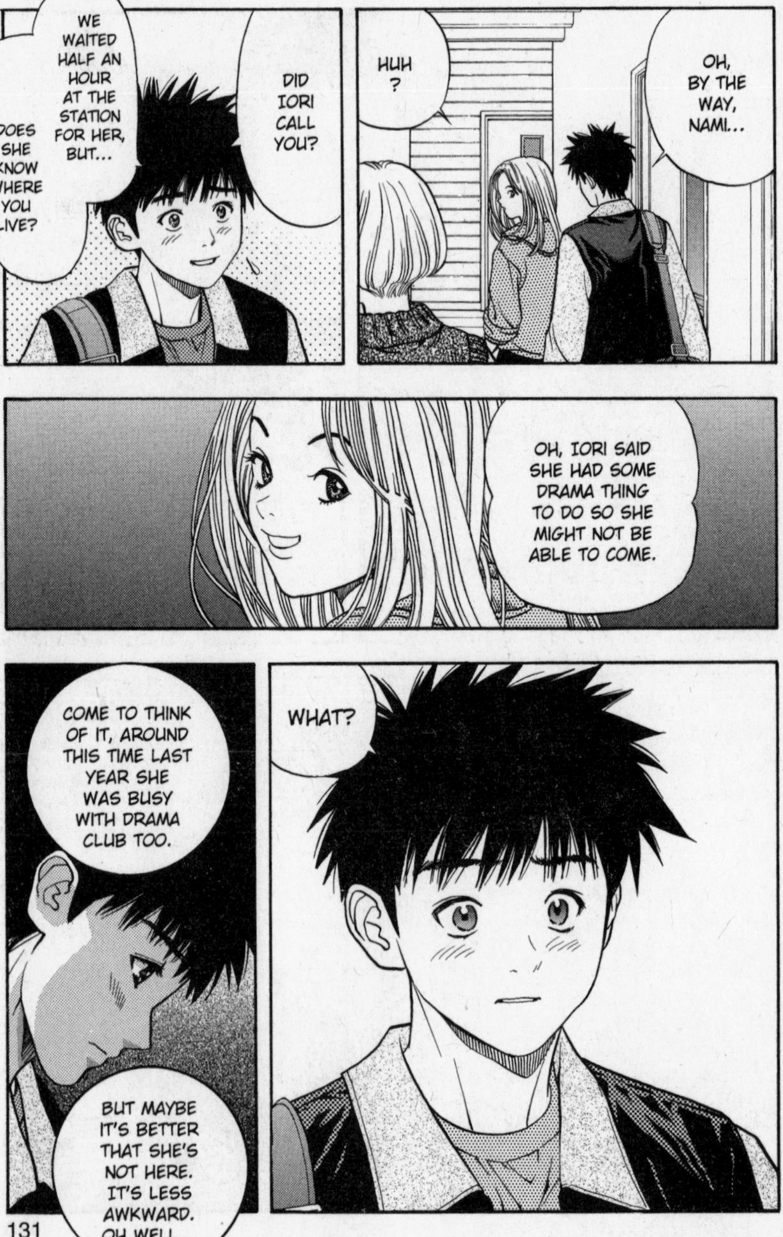
OH, BY THE WAY, NAMI...
HUH?
DID IORI CALL YOU?
WE WAITED HALF AN HOUR AT THE STATION FOR HER, BUT...
DOES SHE KNOW WHERE YOU LIVE?
OH, IORI SAID SHE HAD SOME DRAMA THING TO DO SO SHE MIGHT NOT BE ABLE TO COME.
WHAT?
COME TO THINK OF IT, AROUND THIS TIME LAST YEAR SHE WAS BUSY WITH DRAMA CLUB TOO.
BUT MAYBE IT'S BETTER THAT SHE'S NOT HERE. IT'S LESS AWKWARD. OH WELL...

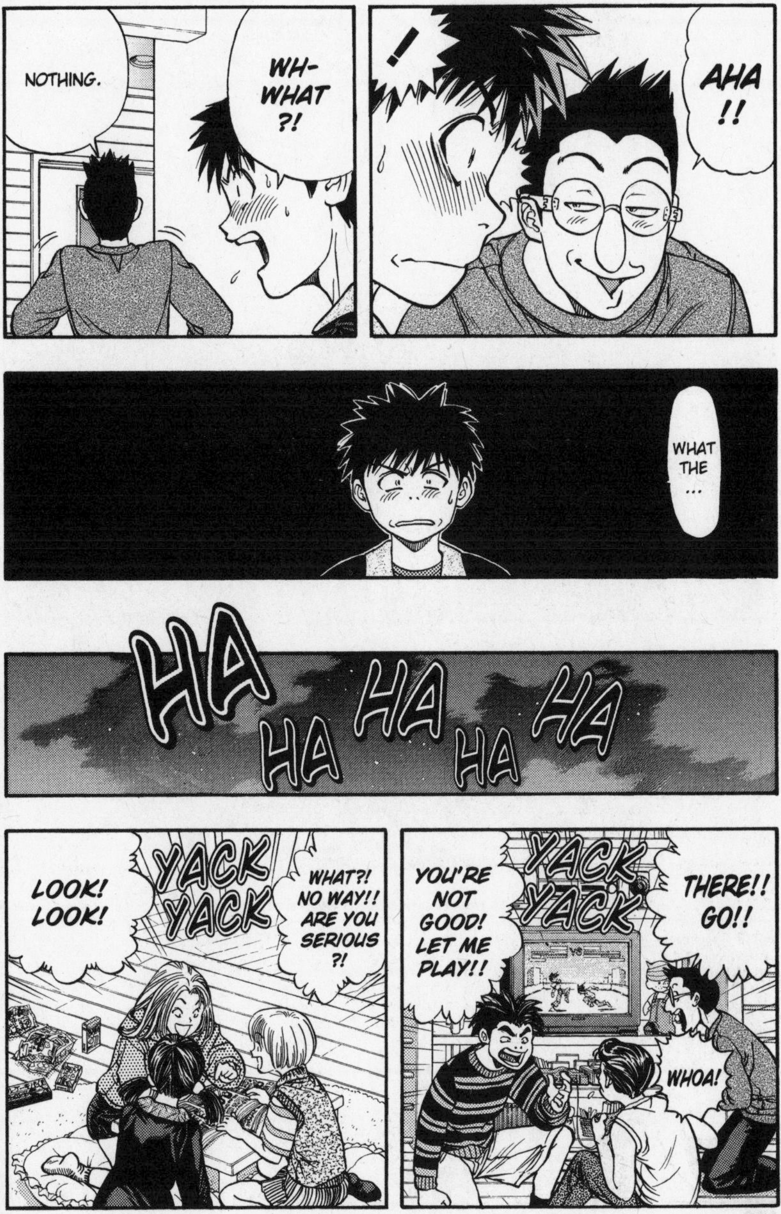
!
AHA!!
WH- WHAT?!
NOTHING.
WHAT THE...
HA HA HA HA HA
THERE!! GO!!
YACK YACK
YOU'RE NOT GOOD! LET ME PLAY!!
WHOA!
WHAT?! NO WAY!! ARE YOU SERIOUS?!
YACK YACK
LOOK! LOOK!

READ THIS WAY

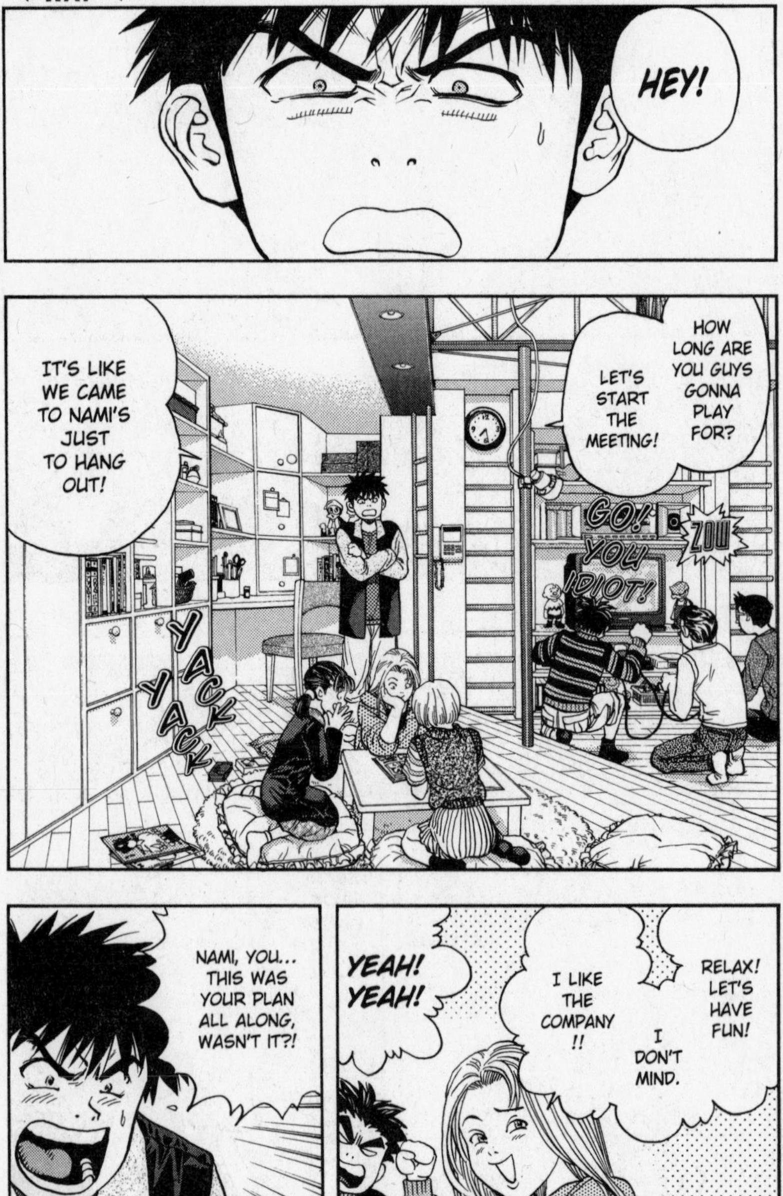
HEY!
HOW LONG ARE YOU GUYS GONNA PLAY FOR?
LET'S START THE MEETING!
ZOU
GO! YOU IDIOT!
YACK YACK
IT'S LIKE WE CAME TO NAMI'S JUST TO HANG OUT!
RELAX! LET'S HAVE FUN!
I DON'T MIND.
I LIKE THE COMPANY!!
YEAH! YEAH!
NAMI, YOU... THIS WAS YOUR PLAN ALL ALONG, WASN'T IT?!

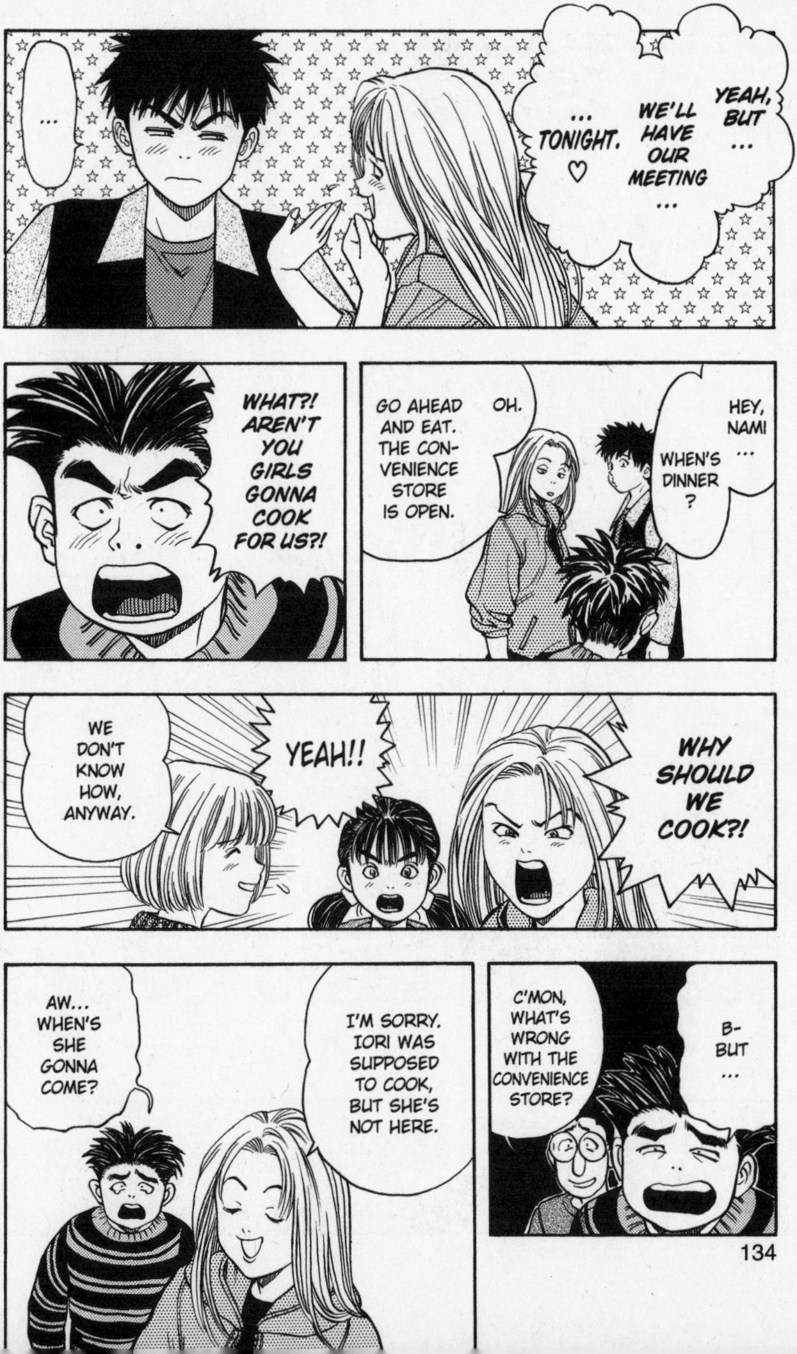
YEAH, BUT ... WE'LL HAVE OUR MEETING ... ... TONIGHT. ♡
...
HEY, NAMI ...
WHEN'S DINNER ?
OH.
GO AHEAD AND EAT. THE CONVENIENCE STORE IS OPEN.
WHAT?! AREN'T YOU GIRLS GONNA COOK FOR US?!
WHY SHOULD WE COOK?!
YEAH!!
WE DON'T KNOW HOW, ANYWAY.
B-BUT ...
C'MON, WHAT'S WRONG WITH THE CONVENIENCE STORE?
I'M SORRY. IORI WAS SUPPOSED TO COOK, BUT SHE'S NOT HERE.
AW... WHEN'S SHE GONNA COME?

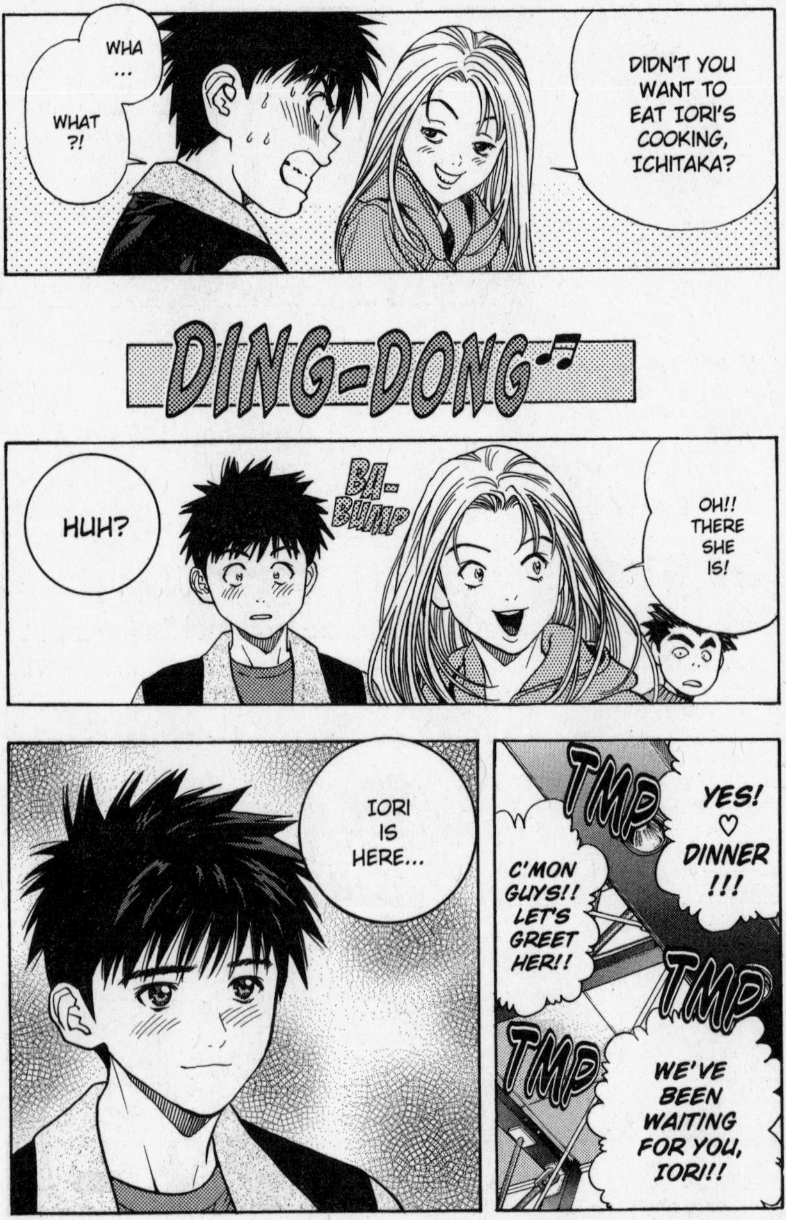
DIDN'T YOU WANT TO EAT IORI'S COOKING, ICHITAKA?
WHA ... WHAT ?!
DING-DONG ♫
OH!! THERE SHE IS!
BA-BUMP
HUH?
YES! ♡ DINNER !!!
TMP
C'MON GUYS!! LET'S GREET HER!!
TMP
TMP
WE'VE BEEN WAITING FOR YOU, IORI!!
IORI IS HERE...

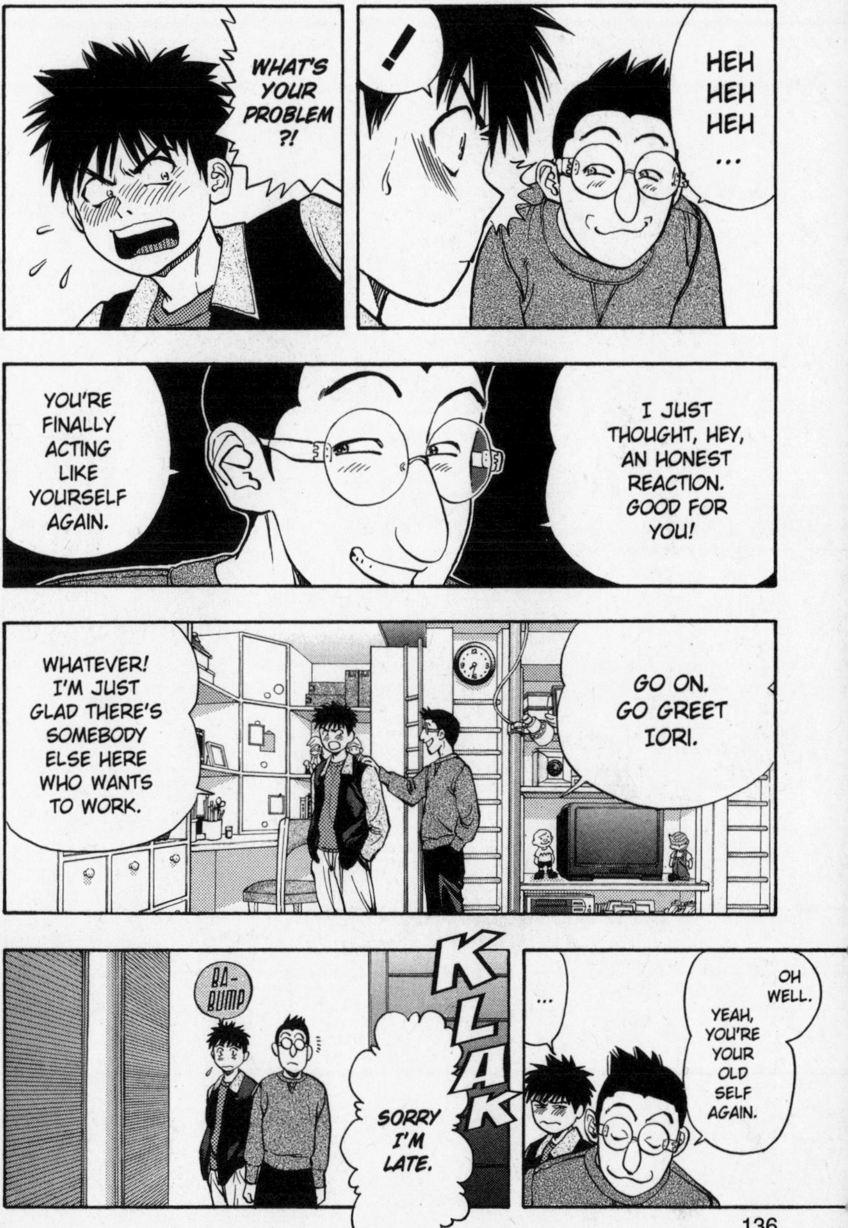
HEH HEH HEH ...
!
WHAT'S YOUR PROBLEM ?!
I JUST THOUGHT, HEY, AN HONEST REACTION. GOOD FOR YOU!
YOU'RE FINALLY ACTING LIKE YOURSELF AGAIN.
GO ON. GO GREET IORI.
WHATEVER! I'M JUST GLAD THERE'S SOMEBODY ELSE HERE WHO WANTS TO WORK.
OH WELL.
YEAH, YOU'RE YOUR OLD SELF AGAIN.
...
KLAK
SORRY I'M LATE.
BA-BUMP

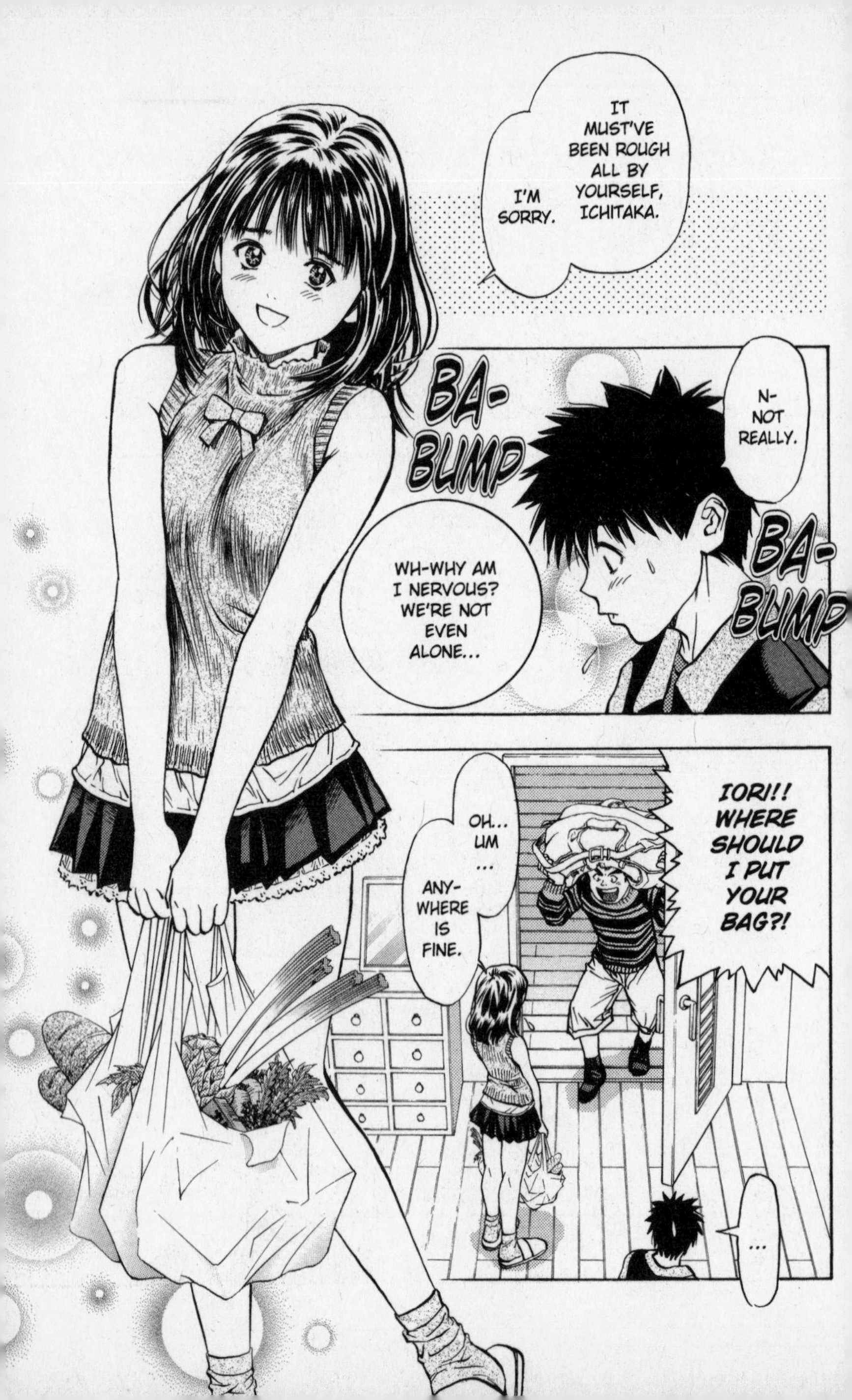
IT MUST'VE BEEN ROUGH ALL BY YOURSELF, ICHITAKA.
I'M SORRY.
BA-BUMP
N-NOT REALLY.
BA-BUMP
WH-WHY AM I NERVOUS? WE'RE NOT EVEN ALONE...
IORI!! WHERE SHOULD I PUT YOUR BAG?!
OH... UM ... ANY-WHERE IS FINE.
...

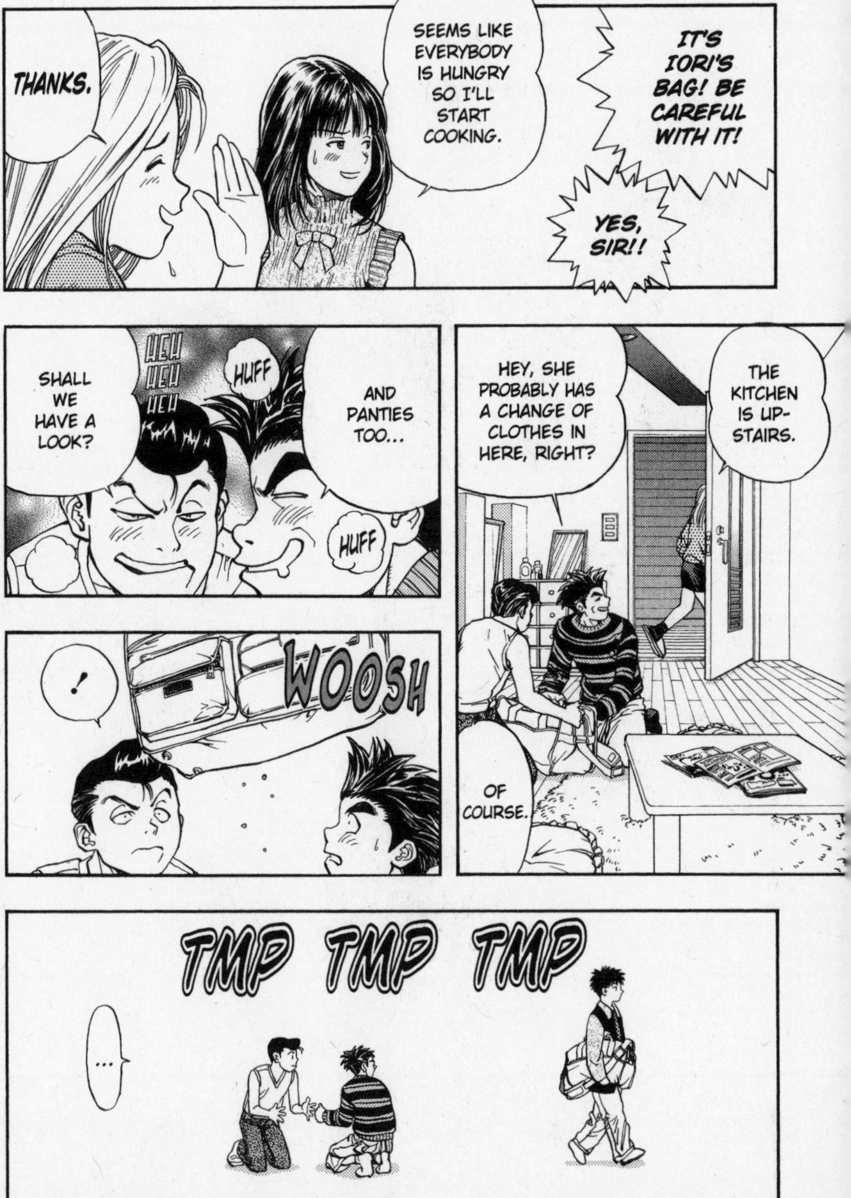
IT'S IORI'S BAG! BE CAREFUL WITH IT!
YES, SIR!!
SEEMS LIKE EVERYBODY IS HUNGRY SO I'LL START COOKING.
THANKS.
THE KITCHEN IS UP-STAIRS.
HEY, SHE PROBABLY HAS A CHANGE OF CLOTHES IN HERE, RIGHT?
OF COURSE.
HUFF
AND PANTIES TOO...
HEH HEH HEH
SHALL WE HAVE A LOOK?
HUFF
WOOSH
!
TMP TMP TMP
...

READ THIS WAY

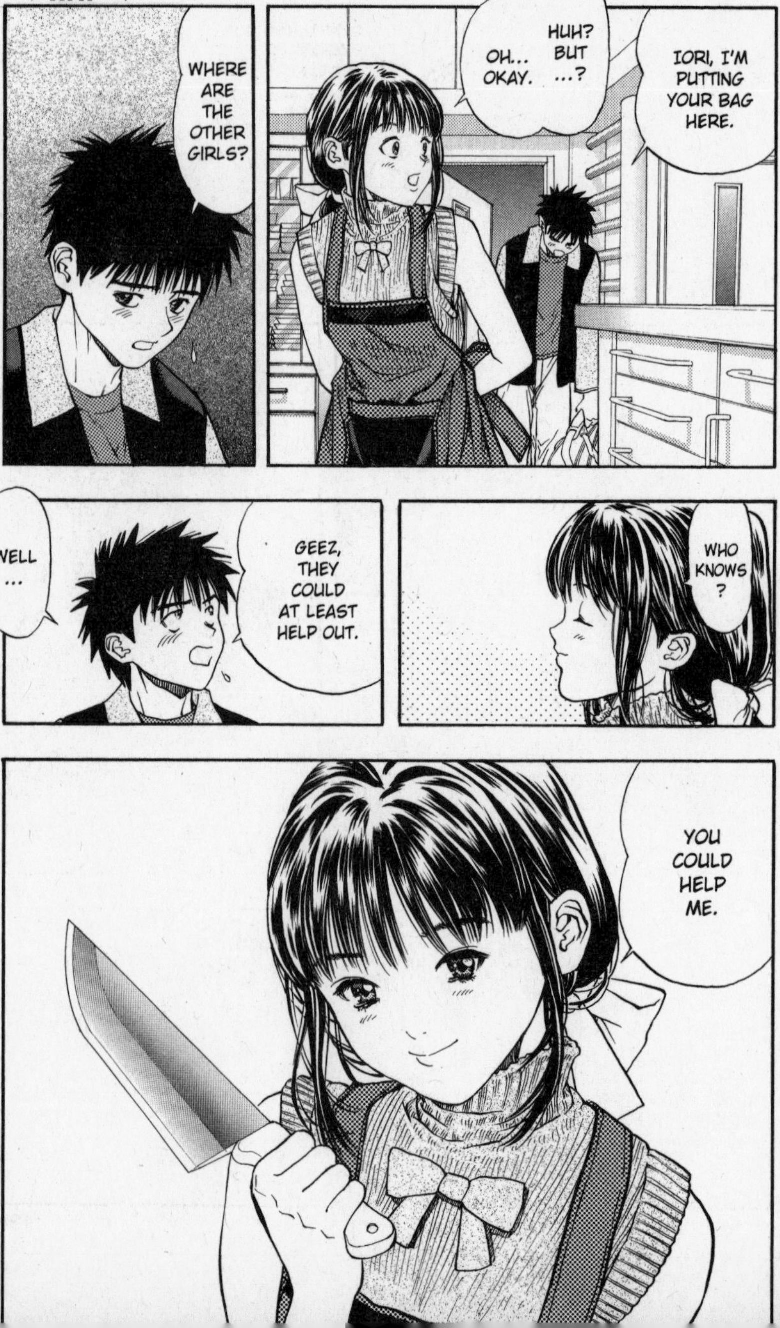
IORI, I'M PUTTING YOUR BAG HERE.
HUH? BUT ...?
OH... OKAY.
WHERE ARE THE OTHER GIRLS?
WHO KNOWS?
GEEZ, THEY COULD AT LEAST HELP OUT.
WELL ...
YOU COULD HELP ME.

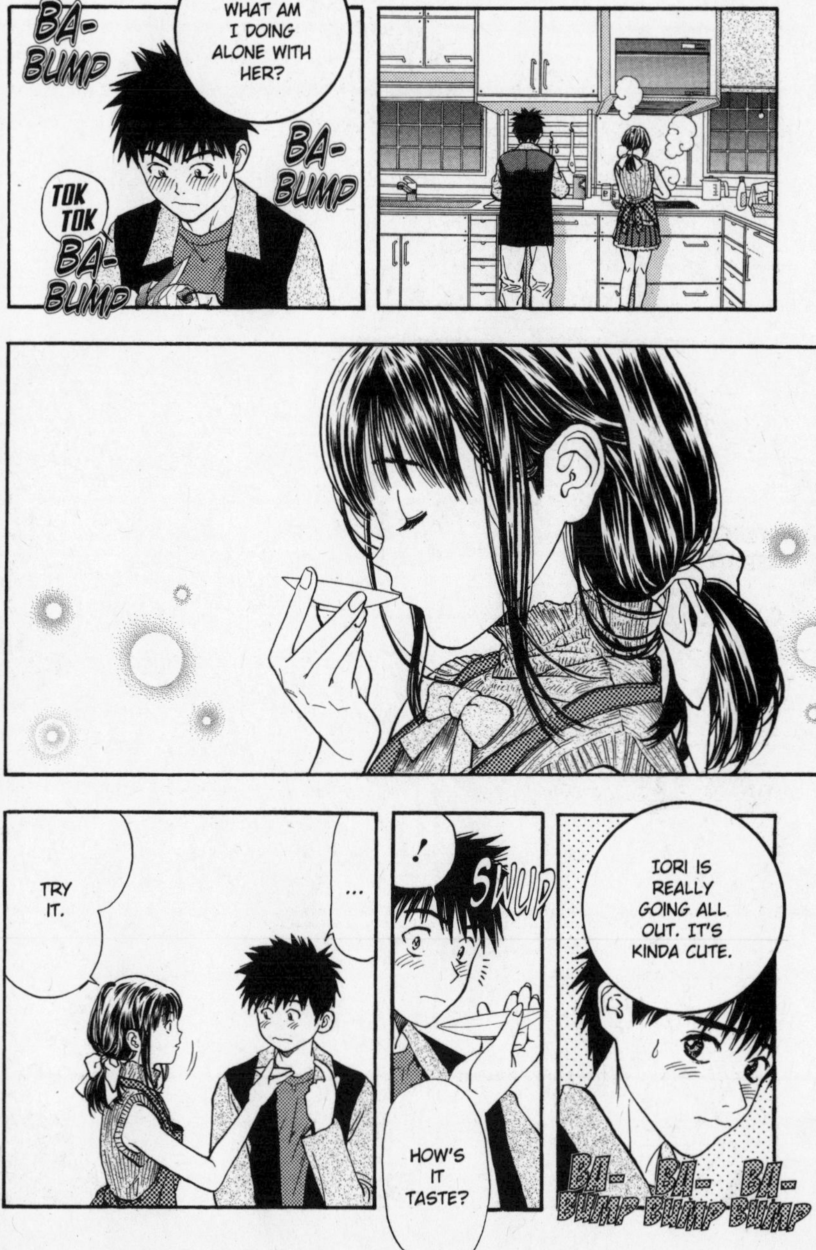
SIGH... WHAT AM I DOING ALONE WITH HER?
BA-BUMP
BA-BUMP
TOK TOK
BA-BUMP
BA-BUMP
IORI IS REALLY GOING ALL OUT. IT'S KINDA CUTE.
BA-BUMP BA-BUMP BA-BUMP
!
SWUP
HOW'S IT TASTE?
...
TRY IT.

READ THIS WAY

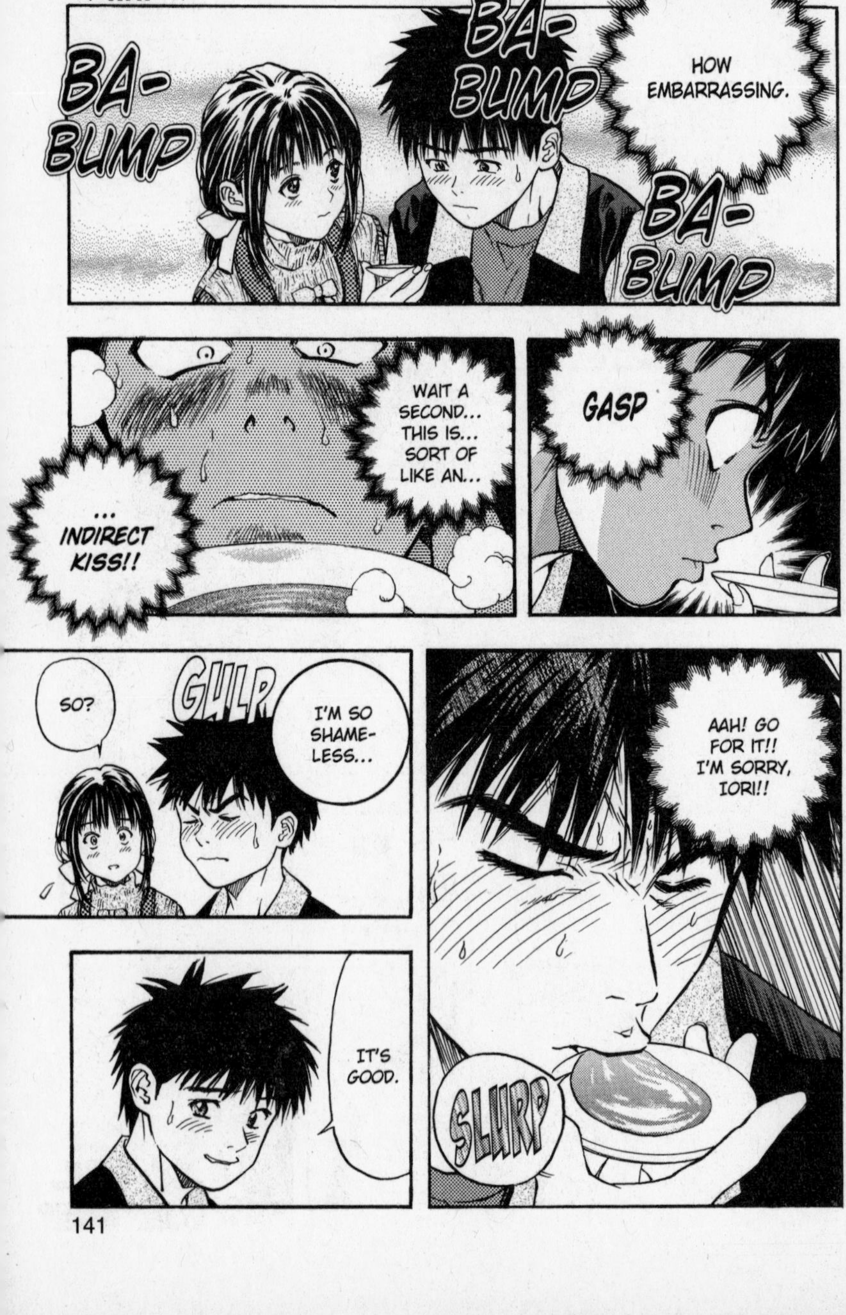
HOW EMBARRASSING.
BA-BUMP
BA-BUMP
BA-BUMP
GASP
WAIT A SECOND... THIS IS... SORT OF LIKE AN...
... INDIRECT KISS!!
AAH! GO FOR IT!! I'M SORRY, IORI!!
SLURP
I'M SO SHAME-LESS...
GULP
SO?
IT'S GOOD.

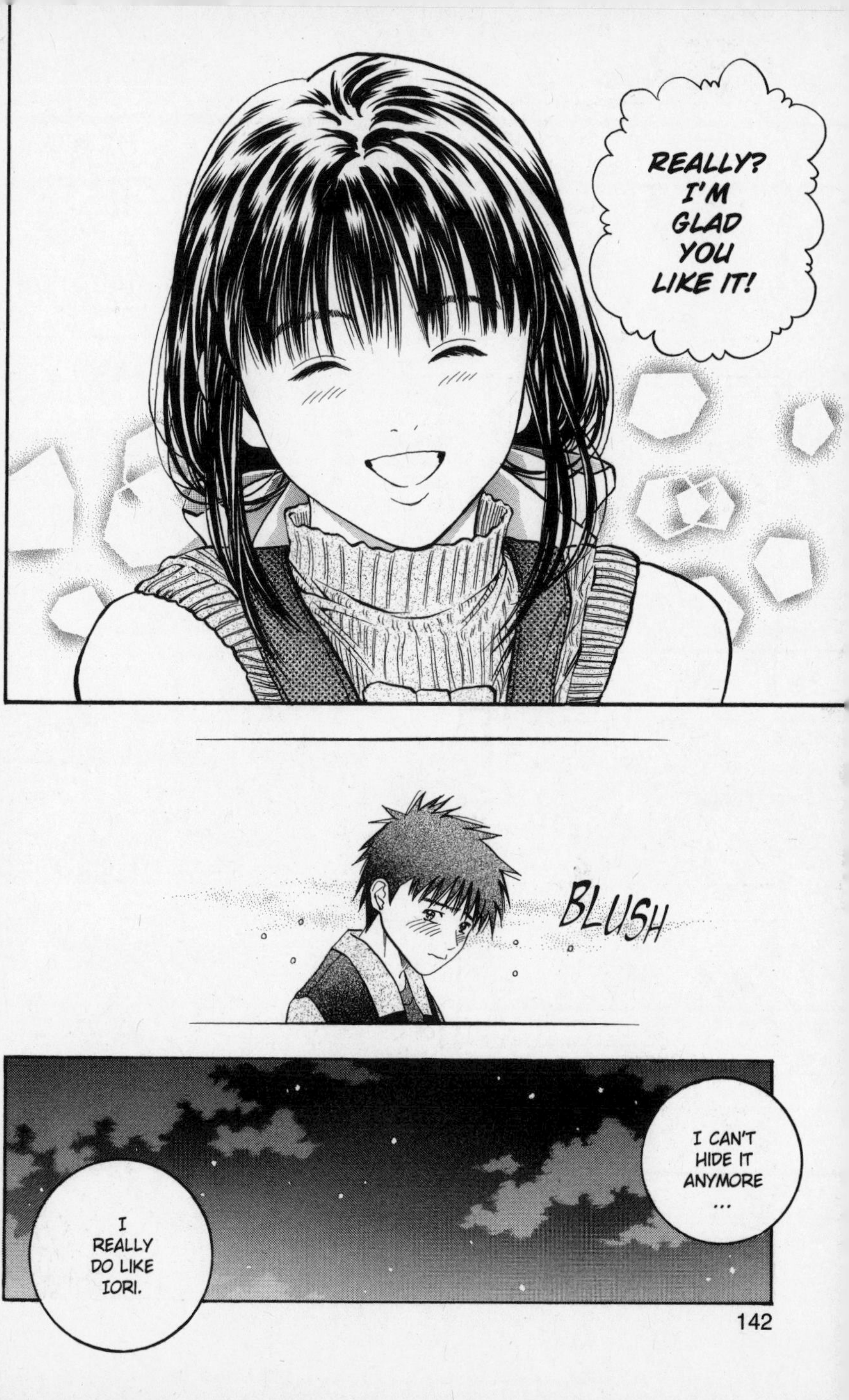
REALLY? I'M GLAD YOU LIKE IT!
BLUSH
I CAN'T HIDE IT ANYMORE ...
I REALLY DO LIKE IORI.

READ THIS WAY

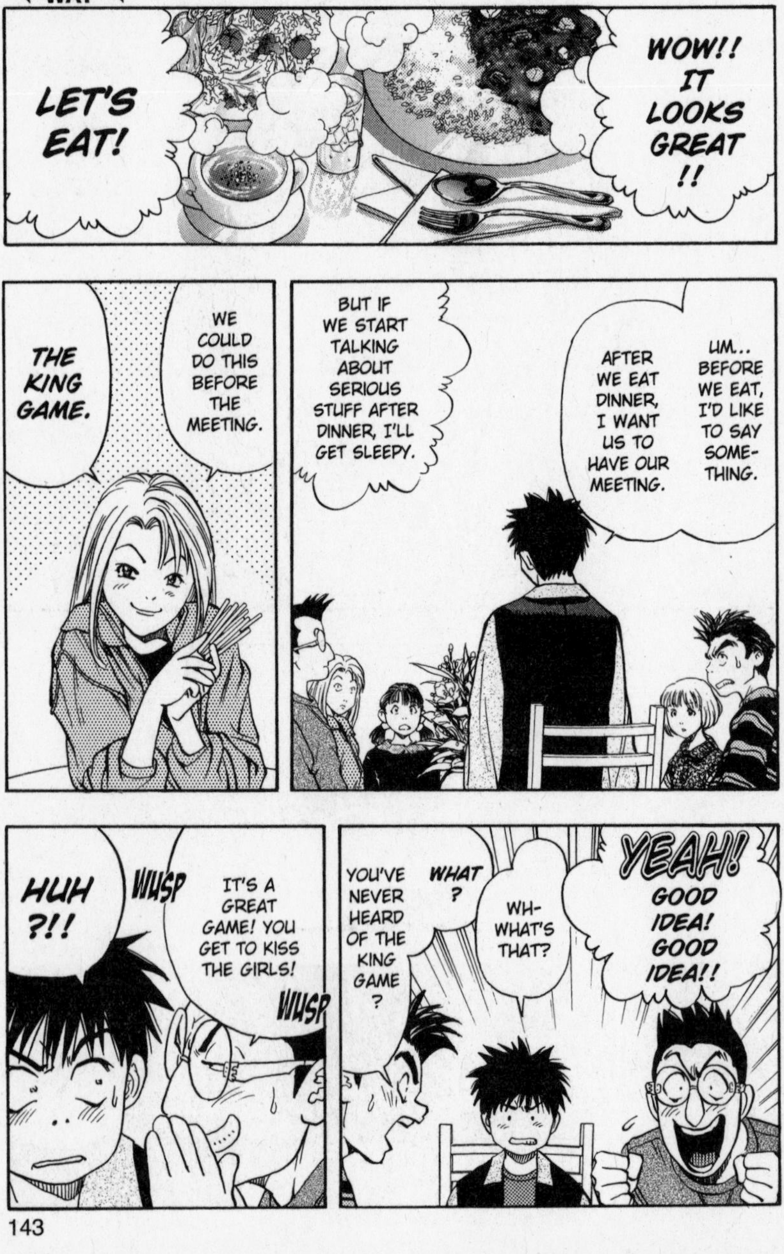
WOW!! IT LOOKS GREAT!!
LET'S EAT!
UM.. BEFORE WE EAT, I'D LIKE TO SAY SOME-THING.
AFTER WE EAT DINNER, I WANT US TO HAVE OUR MEETING.
BUT IF WE START TALKING ABOUT SERIOUS STUFF AFTER DINNER, I'LL GET SLEEPY.
WE COULD DO THIS BEFORE THE MEETING.
THE KING GAME.
YEAH!
GOOD IDEA! GOOD IDEA!!
WH-WHAT'S THAT?
WHAT?
YOU'VE NEVER HEARD OF THE KING GAME?
IT'S A GREAT GAME! YOU GET TO KISS THE GIRLS!
WUSP
WUSP
HUH?!!

I"s

アイズ

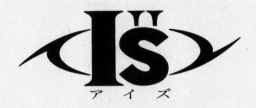

Chapter 53: No Limits

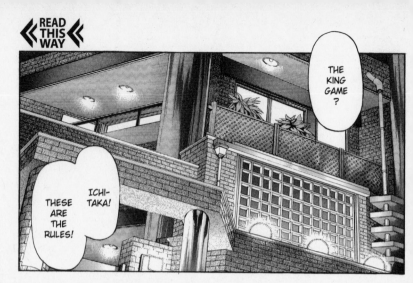

THE KING GAME?

ICHI-TAKA!

THESE ARE THE RULES!

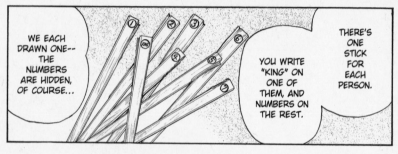

THERE'S ONE STICK FOR EACH PERSON.

YOU WRITE "KING" ON ONE OF THEM, AND NUMBERS ON THE REST.

WE EACH DRAWN ONE-- THE NUMBERS ARE HIDDEN, OF COURSE...

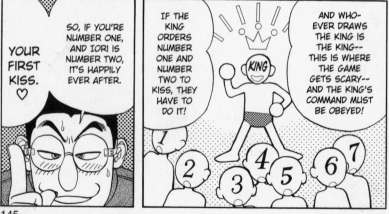

AND WHO-EVER DRAWS THE KING IS THE KING-- THIS IS WHERE THE GAME GETS SCARY-- AND THE KING'S COMMAND MUST BE OBEYED!

KING

IF THE KING ORDERS NUMBER ONE AND NUMBER TWO TO KISS, THEY HAVE TO DO IT!

SO, IF YOU'RE NUMBER ONE, AND IORI IS NUMBER TWO, IT'S HAPPILY EVER AFTER.

YOUR FIRST KISS. ♡

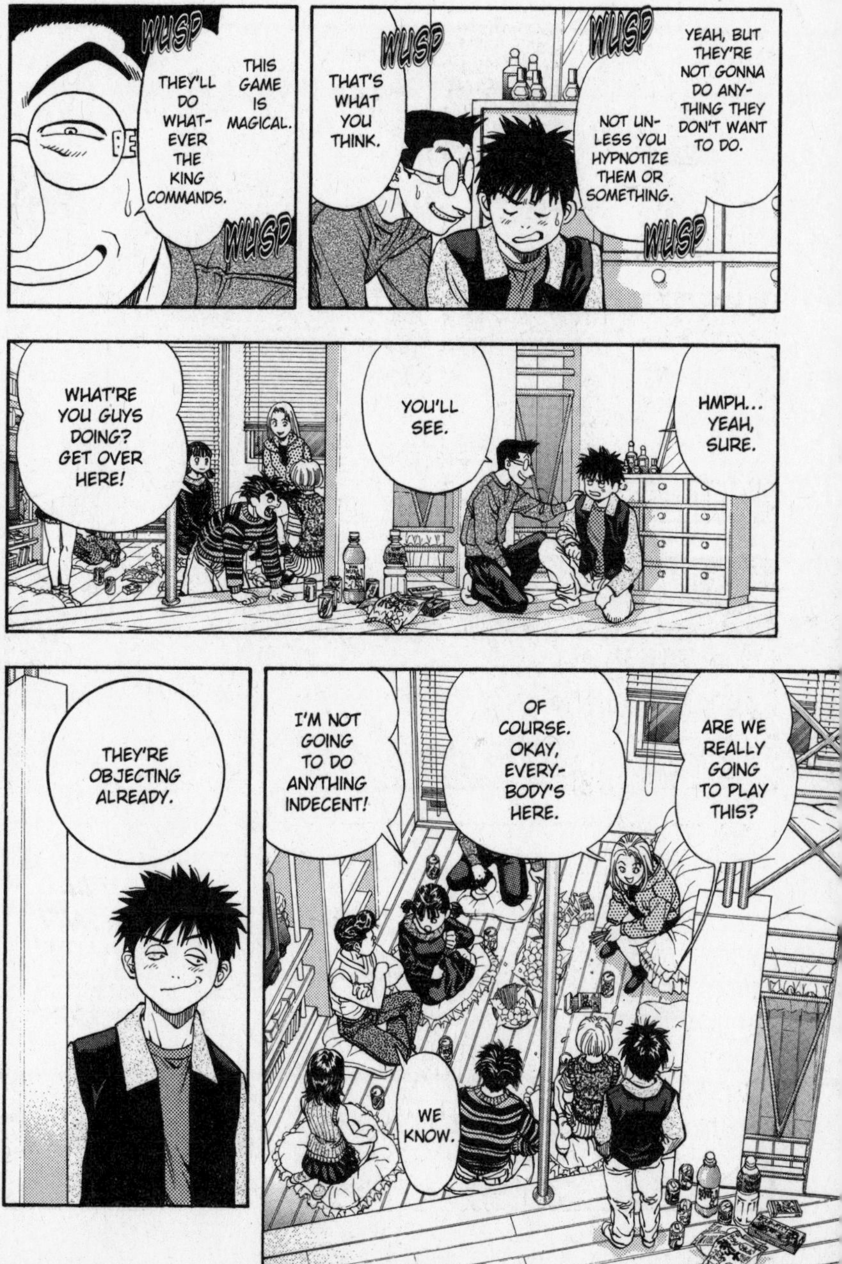
WUSP
YEAH, BUT THEY'RE NOT GONNA DO ANY-THING THEY DON'T WANT TO DO.
NOT UN-LESS YOU HYPNOTIZE THEM OR SOMETHING.
WUSP
WUSP
THAT'S WHAT YOU THINK.
WUSP
THIS GAME IS MAGICAL.
THEY'LL DO WHAT-EVER THE KING COMMANDS.
WUSP
HMPH... YEAH, SURE.
YOU'LL SEE.
WHAT'RE YOU GUYS DOING? GET OVER HERE!
ARE WE REALLY GOING TO PLAY THIS?
OF COURSE. OKAY, EVERY-BODY'S HERE.
I'M NOT GOING TO DO ANYTHING INDECENT!
WE KNOW.
THEY'RE OBJECTING ALREADY.

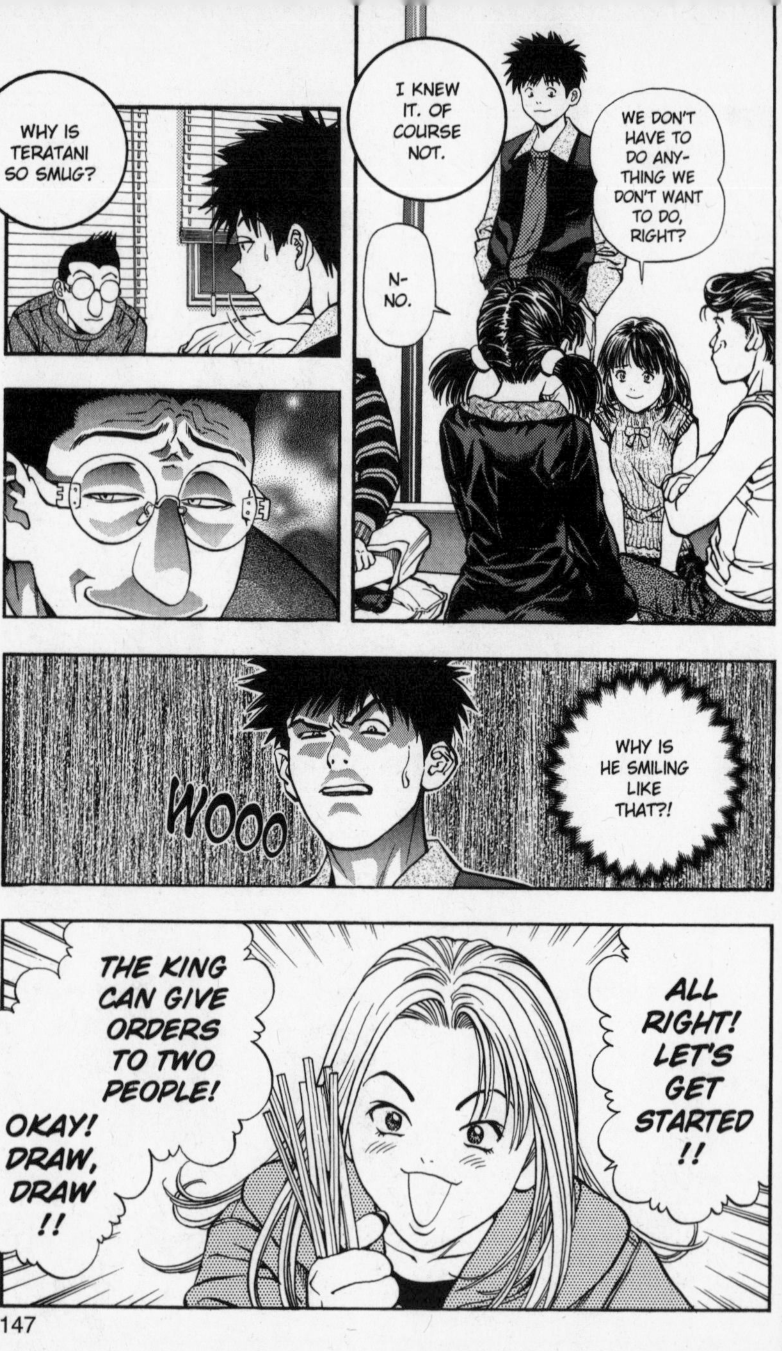
WE DON'T HAVE TO DO ANYTHING WE DON'T WANT TO DO, RIGHT?
I KNEW IT. OF COURSE NOT.
N-NO.
WHY IS TERATANI SO SMUG?
WHY IS HE SMILING LIKE THAT?!
WOOO
ALL RIGHT! LET'S GET STARTED!!
THE KING CAN GIVE ORDERS TO TWO PEOPLE!
OKAY! DRAW, DRAW!!

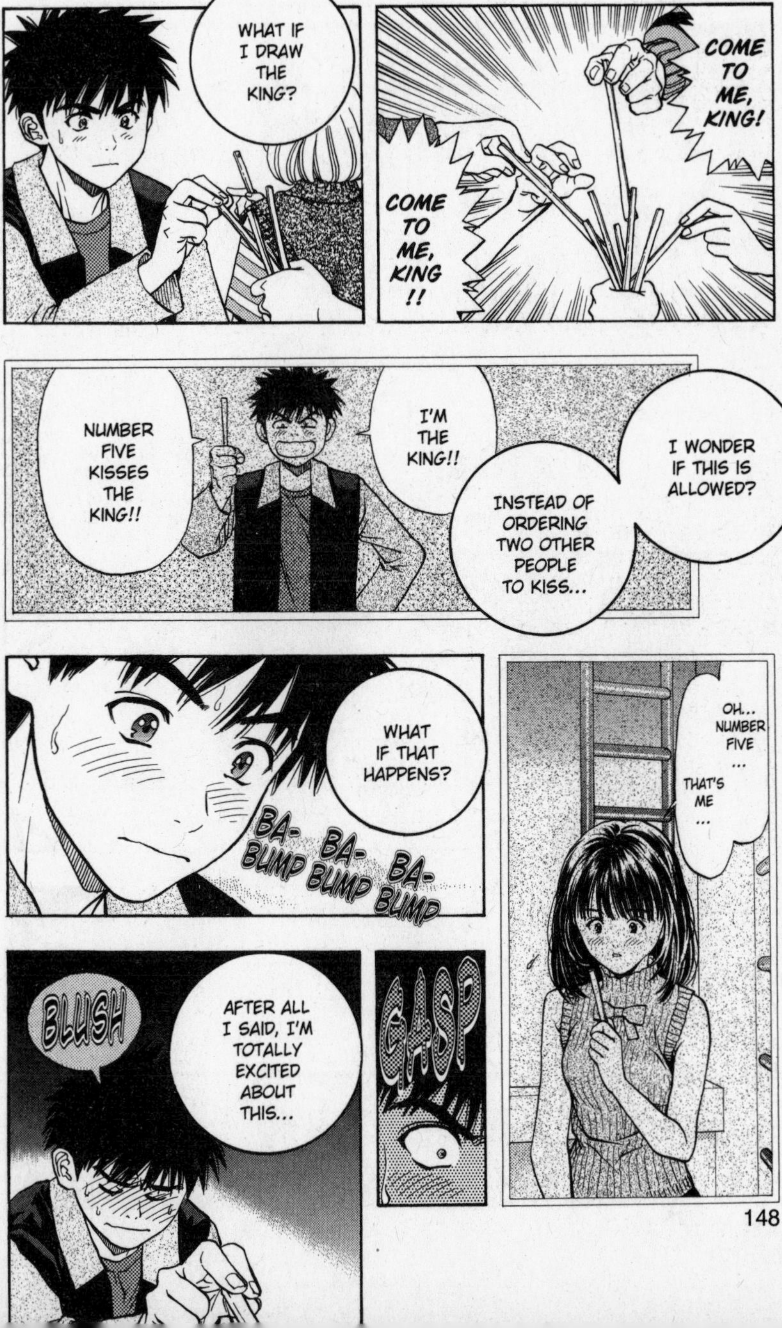
COME TO ME, KING!
COME TO ME, KING !!
WHAT IF I DRAW THE KING?
I WONDER IF THIS IS ALLOWED?
INSTEAD OF ORDERING TWO OTHER PEOPLE TO KISS...
I'M THE KING!!
NUMBER FIVE KISSES THE KING!!
OH... NUMBER FIVE ...
THAT'S ME ...
WHAT IF THAT HAPPENS?
BA-BUMP BA-BUMP BA-BUMP
GASP
BLUSH
AFTER ALL I SAID, I'M TOTALLY EXCITED ABOUT THIS...

READ THIS WAY

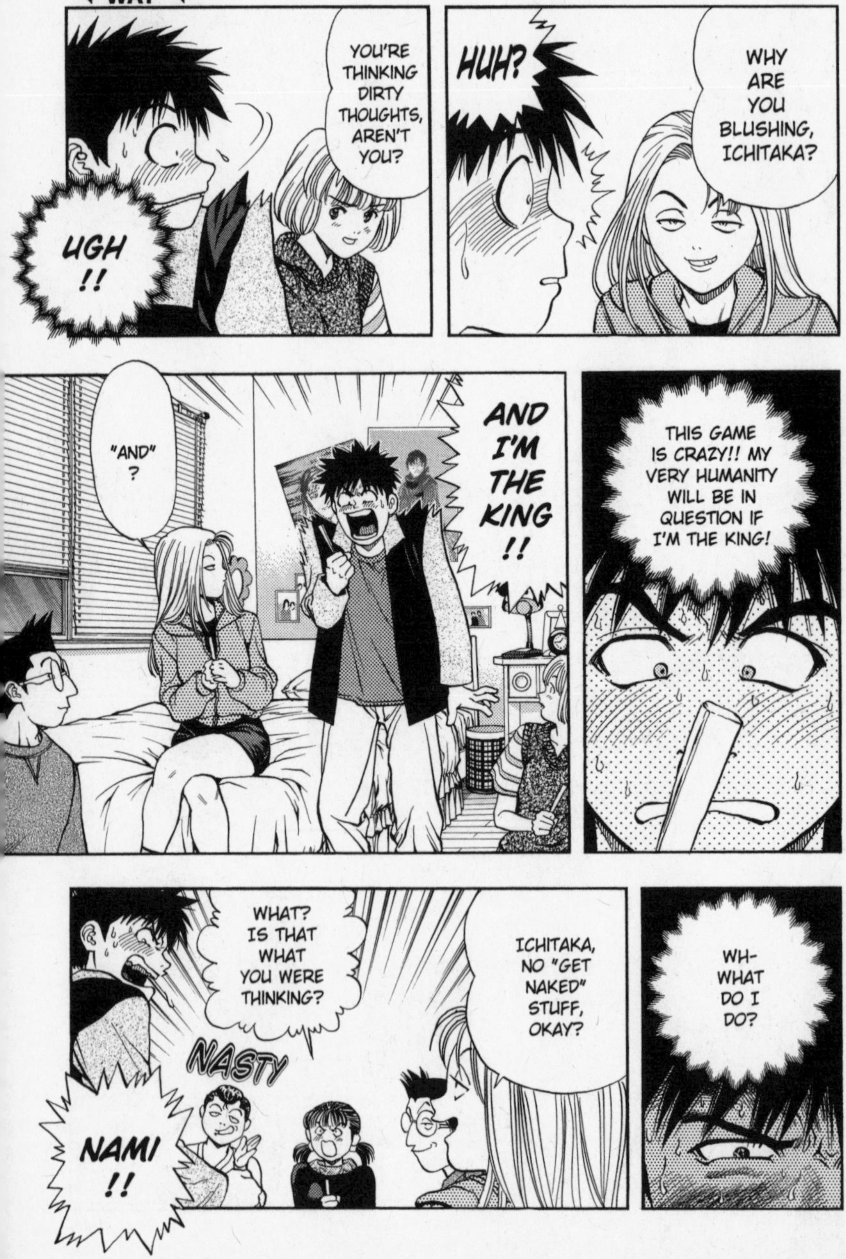

WHY ARE YOU BLUSHING, ICHITAKA?
HUH?
YOU'RE THINKING DIRTY THOUGHTS, AREN'T YOU?
UGH !!
THIS GAME IS CRAZY!! MY VERY HUMANITY WILL BE IN QUESTION IF I'M THE KING!
AND I'M THE KING !!
"AND" ?
WH- WHAT DO I DO?
ICHITAKA, NO "GET NAKED" STUFF, OKAY?
WHAT? IS THAT WHAT YOU WERE THINKING?
NASTY
NAMI !!

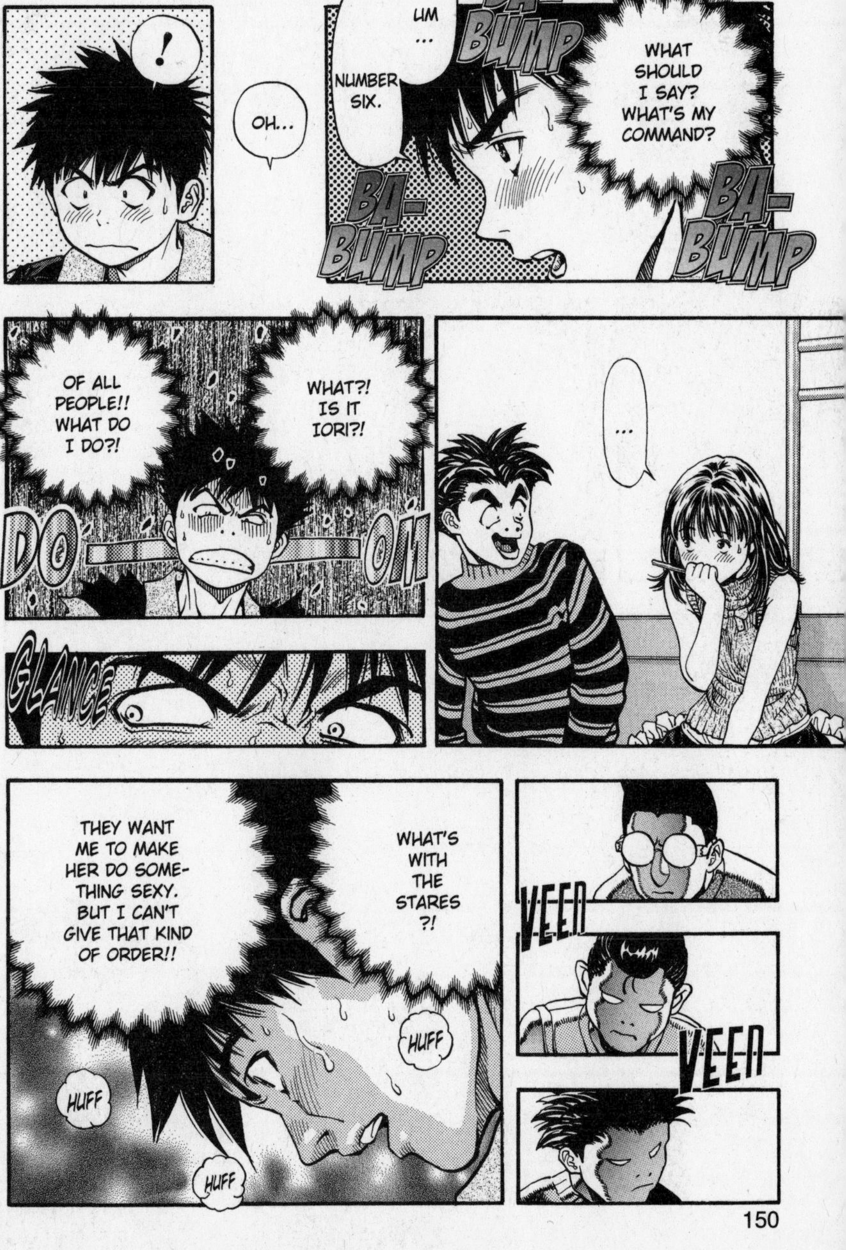
BA-BUMP
WHAT SHOULD I SAY? WHAT'S MY COMMAND?
BA-BUMP
UM ...
NUMBER SIX.
BA-BUMP
OH...
!
...
WHAT?! IS IT IORI?!
OF ALL PEOPLE!! WHAT DO I DO?!
DO-OH
GLANCE
VEEN
VEEN
WHAT'S WITH THE STARES?!
THEY WANT ME TO MAKE HER DO SOME-THING SEXY. BUT I CAN'T GIVE THAT KIND OF ORDER!!
HUFF
HUFF
HUFF

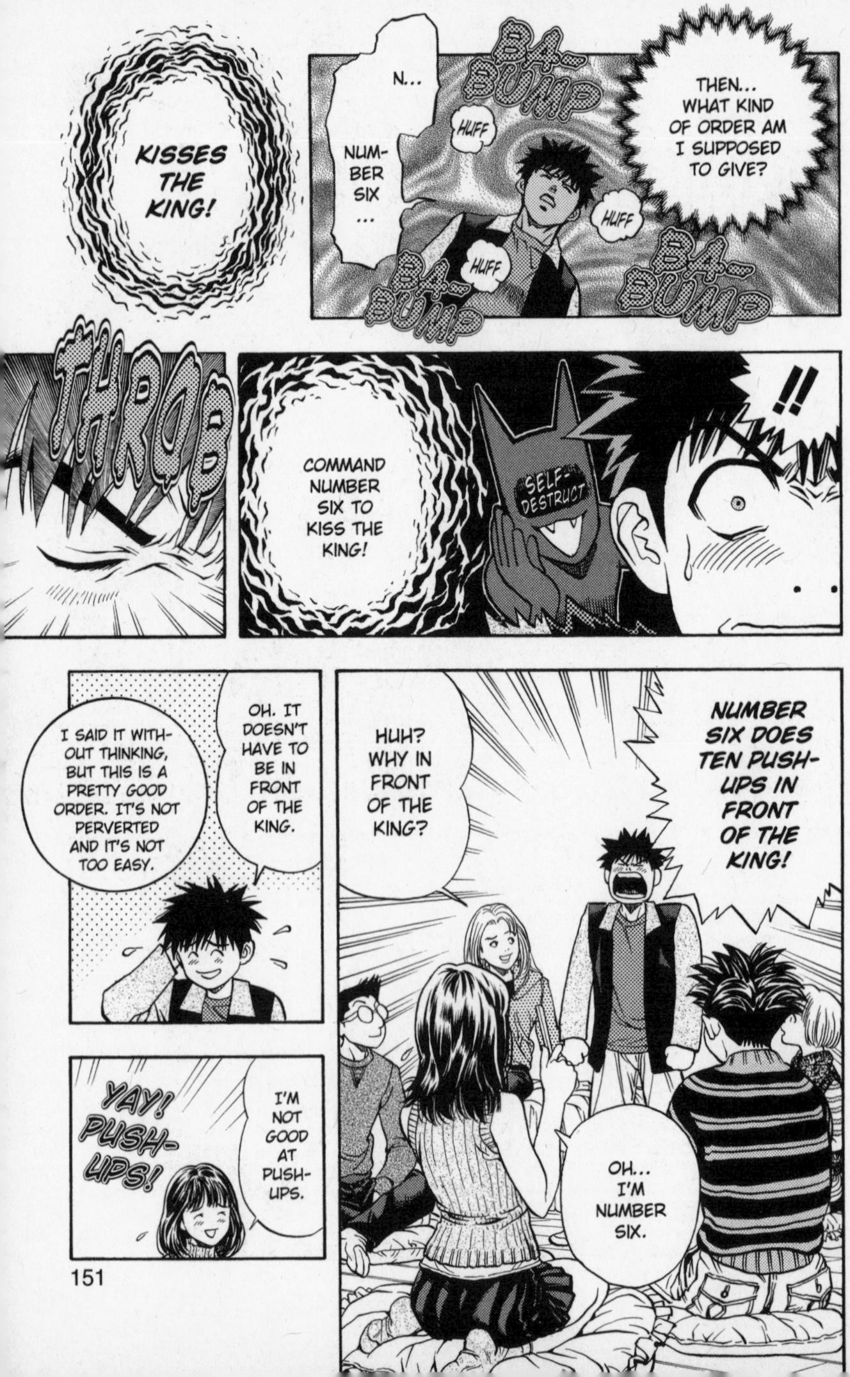
BA-BUMP
THEN... WHAT KIND OF ORDER AM I SUPPOSED TO GIVE?
HUFF
HUFF
HUFF
BA-BUMP
BA-BUMP
N... NUMBER SIX ...
KISSES THE KING!
!!
SELF-DESTRUCT
COMMAND NUMBER SIX TO KISS THE KING!
THROB
NUMBER SIX DOES TEN PUSH-UPS IN FRONT OF THE KING!
HUH? WHY IN FRONT OF THE KING?
OH... I'M NUMBER SIX.
OH. IT DOESN'T HAVE TO BE IN FRONT OF THE KING.
I SAID IT WITHOUT THINKING, BUT THIS IS A PRETTY GOOD ORDER. IT'S NOT PERVERTED AND IT'S NOT TOO EASY.
I'M NOT GOOD AT PUSH-UPS.
YAY! PUSH-UPS!

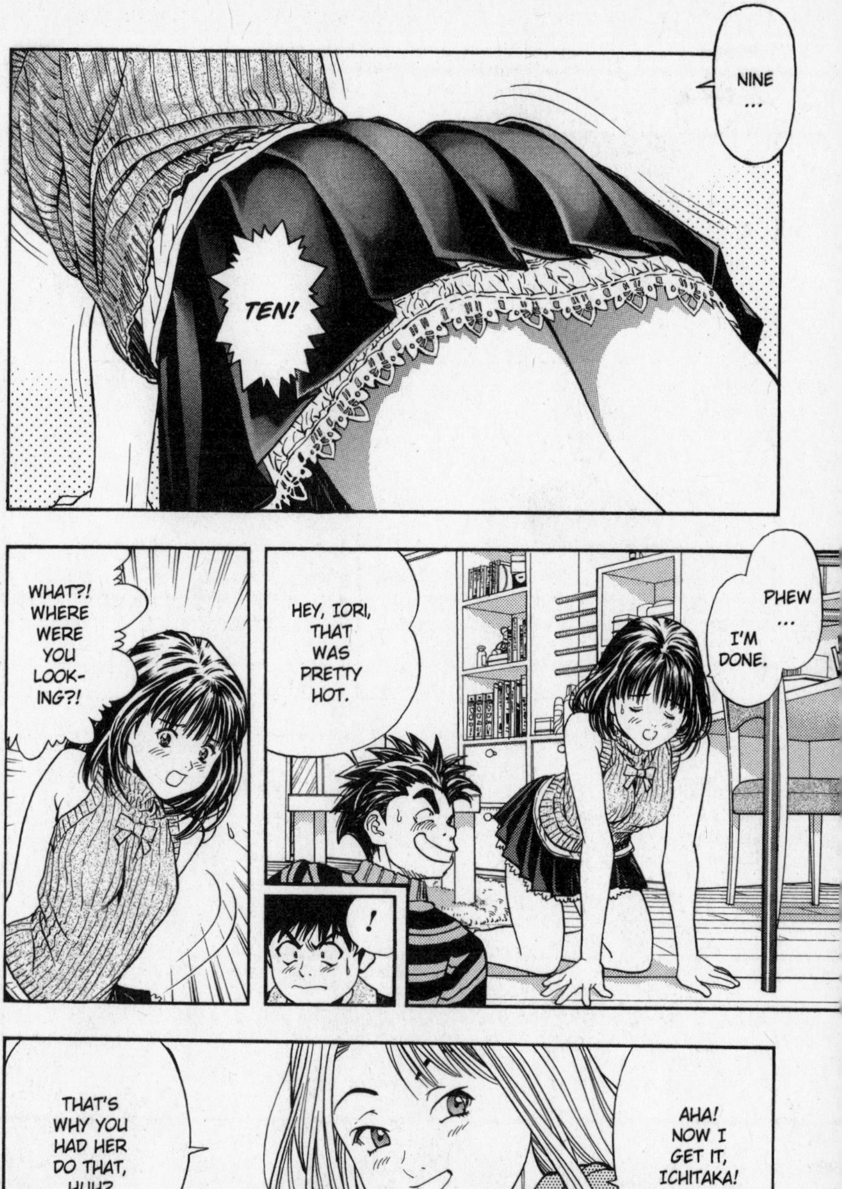
NINE ...
TEN!
PHEW ... I'M DONE.
HEY, IORI, THAT WAS PRETTY HOT.
!
WHAT?! WHERE WERE YOU LOOK-ING?!
AHA! NOW I GET IT, ICHITAKA!
THAT'S WHY YOU HAD HER DO THAT, HUH?

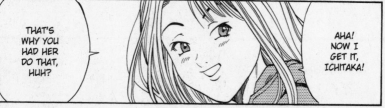

READ THIS WAY

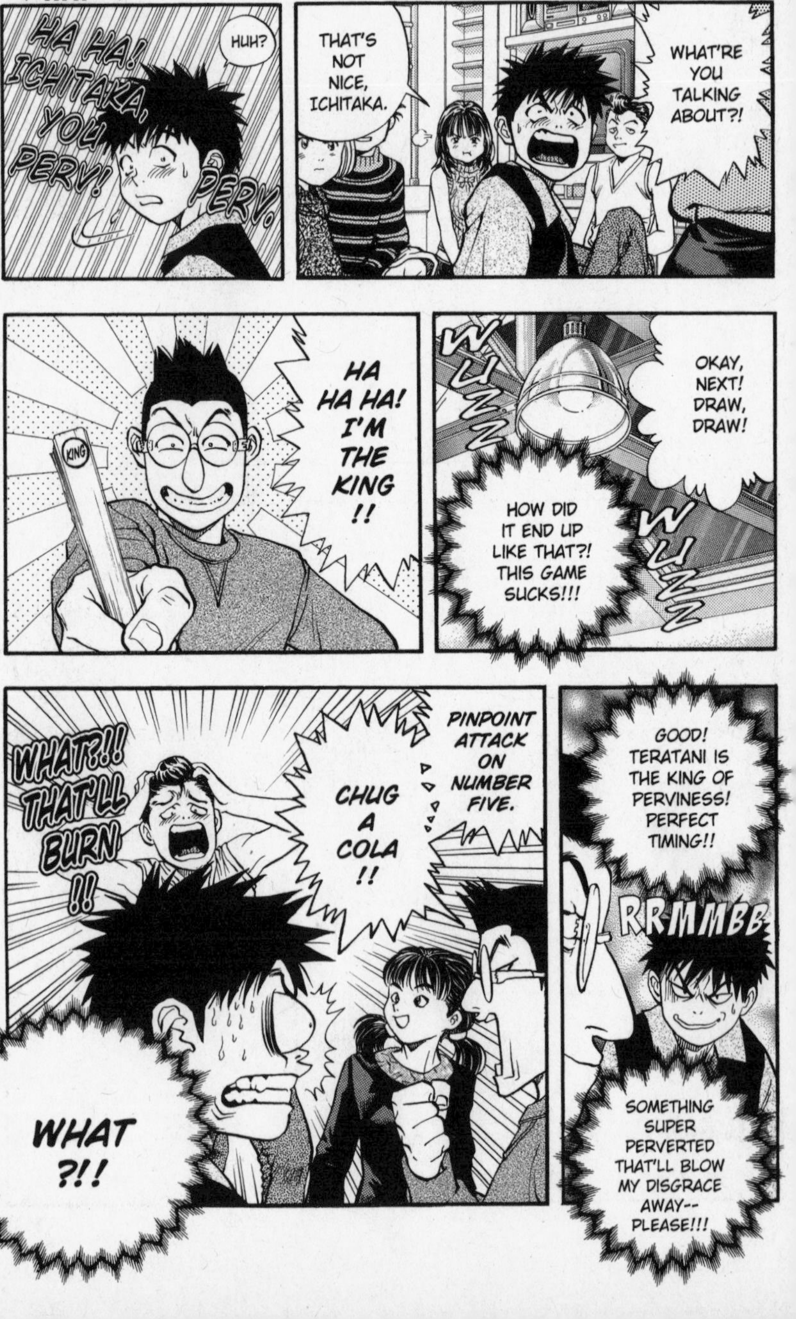
WHAT'RE YOU TALKING ABOUT?!
THAT'S NOT NICE, ICHITAKA.
HUH?
HA HA! ICHITAKA, YOU PERV!
PERV.
OKAY, NEXT! DRAW, DRAW!
WUZZ
HOW DID IT END UP LIKE THAT?! THIS GAME SUCKS!!!
WUZZ
HA HA HA! I'M THE KING!!
KING
GOOD! TERATANI IS THE KING OF PERVINESS! PERFECT TIMING!!
RRMMBB
SOMETHING SUPER PERVERTED THAT'LL BLOW MY DISGRACE AWAY-- PLEASE!!!
PINPOINT ATTACK ON NUMBER FIVE.
CHUG A COLA!!
WHAT?!! THAT'LL BURN!!
WHAT?!!

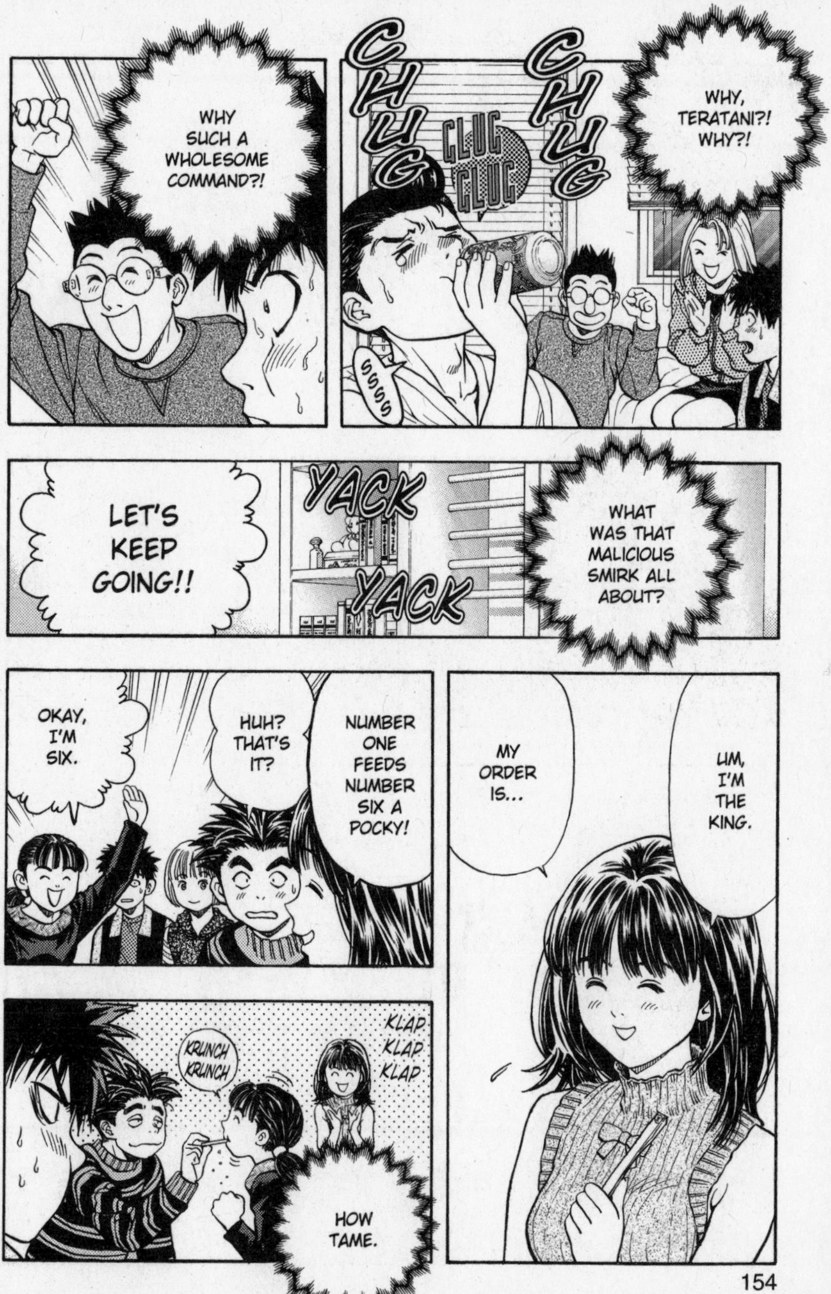
WHY, TERATANI?! WHY?!
CHUG
CLUG CLUG
CHUG
SSSS
WHY SUCH A WHOLESOME COMMAND?!
WHAT WAS THAT MALICIOUS SMIRK ALL ABOUT?
YACK YACK
LET'S KEEP GOING!!
UM, I'M THE KING.
MY ORDER IS...
NUMBER ONE FEEDS NUMBER SIX A POCKY!
HUH? THAT'S IT?
OKAY, I'M SIX.
KLAP KLAP KLAP
KRUNCH KRUNCH
HOW TAME.

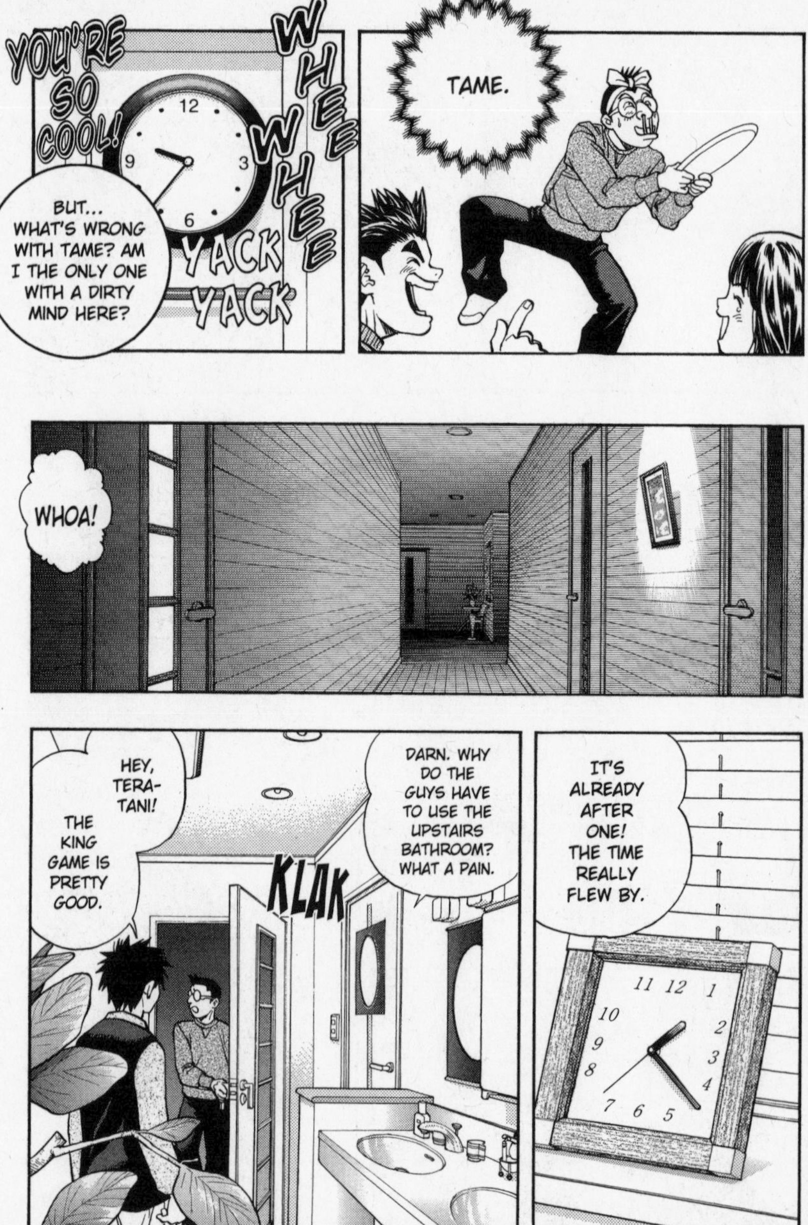
TAME.
YOU'RE SO COOL!
WHEE WHEE
YACK YACK
BUT... WHAT'S WRONG WITH TAME? AM I THE ONLY ONE WITH A DIRTY MIND HERE?
WHOA!
IT'S ALREADY AFTER ONE! THE TIME REALLY FLEW BY.
DARN. WHY DO THE GUYS HAVE TO USE THE UPSTAIRS BATHROOM? WHAT A PAIN.
KLAK
HEY, TERA-TANI!
THE KING GAME IS PRETTY GOOD.

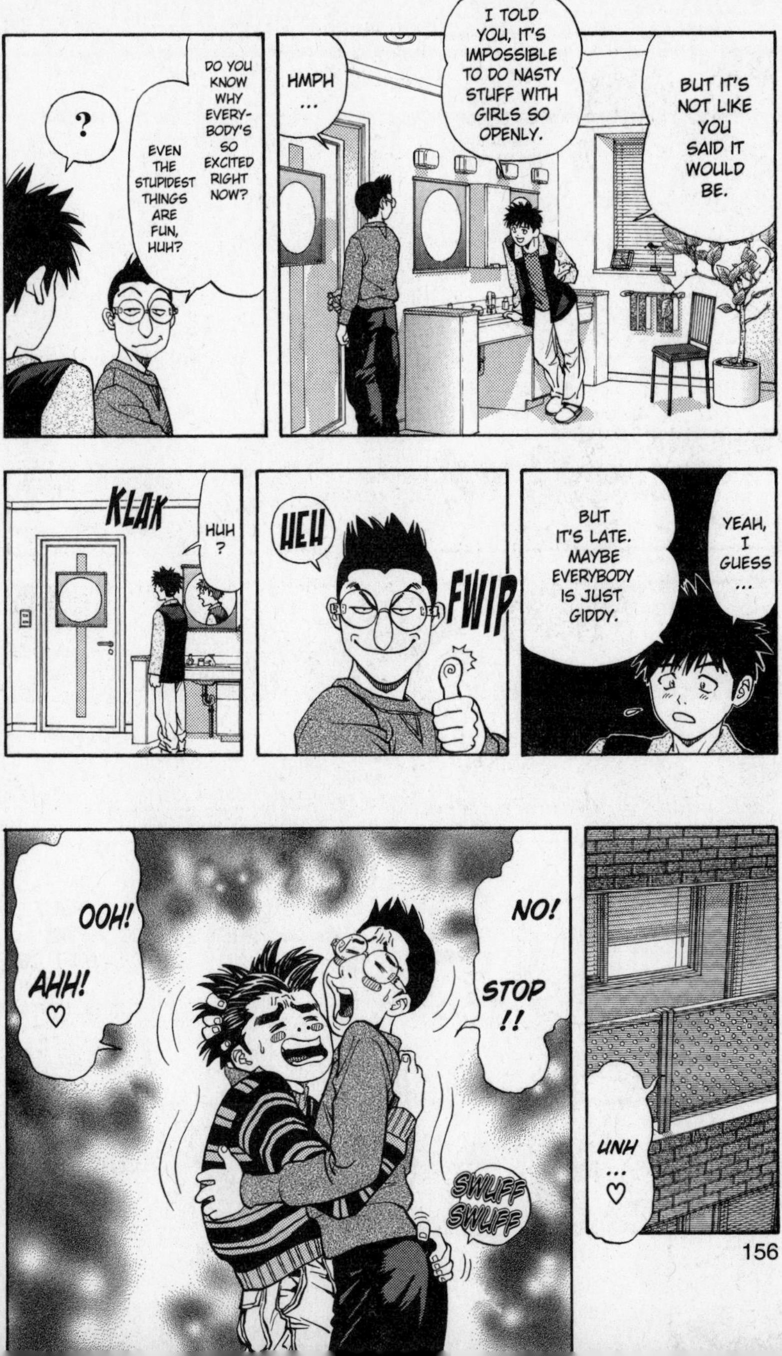
BUT IT'S NOT LIKE YOU SAID IT WOULD BE.
I TOLD YOU, IT'S IMPOSSIBLE TO DO NASTY STUFF WITH GIRLS SO OPENLY.
HMPH ...
DO YOU KNOW WHY EVERYBODY'S SO EXCITED RIGHT NOW?
EVEN THE STUPIDEST THINGS ARE FUN, HUH?
?
YEAH, I GUESS ...
BUT IT'S LATE. MAYBE EVERYBODY IS JUST GIDDY.
FWIP
HEH
HUH?
KLAK
UNH ... ♡
NO!
STOP !!
SWUFF SWUFF
OOH!
AHH! ♡

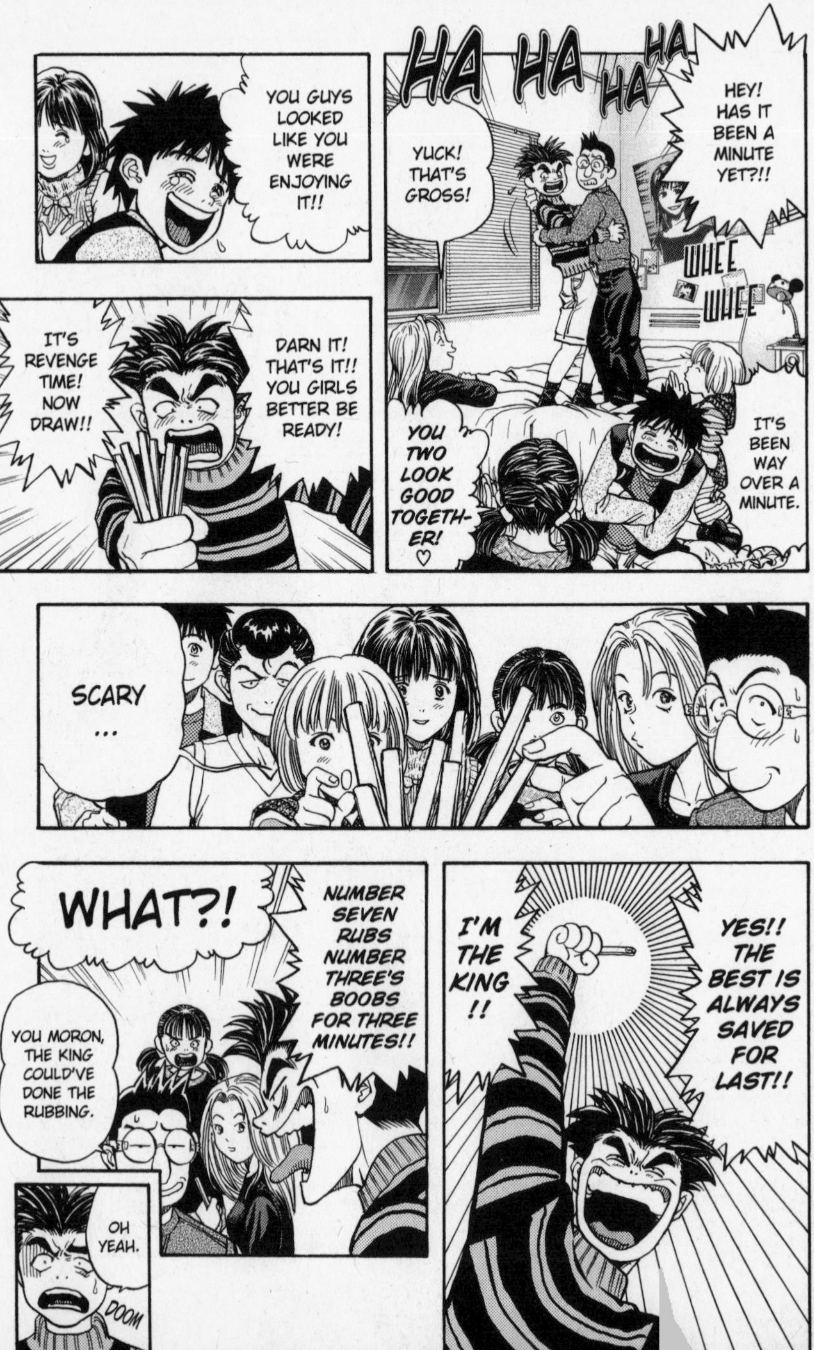
HA HA HA HA
HEY! HAS IT BEEN A MINUTE YET?!!
YUCK! THAT'S GROSS!
WHEE WHEE
IT'S BEEN WAY OVER A MINUTE.
YOU TWO LOOK GOOD TOGETHER! ♡
YOU GUYS LOOKED LIKE YOU WERE ENJOYING IT!!
DARN IT! THAT'S IT!! YOU GIRLS BETTER BE READY!
IT'S REVENGE TIME! NOW DRAW!!
SCARY...
YES!! THE BEST IS ALWAYS SAVED FOR LAST!!
I'M THE KING!!
NUMBER SEVEN RUBS NUMBER THREE'S BOOBS FOR THREE MINUTES!!
WHAT?!
YOU MORON, THE KING COULD'VE DONE THE RUBBING.
OH YEAH.
DOOM

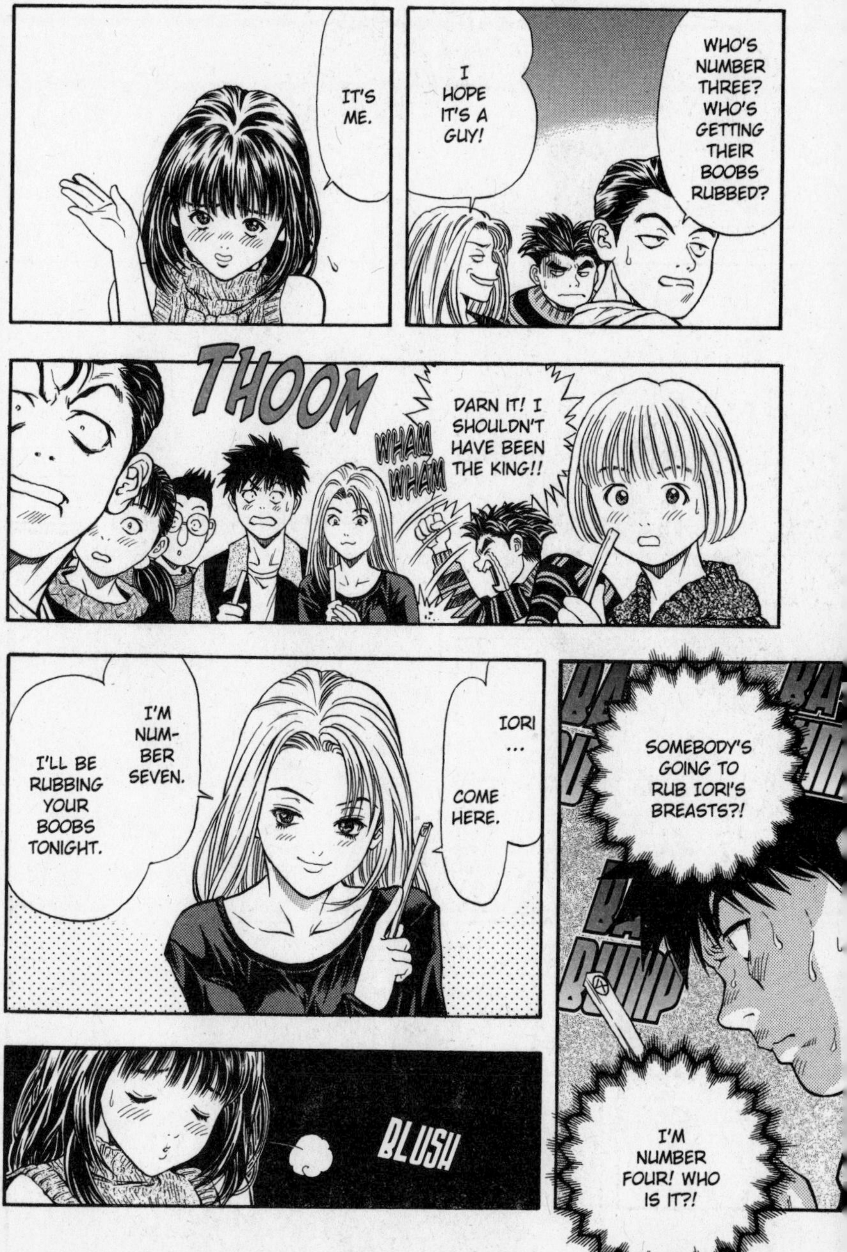
WHO'S NUMBER THREE? WHO'S GETTING THEIR BOOBS RUBBED?
I HOPE IT'S A GUY!
IT'S ME.
THOOM
DARN IT! I SHOULDN'T HAVE BEEN THE KING!!
WHAM WHAM
SOMEBODY'S GOING TO RUB IORI'S BREASTS?!
BUMP
I'M NUMBER FOUR! WHO IS IT?!
IORI ... COME HERE.
I'M NUM-BER SEVEN.
I'LL BE RUBBING YOUR BOOBS TONIGHT.
BLUSH

READ THIS WAY

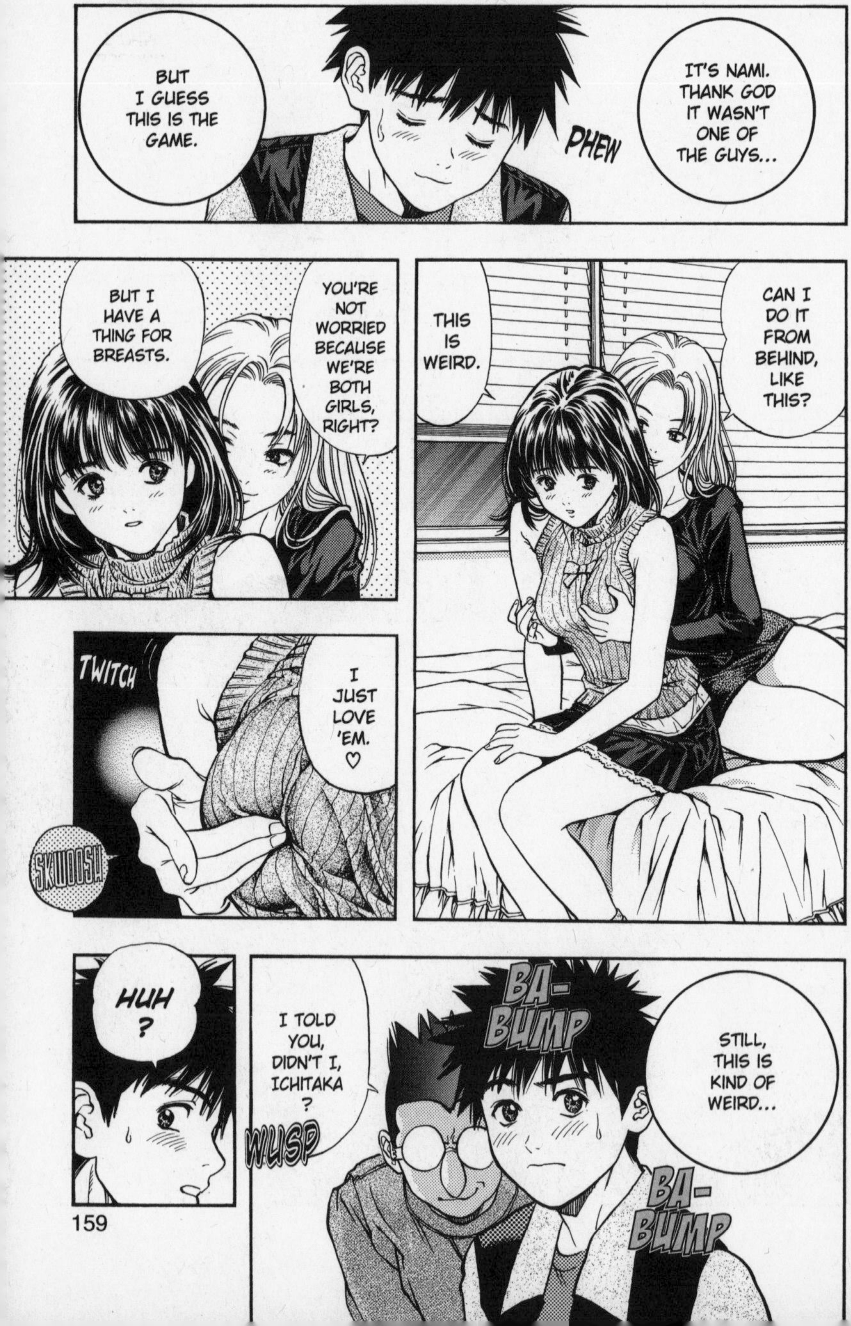

IT'S NAMI. THANK GOD IT WASN'T ONE OF THE GUYS...
PHEW
BUT I GUESS THIS IS THE GAME.
CAN I DO IT FROM BEHIND, LIKE THIS?
THIS IS WEIRD.
YOU'RE NOT WORRIED BECAUSE WE'RE BOTH GIRLS, RIGHT?
BUT I HAVE A THING FOR BREASTS.
I JUST LOVE 'EM. ♡
TWITCH
SKWOOSH
STILL, THIS IS KIND OF WEIRD...
BA-BUMP
BA-BUMP
I TOLD YOU, DIDN'T I, ICHITAKA?
WUSP
HUH?

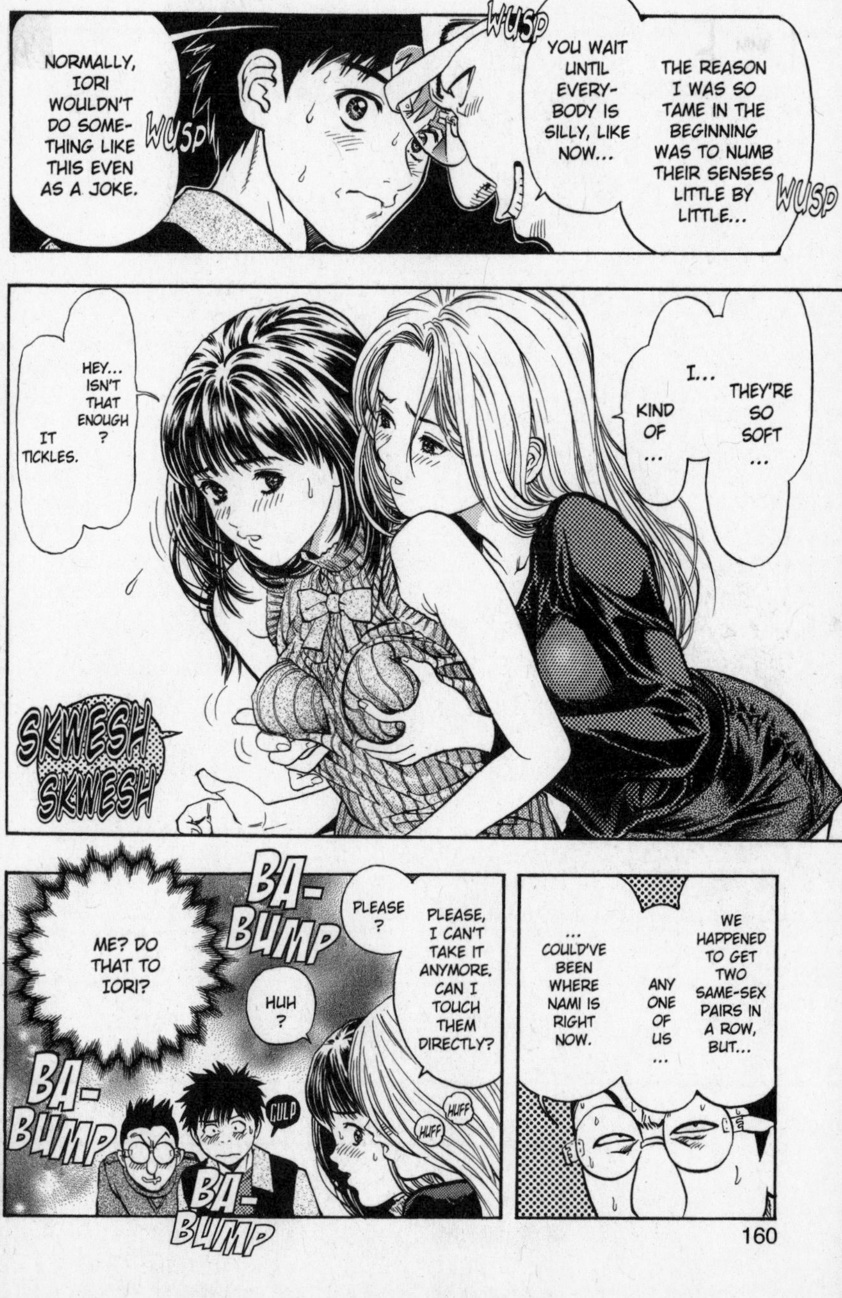

WUSP
THE REASON I WAS SO TAME IN THE BEGINNING WAS TO NUMB THEIR SENSES LITTLE BY LITTLE...
WUSP
YOU WAIT UNTIL EVERY-BODY IS SILLY, LIKE NOW...
WUSP
NORMALLY, IORI WOULDN'T DO SOME-THING LIKE THIS EVEN AS A JOKE.
THEY'RE SO SOFT...
I... KIND OF...
HEY... ISN'T THAT ENOUGH? IT TICKLES.
SKWESH SKWESH
WE HAPPENED TO GET TWO SAME-SEX PAIRS IN A ROW, BUT...
ANY ONE OF US...
... COULD'VE BEEN WHERE NAMI IS RIGHT NOW.
PLEASE, I CAN'T TAKE IT ANYMORE. CAN I TOUCH THEM DIRECTLY?
PLEASE?
BA-BUMP
HUH?
ME? DO THAT TO IORI?
HUFF
HUFF
GULP
BA-BUMP
BA-BUMP

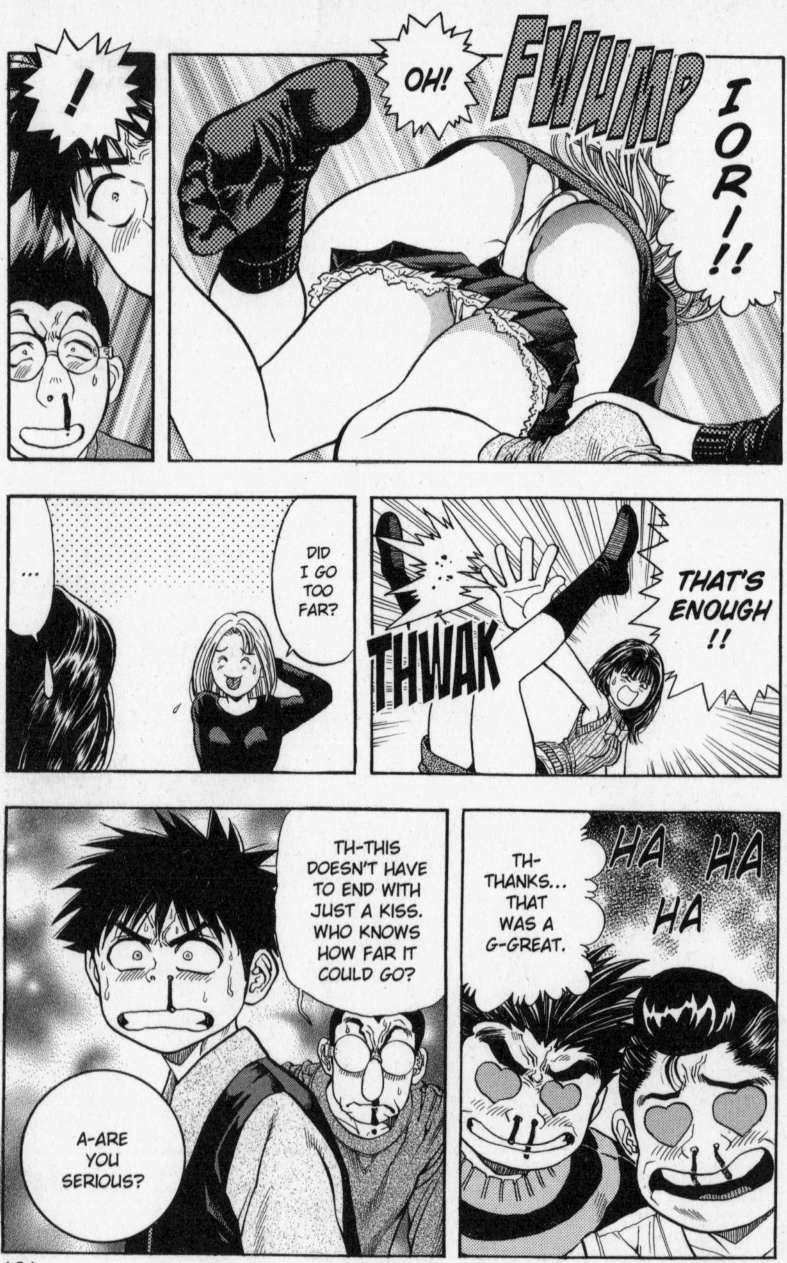
IORI!!
FWUMP
OH!
!
THAT'S ENOUGH!!
THWAK
DID I GO TOO FAR?
...
HA HA HA
TH-THANKS... THAT WAS A G-GREAT.
TH-THIS DOESN'T HAVE TO END WITH JUST A KISS. WHO KNOWS HOW FAR IT COULD GO?
A-ARE YOU SERIOUS?

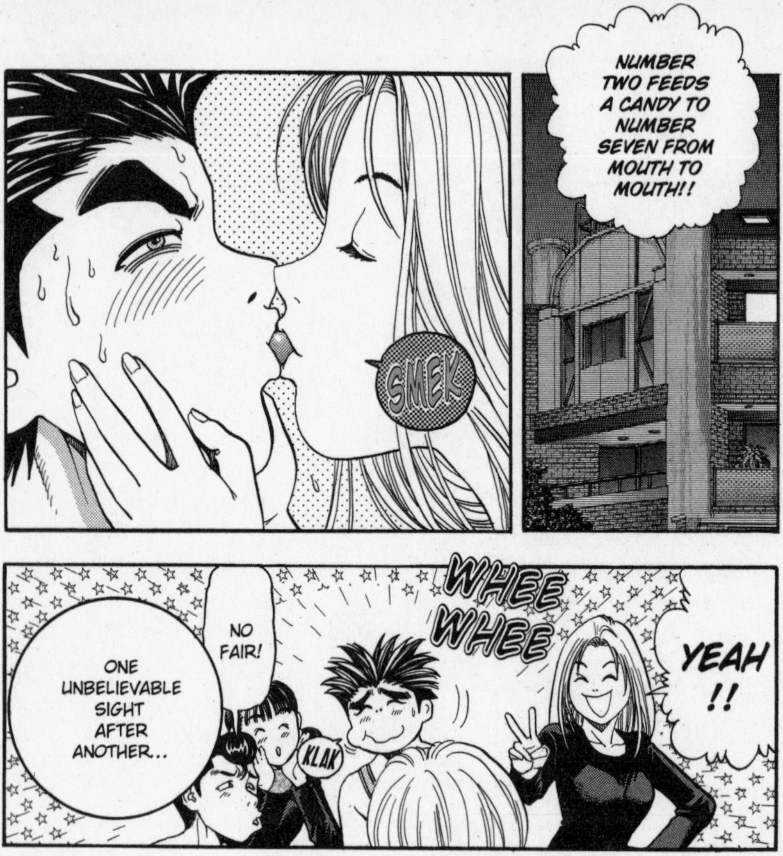
NUMBER TWO FEEDS A CANDY TO NUMBER SEVEN FROM MOUTH TO MOUTH!!
SMEK
YEAH!!
WHEE WHEE
NO FAIR!
ONE UNBELIEVABLE SIGHT AFTER ANOTHER...
KLAK

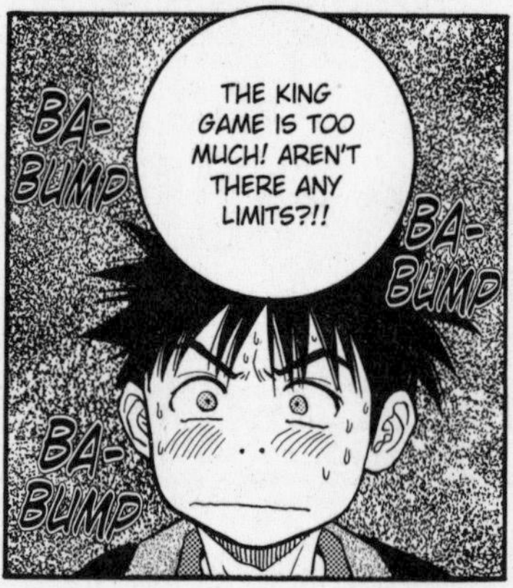
BA-BUMP
THE KING GAME IS TOO MUCH! AREN'T THERE ANY LIMITS?!!
BA-BUMP
BA-BUMP

Chapter 54: No Limits 2

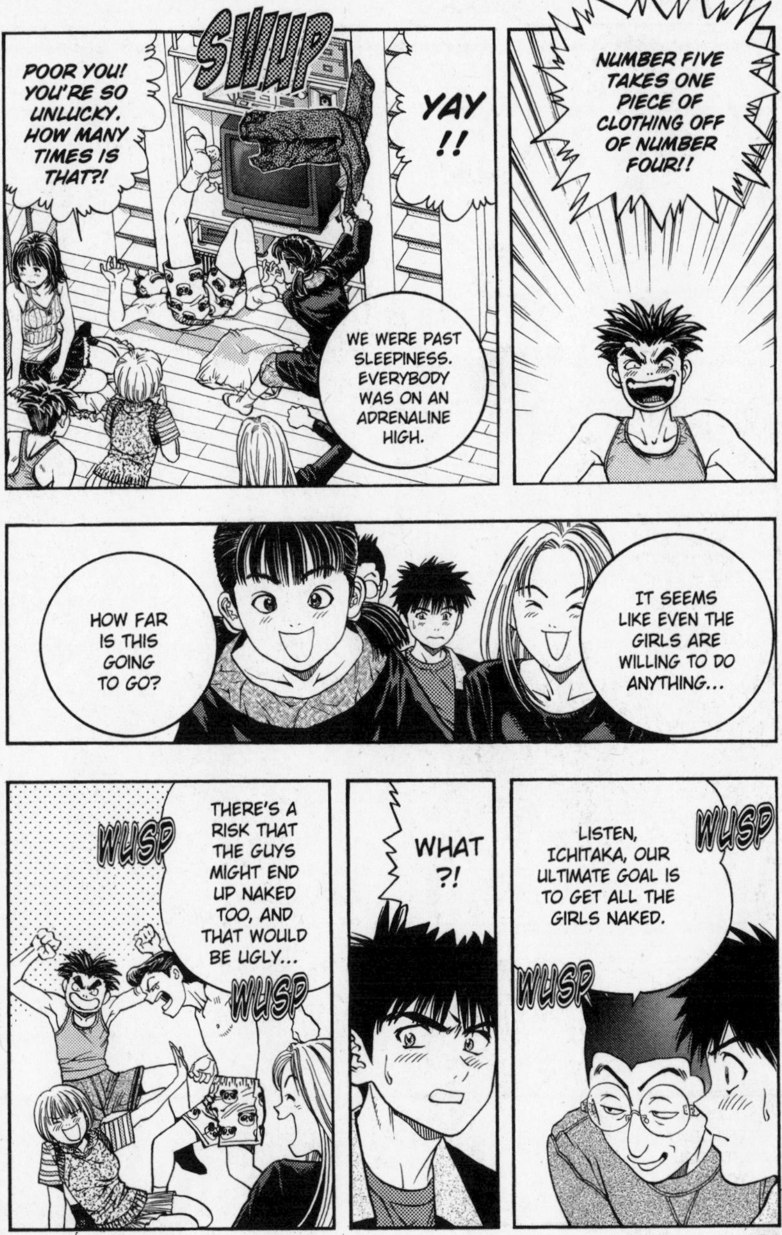
NUMBER FIVE TAKES ONE PIECE OF CLOTHING OFF OF NUMBER FOUR!!
YAY !!
SWUP
POOR YOU! YOU'RE SO UNLUCKY. HOW MANY TIMES IS THAT?!
WE WERE PAST SLEEPINESS. EVERYBODY WAS ON AN ADRENALINE HIGH.
IT SEEMS LIKE EVEN THE GIRLS ARE WILLING TO DO ANYTHING...
HOW FAR IS THIS GOING TO GO?
WUSP
LISTEN, ICHITAKA, OUR ULTIMATE GOAL IS TO GET ALL THE GIRLS NAKED.
WUSP
WHAT ?!
THERE'S A RISK THAT THE GUYS MIGHT END UP NAKED TOO, AND THAT WOULD BE UGLY...
WUSP
WUSP

READ THIS WAY

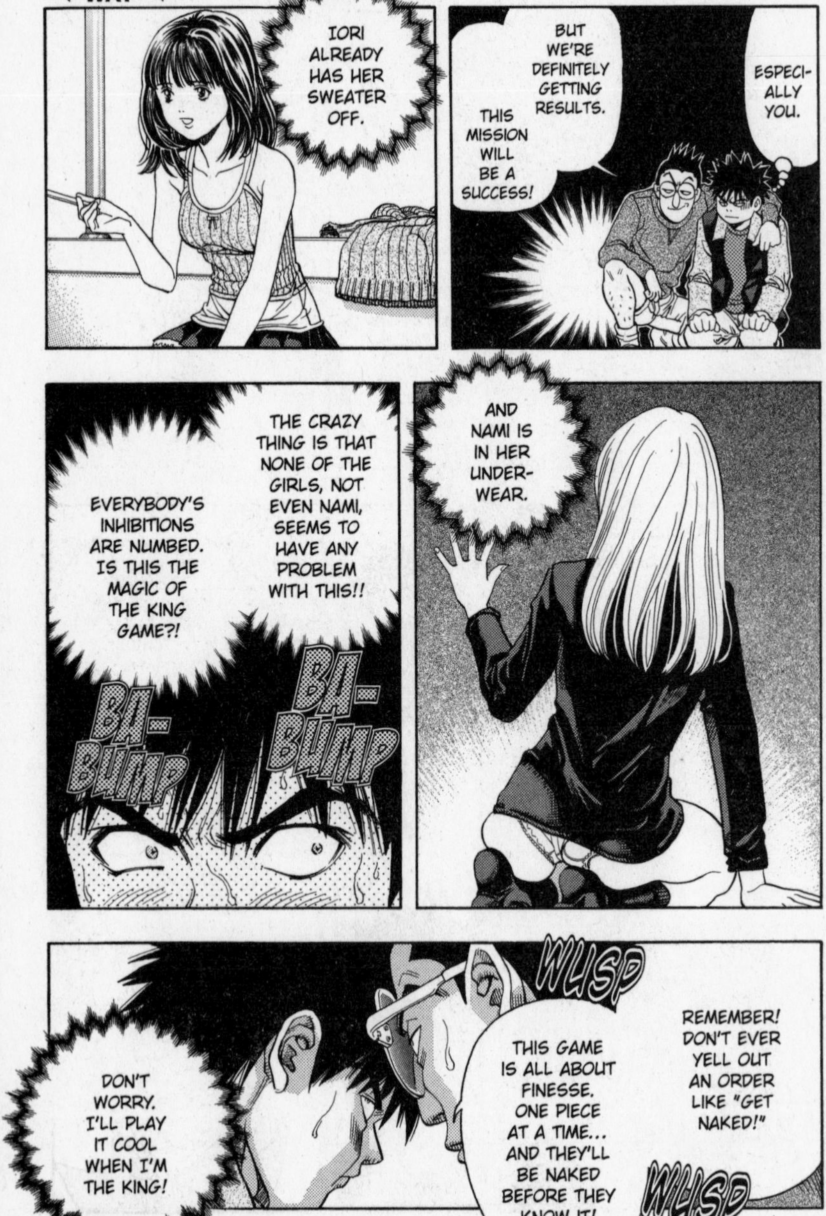

BUT WE'RE DEFINITELY GETTING RESULTS.
THIS MISSION WILL BE A SUCCESS!
ESPECI-ALLY YOU.
IORI ALREADY HAS HER SWEATER OFF.
AND NAMI IS IN HER UNDER-WEAR.
THE CRAZY THING IS THAT NONE OF THE GIRLS, NOT EVEN NAMI, SEEMS TO HAVE ANY PROBLEM WITH THIS!!
EVERYBODY'S INHIBITIONS ARE NUMBED. IS THIS THE MAGIC OF THE KING GAME?!
BA-BUMP
BA-BUMP
WUSP
REMEMBER! DON'T EVER YELL OUT AN ORDER LIKE "GET NAKED!"
THIS GAME IS ALL ABOUT FINESSE. ONE PIECE AT A TIME... AND THEY'LL BE NAKED BEFORE THEY KNOW IT!
WUSP
DON'T WORRY. I'LL PLAY IT COOL WHEN I'M THE KING!

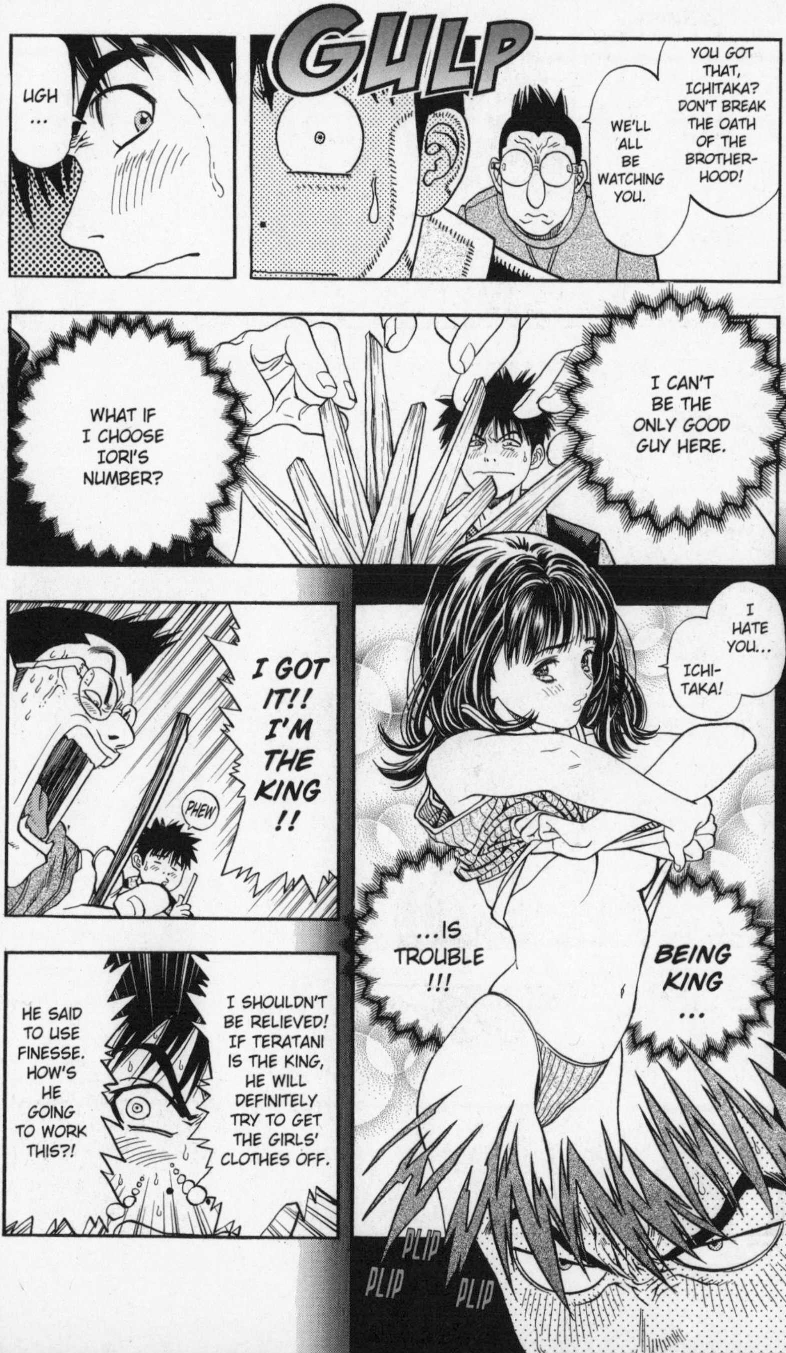
GULP
YOU GOT THAT, ICHITAKA? DON'T BREAK THE OATH OF THE BROTHER-HOOD!
WE'LL ALL BE WATCHING YOU.
UGH ...
I CAN'T BE THE ONLY GOOD GUY HERE.
WHAT IF I CHOOSE IORI'S NUMBER?
I HATE YOU...
ICHI-TAKA!
BEING KING ...
...IS TROUBLE !!!
PLIP
PLIP
PLIP
I GOT IT!! I'M THE KING !!
PHEW
I SHOULDN'T BE RELIEVED! IF TERATANI IS THE KING, HE WILL DEFINITELY TRY TO GET THE GIRLS' CLOTHES OFF.
HE SAID TO USE FINESSE. HOW'S HE GOING TO WORK THIS?!

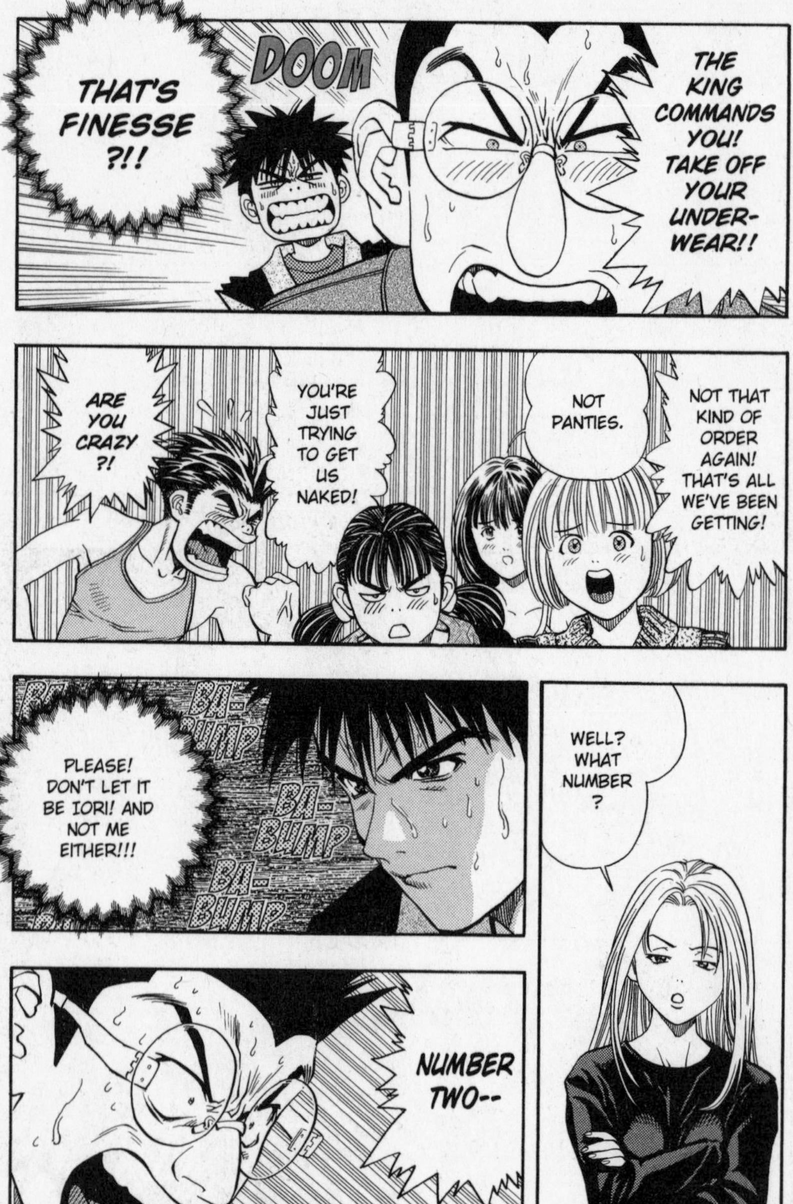

THE KING COMMANDS YOU! TAKE OFF YOUR UNDER-WEAR!!
DOOM
THAT'S FINESSE ?!!
NOT THAT KIND OF ORDER AGAIN! THAT'S ALL WE'VE BEEN GETTING!
NOT PANTIES.
YOU'RE JUST TRYING TO GET US NAKED!
ARE YOU CRAZY ?!
WELL? WHAT NUMBER ?
BA-BUMP
BA-BUMP
BA-BUMP
PLEASE! DON'T LET IT BE IORI! AND NOT ME EITHER!!!
NUMBER TWO--

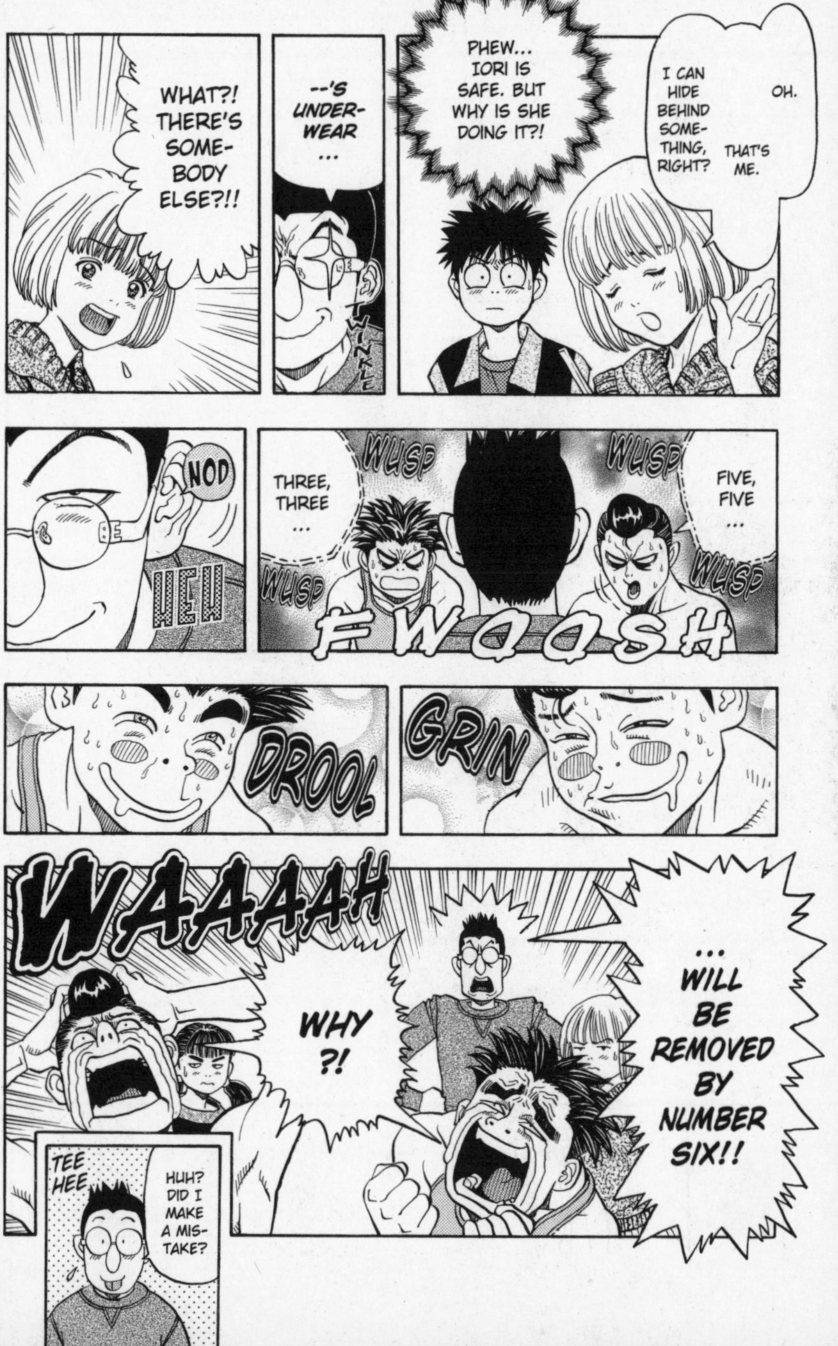
OH. THAT'S ME.
I CAN HIDE BEHIND SOME-THING, RIGHT?
PHEW... IORI IS SAFE. BUT WHY IS SHE DOING IT?!
--'S UNDER-WEAR ...
TWINKLE
WHAT?! THERE'S SOME-BODY ELSE?!!
WUSP
FIVE, FIVE ...
WUSP
WUSP
THREE, THREE ...
WUSP
FWOOSH
NOD
HEH
GRIN
DROOL
... WILL BE REMOVED BY NUMBER SIX!!
WHY ?!
WAAAAAH
HUH? DID I MAKE A MIS-TAKE?
TEE HEE

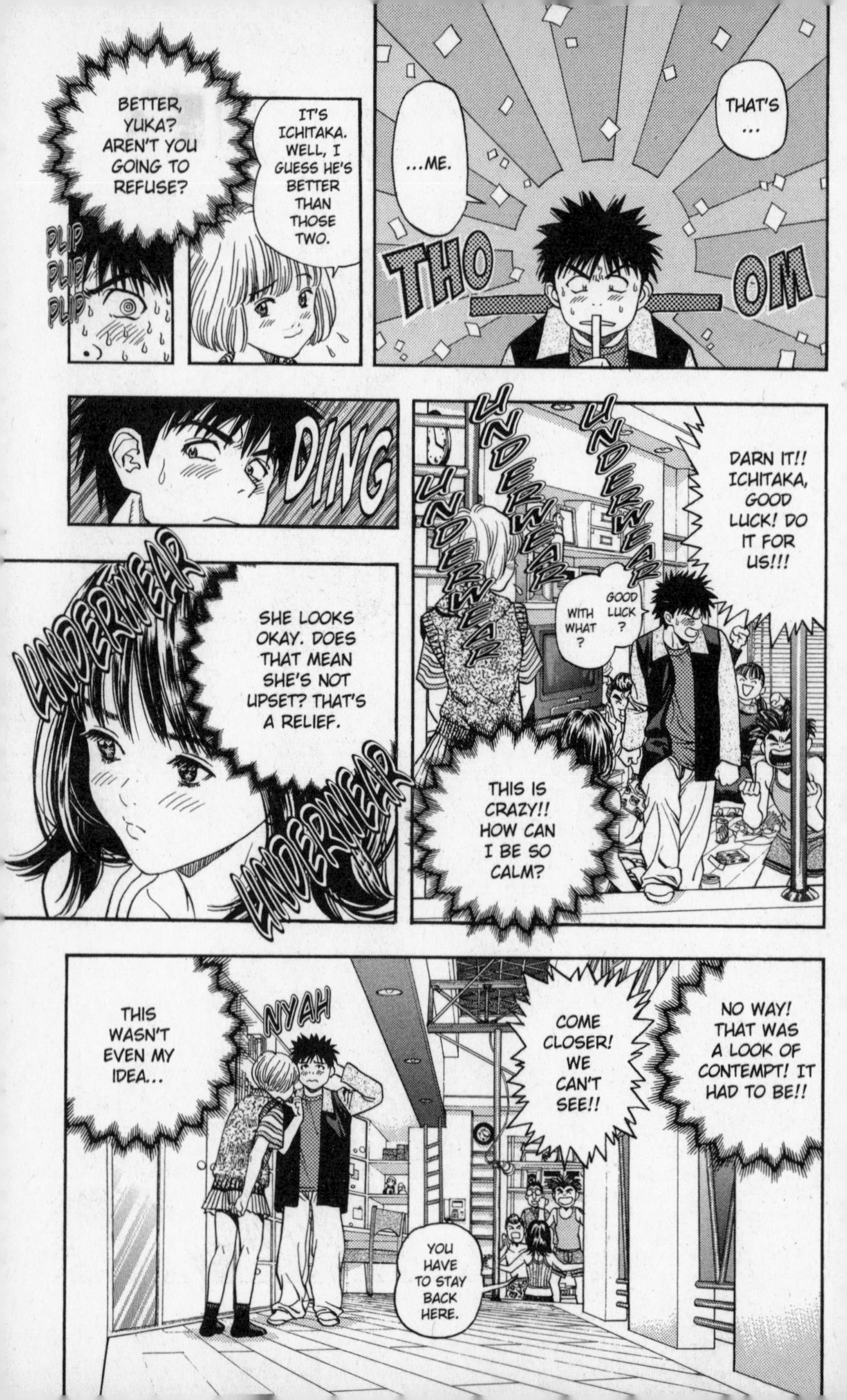
THAT'S ...
...ME.
THO
OM
IT'S ICHITAKA. WELL, I GUESS HE'S BETTER THAN THOSE TWO.
BETTER, YUKA? AREN'T YOU GOING TO REFUSE?
PLIP PLIP PLIP
UNDERWEAR
UNDERWEAR
UNDERWEAR
UNDERWEAR
DARN IT!! ICHITAKA, GOOD LUCK! DO IT FOR US!!!
GOOD LUCK?
WITH WHAT?
THIS IS CRAZY!! HOW CAN I BE SO CALM?
DING
UNDERWEAR
SHE LOOKS OKAY. DOES THAT MEAN SHE'S NOT UPSET? THAT'S A RELIEF.
UNDERWEAR
NO WAY! THAT WAS A LOOK OF CONTEMPT! IT HAD TO BE!!
COME CLOSER! WE CAN'T SEE!!
YOU HAVE TO STAY BACK HERE.
NYAH
THIS WASN'T EVEN MY IDEA...

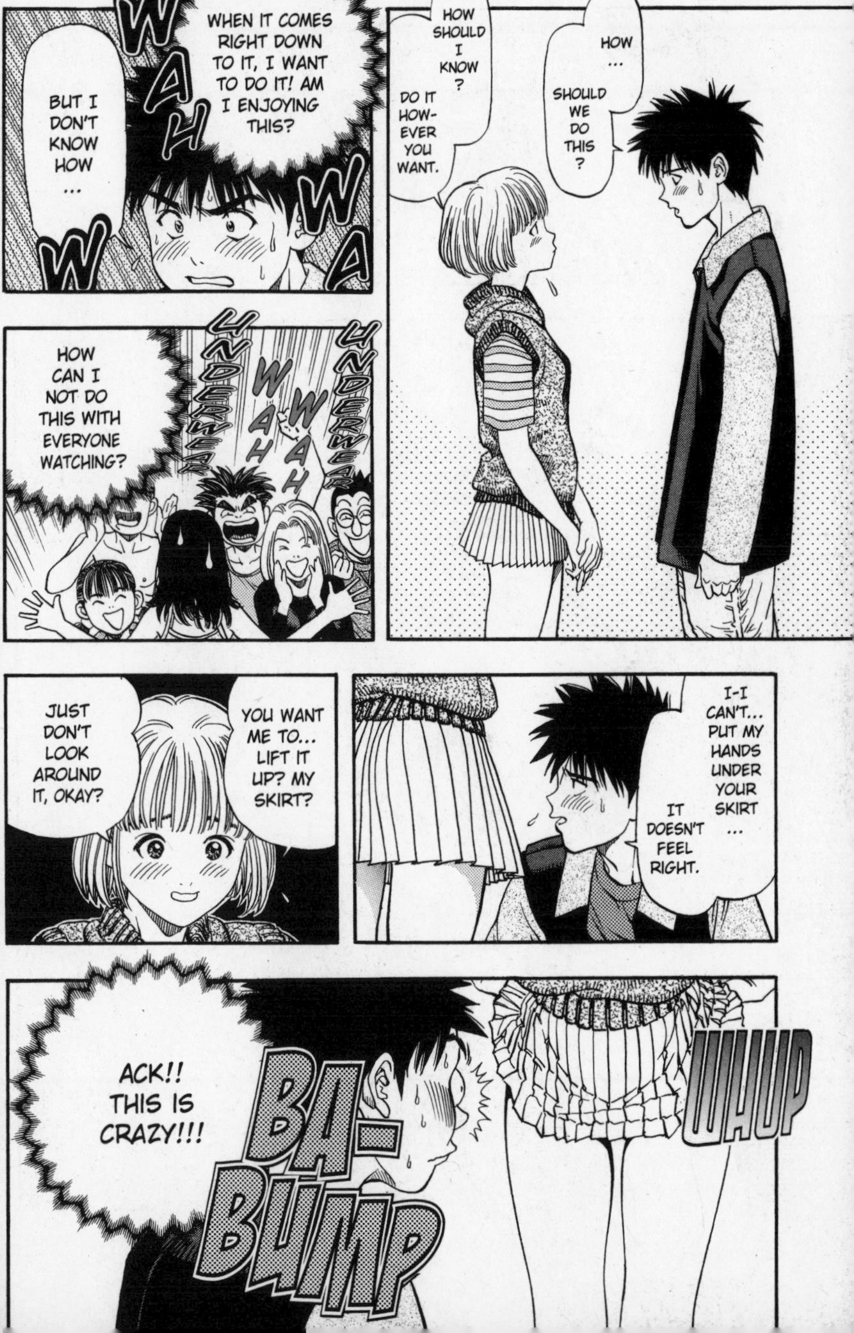
HOW ... SHOULD WE DO THIS ?
HOW SHOULD I KNOW ?
DO IT HOW-EVER YOU WANT.
WAH
WA
WHEN IT COMES RIGHT DOWN TO IT, I WANT TO DO IT! AM I ENJOYING THIS?
BUT I DON'T KNOW HOW ...
W
UNDERWEAR
WAH
WAH
UNDERWEAR
HOW CAN I NOT DO THIS WITH EVERYONE WATCHING?
I-I CAN'T... PUT MY HANDS UNDER YOUR SKIRT ...
IT DOESN'T FEEL RIGHT.
YOU WANT ME TO... LIFT IT UP? MY SKIRT?
JUST DON'T LOOK AROUND IT, OKAY?
WHUP
BA-BUMP
ACK!! THIS IS CRAZY!!!

READ THIS WAY

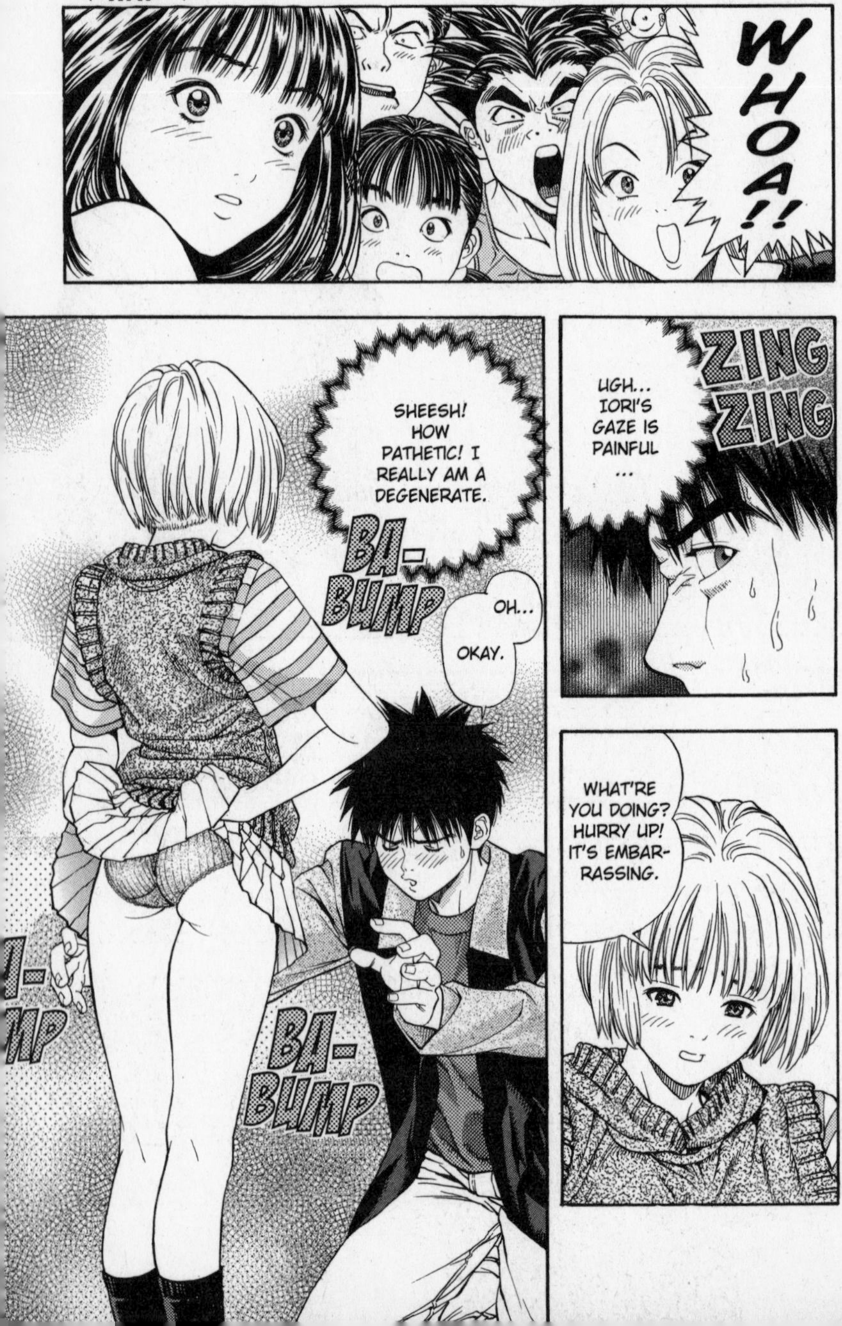
WHOA!!
ZING ZING
UGH... IORI'S GAZE IS PAINFUL ...
WHAT'RE YOU DOING? HURRY UP! IT'S EMBAR-RASSING.
SHEESH! HOW PATHETIC! I REALLY AM A DEGENERATE.
BA-BUMP
OH... OKAY.
BA-BUMP

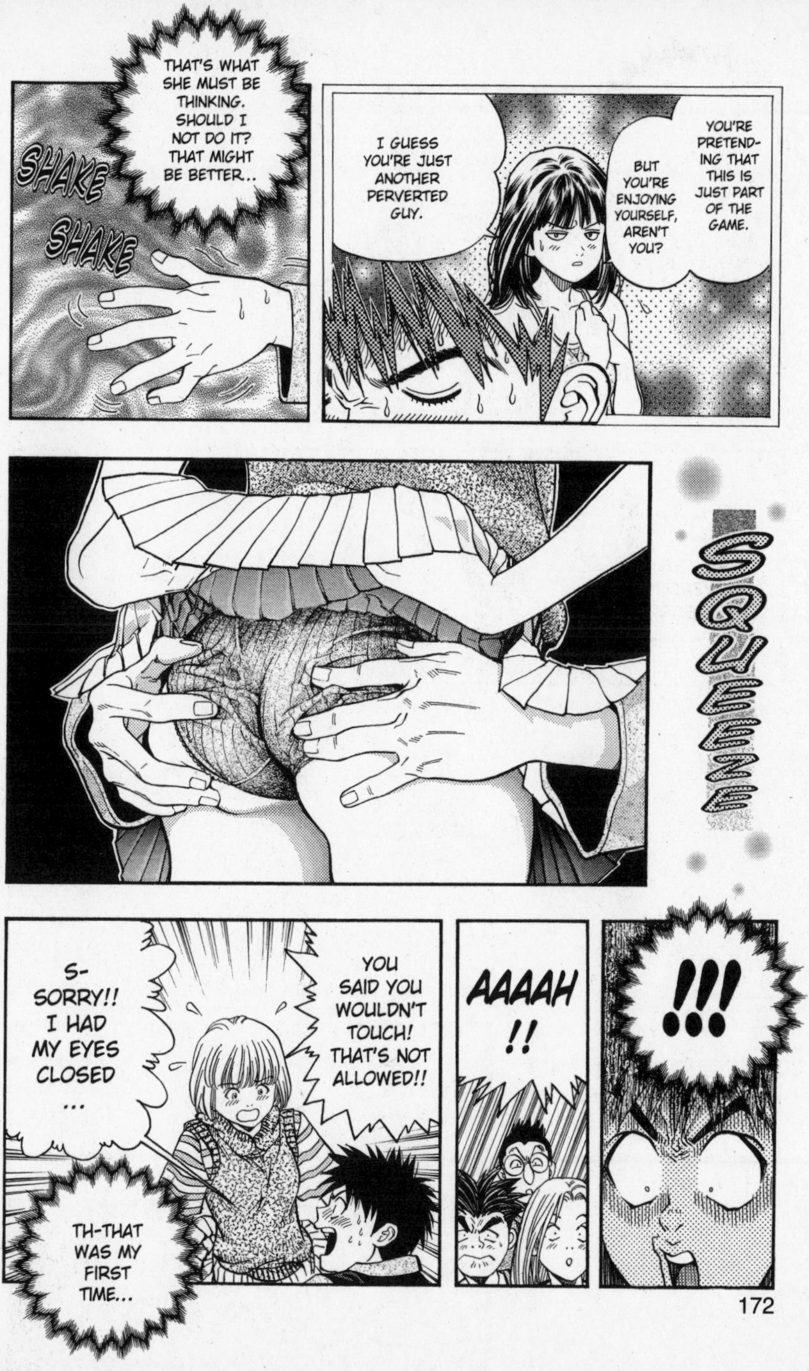
YOU'RE PRETENDING THAT THIS IS JUST PART OF THE GAME.
BUT YOU'RE ENJOYING YOURSELF, AREN'T YOU?
I GUESS YOU'RE JUST ANOTHER PERVERTED GUY.
THAT'S WHAT SHE MUST BE THINKING. SHOULD I NOT DO IT? THAT MIGHT BE BETTER...
SHAKE
SHAKE
SQUEEZE
!!!
AAAAH !!
YOU SAID YOU WOULDN'T TOUCH! THAT'S NOT ALLOWED!!
S-SORRY!! I HAD MY EYES CLOSED...
TH-THAT WAS MY FIRST TIME...

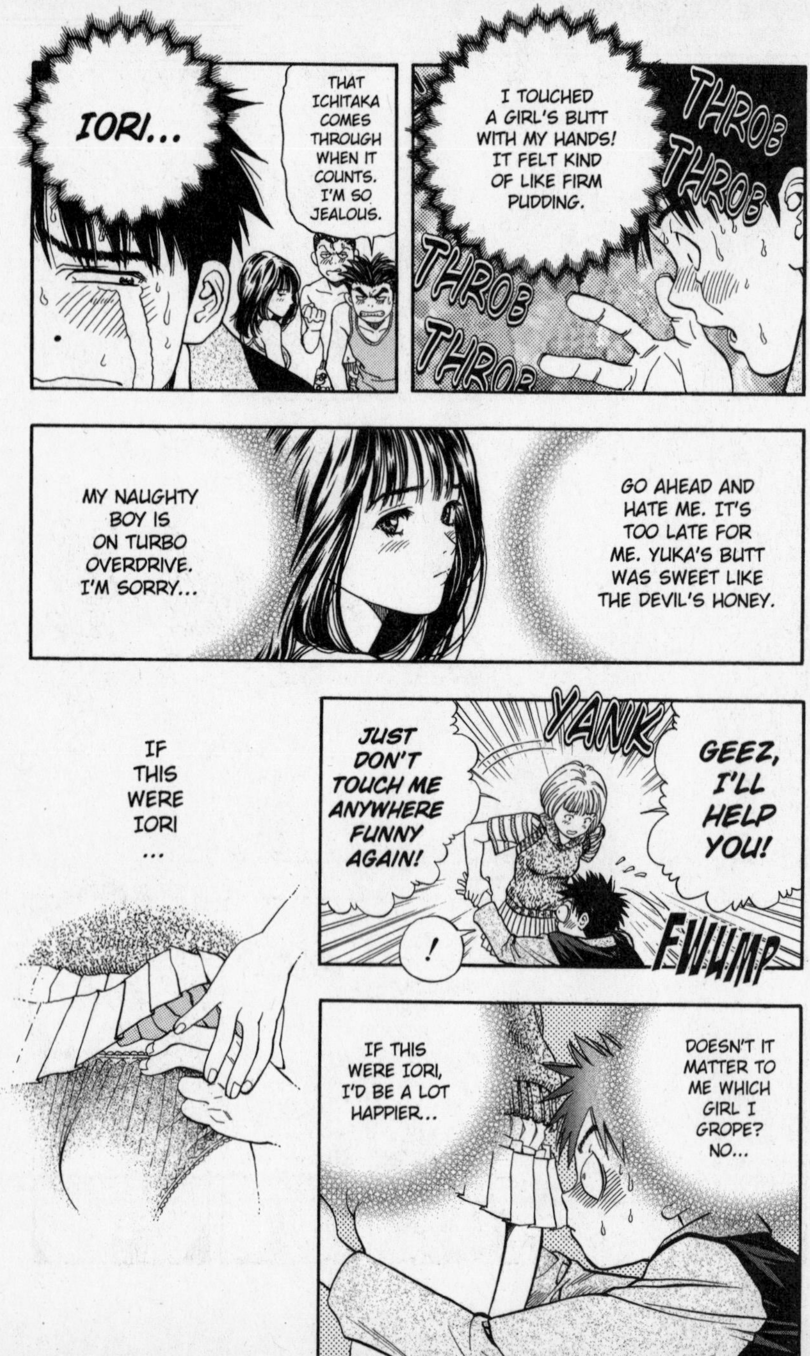
I TOUCHED A GIRL'S BUTT WITH MY HANDS! IT FELT KIND OF LIKE FIRM PUDDING.
THROB THROB
THROB THROB
THAT ICHITAKA COMES THROUGH WHEN IT COUNTS. I'M SO JEALOUS.
IORI...
GO AHEAD AND HATE ME. IT'S TOO LATE FOR ME. YUKA'S BUTT WAS SWEET LIKE THE DEVIL'S HONEY.
MY NAUGHTY BOY IS ON TURBO OVERDRIVE. I'M SORRY...
GEEZ, I'LL HELP YOU!
YANK
JUST DON'T TOUCH ME ANYWHERE FUNNY AGAIN!
FWUMP
!
DOESN'T IT MATTER TO ME WHICH GIRL I GROPE? NO...
IF THIS WERE IORI, I'D BE A LOT HAPPIER...
IF THIS WERE IORI ...

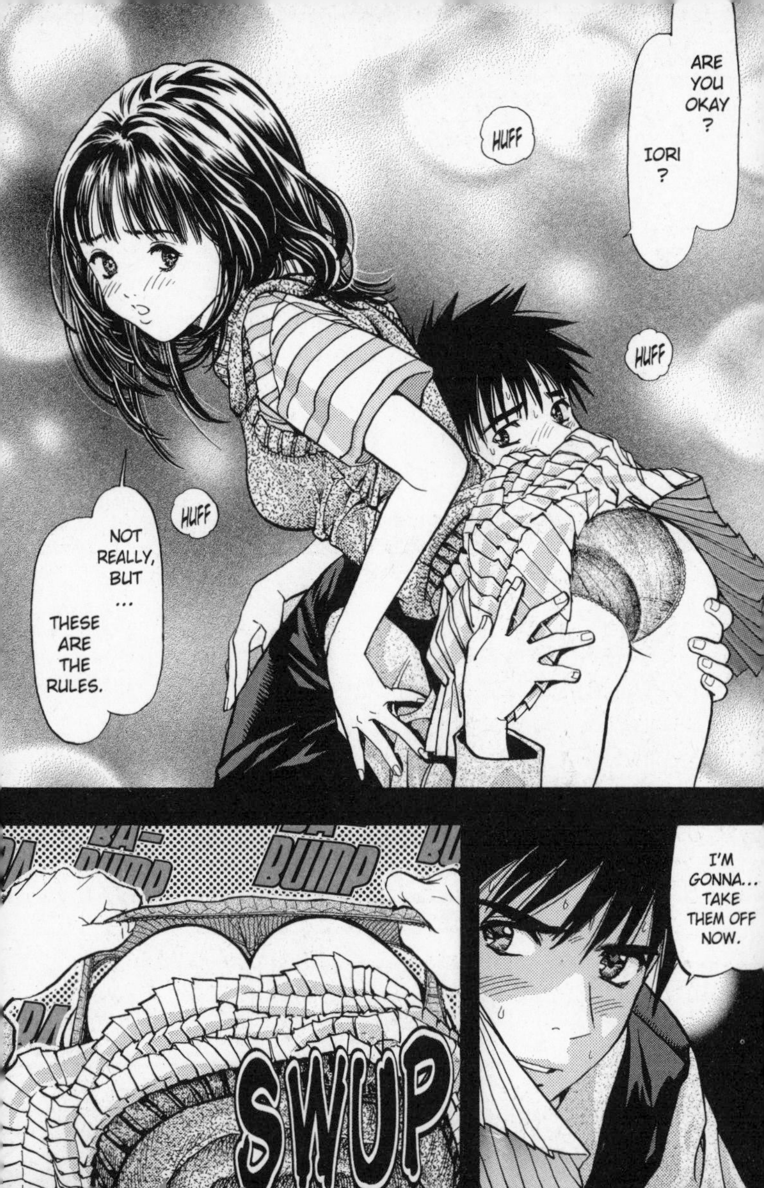
ARE YOU OKAY? IORI?
HUFF
HUFF
HUFF
NOT REALLY, BUT... THESE ARE THE RULES.
I'M GONNA... TAKE THEM OFF NOW.
BUMP
BA-BUMP
SWUP

READ THIS WAY

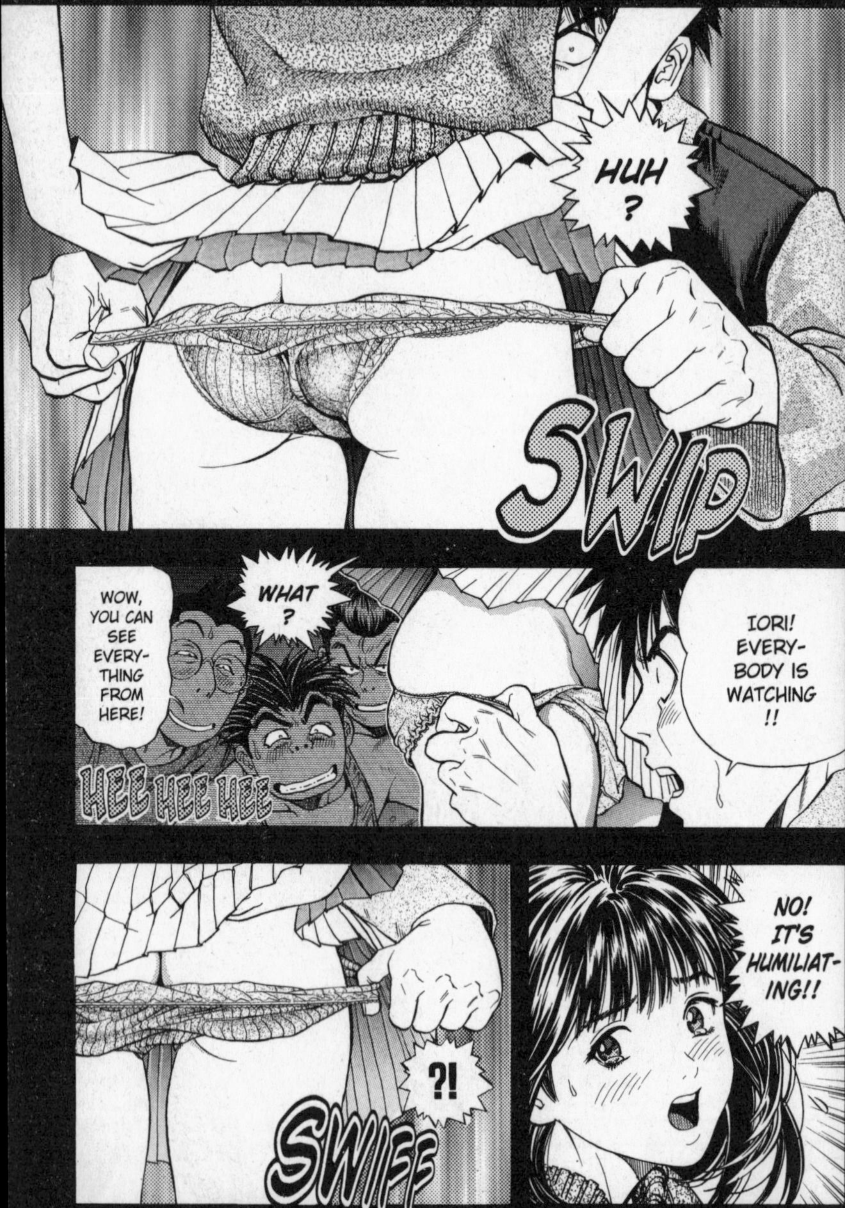
HUH ?
SWIP
IORI! EVERY-BODY IS WATCHING !!
WHAT ?
WOW, YOU CAN SEE EVERY-THING FROM HERE!
HEE HEE HEE
NO! IT'S HUMILIAT-ING!!
?!
SWIFF

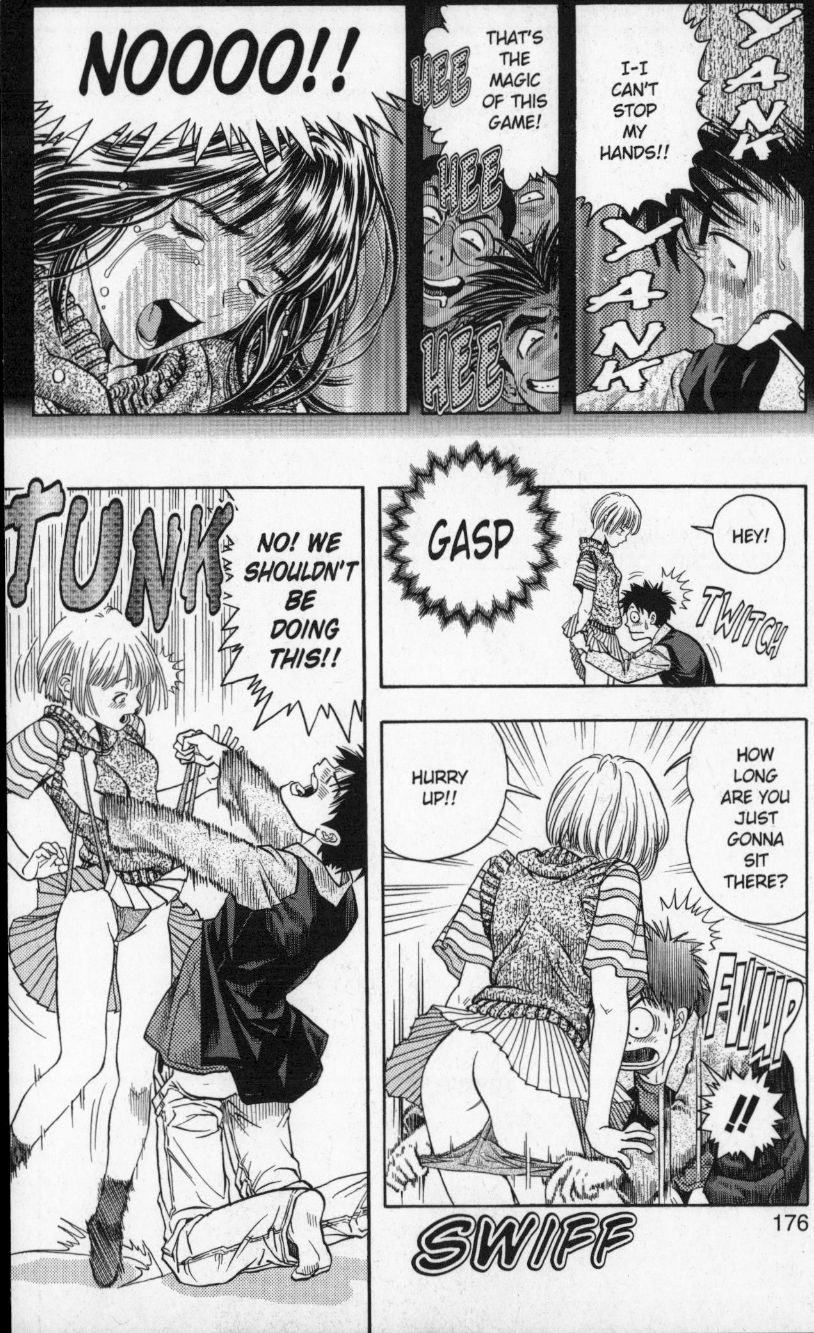

YANK
I-I CAN'T STOP MY HANDS!!
YANK
THAT'S THE MAGIC OF THIS GAME!
HEE
HEE
HEE
NOOOO!!
HEY!
GASP
TWITCH
HOW LONG ARE YOU JUST GONNA SIT THERE?
HURRY UP!!
FWUP
!!
SWIFF
TUNK
NO! WE SHOULDN'T BE DOING THIS!!

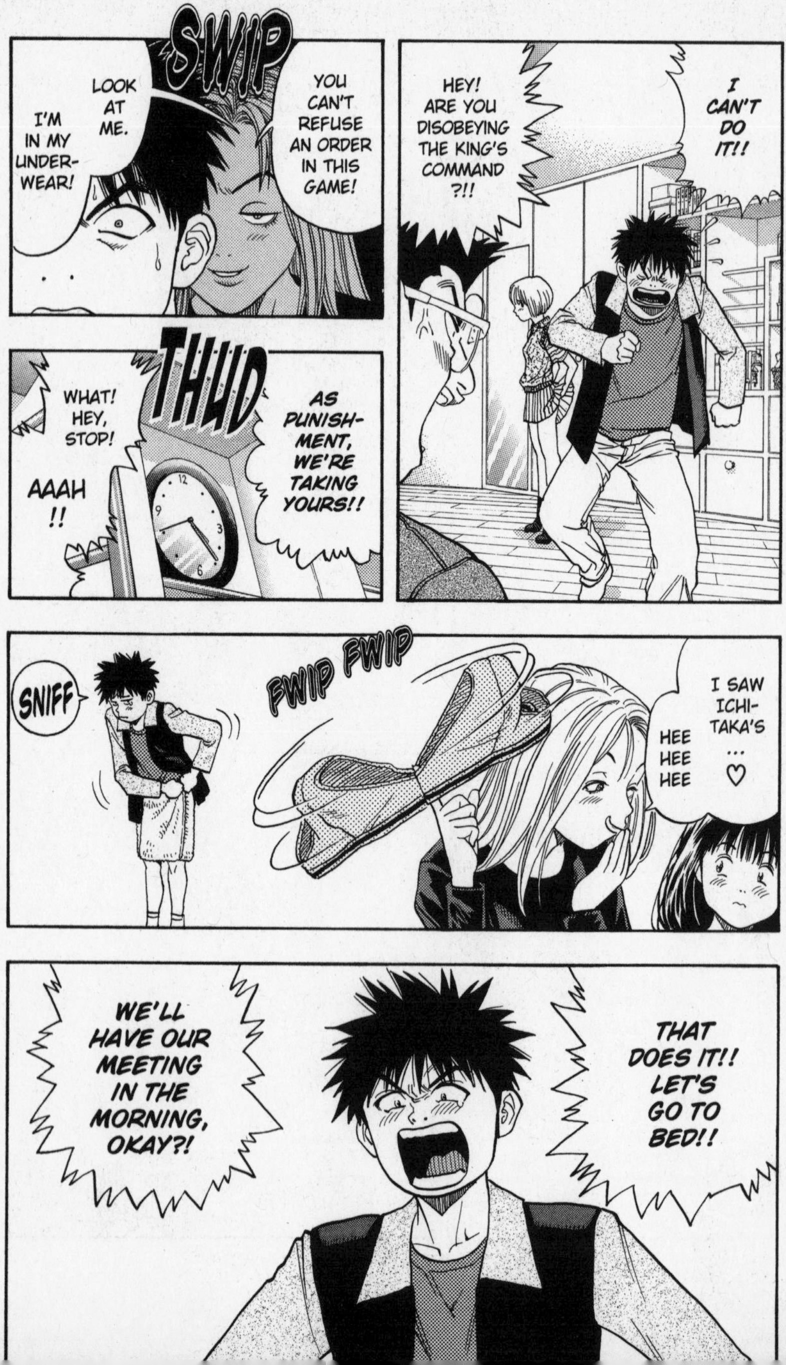
I CAN'T DO IT!!
HEY! ARE YOU DISOBEYING THE KING'S COMMAND ?!!
SWIP
YOU CAN'T REFUSE AN ORDER IN THIS GAME!
LOOK AT ME.
I'M IN MY UNDER-WEAR!
AS PUNISH-MENT, WE'RE TAKING YOURS!!
THUD
WHAT! HEY, STOP!
AAAH !!
I SAW ICHI-TAKA'S ... ♡
HEE HEE HEE
FWIP FWIP
SNIFF
THAT DOES IT!! LET'S GO TO BED!!
WE'LL HAVE OUR MEETING IN THE MORNING, OKAY?!

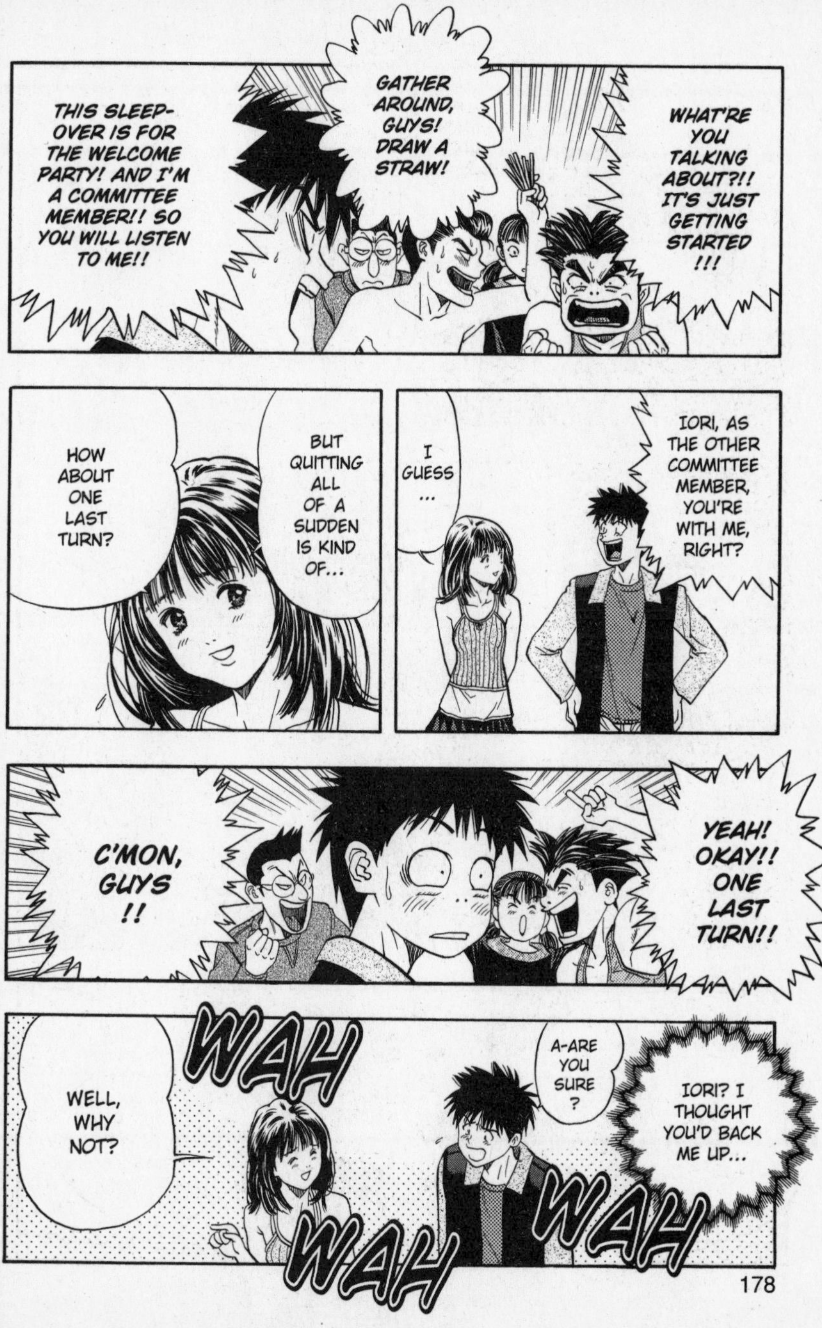
WHAT'RE YOU TALKING ABOUT?!! IT'S JUST GETTING STARTED !!!
GATHER AROUND, GUYS! DRAW A STRAW!
THIS SLEEP-OVER IS FOR THE WELCOME PARTY! AND I'M A COMMITTEE MEMBER!! SO YOU WILL LISTEN TO ME!!
IORI, AS THE OTHER COMMITTEE MEMBER, YOU'RE WITH ME, RIGHT?
I GUESS ...
BUT QUITTING ALL OF A SUDDEN IS KIND OF...
HOW ABOUT ONE LAST TURN?
YEAH! OKAY!! ONE LAST TURN!!
C'MON, GUYS !!
IORI? I THOUGHT YOU'D BACK ME UP...
A-ARE YOU SURE ?
WAH
WELL, WHY NOT?
WAH
WAH
WAH

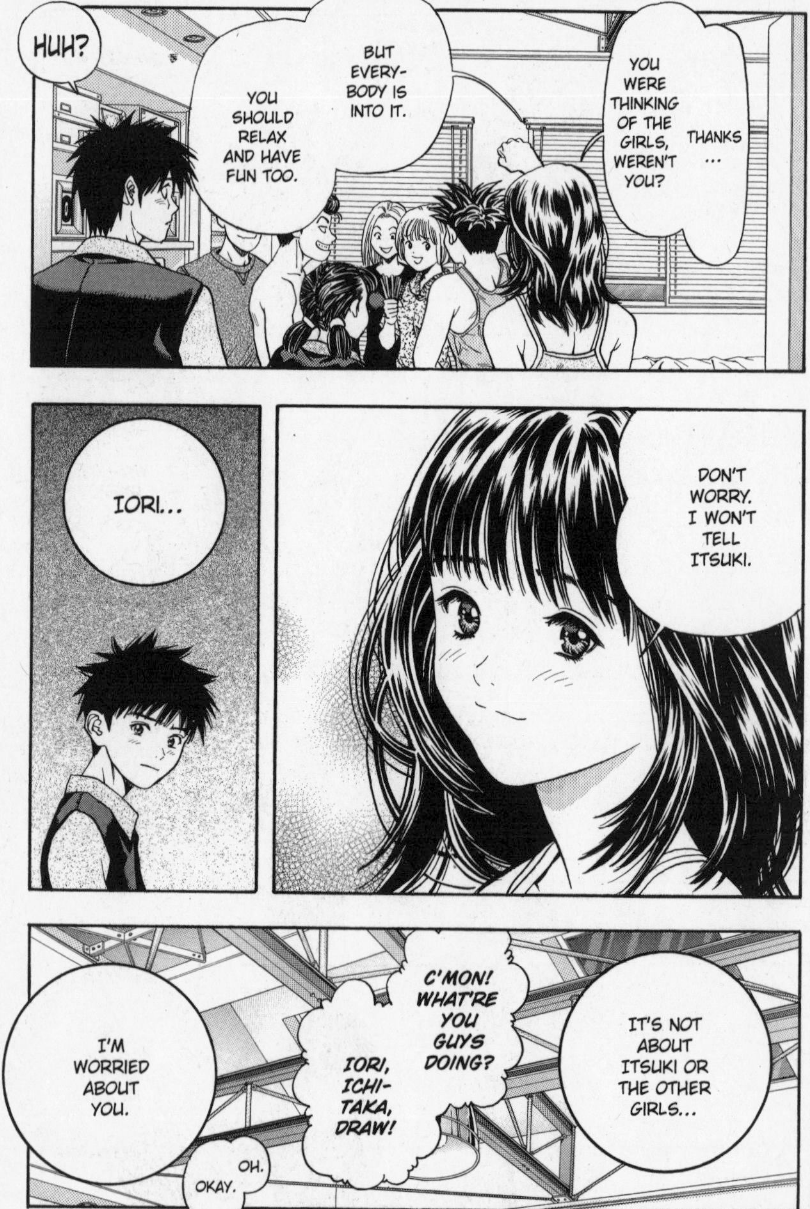
THANKS ...
YOU WERE THINKING OF THE GIRLS, WEREN'T YOU?
BUT EVERY-BODY IS INTO IT.
YOU SHOULD RELAX AND HAVE FUN TOO.
HUH?
DON'T WORRY. I WON'T TELL ITSUKI.
IORI...
IT'S NOT ABOUT ITSUKI OR THE OTHER GIRLS...
C'MON! WHAT'RE YOU GUYS DOING?
IORI, ICHI-TAKA, DRAW!
I'M WORRIED ABOUT YOU.
OH. OKAY.

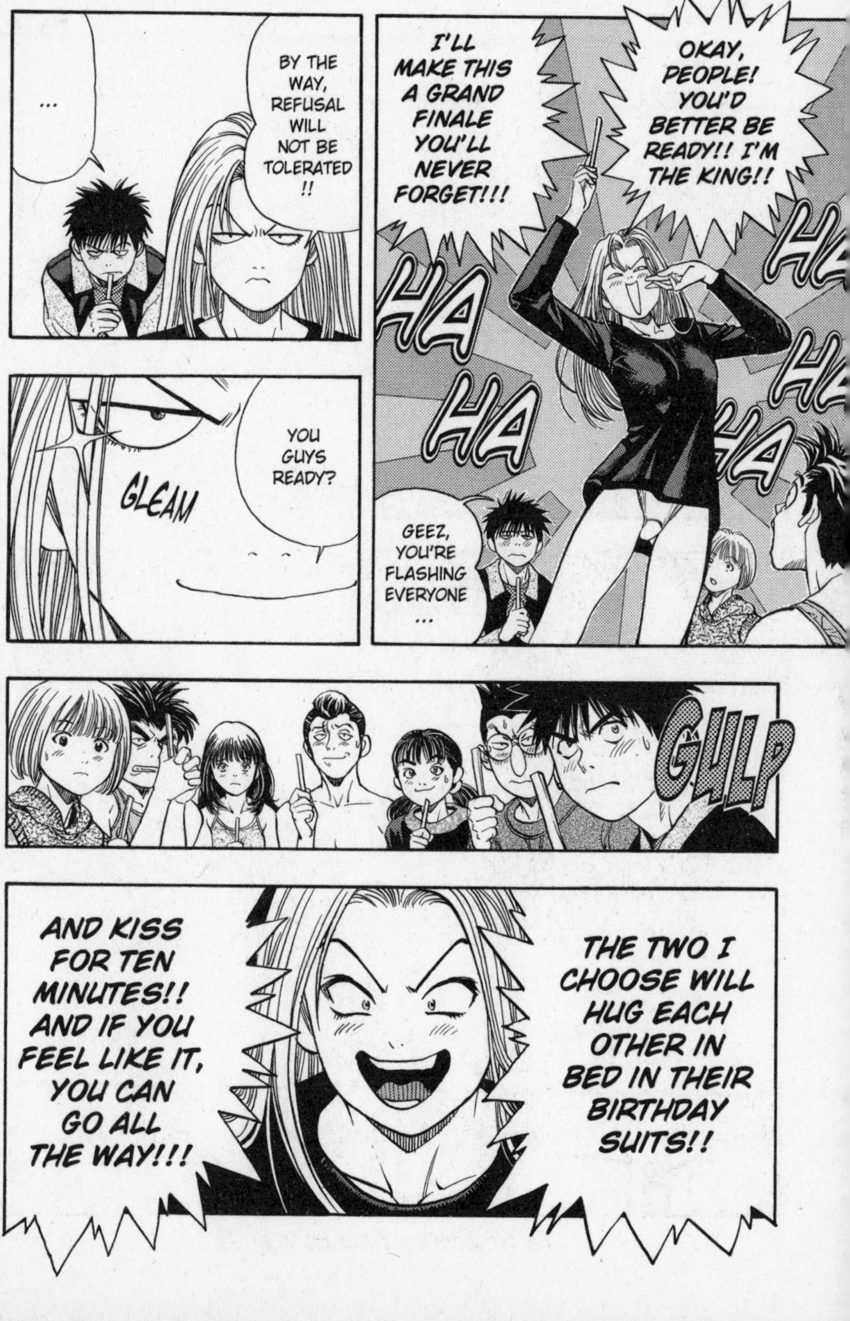
OKAY, PEOPLE! YOU'D BETTER BE READY!! I'M THE KING!!
I'LL MAKE THIS A GRAND FINALE YOU'LL NEVER FORGET!!!
HA HA HA
HA HA
GEEZ, YOU'RE FLASHING EVERYONE ...
BY THE WAY, REFUSAL WILL NOT BE TOLERATED !!
...
YOU GUYS READY?
GLEAM
GULP
THE TWO I CHOOSE WILL HUG EACH OTHER IN BED IN THEIR BIRTHDAY SUITS!!
AND KISS FOR TEN MINUTES!! AND IF YOU FEEL LIKE IT, YOU CAN GO ALL THE WAY!!!

READ THIS WAY

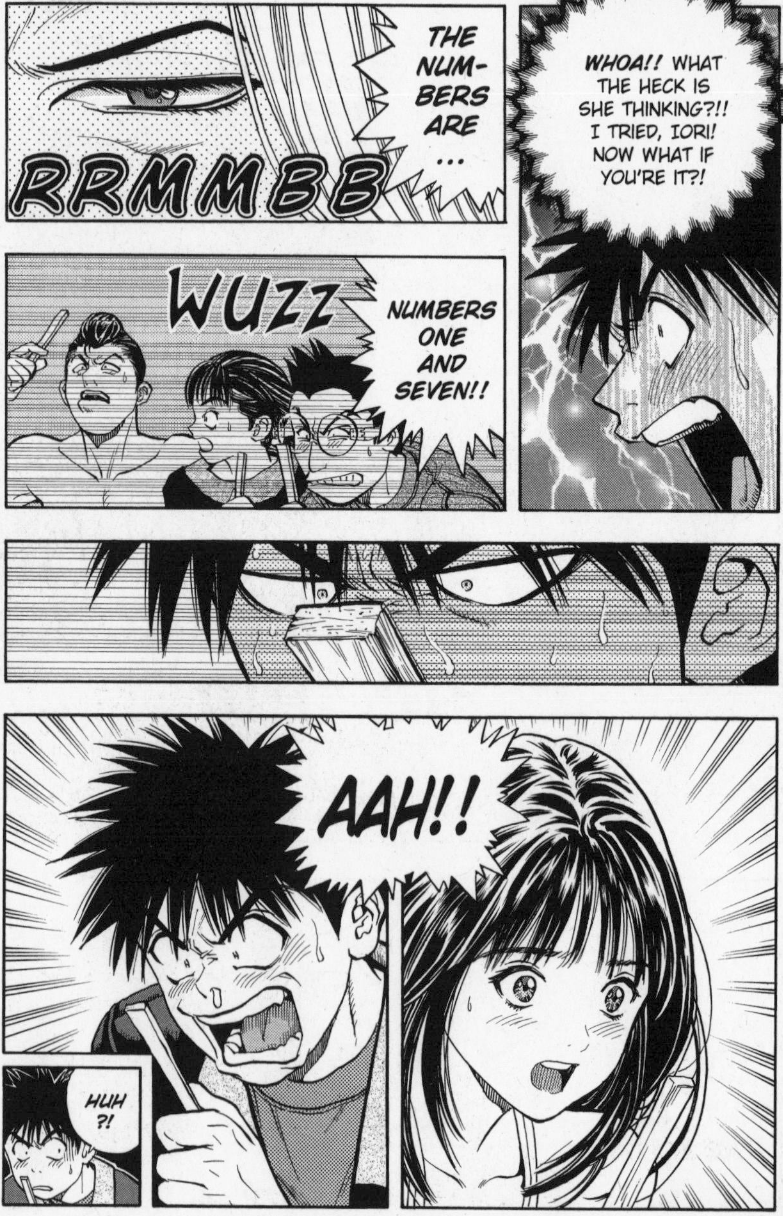

WHOA!! WHAT THE HECK IS SHE THINKING?!! I TRIED, IORI! NOW WHAT IF YOU'RE IT?!
THE NUM-BERS ARE ...
RRMMBB
NUMBERS ONE AND SEVEN!!
WUZZ
AAH!!
HUH ?!

To be continued in vol. 7!

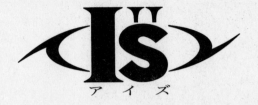

アイズ

I''s Illustration
Collection

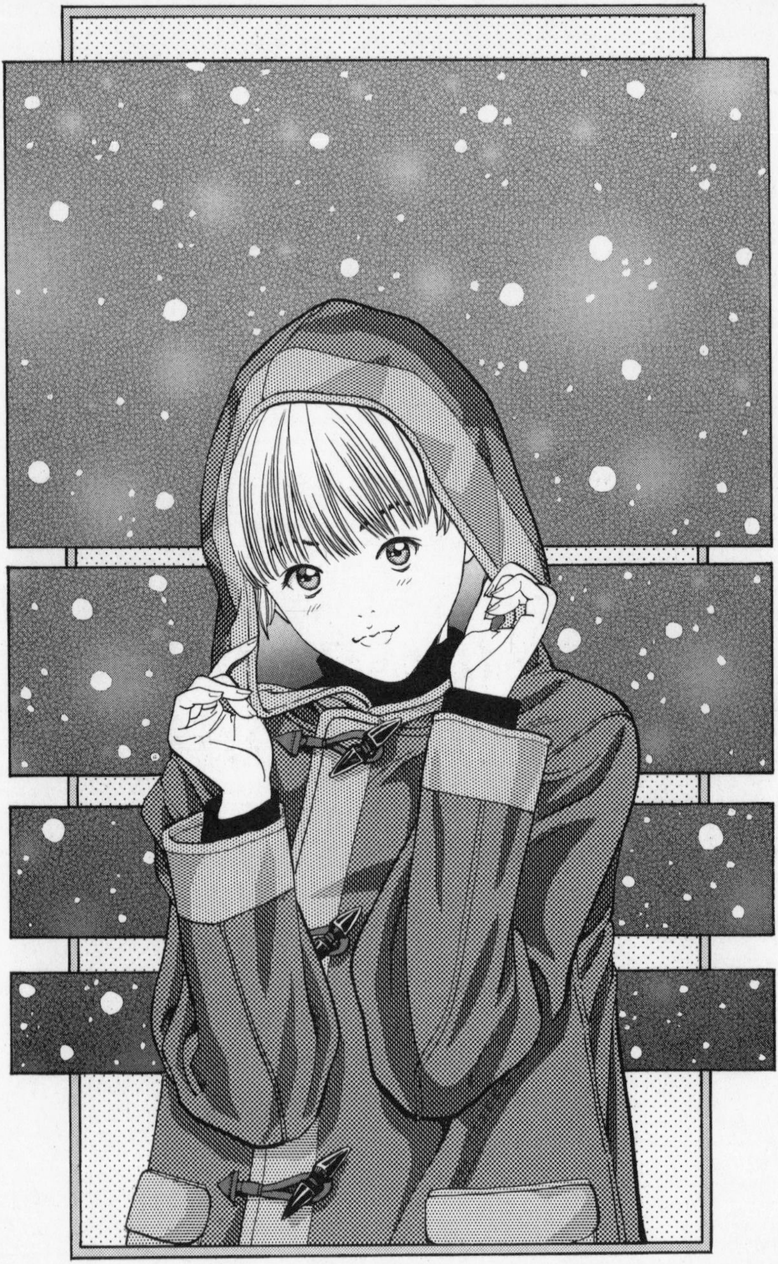

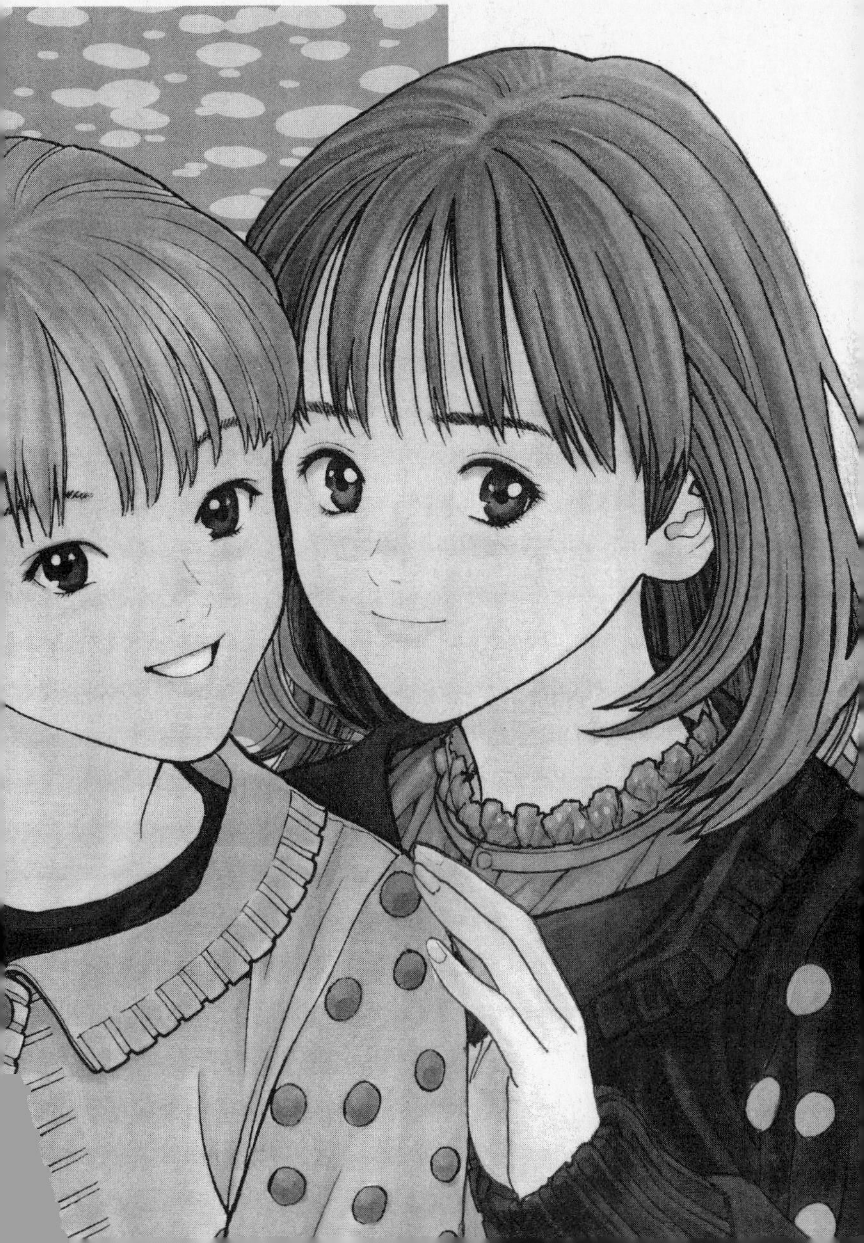

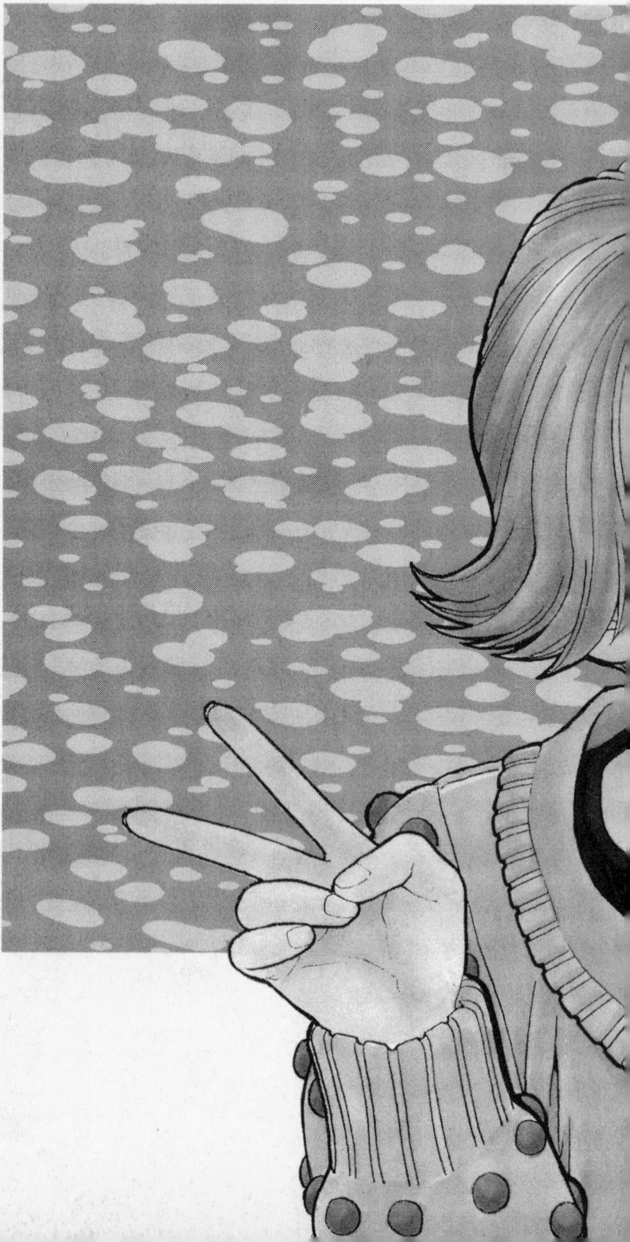

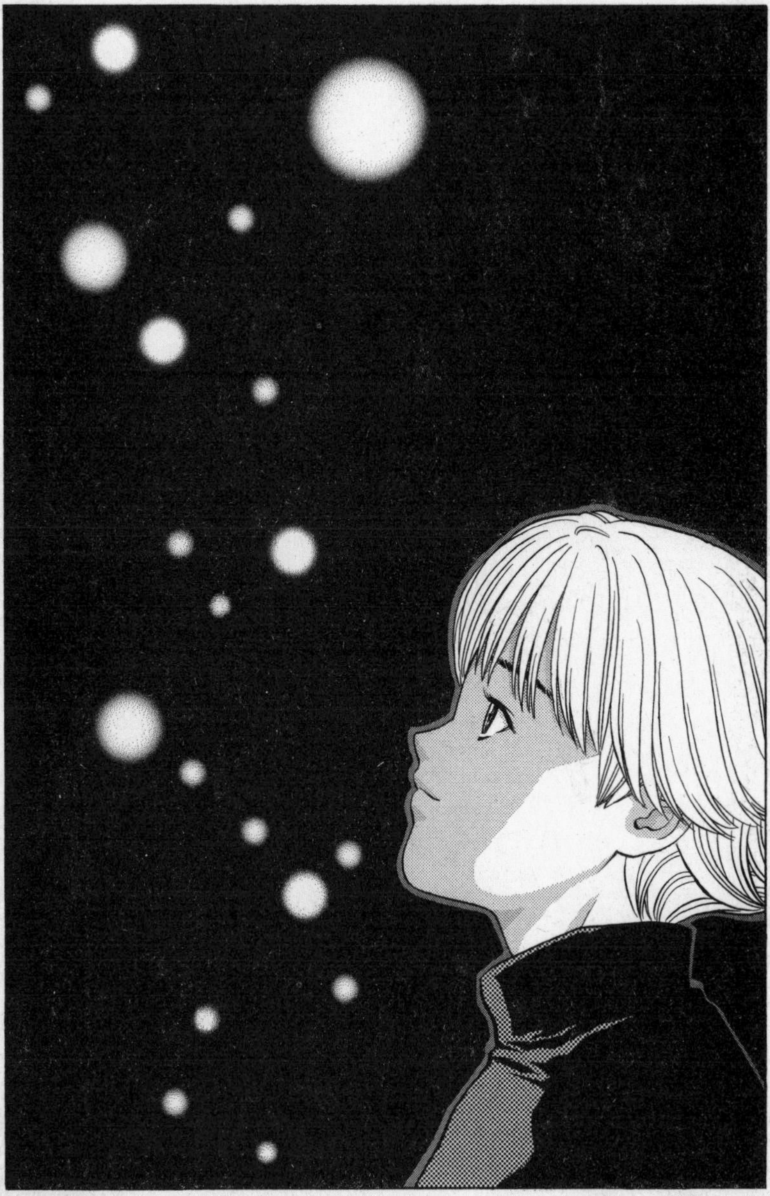

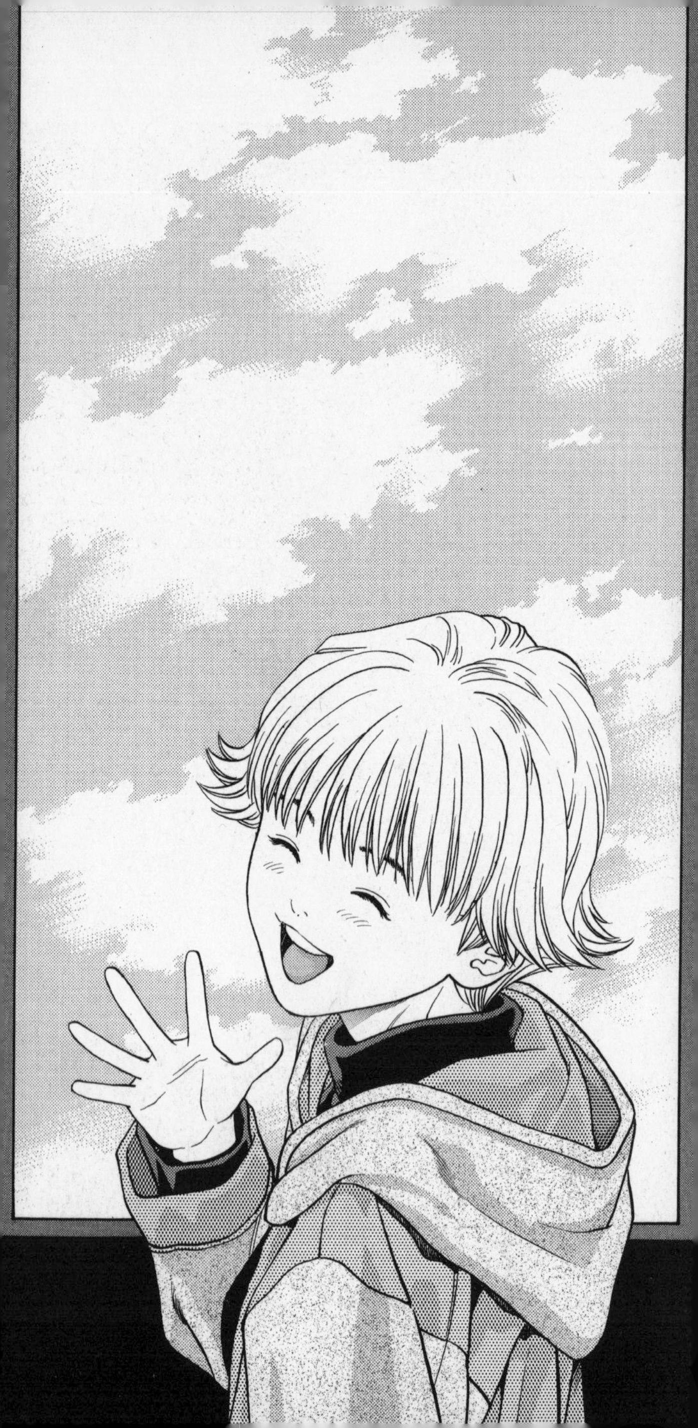

NEXT VOLUME PREVIEW

Ichitaka and Iori reluctantly get into bed together to finish the final round of the King game. Ichitaka is nervous and doesn't know what to do. In the midst of his confusion, the lights go out, and the game is set to end with Ichitaka losing his chance at kissing Iori. But in the darkness, Ichitaka feels a light touch of lips...

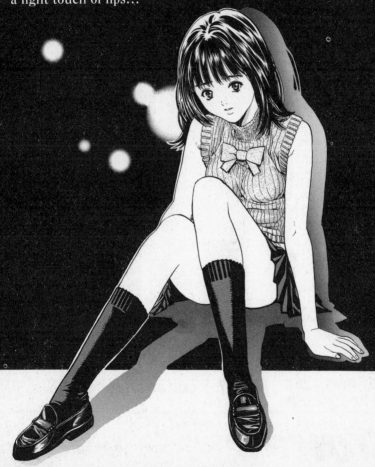

Available in May 2006

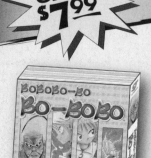

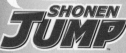

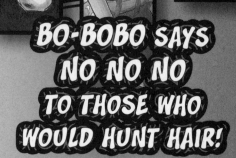

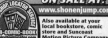

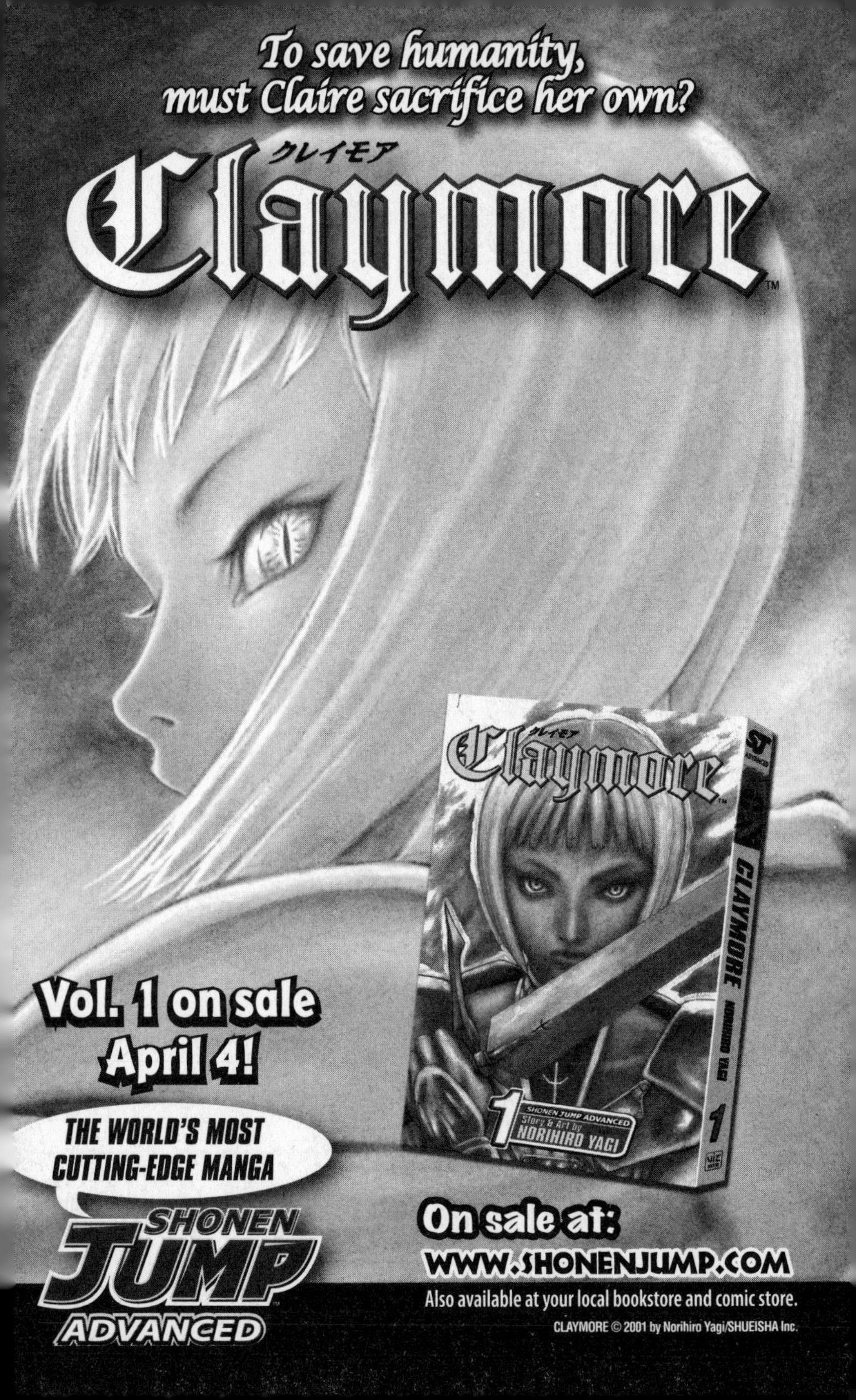
To save humanity,
must Claire sacrifice her own?
クレイモア
Claymore™
Vol. 1 on sale
April 4!
THE WORLD'S MOST
CUTTING-EDGE MANGA
SHONEN JUMP ADVANCED
Claymore
CLAYMORE
NORIHIRO YAGI
1 SHONEN JUMP ADVANCED
Story & Art by
NORIHIRO YAGI
On sale at:
WWW.SHONENJUMP.COM
Also available at your local bookstore and comic store.
CLAYMORE © 2001 by Norihiro Yagi/SHUEISHA Inc.

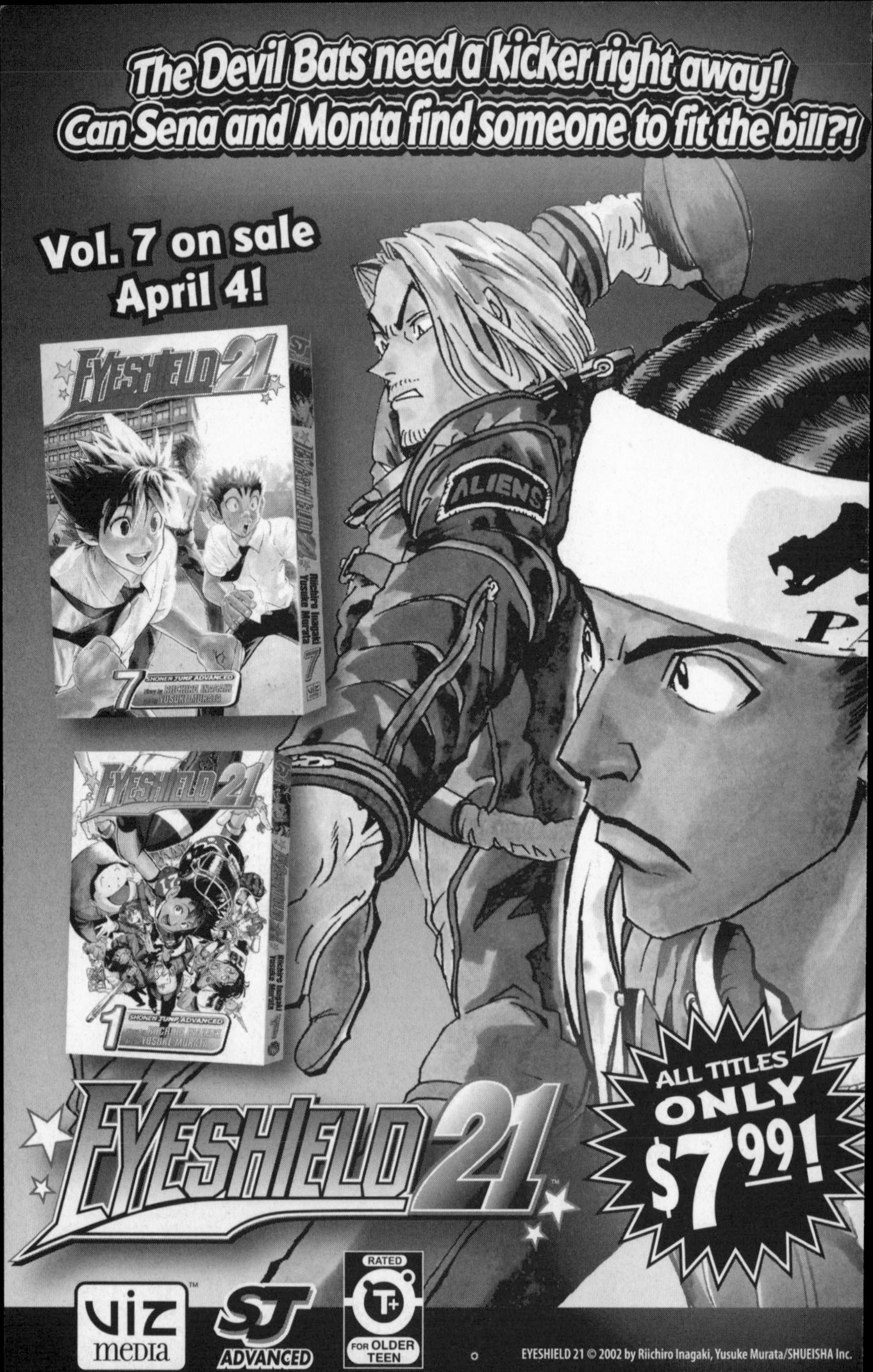

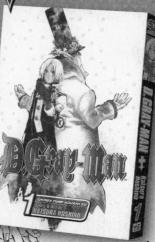

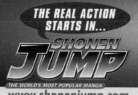
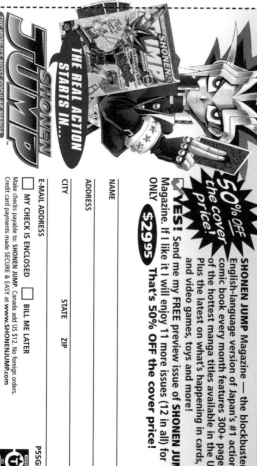
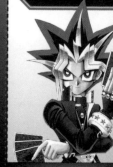

Check us out
on the web!

www.shonenjump.com

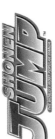

SHONEN JUMP
THE WORLD'S MOST POPULAR MANGA

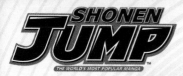

COMPLETE OUR SURVEY AND LET US KNOW WHAT YOU THINK!

☐ Please do NOT send me information about VIZ Media and SHONEN JUMP products, news and events, special offers, or other information.

☐ Please do NOT send me information from VIZ Media's trusted business partners.

Name: ______________________________

Address: ______________________________

City: ______________ **State:** ________ **Zip:** ____________

E-mail: ______________________________

☐ **Male** ☐ **Female** **Date of Birth** (mm/dd/yyyy): ___/___/______ (**Under 13? Parental consent required.**)

1 Do you purchase SHONEN JUMP Magazine?

☐ Yes ☐ No

If **YES**, do you subscribe?

☐ Yes ☐ No

If **NO**, how often do you purchase SHONEN JUMP Magazine?

☐ 1-3 issues a year ☐ 4-6 issues a year ☐ more than 7 issues a year

2 Which SHONEN JUMP Manga did you purchase this time? (please check only one)

☐ Beet the Vandel Buster ☐ Bleach ☐ Bobobo-bo Bo-bobo
☐ Death Note ☐ Dragon Ball ☐ Dragon Ball Z
☐ Dr. Slump ☐ Eyeshield 21 ☐ Hikaru no Go
☐ Hunter x Hunter ☐ I"s ☐ JoJo's Bizarre Adventure
☐ Knights of the Zodiac ☐ Legendz ☐ Naruto
☐ One Piece ☐ Rurouni Kenshin ☐ Shaman King
☐ The Prince of Tennis ☐ Ultimate Muscle ☐ Whistle!
☐ Yu-Gi-Oh! ☐ Yu-Gi-Oh!: Duelist ☐ Yu-Gi-Oh!: Millennium World
☐ YuYu Hakusho ☐ Other ______________

Will you purchase subsequent volumes?

☐ Yes ☐ No

3 How did you learn about this title? (check all that apply)

☐ Favorite title ☐ Advertisement ☐ Article
☐ Gift ☐ Read excerpt in SHONEN JUMP Magazine
☐ Recommendation ☐ Special offer ☐ Through TV animation
☐ Website ☐ Other ______________

4 Of the titles that are serialized in SHONEN JUMP Magazine, have you purchased the paperback manga vo

- ☐ Yes

If **YES**, which ones hav

- ☐ Hikaru no Go
- ☐ Naruto
- ☐ One Piece
- ☐ Shaman King
- ☐ Yu-Gi-Oh!: Millennium World
- ☐ YuYu Hakusho

If **YES**, what were your reasons for purchasing? (please pick up to 3)

- ☐ A favorite title
- ☐ A favorite creator/artist
- ☐ I want to read it in one go
- ☐ I want to read it over and over again
- ☐ There are extras that aren't in the magazine
- ☐ The quality of printing is better than the magazine
- ☐ Recommendation
- ☐ Special offer
- ☐ Other

If **NO**, why did/would you not purchase it?

- ☐ I'm happy just reading it in the magazine
- ☐ It's not worth buying the manga volume
- ☐ All the manga pages are in black and white, unlike the magazine
- ☐ There are other manga volumes that I prefer
- ☐ There are too many to collect for each title
- ☐ It's too small
- ☐ Other ______________________

5 Of the titles NOT serialized in the magazine, which ones have you purchased?
(check all that apply)

- ☐ Beet the Vandel Buster
- ☐ Bleach
- ☐ Bobobo-bo Bo-bobo
- ☐ Death Note
- ☐ Dragon Ball
- ☐ Dragon Ball Z
- ☐ Dr. Slump
- ☐ Eyeshield 21
- ☐ Hunter x Hunter
- ☐ I"s
- ☐ JoJo's Bizarre Adventure
- ☐ Knights of the Zodiac
- ☐ Legendz
- ☐ The Prince of Tennis
- ☐ Rurouni Kenshin
- ☐ Ultimate Muscle
- ☐ Whistle!
- ☐ Yu-Gi-Oh!
- ☐ Yu-Gi-Oh!: Duelist
- ☐ None
- ☐ Other ______________________

If you did purchase any of the above, what were your reasons for purchasing?

- ☐ A favorite title
- ☐ A favorite creator/artist
- ☐ Read a preview in SHONEN JUMP Magazine and wanted to read the rest of the story
- ☐ Recommendation
- ☐ Other

Will you purchase subsequent volumes?

- ☐ Yes
- ☐ No

6 What race/ethnicity do you consider yourself? (please check one)

- ☐ Asian/Pacific Islander
- ☐ Black/African American
- ☐ Hispanic/Latino
- ☐ Native American/Alaskan Native
- ☐ White/Caucasian
- ☐ Other

THANK YOU! Please send the completed form to:

VIZ Media Survey
42 Catharine St.
Poughkeepsie, NY 12601

All information provided will be used for internal purposes only. We promise not to sell or otherwise divulge your information.